Peter,

*Data Communications*

# The Saunders College Publishing Series in Electronics Technology

**Bennett**
*Advanced Circuit Analysis*
ISBN: 0-15-510843-4

**Brey**
*The Motorola Microprocessor Family: 68000, 68010, 68020, 68030, and 68040; Programming and Interfacing with Applications*
ISBN: 0-03-026403-5

**Carr**
*Elements of Microwave Technology*
ISBN: 0-15-522102-7

**Carr**
*Integrated Electronics: Operational Amplifiers and Linear IC's with Applications*
ISBN: 0-15-541360-0

**Driscoll**
*Data Communications*
ISBN: 0-03-026637-8

**Filer/Leinonen**
*Programmable Controllers and Designing Sequential Logic*
ISBN: 0-03-032322-3

**Garrod/Borns**
*Digital Logic: Analysis, Application and Design*
ISBN: 0-03-023099-3

**Grant**
*Understanding Lightwave Transmission: Applications of Fiber Optics*
ISBN: 0-15-592874-0

**Greenfield**
*The 68HC11 Microcontroller*
ISBN: 0-03-0515882

**Harrison**
*Transform Methods in Circuit Analysis*
ISBN: 0-03-020724-X

**Hazen**
*Exploring Electronic Devices*
ISBN: 0-03-028533-X

**Hazen**
*Fundamentals of DC and AC Circuits*
ISBN: 0-03-028538-0

**Hazen**
*Experiencing Electricity and Electronics*
*Conventional Current Version*
ISBN: 0-03-007747-8
*Electron Flow Version*
ISBN: 0-03-03427-2

**Ismail/Rooney**
*Digital Concepts and Applications*
ISBN: 0-03-026628-9

**Laverghetta**
*Analog Communications for Technology*
ISBN: 0-03-029403-7

**Leach**
*Discrete and Integrated Circuit Electronics*
ISBN: 0-03-020844-0

**Ludeman**
*Introduction to Electronic Devices and Circuits*
ISBN: 0-03-009538-7

**McBride**
*Computer Troubleshooting and Maintenance*
ISBN: 0-15-512663-6

**Oppenheimer**
*Survey of Electronics*
ISBN: 0-03-020842-4

**Prestopnik**
*Digital Electronics: Concepts and Applications for Digital Design*
ISBN: 0-03-026757-9

**Seeger**
*Introduction to Micro-processors with the Intel 8085*
ISBN: 0-15-543527-2

**Spiteri**
*Robotics Technology*
ISBN: 0-03-020858-0

**Wagner**
*Digital Electronics*
ISBN: 0-15-517636-6

**Winzer**
*Linear Integrated Circuits*
ISBN: 0-03-03246-8

**Yatsko/Hata**
*Circuits: Principles, Analysis, and Simulation*
ISBN: 0-03-00933-2

# Data Communications

Frederick F. Driscoll
*Wentworth Institute of Technology*

**SAUNDERS COLLEGE PUBLISHING**
*A Harcourt Brace Jovanovich College Publisher*

Fort Worth   Philadelphia   San Diego   New York   Orlando
San Antonio   Toronto   Montreal   London   Sydney   Tokyo

Text Typeface: Times Roman
Compositor: Ruttle, Shaw & Wetherill
Acquisitions Editor: Barbara Gingery
Assistant Editor: Laura Shur
Managing Editor: Carol Field
Project Editor: Anne Gibby
Copy Editor: Jennifer Holness-Harze
Manager of Art and Design: Carol Bleistine
Associate Art Director: Doris Bruey
Text Designer: Rebecca Lemna
Cover Designer: Lawrence R. Didona
Text Artwork: GRAFACON, Inc.
Director of EDP: Tim Frelick
Production Manager: Charlene Squibb

Cover Credit: Artwork provided by Lawrence R. Didona

Printed in the United States of America

DATA COMMUNICATIONS

ISBN: 0-03-026637-8

Library of Congress Catalog Card Number: 91-050656

1 2 3 4  0 1 6  9 8 7 6 5 4 3 2 1

*In loving memory of my mother,*
*Margaret A. Driscoll*
*and*
*in honor of my father,*
*Fred F. Driscoll*

# *Preface*

Every day, more and more businesses, government agencies, and academic departments require accurate and faster transmission of computer information and data. Thus, the field of data communications has become a rapidly growing area.

## Approach/Audience

Like other computer-based equipment, this area of study can be approached either from a software or hardware point of view. Since this text is primarily written for electronic technicians, technologists, and engineers, a hardware approach is used, that is, an approach from "the bottom up." This text introduces the general theory of data communications as well as some of the integrated circuits that implement the theory. Although there are many manufacturers selling ICs for the data communications market, this author has chosen many Motorola products. They are universally available, well documented and cover a wide range of data communication applications. Although some of the devices may not be recommended for new designs, they are still available and can be used in the laboratory to learn the fundamental principles of data communication. Those principles, learned in this text, can easily be carried over to future devices and to devices produced by other manufacturers.

This book is written so that a reader with a background in basic digital electronics and some microprocessor theory can understand the concepts presented. Familiarity with modulation techniques may be helpful, but is not required because sufficient information and examples are provided in the chapters.

The field of data communications is very broad. This text takes the reader through the fundamentals and details of a hardware approach and will provide the groundwork for further study in this burgeoning new technology. The text will be most useful at the two-year technical college level for students majoring in computer engineering technology, electronic engineering technology, or computer science.

In order for this text to provide an easy learning environment for the students, each chapter begins with a list of objectives and an introduction to familiarize the reader with terms and concepts that will be introduced. Also, an end-of-chapter summary is provided so that readers may refresh themselves with principles that have been covered. Each chapter includes worked-out examples that stress points covered in the text. Also, a set of problems at the end of each chapter reinforces what the student has learned. Answers to selected problems are given at the end of the book.

There are a number of data sheets in the Appendix for reference purposes. Because of limited space, the data sheets for a particular device may not include all of its electrical characteristics but they do provide a reference for many of the device's functional characteristics and pin designations. Complete data sheets can be obtained from the manufacturer.

The instructor's manual includes worked-out solutions to all of the text problems as well as a listing of suggested laboratory experiments which will give instructors ideas for conducting some basic experiments.

## Contents Overview

Chapter 1 is an overview to data communications. It begins with a definition of data communications and shows how a system to transmit and receive data expands from one terminal and a computer to several terminals communicating to a host computer.

Chapter 2 describes the most common binary pattern codes the user encounters in the data communication field. The majority of this chapter is devoted to the ASCII character set because of its wide usage in microcomputers.

Chapter 3 covers one type of transmission—asynchronous transmission. The advantages of using asynchronous transmission as well as its format are introduced in the first part of the chapter. The second part covers some practical ways to compensate for distorted transmitted waveforms.

Chapter 4 introduces the general concepts of Universal Asynchronous Receiver/Transmitters (UARTs), both the reasons for needing them and their operation. Motorola's Asynchronous Communication Interface Adapter (ACIA) is also introduced in this chapter to show how a specific UART device functions and how to interface it to an MC68000 microprocessor.

Chapters 5 and 6 cover one of the most widely used interface standards, the RS–232–C. Although the D version, known as EIA–232–D, has been published, and the E–version should be released shortly, the term RS–232–C or simply RS–232 is used so often, even by manufacturers, it has been chosen in this text and differences between the standards are pointed out where they occur. The mechanical and electrical characteristics of the RS–232 are covered in Chapter 5. Chapter 6 introduces the RS–232 functional characteristics and some typical applications.

Because the RS–232 standard was introduced a number of years ago and has limitations as to the rate of data transfer and a maximum distance between its end points, newer standards have emerged. Some of these standards are covered in Chapter 7.

The ever-present telephone line is a very convenient system to connect terminals and computers. Interface devices for sending and receiving asynchronous data over telephone lines are covered in Chapters 8 and 9. Chapter 8 introduces many of the general concepts, terms, and definitions. Chapter 9 discusses specific devices and design considerations for a slow-speed frequency shift keying (FSK) type modem.

If the logic state of a single bit changes during transmission, an error has occurred. Chapter 10 explains the three techniques used to detect errors at the receiver and a hardware approach for error detection.

When large blocks of data must be sent, synchronous transmission is more efficient than asynchronous transmission. In order to provide an orderly transfer of data between transmitter and receiver, a set of rules is needed. These rules are called protocols. Protocols for synchronous communication fall into two categories—character oriented and bit oriented. These are covered in Chapters 11 and 12, respectively.

Chapter 13 begins with three types of multiplexing: frequency, time, and statistical time. The remaining sections introduce systems that use multiplexing as a way of transmitting data. This chapter also introduces ways that systems may be expanded using not only multiplexers but also port selectors and port concentrators. Principles of digital service units as well as the T1 carrier service and different types of line coding techniques are also introduced.

Modems do not allow simultaneous transmission of voice and data over telephone lines although such applications are often required within a company. Some of the newest LSI chips allow an all digital system to be designed at a reasonable cost. Chapter 14 shows how such a system can be designed.

## Acknowledgments

I would like to give a special thank you to my colleagues Robert F. Coughlin and Robert S. Villanucci who, as always, provided valuable support and assistance, and assurance that the text is written with the student in mind. I would also like to thank the reviewers for their comments and helpful suggestions:

Bill Martin
Oklahoma State University

Bradley Jenkins
St. Petersburg Junior College

Clay Laster
San Antonio College

Ellis Nuckols
Oklahoma State University

A grateful acknowledgment must go to the professional staff at Saunders College Publishing for their patience, guidance, and advice throughout this project: Barbara Gingery, Senior Acquisitions Editor; Laura Shur, Assistant Editor, and Anne Gibby, Project Editor. Personnel at Motorola and Hewlett-Packard companies as well as the professional organization of the Electronic Industries Association have been extremely helpful to me in obtaining permission to use their data sheets or standards. Finally, I thank my wife, Jean, for the patience, organization, and love that make my efforts possible.

Frederick F. Driscoll
September 1991

*Tests are open notebook no textbooks.*

# Contents

## Chapter 3
### Asynchronous Transmission   34

## Chapter 4  *Substitute use 8250, 16250 etc.*
### Universal Asynchronous Receiver/Transmitter   55

## Chapter 5
## RS–232–C Mechanical and Electrical Characteristics   79

*Comp Com I will emphasize point-to-point communication*

# An Overview of Data Communications

# 1

Upon completion of this introductory chapter on data communications, the student will be able to

- Define the term "data communications."

- Explain the difference between serial and parallel transfer of data.

- Know the advantages and disadvantages of asynchronous transmission versus synchronous transmission.

- Compare the percent overhead required for asynchronous and synchronous transmission.

- Briefly describe the difference between a character oriented and a bit oriented frame.

- Define the terms "modem" and "multiplexer."

- Give examples of simplex, half-duplex, and full-duplex communication.

- Describe the difference between point-to-point and multipoint systems.

- Explain the terms "bit rate" and "baud rate."

- Realize that there are national and international organizations that develop and publish data communication standards.

## Introduction

Many data communications textbooks begin with a history of the subject. Instead, this chapter will give an overview of many of the topics encountered in the field of engineering today. Some of these may be familiar; others will be completely new. The remaining chapters will expand each topic and introduce some of the available large-scale integration (LSI) chips used as interface devices to perform various functions. These chips allow data to be transferred easily

1. From one computer to another.

2. From peripheral equipment to a computer.

**3.** From a computer to peripheral equipment.

**4.** Between pieces of peripheral equipment.

In all cases, they free the central processing unit (CPU) from the mundane task of sending and receiving data.

As computer systems become more advanced, an ever increasing volume of information will be exchanged and users will want to be able to transfer data at a much faster rate. Thus, new chips are designed to incorporate two or more functions that their predecessors were not capable of performing. These newer devices usually have some advantages: lower cost, lower power consumption, less weight, and less printed circuit board area. Although the newer devices are more efficient, some of the older chips are still excellent devices for demonstrating certain theories. Many older chips are still available at a reasonable cost and are incorporated into many systems that can be found in the field even today.

In the following chapters, the fundamental principles of how data is transferred between pieces of electronic equipment will be explained. To begin, the general definitions of ''communication'' and ''data communication'' will be compared.

## 1-1    What is Data Communication?

**Communication** is the act or process of exchanging or sharing information. In order to communicate, three things are needed: a sender, a receiver, and a medium. Consider some everyday examples. In face-to-face oral communication, one person speaks (the sender), another listens (the receiver), and the air is the medium. In a telephone conversation, the sender speaks, the receiver listens, and the telephone system is the medium. These are examples of voice communications. People also share information by letter (written communication), video (television), or even sign language. In all of these examples, information is either shared or exchanged by humans.

Data communication has a more restrictive definition. **Data communication** is the process of sharing or exchanging encoded information between two or more pieces of equipment. For data communication, the sender and receiver are machines. The term **encoded information** means that the data is transferred as a sequence of electrical signals. For example, when a computer operator presses the letter D on a keyboard, a sequence of electrical signals is sent to the computer. If the electrical signals are represented in terms of logic 1s and 0s, the letter D could be represented by 01000100. This binary pattern would be sent from the keyboard (sender), across a wire or wires (medium) to a computer (receiver). The computer would ''interpret'' the binary pattern to be the letter D. The electrical signals or the binary pattern is known as **encoded data.** Encoded data can be sent in either analog or digital form. In some data communication systems, the encoded data may be sent part way as digital signals and part way as analog signals. Whether the data is being transferred in digital or in analog form, the source (or sender) and the receiver are pieces of electronic equipment.

Be careful not to confuse data communication with digital transmission. Data communication is the transfer of encoded data between electronic equipment in either digital or analog form. In digital transmission, voice, data, video, or a combination of these is first converted to digital signals, which are then transmitted. A data communication application may use digital transmission but it is presently not limited to this form. As the information age continues to grow, data communication applications will increasingly use digital transmission techniques. There are two ways to transfer data, as discussed in the next section.

## 1-2 Serial Versus Parallel

Data may be transferred either by serial transmission over a single line or by parallel transmission over many lines. In **serial transmission,** binary data is sent

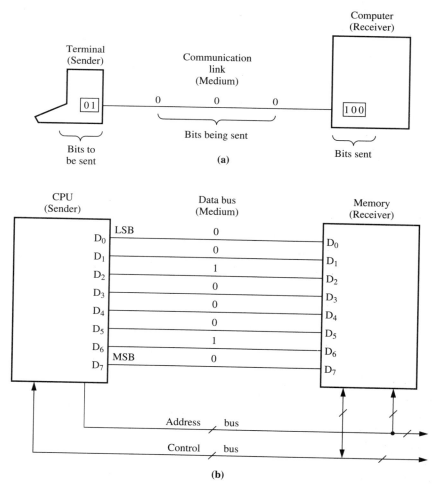

**Figure 1-1    Example of (a) Serial Transmission and (b) Parallel Transmission**

down a single wire 1 bit at a time. In **parallel transmission,** each bit has its own wire and all the data is sent at the same time. Figure 1-1a shows an example of serial transmission from a terminal to a computer for the binary pattern 01000100. The data bus within a computer system is an example of parallel transmission as shown in Figure 1-1b.

As expected, parallel transmission is faster because all bits are sent at once. Therefore, parallel transmission is used within the computer for functions such as transferring data between the CPU and memory, between the CPU and I/O chips, and between memory and I/O chips. However, multiple wires can become extremely cumbersome, costly, and susceptible to noise if parallel transmission is used between computers or between a computer and its peripheral equipment (such as keyboards, CRT displays, printers, plotters, etc.). Although some systems do use parallel transmission to transfer data to peripheral equipment, the majority use a serial format. There are available I/O chips that can convert the CPU's parallel data to serial format and transmit it. These I/O chips can also receive serial data and convert it to a parallel format so that it can be read by the CPU or memory. Because data communication occurs between computers or computers and peripheral equipment, the primary concern of this text is serial rather than parallel transmission. The next section discusses the different types of serial transmission.

## 1-3   Asynchronous Versus Synchronous

There are two methods of transmitting data serially: **asynchronous transmission** and **synchronous transmission.** In order for the transmitter and receiver to work together, both units must use the same transmission method. The receiver must also be able to detect the beginning and end of a character for asynchronous transmission and the beginning and end of a block of characters for synchronous transmission.

### 1-3.1   Asynchronous Transmission

**Asynchronous** means that a character may be transmitted at any time. Asynchronous transmission is used primarily for slow speed (less than 19,200 bits per second [bps]) and inexpensive data equipment such as CRT terminals, printers, and plotters. It is a popular method of sending data because the logic circuitry is simple, thus reducing the cost. It also allows for variable bursts of data; that is, the time between characters does not have to be equal. Using a computer for word processing is an example of asynchronous transmission. For any typist, the time between each key stroke varies. This variation may be due to the word being typed, the location of the characters on the keyboard, whether or not the shift key is used, and whether or not the character is typed with the person's stronger hand. Figure 1-2 shows an example of the word "DATA" being transmitted from a terminal to a computer with different time intervals between each letter. "Asynchronous" is a somewhat misleading term because it implies that there is no synchronization between transmitter and receiver. The receiver actually resynchronizes on each new character using the start bit. This will be studied in Chapter 3.

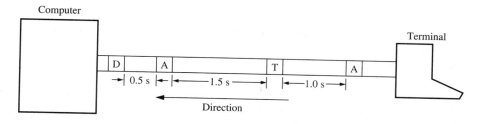

**Figure 1-2   The Characters in Asynchronous Communication Can Be Sent at Any Time**

Figure 1-3 shows the format of asynchronous transmission. There are four parts to each asynchronous character: start bit; data bits; parity bit; and stop bit or bits. Although the parity bit is optional, many systems use it; we will study examples with and without the parity bit.

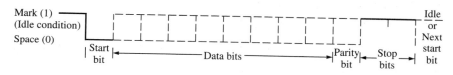

**Figure 1-3   Character Format for Asynchronous Transmission**

Although asynchronous communication systems are easy to design, build, and use, they are an inefficient method of transmitting data, because at least one start and stop bit have to be transmitted for each character. This results in an overhead factor. Expressed as a percent, the overhead is given by

$$\text{Percent overhead} = \frac{\text{nondata bits}}{\text{total bits}} \times 100\% \qquad (1\text{-}1)$$

E X A M P L E   1 - 1

Determine the overhead in percent for asynchronous transmission if the character is being transmitted as

**(a)** Start bit, 8 data bits, no parity bit, and a stop bit.

**(b)** Start bit, 7 data bits, a parity bit, and a stop bit.

**Solution**

**(a)** There are two nondata bits, the start and stop bits. Applying Equation (1-1) yields

$$\text{Percent overhead} = \frac{2}{10} \times 100\% = 20\%$$

**(b)** Although there are still 10 bits per character, there are only 7 data bits of data. The start, parity, and stop bits are the nondata bits. Therefore, Equation (1-1) yields

$$\text{Percent overhead} = \frac{3}{10} \times 100\% = 30\%$$

A more efficient method of transmitting data requires reduced overhead. This reduction can be achieved by synchronous transmission.

## 1-3.2   Synchronous Transmission

Synchronous transmission does not require a start and stop bit to frame each character. Instead, large blocks of data are transmitted at one time.

Remember that in asynchronous transmission, the start bit identifies the beginning of a new character and allows the receiver clock to be resynchronized. In synchronous transmission, the receiver must be able to identify each new frame of data as well as each bit within the frame. Figure 1-4 shows two different synchronous formats: a **character oriented frame** and a **bit oriented frame.** A character oriented transmission frame begins with one or more special synchronization (SYN) characters. A SYN character is a unique binary pattern. The beginning SYN characters are followed by control information, data, more control characters, and finally error checking characters. Another approach to character oriented transmission is to include the number of bytes of data within the first set of control information. The receiver detects this information and uses it to count the number of data bytes.

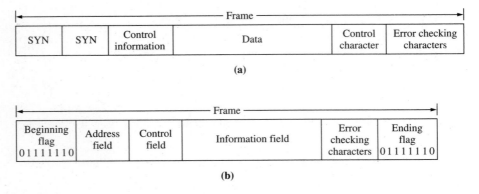

**Figure 1-4   Examples of Synchronous Format (a) Character Oriented Frame and (b) Bit Oriented Frame**

A bit oriented frame also has special bit patterns at the beginning and ending of each frame. These special patterns are 8 bits long and are referred to as **flags.** The same flag (01111110) is used at the beginning and end. As Figure 1-4b shows, the beginning or opening flag is followed by address information, control information, data, error checking information, and finally the ending flag.

At first glance, both types of synchronous frames, character oriented and bit oriented, appear similar. They both have special binary patterns to identify the frame boundaries. They also have control and data fields. The differences between them are in their overall formats and the interpretation of control information. Synchronous communication frames will be further addressed in Chapters 11 and 12.

In addition to frame boundaries, the receiver in synchronous transmission must have a method of identifying the location of each bit within the frame; otherwise, a problem known as **drifting** may occur between the transmitter and receiver. Drifting occurs when the transmitter's and receiver's clock signals are not synchronized. Every small error in the clock signal is cumulative. Therefore, for long blocks of data the receiver may not be sampling the line at the right time. One solution to this problem is to provide a separate clock line between transmitter and receiver. This ensures that the transmitter and receiver are getting the same clock signal. In most applications, though, a separate clock line is impossible. If data is to be sent via a telephone network, for example, there is no separate line. For this and most other synchronous applications, the clock signal is embedded into the data to maintain bit synchronization. The transmitter encodes a clock signal into the bit stream and the receiver removes it so the transmitter and receiver stay in synchronization. The reasons synchronous transmission is more efficient than asynchronous transmission will be examined next.

## E X A M P L E   1 - 2

Assume that 1024 data bits are to be transmitted. What is the percent overhead if the data is transmitted using

(a) Asynchronous transmission?

(b) Synchronous transmission using a bit oriented frame?

**Solution**

(a) Using asynchronous transmission, the 1024 data bits would be sent as individual characters. Assume that each character is 8 bits with no parity bit. This results in 128 characters ($1024/8 = 128$). Now each character must be framed by a start and a stop bit; therefore, there will be a total of 256 nondata bits ($128 \times 2 = 256$). Equation (1-1) yields

$$\text{Percent overhead} = \frac{256}{1024 + 256} \times 100\% = 20\%$$

(b) A typical bit oriented frame would have a total of 48 nondata bits for the opening flag, address, control, error checking fields, and closing flag. (These individual fields will be studied in Chapter 12.) Assume that the 1024 data bits comprise the entire information field. Now applying Equation (1-1) yields

$$\text{Percent overhead} = \frac{48}{1024 + 48} \times 100\% = 4.5\%$$

Note that the 48 bits that identified the flags and noninformation fields for the synchronous transmission example do not change regardless of the number of bits in the data field. Therefore, if the data field is very small, synchronous transmission techniques could be less efficient than asynchronous transmission. The problems at the end of this chapter will allow the reader to verify this point. Note that the type of transmission chosen and the amount of data to be transmitted have had a direct effect on the efficiency. However, there are also many other trade-offs including cost and application that determine which type of transmission is used.

*Ask - What is analog? digital?*

## 1-4   Modems and Multiplexers

The most direct approach for transmitting data to and from a computer is in digital form. This may be easy if the transmitter and receiver are close together or if a specific digital link has been connected between them. (This topic is covered in Chapter 13.) If there is a long distance between the transmitter and receiver or if a digital link is not available, then another convenient medium is needed.

One of the most available links is the telephone network. Since much of the telephone system is analog, what is needed is a piece of equipment that can convert digital data at the transmitter to an analog signal and that can reconvert this analog signal to digital data at the receiver. A **modem** is such a piece of equipment. The word "modem" is a contraction of two words, *mo*dulation and *dem*odulation. As will be studied in Chapters 8 and 9, the digital data modulates (varies) an analog *carrier* signal. It is the modulated signal that is transmitted and received by the modem at the other end. The receiving modem demodulates the signal and recovers the digital data. Figure 1-5a illustrates the fundamental concepts of using modems.

*briefly define*

Figure 1-5b expands the system of Figure 1-5a to show how the original data can appear at different stages in a long telephone transmission link. Note that the digital data that is being transmitted from central office #1 to central office #2 is not the same as the original data. This is because the circuitry at central office #1 is sampling an input analog signal, converting it to digital form, and then trans-mitting it. The circuitry at central office #2 reconverts the digital data to an analog signal and sends it to the modem. The modem at the receiving end can recover the original data. Modems are designed to be used either for asynchronous or synchronous transmission.

These examples so far have dealt with one terminal connected to a computer. This system can be expanded.

As a company grows, more computer terminals will be needed to keep pace with that growth. Figure 1-6 shows the system of Figure 1-5 expanded from one to four terminals. Since the systems of Figures 1-5 and 1-6 require two modems and one phone line for each terminal, multiterminal systems can get very expensive, especially if the modems are designed for 9600 bits per second (bps) and the phone lines are used extensively. To reduce costs, a pair of **multiplexers** and modems can be used as shown in Figure 1-7. Although Figure 1-7 shows the multiplexers and modems as separate units, they can be purchased as a single unit.

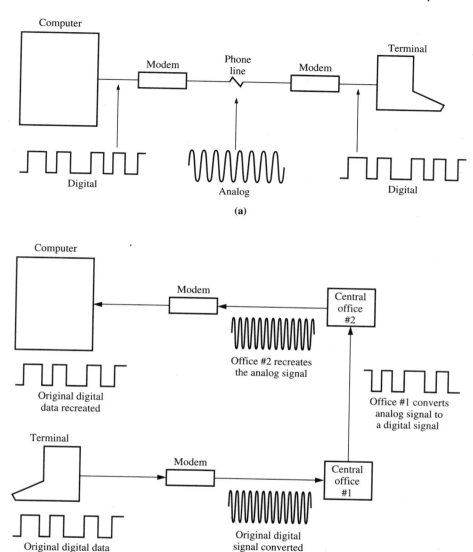

**Figure 1-5** **(a) A Phone Line Is Used to Transmit Digital Data. (b) Original Data May Appear in Different Forms from Terminal to Computer**

Like modems, multiplexers are used in pairs. The unit at the transmitting end takes the data from four terminals and combines it to be outputted on a single line. The receiving unit undoes what the first one did. This process is called demultiplexing. Regardless of the function performed, the units are simply referred to as multiplexers. In Chapter 13, multiplexing will be studied in more detail.

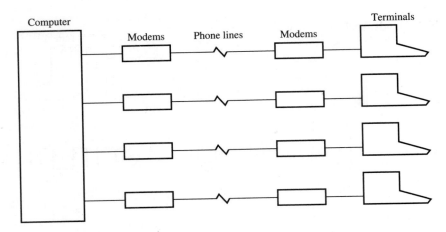

**Figure 1-6   Each Terminal Is Linked to the Computer by Its Own Pair of Modems and Phone Line**

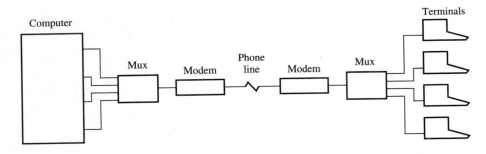

**Figure 1-7   A Pair of Multiplexers (Muxes) and Modems Can Reduce Costs Associated with Expanding a System**

## 1-5   Channel Limitations

As mentioned earlier, three things are needed in order to communicate: a sender, a receiver, and a medium. In data communication, the medium is referred to as a **data link, data channel,** or simply **channel.** The channel is the pathway for the flow of electrical signals. It may be a single wire, a wire pair, a coaxial or fiber optic cable, or a satellite link. In some applications, the channel is a specific frequency band. The electrical and physical characteristics of a channel limit the rate at which data can be transmitted.

The frequency range of the human ear will be compared with that of a telephone circuit. The ideal range for human hearing is 20 to 20,000 hertz. Most people do not have this wide a range and 40 to 14,000 hertz may be more typical. Normal conversation is heard at a frequency between 300 and 4000 hertz, with most of the energy occurring in the range 1000 to 2000 hertz. The other parts of the ear's frequency response (below 300 and above 4000 hertz) allow us to hear low and high sounds, such as the low bass tones and rich treble tones of an orchestra. Since the telephone network was designed for conversation and not music, it has a frequency response from only 300 to 3300 hertz. Thus, a telephone network is a poor medium for transmitting high fidelity music.          *good*

In a similar way, a telephone system also limits the rate at which digital data can be sent. However, many data communication applications force us to make a compromise between data rate versus convenience and cost. Telephone lines are everywhere and provide convenient (because they are already installed) data channels. Their disadvantage is that for the readily available dial-up line the data rate is usually less than 1200 bps. The next section discusses how channels are used for data communication.

## 1-6  Communication Modes

There are three types of communication modes: **simplex, half-duplex,** and **full-duplex** transmission. Figure 1-8 shows an example of each type. In simplex transmission, data always flows in the same direction. Figure 1-8a shows that the data transmission is from point A to point B. Since there is no return path, there is no way for the equipment at point B to signal point A. Two everyday examples of simplex transmission applications are radio and television. Information is sent only in one direction: there is no way of sending information from the receiver to the station.

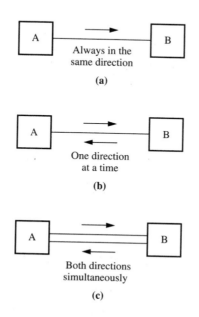

**Figure 1-8   Types of Channels: (a) Simplex; (b) Half-duplex; and (c) Full-duplex**

Half-duplex communication permits transmissions from point A to point B and from point B to point A, but not at the same time. Therefore, in a half-duplex transmission application, the channel must be "turned around." This is a disadvantage in many applications because the equipment at point A has to stop transmitting before point B can transmit. A two-way radio is an example of a half-duplex channel because one person has to "give up" the channel before the second person can transmit.

Full-duplex communication allows transmission from A to B and from B to A simultaneously. A telephone network is a full-duplex channel. Although it is not polite, both parties can talk at the same time.

## 1-7    Terminals

The most often used piece of peripheral equipment for communicating with a computer is a video terminal, consisting of a keyboard and a CRT display. Although terminals come in a variety of sizes and shapes and from a number of manufacturers, an attempt will be made to group them in three categories: dumb, smart, and intelligent.

**Dumb terminals** are usually low-cost units that transmit data asynchronously. Characters are sent to a host CPU as they are typed. These terminals usually do not contain computer power, are unable to be polled (*see* Section 1-8), and do not contain circuitry to "announce" any transmission errors received by the host computer.

**Smart terminals** usually have some computing power such as editing text, storing data in a memory buffer, and performing handshaking control signals to acknowledge that data is received without errors. They can be used in a polled or multidrop line application (*see* Section 1-8). Smart terminals store the data in an internal memory buffer and send the data synchronously. This can make maximum use of channel capacity. These devices are not user programmable. The computing power built into these terminals is fixed by the manufacturer.

**Intelligent terminals** have the maximum flexibility and may be stand-alone microcomputers. They are user programmable and may use only a host computer to access a large data base or for additional computing power. Intelligent terminals are also referred to as user programmable. Many personal computers are used in this application.

## 1-8    Point-to-Point and Multipoint Systems

A **point-to-point** system has equipment at each end of a connection. Examples include the following:

1. One terminal connected to a computer.

2. Several terminals connected to one computer where each terminal has its own link.

**3.** A computer connected to a computer or several terminals connected to a computer through multiplexers.

Figures 1-5 to 1-7 are examples of point-to-point configurations.

A **multipoint** system has one primary station (usually a computer) and several secondary stations (usually terminals) that share the same communication line. Figure 1-9 shows a multipoint configuration. This system requires smart or intelligent terminals and usually a polling scheme, where, for example, the computer addresses each terminal in sequence.

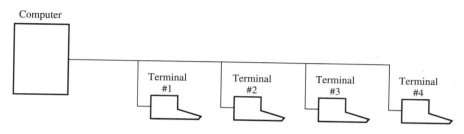

**Figure 1-9   Example of a Multipoint System**

Both point-to-point and multipoint systems use either half-duplex or full-duplex transmission. Simplex transmission schemes usually are not used in data communication applications.

In both point-to-point and multipoint systems, a set of rules must be followed to guarantee that an orderly transfer of data occurs:

**1.** The transmitter must know the receiver is ready.

**2.** Data must be transferred.

**3.** The transmitter must know that data has been received correctly.

**4.** The transmitter and receiver must be able to terminate the connection.

These rules are grouped together and referred to as protocols. They are introduced in Chapters 11 and 12.

## 1-9   Bit Rate Versus Baud Rate

The term **bit rate** means the number of binary digits transmitted in 1 second. Typical bit rates are 300, 1200, 2400, 4800, and 9600 bps. Often the term **baud rate** is confused with bit rate. Baud rate is defined as the number of signaling elements per unit time. The relationship between signal elements and bits will be examined. Consider the following two examples:

**1.** If a transmitter sends one signal to the receiver and it represents 1 bit, then the bit rate equals the baud rate.

**2.** If the transmitter sends one signal and it represents 2 bits, then the bit rate is twice the baud rate.

One of the main applications for encoding 2 or more bits into one signal is to increase the data rate over the telephone system. The bandwidth of the telephone system is 3000 hertz (3300 − 300 = 3000). This results in a practical maximum full-duplex data rate of 1200 baud. If a modem has been designed so that it encodes 2 bits for each baud, then the bit rate is 2400 bps (2 bits/baud × 1200 baud/ second = 2400 bps). Another modem may be designed to encode 4 bits for each baud. This results in a bit rate of 4800 bps (4 bits/baud × 1200 baud/second = 4800 bps).

At low data rates, usually less than 1200 bps, the baud rate and bit rate are equal. Some examples include 300 bps = 300 baud; 600 bps = 600 baud; and 1200 bps = 1200 baud. Because the number of bits transmitted is of primary concern, bit rate will be mainly used in this text to avoid confusion.

## 1-10    National and International Standards Organizations

Today there are many companies, government agencies, organizations, and professional societies involved with the field of data communications. Some are national and others are international groups. In order for manufacturers to design equipment that can be used by as many buyers as possible, standards had to be established. Some of the more widely known national and international organizations established committees to make recommendations and to publish and distribute the results. They are

**1.** The American National Standards Institute (ANSI).

**2.** The Electronic Industries Association (EIA).

**3.** The Consultative Committee International Telegraph and Telephone (CCITT) of the International Telecommunications Union (ITU).

**4.** The International Standards Organization (ISO).

ANSI is a nonprofit, nongovernmental organization comprising companies, organizations, and professional societies. It is the principal development body for data communication standards in the United States. ANSI is the coordinator and clearing house for all voluntary data communication standards and is a member of ISO. Many of the standards ANSI publishes are the result of its own technical committees, which are made up of technically qualified individuals rather than representatives from companies or societies. Other standards published by ANSI come from its member organizations such as EIA. EIA is a trade association of electronic companies, some of which manufacture data communication hardware equipment such as connectors, cables, modems, multiplexers, and digital line drivers.

The ITU, which is headquartered in Geneva, Switzerland, is a specialized agency of the United Nations. There are over 160 member countries in the ITU.

The ITU has two committees that deal with technical issues and development of standards. One committee is the International Radio Consultative Committee (CCIR) and the other is the International Telegraph and Telephone Consultative Committee (CCITT). It is the CCITT that deals with data communication standards. Within CCITT there are 18 Study Groups, each responsible for a specific area. The recommendations in this text are from Study Groups VII and XVII. These recommendations are the international equivalent of EIA recommendations, which are also covered in this text. Within member countries, it is the Post, Telegraph, and Telephone authorities that are responsible for data communications. Companies can belong to the CCITT but as nonvoting members.

The ISO is also based in Geneva, Switzerland. It is an independent organization that coordinates the efforts of other national bodies such as ANSI and the British Standards Institution (BSI) and generates worldwide standards for local area networks. The ISO has developed and published a seven-level hierarchy of protocols for networks known as the Open Systems Interconnect (OSI) model. The goal of the OSI model is to develop a standard by which businesses can easily share and exchange information using computers and purchase communication equipment from a variety of vendors. The material in this text covers the first two levels, the physical layer and the data link layer. The Institute of Electrical and Electronic Engineers (IEEE), through their affiliation with ANSI, has developed and published a number of standards in the OSI model.

In addition to these organizations, there are a number of government agencies and private companies that have established data communication standards, some of which have been accepted by a number of manufacturers and have become a de facto standard. Other proposed documents are going through the process of being accepted by one of the national organizations or professional societies.

## Summary

This chapter is a building block for many concepts used in data communications. We began by comparing a general definition of communication with data communication and then introduced two types of serial communication—asynchronous and synchronous. Often, computers and terminals are not next to one another and thus a convenient link between them is needed. Telephone systems are convenient but they were originally designed for analog transmission and not for digital transmission. A modem converts a digital signal to an analog signal to be sent over the telephone network. A modem at the receiver end reverses the process. As data communication systems expand, multiplexers may be more cost effective than a modem pair for each terminal and computer link.

Although there are three modes of communication—simplex, half-duplex, and full-duplex—the last two are the most often used modes for data communications. The two most common ways of configuring a system—point-to-point and multipoint—use both half-duplex and full-duplex operation. The majority of this textbook will demonstrate point-to-point applications. Regardless of how a system is configured, a user is always interested in the number of bits that are transmitted in 1 second—the bit rate. The limited bandwidth of a telephone network requires 2 or more bits to be sent as one signal element. Thus, a new term must be defined—baud rate—the number of signal elements per unit time. In order for business to purchase computing and communicating equipment from multivendors, standards are necessary. Several national and international organizations that develop and publish these standards are the subject of Section 1-10.

## Problems

**1.1** Define the following terms:

    **(a)** Data communication        **(f)** Half-duplex transmission
    **(b)** Serial transmission           **(g)** Full-duplex transmission
    **(c)** Asynchronous transmission   **(h)** Dumb terminals
    **(d)** Synchronous transmission    **(i)** Point-to-point systems
    **(e)** Modems                **(j)** Bit rate

**1.2** Calculate the overhead in percent for each of the following asynchronous characters:

    **(a)** 6 data bits, no parity bit     **(c)** 7 data bits, no parity bits
    **(b)** 8 data bits plus a parity bit  **(d)** 5 data bits plus parity

    Each asynchronous character has one start and stop bit.

**\*1.3** What is the overhead in percent to transmit 256 data bits using synchronous transmission with a bit oriented frame? Assume that the flags and other nondata fields require 48 bits.

**1.4** If the 256 data bits of Problem 1.3 are sent using asynchronous transmission, calculate the overhead in percent. Assume that each character is framed by one start and one stop bit and the character consists of 8 bits and no parity bit.

**\*1.5** If the percentage overhead for a bit oriented frame is 25% and there are 48 nondata bits, calculate the number of data bits in the information field.

**1.6** Explain why modems have to be used in pairs.

**\*1.7** Identify each of the following situations as either simplex, half-duplex, or full-duplex transmission:

    **(a)** Walkie-talkies
    **(b)** Lecture only
    **(c)** Question/answer period
    **(d)** Keyboard portion of a computer terminal

\* *See* Answers to Selected Problems.

# *Data Codes* 2

Upon completion of this chapter on data codes, the student will be able to

- Use the ASCII character matrix.
- Convert a 7-bit pattern to an ASCII symbol.
- Understand the reason for needing a data code standard.
- Know the reason for control characters.
- Be able to group the ASCII control characters into different categories.
- Understand a handshake procedure between pieces of equipment.
- Be familiar with the EBCDIC standard.

## Introduction

Digital equipment processes only binary digits, 0 and 1. To transmit a message, bits are grouped together to form alphanumerical characters (numbers or letters), punctuation marks, special characters, or control characters. The circuitry within printers and terminals then converts each group of binary digits into a familiar character or symbol so we can read the information that has been transmitted. To do this, the equipment that is sending and receiving the data must be designed so each unique group of bits always represents the same character or symbol. Thus, a standard is required. A standard ensures that equipment purchased from different manufacturers will be compatible. Bits that are grouped together to represent a particular character or symbol are known as **transmission codes, data codes,** or simply **codes.** Several data codes are important in data communication because they are used so often. The code encountered the most is the **ASCII** character set. This chapter primarily focuses on this code. Section 2-4 summarizes IBM's Extended Binary Coded Decimal Information Code known as **EBCDIC** (pronounced "eb-see-dik"), which is used in their miniframe and largeframe computers.

## 2-1  ASCII

The American National Standards Institute (ANSI) wanted to establish compatibility between equipment transmitting and receiving digital data. It published a 7-bit coded character set in 1963. Since then it has been updated and revised. In the United States, this character set is known as the American Standard Code for Information Interchange, abbreviated ASCII (pronounced "as-key"). Along with an international code that is almost identical, it is probably the most widely used information code in the world. The 7 bits allow for 128 ($2^7$ = 128) different characters or symbols. An eighth bit may be added for parity. The choice of parity is left to equipment designers. Therefore, you may find equipment that is designed to transmit or receive ASCII characters with odd parity, ASCII characters with even parity, or ASCII characters without parity. Examples of each are given in Chapter 3.

Section 2-3 discusses some of the characteristics of a useful standard and shows how the ASCII character set fits many needs. First, the ASCII character set will be discussed.

A common way of displaying all 128 characters and symbols is in a matrix format as shown in Figure 2-1. Each character or symbol in the matrix is represented by its binary pattern. The most significant bits (MSB) (bits 7, 6, and 5) are at the top and the least significant bits (LSB) (bits 4, 3, 2, and 1) are in the left hand column. Since the hexadecimal code is used so often it is also included in Figure 2-1. Remember, if parity is used, it will be added to the binary pattern as the eighth bit.

To learn how to read the matrix, use the capital letter E. The most significant hex digit is 4 and the least significant hex digit is 5. Therefore the ASCII code for E in hex is 45 or in binary is 1000101. Sometimes you may find the binary pattern written as P1000101 where P represents the location of the parity bit.

---

E  X  A  M  P  L  E    2 - 1

---

Convert the following binary patterns to the character symbols: (a) 1101010; (b) 1010000; (c) 0100101.

**Solution**

The bits are arranged from MSB to LSB as

|     | MSB | | | | | | LSB | ASCII |
|-----|-----|-----|-----|-----|-----|-----|-----|-----------|
|     | $b_7$ | $b_6$ | $b_5$ | $b_4$ | $b_3$ | $b_2$ | $b_1$ | Character |
| (a) | 1 | 1 | 0 | 1 | 0 | 1 | 0 | j |
| (b) | 1 | 0 | 1 | 0 | 0 | 0 | 0 | P |
| (c) | 0 | 1 | 0 | 0 | 1 | 0 | 1 | % |

Most Significant Bits
b₇ b₆ b₅

| | Hex Codes → | 000<br>0 | 001<br>1 | 010<br>2 | 011<br>3 | 100<br>4 | 101<br>5 | 110<br>6 | 111<br>7 |
|---|---|---|---|---|---|---|---|---|---|
| 0000 | 0 | NUL | DLE | SP | 0 | @ | P | ` | p |
| 0001 | 1 | SOH | DC1 | ! | 1 | A | Q | a | q |
| 0010 | 2 | STX | DC2 | " | 2 | B | R | b | r |
| 0011 | 3 | ETX | DC3 | # | 3 | C | S | c | s |
| 0100 | 4 | EOT | DC4 | $ | 4 | D | T | d | t |
| 0101 | 5 | ENQ | NAK | % | 5 | E | U | e | u |
| 0110 | 6 | ACK | SYN | & | 6 | F | V | f | v |
| 0111 | 7 | BEL | ETB | ' | 7 | G | W | g | w |
| 1000 | 8 | BS | CAN | ( | 8 | H | X | h | x |
| 1001 | 9 | HT | EM | ) | 9 | I | Y | i | y |
| 1010 | A | LF | SUB | * | : | J | Z | j | z |
| 1011 | B | VT | ESC | + | ; | K | [ | k | { |
| 1100 | C | FF | FS | , | < | L | \ | l | \| |
| 1101 | D | CR | GS | – | = | M | ] | m | } |
| 1110 | E | SO | RS | . | > | N | ^ | n | ~ |
| 1111 | F | SI | US | / | ? | O | — | o | DEL |

Least Significant Bits
b₄ b₃ b₂ b₁

$b_7\ b_6\ b_5$ — Most Significant Bits.
$b_4\ b_3\ b_2\ b_1$ — Least Significant Bits.

**Figure 2-1** ASCII Character Set. This Set Is the U.S. Version of the International Telegraph and Telephone Consultative Committee (CCITT) International Alphabet Study Group V *printable*

The ASCII character set can be divided into two major categories: control characters (columns 0 and 1) and graphical characters (columns 2 to 7). A control character is defined in the standard as a character that initiates, modifies, or stops the recording, processing, transmission, or interpretation of data. The control characters are covered in Section 2-2. Graphical characters refer to printable characters and not to computer drawings. The ASCII graphical characters are found in the last six columns except for the DEL character, which is a control character.

The columns within the matrix of Figure 2-1 are organized in the following way:

| Columns | Organization |
| --- | --- |
| 0 and 1 | Control characters |
| 2 and 3 | Numbers, punctuation marks, and symbols |
| 4 and 5 | Uppercase letters and symbols |
| 6 and 7 | Lowercase letters and symbols |

The matrix highlights some easy ways to remember how to convert from an ASCII character or symbol to its hex equivalent. For example, all the numerical values are in column 3. Therefore, the conversion from a numerical value to its ASCII hex equivalent is given by

$$\text{ASCII value in hex} = 30_{hex} + \text{Numerical value} \qquad (2\text{-}1)$$

E X A M P L E   2 - 2

Convert the following decimal numbers to their ASCII hex equivalent values: (a) 5; (b) 0; (c) 14.

**Solution**

(a) Applying Equation (2-1) yields

$$\text{ASCII value in hex} = 30_{hex} + 5 = 35_{hex}$$

(b) Applying Equation (2-1) yields

$$\text{ASCII value in hex} = 30_{hex} + 0 = 30_{hex}$$

(c) Each decimal number must be converted to its ASCII value. Therefore, applying Equation (2-1) twice yields

$$\text{ASCII value in hex} = 30_{hex} + 1 = 31_{hex}$$
$$\text{ASCII value in hex} = 30_{hex} + 4 = 34_{hex}$$

The decimal number 14 is 31 34 in the ASCII hex equivalent. The binary pattern can also be obtained from Figure 2-1 or by converting the hexadecimal value to binary such as $31_{hex} = 0110001_{binary}$ and $34_{hex} = 0110100_{binary}$. Therefore, the decimal number 14 would be transmitted as the binary sequence 01100010110100. Parity bits have not been included yet. If they were included, there would be a parity bit for each 7 bits of data. The capital letter P in the following binary sequence shows the location of the parity bits P0110001P0110100.

We also see that the ASCII matrix of Figure 2-1 is organized so that uppercase and lowercase letters differ by two columns or $20_{hex}$. In equation form this is written as

$$\text{Lowercase letters in hex} = \text{uppercase letters in hex} + 20_{hex} \qquad (2\text{-}2)$$

E  X  A  M  P  L  E      2 - 3

Use Equation (2-2) to convert "DATA" from its uppercase ASCII hex values to lowercase hex values. $D = 44_{hex}$, $A = 41_{hex}$, and $T = 54_{hex}$.

**Solution**

From Equation (2-2), the following hex values for the lowercase letters are obtained:

$$d = 44_{hex} + 20_{hex} = 64_{hex}$$

$$a = 41_{hex} + 20_{hex} = 61_{hex}$$

$$t = 54_{hex} + 20_{hex} = 74_{hex}$$

$$a = 41_{hex} + 20_{hex} = 64_{hex}$$

Although uppercase and lowercase letters differ by $20_{hex}$ or two columns in the matrix table, a closer examination shows that only 1 bit (bit 6) changes state. This allows logic circuitry to distinguish between uppercase and lowercase letters easily.

In addition to the alphanumerical characters, punctuation marks, and symbols that are familiar to us, the ASCII table includes special characters for transmitting data more efficiently. These special characters are known as control characters.

## 2-2   Control Characters

As previously mentioned, ASCII's definition of a **control character** is a character whose occurrence in a particular context initiates, modifies, or stops the recording, processing, transmission, or interpretation of data. Control characters provide for an orderly flow of data.

Many of these control characters are automatically generated by software routines and therefore a computer user is unaware that control characters are being transmitted. In some applications, a user may want to insert a particular control character from the keyboard. This is done by depressing one key labeled "control key" and at the same time another graphical key. On many keyboards, the control key is labeled as CONTROL or CTRL. When this key is depressed along with a graphical key, a control character is generated. In Figure 2-1, the control characters (except for DEL) are located in columns 0 and 1. Some of the control characters are separate keys on a keyboard while others may be generated by using the control key along with a particular graphical key. In Figure 2-1 these control characters are $40_{hex}$ less than the uppercase graphical keys.

$$\text{Control character in hex} = \text{graphical key in hex} - 40_{hex} \qquad (2\text{-}3)$$

Before studying the function of the control characters, do the following example using Equation (2-3).

E X A M P L E    2 - 4

Suppose your computer terminal has a bell that you want to use. Which key must be pressed along with the control key to ring the bell and what is the binary pattern that is transmitted from the keyboard to the computer?

**Solution**

From Figure 2-1, the word "bell" is listed as BEL and its ASCII equivalent value is $07_{hex}$. Rearranging Equation (2-3) yields

$$\text{Graphical key in hex} = 40_{hex} + 07_{hex} = 47_{hex}$$

and the capital letter that would be pressed along with the control key is G ($47_{hex}$). The binary pattern that is transmitted is 1000111. (Remember, not all keyboards generate a bell sound.)

E X A M P L E    2 - 5

Which control characters are generated if the following keys are pressed along with the control key: (a) H, (b) I, (c) [?

**Solution**

Another way of understanding Equation (2-3) is that the control character and the capital letter reference key are separated by four columns. For this example, use Figure 2-1 and enter the matrix at the graphical key and then move to the left four columns.

|      | Graphical Key | Move Left Four Columns | Control Character |
|------|---------------|------------------------|-------------------|
| (a)  | H             | $- 40_{hex}$           | BS (backspace)    |
| (b)  | I             | $- 40_{hex}$           | HT (horizontal tab) |
| (c)  | [             | $- 40_{hex}$           | ESC (escape)      |

Some control characters are used so often that manufacturers have included a key for that specific function. Examples are ESC (escape), BEL (bell), and CR (carriage return). On many computer terminals, these functions can also be generated by holding down the control key and pressing the correct graphical key.

Most of the control characters fall into one of the following categories: **format effectors, communication control, information separators,** and **device control** as shown in Figure 2-2. However, there are still nine other control characters that the standard does not put into one of these four categories. These characters are listed in Figure 2-2 as **other control characters.**

| Control Characters | | Format effectors | Communication control | Information separators | Device control | Other control characters |
|---|---|---|---|---|---|---|
| NUL | Null | | | | | X |
| SOH | Start of Header | | X | | | |
| STX | Start of Text | | X | | | |
| ETX | End of Text | | X | | | |
| EOT | End of Transmission | | X | | | |
| ENQ | Enquiry | | X | | | |
| ACK | Acknowledge | | X | | | |
| BEL | Bell | | | | | X |
| BS | Backspace | X | | | | |
| HT | Horizontal Tabulation | X | | | | |
| LF | Line Feed | X | | | | |
| VT | Vertical Tabulation | X | | | | |
| FF | Form Feed | X | | | | |
| CR | Carriage Return | X | | | | |
| SO | Shift Out | | | | | X |
| SI | Shift In | | | | | X |
| DLE | Data Link Escape | | X | | | |
| DC1 | Device Control 1 | | | | X | |
| DC2 | Device Control 2 | | | | X | |
| DC3 | Device Control 3 | | | | X | |
| DC4 | Device Control 4 | | | | X | |
| NAK | Negative Acknowledge | | X | | | |
| SYN | Synchronous Idle | | X | | | |
| ETB | End of Transmission Block | | X | | | |
| CAN | Cancel | | | | | X |
| EM | End of Medium | | | | | X |
| SUB | Substitute | | | | | X |
| ESC | Escape | | | | | X |
| FS | File Separator | | | X | | |
| GS | Group Separator | | | X | | |
| RS | Record Separator | | | X | | |
| US | Unit Separator | | | X | | |
| DEL | Delete | | | | | X |

**Figure 2-2   ASCII Control Characters and Their Categories**

## 2-2.1   Format Effectors

Format effectors are control characters that determine how a particular message will be displayed either on a video terminal or printout. They are intended to be used to make a neat and orderly layout of the message for easy reading. Format effectors are used by data communication equipment to separately control the horizontal and vertical placement of the cursor or printhead. The six format effector characters are BS, HT, LF, VT, FF, and CR.

---

**BS (Backspace) 08$_{hex}$**   A control character that moves the cursor or printhead back one position on the same line.

**HT (Horizontal Tabulation) 09$_{hex}$**   A control character that moves the cursor or printhead right to the next predetermined character position on the same line.

**LF (Line Feed) 0A$_{hex}$**   A control character that moves the cursor or printhead down to the next line at the same position.

**VT (Vertical Tabulation) 0B$_{hex}$**   A control character that moves the cursor or printhead to the next predetermined line at the same character position. The next predetermined line does not necessarily imply the next line but may be several lines away.

**FF (Form Feed) 0C$_{hex}$**   A control character that moves the cursor or printhead to the same character position on a predetermined line on the next page. Often the sender and receiver have agreed that the cursor or printhead should be moved to the first character position on the next page.

**CR (Carriage Return) 0D$_{hex}$**   A control character that moves the cursor or printhead to the first position on the same line. In most systems, a carriage return generates both a carriage return and a line feed. Thus depressing a ''return'' key on most keyboards moves the cursor or printhead to the first active position on the next line.

---

## 2-2.2   Communication Control

The ASCII standard defines communication control characters as those characters intended to control or facilitate transmission of information over communication networks. As shown in Figure 2-2, there are ten communication control characters. Listing them in alphabetical order they are ACK, DLE, ENQ, EOT, ETB, ETX, NAK, SOH, STX, and SYN. This section gives a brief description of each character. However, they are used primarily for synchronous transmission applications and therefore will be studied in more detail in Chapter 11. Figure 2-3 is an expanded version of Figure 1-4a and is an aid in understanding where these control characters occur in a character oriented frame.

---

**ACK (Acknowledge) 06$_{hex}$**   This control character verifies that a block of data was received correctly by the receiving station. The ACK control character is transmitted from the receiver to the sender as an affirmative or positive acknowledgment that the previous block was received error free.

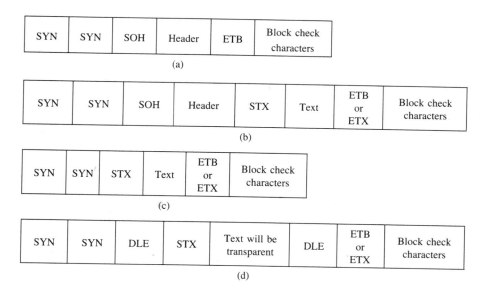

**Figure 2-3   Applications of Communication Control Characters Used in Different Character Oriented Frames**

**DLE (Data Link Escape) 10$_{hex}$**   This control character is used to change the meaning of a limited number of characters immediately following it. In Chapter 11, the DLE character will be used to provide transparent transmission for certain synchronous applications. The DLE character is also intended to provide supplementary data transmission control functions. You may obtain information on this material from ANSI X3.28 publication.

**ENQ (Enquiry) 05$_{hex}$**   This control character is used by a primary station asking for identification, status, or both from a remote station. Often it is used by the primary to ask the question "Who are you?" (WRU). It can be used in a point-to-point system or a specifically addressed station in a multipoint system.

**EOT (End of Transmission) 04$_{hex}$**   This control character is used to indicate the end of the transmission. The entire transmission may have contained one or more texts along with associated headings. In a multipoint system, this control character can inform the other stations to check the line for messages that may be addressed to them.

**ETB (End of Transmission Block) 17$_{hex}$**   Long messages are often divided into multiple blocks for the purpose of transmission. This control character identifies the end of a block of data and is followed by the error checking characters.

**ETX (End of Text) 03$_{hex}$**   This control character indicates to the receiver that the end of a text has occurred. The functions of ETB and ETX are similar but the ETX character indicates that there are no more data blocks to follow. The error checking characters follow the ETX control character.

**NAK (Negative Acknowledge) 15$_{hex}$**   This control character is transmitted by a receiving station indicating that the message was not received correctly. As will be studied in Chapter 11, a negative acknowledge usually causes the sender to retransmit the message.

**SOH (Start of Header) $01_{hex}$**   This control character indicates the beginning of the header portion of an information message.

**STX (Start of Text) $02_{hex}$**   This control character indicates the beginning of the main body of the information that is being transmitted. It also indicates the end of the header.

**SYN (Synchronous Idle) $16_{hex}$**   This control character provides message framing and synchronization. It is also used when no other characters are being sent.

---

### 2-2.3   Information Separators

There are four control characters that are categorized as information separators: FS (File Separator), GS (Group Separator), RS (Record Separator), and US (Unit Separator). These control characters may be used as information separators. If they are used, they have a hierarchical relationship. FS is the most inclusive, then GS, then RS, and then US is the least inclusive. The information and length contained within each part are not specified by the standard.

### 2-2.4   Device Control

The ASCII standard includes four device control characters: DC1, DC2, DC3, and DC4. These characters allow manufacturers to use them for a variety of applications. Control characters DC1 and DC3 are used primarily for flow control. For example, assume that a computer is sending data to a printer. Although most printers have a memory buffer to temporarily store data while waiting for the print mechanism, the printer's mechanical parts operate much slower than the rate at which the computer can send data, thus overflowing the memory buffer. Flow control is a solution to this problem. It allows the printer's circuitry to determine the rate at which it can accept data from the computer. The convention is to use DC1 and DC3 as transmission on and transmission off, respectively.

DC1 = XON (transmission on)

DC3 = XOFF (transmission off)

The handshake procedure between the computer and the printer works in the following way. Assume that the printer's buffer is empty. As data comes from the computer, the buffer begins to fill. When the buffer is approximately 75% full, the printer sends a DC3 control character (XOFF) back to the computer. As soon as the computer recognizes the character, transmission stops. To work in this way, there must be either half- or full-duplex operation between the computer and the printer. A set point of approximately 75% rather than 100% is used to prevent the buffer from overflowing, thus causing data to be lost before the computer receives the XOFF command. As the printer's circuitry removes data from the buffer, at some point the buffer will decrease to 25%. Then the printer sends a DC1 control character (XON) back to the computer. This notifies the computer to send more data. This handshake procedure continues until the entire message is transmitted.

## 2-2.5   Other ASCII Control Characters

As shown in Figure 2-2, there are nine control characters that are not grouped into one of the defined categories: NUL, BEL, SO, SI, CAN, EM, SUB, ESC, and DEL.

---

**NUL (Null) 00$_{hex}$**   This control character is a nonprintable character used for time delay or layout purposes. For example, if an additional time interval is needed for a print mechanism to respond to a carriage return-line feed operation, then a series of NUL characters can provide the appropriate delay. A NUL character or characters may be inserted into or removed from a data stream without affecting the content. It may, however, affect the layout of the data. At some time a worker at a terminal may be prompted by the computer to ''Enter the number of nulls.'' This is so the computer transfers data at an appropriate rate to the receiver (such as a printer or other computer) to ''handle'' it.

**BEL (Bell) 07$_{hex}$**   This control character is used when it is necessary to alert somebody. It may be used as an alarm or simply an attention-getting device.

**SO (Shift Out) 0E$_{hex}$**   This control character is used to extend the graphical character set. It allows the bit combinations in columns 2 to 7 (except for SP and DEL) to have different meanings until a ''Shift in character'' is received. Thus non-English characters may be transmitted by using the SO and SI control characters. Of course, the sender and receiver must have established beforehand the meaning of each binary pattern following the SO character.

**SI (Shift In) 0F$_{hex}$**   This control character reinstates the standard ASCII character set for all bit combinations after it is received.

**CAN (Cancel) 18$_{hex}$**   This control character indicates to the receiver that the data that it is receiving is incorrect or should be disregarded. The transmitter has determined that something has ''gone wrong'' and wishes to warn the receiver. The receiver does not automatically reject all the data on receiving a CAN character unless it is programmed to do so. Instead, the receiver may be programmed to reject only part or none of the data. Therefore, the specific meaning of the CAN character must be defined for each application.

**EM (End of Medium) 19$_{hex}$**   As the name implies, this control character identifies an ending. There are three possible endings that this control identifies.

1. The physical end of the medium.

2. The end of the used portion of the medium.

3. The end of the wanted portion of recorded data on the medium.

Figure 2-4 illustrates the location where the EM control character could be used.

**SUB (Substitute) 1A$_{hex}$**   A control character that may be substituted for a character that is determined to be invalid or incorrect.

**ESC (Escape) 1B$_{hex}$**   This control character provides for code extension. The 7 bits allow for 128 ASCII characters. This number of bits was decided to be the best size to fit most applications. However, some users find themselves being too restricted and need more characters.

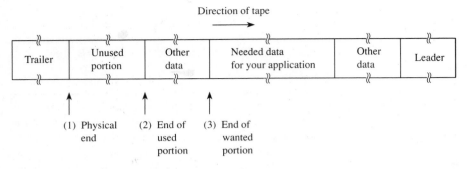

Figure 2-4   **Example of Using an EM Character**

**DEL (Delete) 7F$_{hex}$**   This control character is used primarily to erase an unwanted character. Another use of this control character is for time fill. A DEL character may be inserted into or removed from a data stream without affecting the content of the information. What may be affected, as DEL characters are inserted and removed, is the layout or control of equipment. This secondary use of the DEL character is similar to the NUL character.

## 2-3   Need for a Standard

Section 1-10 introduced some of the national and international organizations that develop and publish standards. Since the basic components of the ASCII standard have been discussed, some of the more important characteristics in designing such a standard can now be examined.

There are many considerations that determine what must be included in a standard character set. We need to know whether there are enough graphical and control characters, whether each code has a unique interpretation, whether the classes of characters can be easily identified, whether it conforms to international standards, whether it can be used by existing programming languages, and whether it conforms to collating and keyboard conventions.

The ASCII graphical set includes the digits 0 to 9, both the uppercase and lowercase Latin letters A to Z, as well as punctuation marks, mathematical symbols, and the most frequently used business symbols. Languages other than English are accommodated because the set includes two accent marks and other diacritical marks. The set also includes the characters commonly encountered in programming languages, in particular COBOL and FORTRAN.

The location of the graphical characters within the set has been arranged to minimize the hardware and operating time. For example, keyboard hardware devices are simplified by having the uppercase and lowercase letter differ by only 1 bit—bit 6. For uppercase letters, bit 6 is a logic 0 and for lowercase letters bit 6 is a logic 1. For collating purposes, SP (space) collates before other graphical characters and is therefore the first graphical character. Similarly, a comma collates before the alphabet.

Even the location of particular control characters has been carefully considered. For example, the ACK and NAK characters are located to provide protection against transmission errors. Another example is the location of the information separators that are at the end of the control characters and before SP (space). The reason is that SP is sometimes used as a separator.

You may learn more about the design considerations by reading the Appendices for the American National Standard Code for Information Interchange.

## 2-4   EBCDIC

In the 1960s, IBM devised a proprietary 8-bit code to be used on their mainframe computers. Although the code is not detailed in national or international standards' publications, EBCDIC may be easily found because IBM equipment is so prevalent. Therefore, the EBCDIC code is summarized in this section.

An 8-bit code provides for 256 ($2^8 = 256$) different binary combinations. Although there are 256 possible binary combinations in the EBCDIC character set, there are many unassigned bit patterns as shown in Figure 2-5. The empty spaces may be assigned for particular applications needing to transmit other symbols or control functions. Therefore, if the additional control characters are not being used, there is a significant overhead factor using a basic 8-bit code rather than a 7-bit code. However, IBM designed their code primarily for synchronous communication and needed the additional control characters. A note of caution: IBM identifies the LSB as bit 7 and the MSB as bit 0. In Figure 2-5, the MSBs ($b_0$ to $b_3$) are at the left along with their hexadecimal equivalent codes. The LSBs ($b_4$ to $b_7$) and their hexadecimal equivalent codes are at the top. Figure 2-5 shows those characters that correspond to most of the universal codes used in other standards.

### E X A M P L E   2 - 6

Obtain the binary and hexadecimal digits for the following alphanumerical characters using the EBCDIC character set: (a) A; (b) n; (c) 3; (d) R.

**Solution**

Using Figure 2-5, the following is obtained:

|     | Character | Binary | Hex |
|-----|-----------|--------|-----|
| (a) | A | 11000001 | C1 |
| (b) | n | 10010101 | 95 |
| (c) | 3 | 11110011 | F3 |
| (d) | R | 11011001 | D9 |

Bits: b0 b1 b2 b3 — Most Significant (columns, hex 0–F); b4 b5 b6 b7 — Least Significant (rows, hex 0–F)

| LSN \ MSN | 0 | 1 | 2 | 3 | 4 | 5 | 6 | 7 | 8 | 9 | A | B | C | D | E | F |
|---|---|---|---|---|---|---|---|---|---|---|---|---|---|---|---|---|
| 0 | NUL | DLE | DS |  | SP | & | - |  |  |  |  |  | { | } | \ | 0 |
| 1 | SOH | DC1 | SOS |  |  |  | / |  | a | j | ~ |  | A | J |  | 1 |
| 2 | STX | DC2 | FS | SYN |  |  |  |  | b | k | s |  | B | K | S | 2 |
| 3 | ETX | DC3 |  |  |  |  |  |  | c | l | t |  | C | L | T | 3 |
| 4 | PF | RES | BYP | PN |  |  |  |  | d | m | u |  | D | M | U | 4 |
| 5 | HT | NL | LF | RS |  |  |  |  | e | n | v |  | E | N | V | 5 |
| 6 | LC | BS | ETB | UC |  |  |  |  | f | o | w |  | F | O | W | 6 |
| 7 | DEL | IL | ESC | EOT |  |  |  |  | g | p | x |  | G | P | X | 7 |
| 8 |  | CAN |  |  |  |  |  |  | h | q | y |  | H | Q | Y | 8 |
| 9 | RLF | EM |  |  |  |  |  |  | i | r | z |  | I | R | Z | 9 |
| A | SMM | CC | SM |  | ¢ | ! | \| | : |  |  |  |  |  |  |  |  |
| B | VT |  |  |  | . | $ | , | # |  |  |  |  |  |  |  |  |
| C | FF | IFS |  | DC4 | < | * | % | @ |  |  |  |  |  |  |  |  |
| D | CR | IGS | ENQ | NAK | ( | ) | _ | ' |  |  |  |  |  |  |  |  |
| E | SO | IRS | ACK |  | + | ; | > | = |  |  |  |  |  |  |  |  |
| F | SI | IUS | BEL | SUB | \| | ¬ | ? | " |  |  |  |  |  |  |  |  |

**Figure 2-5** EBCDIC Character Set Showing the Most Commonly Used Codes

From Figure 2-5 we observe that the control functions are grouped in the upper four rows (rows 0 to 3). Rows 4 to 7 contain punctuation marks and other commonly used symbols. The lowercase letters are grouped in rows 8 to A and the uppercase letters are in rows C to E. The last row (row F) contains the numerals 0 to 9. Like the ASCII matrix, the EBCDIC matrix shows a logical pattern between uppercase and lowercase letters and all the numerals are arranged in a single row. For EBCDIC characters, the uppercase and lowercase letters are separated by four rows or $40_{hex}$, but only 1 bit needs to change state. If bit 1 is a logic 0, lowercase letters are being transmitted, and if bit 1 is a logic 1, then uppercase letters are being sent. Since the digits 0 to 9 are in a single row (row F), the conversion for numerals is easy and is given by

$$\text{EBCDIC value} = F0_{hex} + \text{numerical value} \qquad (2\text{-}4)$$

**E X A M P L E 2 - 7**

Convert the following numerical values to their EBCDIC hexadecimal value: (a) 4; (b) 50; (c) 128.

**Solution**

Using Equation (2-4)

(a) $F0_{hex} + 4 = F4_{hex}$

(b) $F0_{hex} + 5 = F5_{hex}$
and
$F0_{hex} + 0 = F0_{hex}$
50 in EBCDIC $= F5F0_{hex}$

(c) $F0_{hex} + 1 = F1_{hex}$
$F0_{hex} + 2 = F2_{hex}$
$F0_{hex} + 8 = F8_{hex}$
128 in EBCDIC $= F1F2F8_{hex}$

## Summary

Many different code sets are used in the field of computers and data communications. This chapter concentrated on one of the most widely used code sets—the ASCII character set. In this set, letters, numbers, punctuation marks, symbols, and nonprintable control characters are represented by a 7-bit binary pattern. An eighth bit may be added for parity. The choice of parity is left to the users or equipment designers.

A matrix format is one of the most common ways of displaying the characters within a code set because relationships between characters can be quickly observed. The ASCII character set can be divided into two major categories: control characters and graphical characters. Control characters initiate, modify, or stop the recording, processing, transmission, or interpretation of data. Control characters are not printed or displayed on a CRT screen. These characters are grouped into one of the following categories: format effectors; communication control; information separators; device control; and other control characters. Graphical characters refer to printable characters. This chapter also introduced the EBCDIC. This code set is used primarily by IBM and similar equipment. This set uses 8 bits to represent each character.

## Problems

\* **2.1** Given the following binary patterns, what are the ASCII characters?
  (a) 0100000
  (b) 0111100
  (c) 1011100
  (d) 1111000

**2.2** Convert the following decimal numbers to their ASCII hexadecimal equivalent values:
  (a) 7  (b) 12  (c) 483

\* **2.3** What is the relationship between the uppercase and lowercase letters in (a) hex (b) binary?

**2.4** Refer to Problem 2.1(a). If bit 6 is damaged during transmission and is received as a logic 0, which ASCII character is interpreted at the receiver?

\* **2.5** Using the ASCII character set, represent the expression "Data Communication" in hexadecimal.

**2.6** Using the ASCII character set, represent the word "Data" in binary.

\* **2.7** Which control characters are generated if the following graphical keys are pressed with the control key: (a) @; (b) J; (c) Q?

**2.8** What is the function of the format effectors?

\* **2.9** According to the ASCII standard, does a carriage return automatically generate a line feed?

**2.10** Which bit or bits change state to generate control characters DC1 and DC3?

\***2.11** Is the EBCDIC character set an ANSI standard?

**2.12** The following binary string is being transmitted using EBCDIC code. Determine the message. The LSB of each 8-bit pattern is at the left and the first character being transmitted is the leftmost binary pattern.

\* *See* Answers to Selected Problems.

1st character

LSB  0010001110000001110001011000000100000010
     11000011011010010010000110100001010000101

*2.13 Explain how a memory look-up table could be used to convert from ASCII characters to EBCDIC characters.

2.14 What problems do you foresee when a look-up table is used to convert from EBCDIC to ASCII? What solution to this problem could you propose?

# 3

# *Asynchronous Transmission*

Upon completion of this chapter on asynchronous transmission, the student will be able to

- Understand the function of UARTs.
- Know the asynchronous character format.
- Draw the asynchronous waveform given a binary pattern.
- Write the binary pattern and determine the ASCII character given the asynchronous waveform.
- Calculate the bit rate, the type of parity, and the number of characters per second given the asynchronous waveform.
- List some of the practical considerations that exist on a communication line.
- Define the terms "marking distortion" and "space distortion."
- Know the need for hysteresis in a receiving unit.
- Identify the upper and lower threshold voltages on the output/input characteristics of the receiving circuitry.
- Know when a UART's circuitry should sample the line to identify the logic state of an incoming bit.
- Calculate receiver distortion tolerance.
- Calculate clock speed distortion.
- Determine the type and amount of bias distortion.

## Introduction

As discussed in Chapter 1, digital data is transferred either by serial transmission over a single line or by parallel transmission over many lines. In serial transmission, the binary data is sent down a single wire 1 bit at a time. In parallel transmission, each bit has its own wire and all the data is sent at the same time. Refer to Figure 1-1.

Remember that parallel transmission is faster because all bits are sent at once. It is the method used within the computer. External to the computer, however, serial transmission is more cost-effective. Therefore, an I/O chip is needed to convert the central processing unit's (CPU's) parallel data to serial format and to transmit it. The I/O chip must also be able to receive serial data and convert it to a parallel format to be put onto the computer's data bus.

Two methods of serial transmission were introduced in Chapter 1, asynchronous and synchronous. This chapter concentrates on the rules (known as <u>protocols</u>) for asynchronous transmission while synchronous transmission protocols are covered in Chapters 11 and 12. Chapter 4 examines an I/O chip that is capable of transmitting and receiving serial data. These devices are generally known as universal asynchronous receiver/transmitters (UARTs). Intel's device can be used for synchronous and asynchronous communication and it is known as a universal synchronous asynchronous receiver/transmitter (USART). Intel has other synchronous devices that have more features than the USART. Motorola has separate devices for synchronous and asynchronous communication. Their asynchronous device, known as an asynchronous communication interface adapter (ACIA) will be covered in Chapter 4. Motorola's synchronous devices are their Synchronous Serial Data Adapter and their Advanced Data Link Controller. A UART or ACIA is *not* a modem but rather a programmable parallel-to-serial and serial-to-parallel converter, along with other built-in features. As Figure 3-1 shows, the device is an interface chip connected between a computer's bus lines and a modem or other data channel devices. Manufacturers other than Intel and Motorola also market similar products, usually under the general name of UART. Asynchronous character format will be examined first.

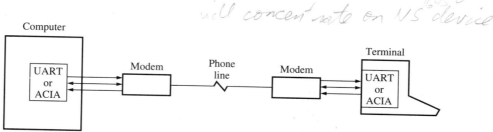

Figure 3-1    UARTs or ACIAs Are Interface Chips Connected Between the Computer's Parallel Data Bus and a Serial Device Such as a Modem

## 3-1   Asynchronous Character Format

Although asynchronous transmission has its roots in electromechanical devices, it is still a popular method of transmitting data today. For low-speed (less than 19,200 bits per second [bps]), inexpensive data equipment, asynchronous transmission is still widely used.

Early teleprinters operated on the notion that an idle line (no data being sent) is one through which current flows. In these teleprinter systems, data was transmitted when the current was interrupted. The idle state became known as the **mark condition** or **"1" state.** The absence of current on the line was called the **space condition** or **"0" state.** Most of today's data transmission systems rely on voltage changes. However, the terms "mark" and "space" are still used. For transistor-transistor logic levels, a logic 1 is the mark condition and a logic 0 is the space condition. The terms "mark" and "space" come from early pen and ink telegraph recorders. The pen traced a line on a moving paper strip. Whenever the current stopped, a spring lifted the pen—leaving a "space." A flow of current restored the "mark." Morse code looks like long and short marks separated by spaces.

Asynchronous transmission begins when the line is brought from mark to space. This first bit is called the **start bit.** The start bit is immediately followed by the data bits. Depending on the application, there are between 5 and 8 data bits. A parity bit is often used, and this bit follows the data bits. Each character in asynchronous transmission ends with a stop bit or bits. Figure 3-2 illustrates the character format. Each part will now be reviewed in more detail.

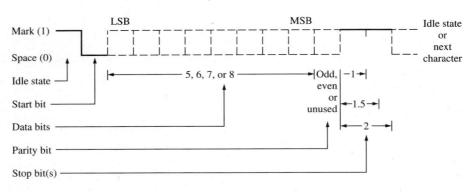

**Figure 3-2   Character Format for Asynchronous Communication**

### 3-1.1   Start Bit

When data is not being transmitted, the communication line is said to be in the idle or mark state (a logic 1 state). When a character is going to be sent, the transmitter brings the line to a logic 0 for 1 bit time, the **start bit.** It is this bit that is used by the receiver to resynchronize its receiving circuitry. The asynchronous receiver is designed to detect the transition from logic 1 to logic 0. Since noise is a problem on a communication line, receivers are designed to sample the line several times before recognizing the beginning of the data bits. This topic of sampling will be discussed in more detail in Section 3-4.

### 3-1.2   Data Bits

The data bits follow the start bit. The least significant bit (LSB) of the data follows the start bit. The data bits contain the information to be transmitted and received. Some transmitters and receivers are designed for 5, 6, 7, or 8 bits. The most often used number of data bits is 7 or 8. The number of possible characters that can be represented is given by

$$\text{Number of possible characters} = 2^n \qquad (3\text{-}1)$$

where n is the number of data bits. This information can be summarized as follows:

| Number of Bits | Power of $2^n$ | Possible Number of Characters |
|---|---|---|
| 5 | $2^5$ | 32 |
| 6 | $2^6$ | 64 |
| 7 | $2^7$ | 128 |
| 8 | $2^8$ | 256 |

The 32-character set produced by 5 bits is known as the Baudot code. This code is used by Model 28 Teletypes. The 6 bits have been used for stock market quotes. The 7 bits produce the popular character set known as American Standard Code for Information Interchange (ASCII), which was covered in Chapter 2. IBM uses an 8-bit code called Extended Binary Coded Decimal Information Code (EBCDIC), which was also summarized in Chapter 2. *and extended ASCII / ANSI*

### 3-1.3 Parity Bit

Parity is a method of error detection. A parity bit is an optional bit that follows the data bits. If parity is used, there are two types, even and odd. Even parity means that the total number of logic 1s in the data bits plus the parity bit is an even number. The examples in Figure 3-3 show 7 bits of data being transmitted using even parity.

| | 7 Bits of data | | | | | | | Parity bit for even parity checking |
|---|---|---|---|---|---|---|---|---|
| (a) | 1 | 0 | 0 | 1 | 1 | 1 | 0 | 0 |
| (b) | 0 | 0 | 1 | 1 | 1 | 0 | 0 | 1 |
| (c) | 1 | 1 | 1 | 1 | 1 | 1 | 1 | 1 |
| (d) | 0 | 0 | 1 | 0 | 0 | 1 | 0 | 0 |
| (e) | 1 | 1 | 0 | 1 | 1 | 0 | 1 | 1 |

↑
LSB

**Figure 3-3 Examples of Even Parity**

Examples a and d of Figure 3-3 already have an even number of logic 1s in the data. Therefore, the parity bit is a logic 0 so that the total number of logic 1s is an even number. Examples b, c, and e in Figure 3-3 illustrate that the parity bit must be a logic 1 so that the total number of logic 1s in the data plus the parity bit is an even number.

*Good!*

If the transmitter and receiver are programmed to use odd parity, then the total number of logic 1s in the data plus the parity bit is an odd number. For comparison, Figure 3-4 uses the same binary patterns as in Figure 3-3, but with odd parity.

The parity bit for examples a and d must be a logic 1 so that the total number of logic 1s is an odd number. Since the number of logic 1s in examples b, c, and e of Figure 3-4 is already an odd number, then the parity bit will be a logic 0.

|  | 7 Bits of data | Parity bit for odd parity checking |
|---|---|---|
| (a) | 1  0  0  1  1  1  0 | 1 |
| (b) | 0  0  1  1  1  0  0 | 0 |
| (c) | 1  1  1  1  1  1  1 | 0 |
| (d) | 0  0  1  0  0  1  0 | 1 |
| (e) | 1  1  0  1  1  0  1 | 0 |

↑
LSB

**Figure 3-4   Examples of Odd Parity**

Parity is used so that the receiver can test for errors in transmission. That is, is the data received the same as the data sent? Consider Example a of Figure 3-4 as the information to be transmitted. Noise on the communication line has caused a logic 0 to be received as a logic 1.

|  | LSB | Parity bit |
|---|---|---|
|  | ↓ | ↓ |
| Transmitted binary pattern | 1 0 0 1 1 1 0 1 | |
| Received binary pattern | 1 1 0 1 1 1 0 1 | |
| Noise on the line has caused a bit change ⌐ | | |

As previously mentioned, before data can be transmitted, the transmitter and receiver must agree on a number of things, one of which is parity. In this example, the receiver's logic circuitry determines that there is an even number of logic 1s; hence an error has occurred. The receiver then may request the sender to retransmit the data.

Although parity is used in slow-speed asynchronous communication, it is a limited error detection scheme. As will be shown in Problems 3.8 and 3.9 and in Chapter 10, parity is not foolproof and more sophisticated methods are often used. *not used very often anymore. Usually set no parity.*

### 3-1.4   Stop Bit

Following the data bits and the parity bit (if used), the transmitter sends a stop bit or bits. These bits are logic 1s and indicate the end of the character. The duration of the stop bits generated by UARTs and ACIAs is either 1, 1.5, or 2 bit times.

As shown in Figure 3-2, stop bit(s) are a mark or idle state. Thus, the transmitter is ready to send another character and the next transition from logic 1 to logic 0 indicates a start bit.

Although early mechanical devices required 1.42, 1.5, or 2.0 stop bits in order for the printhead to settle, only 1 stop bit is needed to indicate the end of the character for a computer. A stop bit(s) ensures that the character is properly framed, a topic that will be discussed in Chapter 4.

E  X  A  M  P  L  E      3 - 1

Draw the asynchronous character waveform for the capital letter D. Use the 7-bit ASCII binary pattern with odd parity and 1 stop bit.

**Solution**

From the ASCII matrix of Figure 2-1, the following is found:

$$D = 44_{hex} = \quad 1000100$$
$$\nearrow \qquad \qquad \nwarrow$$
$$\text{MSB} \qquad \text{LSB}$$

Rearranging the binary pattern so that the LSB is at the left and using odd parity, the following is obtained:

$$D = 00100011$$
$$\uparrow \qquad \uparrow\uparrow$$
$$\text{LSB} \quad \text{MSB  P}$$

The waveform of this character is shown in Figure 3-5. The parity bit must be a logic 1, so the total number of 1s in the data plus the parity bit is an odd number. Note: the conventional way of drawing an asynchronous character waveform is to have the start bit on the left, followed by the LSB of data. The most significant bit (MSB) of data, parity, and stop bit are at the right. This causes a reversal of the order of the binary pattern. Be sure to examine Figure 3-5 carefully.

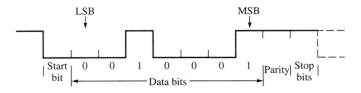

**Figure 3-5    Asynchronous Format for the Letter D**

ASCII characters are usually stored in memory as 8 bits. The eighth bit may be a "don't-care" condition. Although all 8 bits are sent by the CPU to the UART, the UART may be programmed to send only the first 7 bits or the first 7 bits plus the parity bit. At this time, don't worry about the start, parity, or stop bit(s); these are all inserted automatically by the UART.

In any asynchronous transmission, the transmitter and receiver must be set not only for the same character format but also for the same rate of transfer. The rate at which bits are transferred is referred to as the bit rate.

## 3-2  Bit Rate

The time to transmit (or receive) a bit is known as **bit time, time per bit,** or **bit interval,** as shown in Figure 3-6. The start, data, parity, and stop bits all have the same bit times. The reciprocal of the bit time is known as **bit rate, bits per second** (bps), or **line speed.** In equation form, this is expressed as

$$\text{Bit rate} = \frac{1}{t_b} \tag{3-2}$$

where $t_b$ is the bit time. Other relationships for asynchronous transmission are as follows:

$$\text{Character time} = \text{total number of bits in a character} \times \text{bit time} \tag{3-3}$$

$$\text{Characters per second} = \frac{1}{\text{character time}} \tag{3-4}$$

$$\text{Data bps} = \text{data bits/character} \times \text{character/second} \tag{3-5}$$

Example 3-2 shows how Equations (3-2) to (3-5) apply to a waveform similar to Figure 3-6.

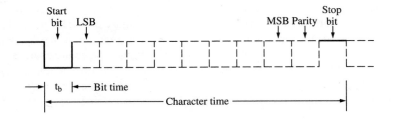

**Figure 3-6   Comparison of Bit Time and Character Time Using 1 Stop Bit**

E  X  A  M  P  L  E    3 - 2

If the bit time in Figure 3-7 is 0.833 ms, determine (a) bit rate, (b) time to transmit one character, (c) number of characters per second, and (d) number of data bps.

**Solution**

**(a)** Applying Equation (3-2) yields

$$\text{Bit rate} = \frac{1}{0.833 \text{ ms}} = 1200 \text{ bps}$$

**(b)** In Figure 3-7, the character contains 10 bits (1 start bit, 7 data bits, 1 parity bit, and 1 stop bit). Using Equation (3-3) the following is obtained:

$$\text{Character time} = 10 \text{ bits} \times 0.833 \text{ ms} = 8.33 \text{ ms}$$

**(c)** Applying Equation (3-4) yields

$$\frac{1}{8.33 \text{ ms/character}} = 120 \text{ characters/second}$$

**(d)** In Figure 3-7, there are 7 data bits. Using Equation (3-5), the following is obtained:

$$\text{Data bps} = 7 \text{ bits/character} \times 120 \text{ characters/second} = 840 \text{ bits/second}$$

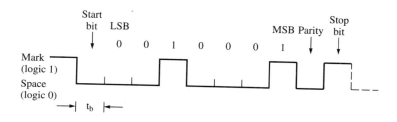

**Figure 3-7   Waveform for Example 3-2**

Bit rate refers to the total number of bits being transmitted (or received) in 1 second. In Example 3-2, the bit rate is 1200, but only 840 bits actually carried data. The remaining 360 bits (1200 − 840) are overhead. Remember that this overhead is a disadvantage of asynchronous communication. The advantages of asynchronous communication are that the hardware and software designs are easier than for synchronous communication.

Figure 3-8 lists the characteristics of the most commonly used bit rates for a character format of 1 start bit, 7 data bits, 1 parity bit, and 1 stop bit.

| Bit rate | Bit time (ms) | Character time (ms) | Characters/second | Data Bits/second |
|---|---|---|---|---|
| 110 | 9.09 | 90.9 | 11 | 77 |
| 150 | 6.99 | 66.6 | 15 | 105 |
| 300 | 3.33 | 33.3 | 30 | 210 |
| 600 | 1.666 | 16.66 | 60 | 420 |
| 1200 | 0.833 | 8.33 | 120 | 840 |
| 2400 | 0.416 | 4.16 | 240 | 1680 |
| 4800 | 0.208 | 2.08 | 480 | 3360 |
| 9600 | 0.104 | 1.04 | 960 | 6720 |
| 19.2K | 0.052 | 0.52 | 1920 | 13,440 |
| 38.4K | 0.026 | 0.26 | 3840 | 26,880 |

**Figure 3-8   Comparison of Different Bit Rates Using 10 Bits per Character (1 Start Bit, 7 Data Bits, 1 Parity Bit, and 1 Stop Bit)**

E X A M P L E   3 - 3

Refer to Figure 3-7 and determine the (a) data bit pattern, (b) ASCII character, and (c) type of parity.

**Solution**

**(a)** Since the LSB is the first bit sent after the start bit, the bit pattern must be reversed to conform to ASCII convention. From Figure 3-7, the data bits are

1000100

MSB    LSB

**(b)** Now use Figure 2-1 to find this ASCII binary pattern of 1000100 is $44_{hex}$ or the capital letter D.

**(c)** Since the total number of 1s in the data bits and parity bit is an even number, then the character format uses even parity.

E X A M P L E   3 - 4

Consider that the phrase "Data Comm." is to be transmitted asynchronously with odd parity from a computer to a printer. Draw the pulse waveform for the first two letters and the last punctuation mark.

**Solution**

From Chapter 2, the ASCII binary pattern for each letter, as well as the space and period codes are given by

|        | Hex Code | 7 Bit ASCII | Parity Bit |
|--------|----------|-------------|------------|
| D      | 44       | 1000100     | 1          |
| a      | 61       | 1100001     | 0          |
| t      | 74       | 1110100     | 1          |
| a      | 61       | 1100001     | 0          |
| space  | 20       | 0100000     | 0          |
| C      | 43       | 1000011     | 0          |
| o      | 6F       | 1101111     | 1          |
| m      | 6D       | 1101101     | 0          |
| m      | 6D       | 1101101     | 0          |
| period | 2E       | 0101110     | 1          |
|        |          | MSB LSB     |            |

Figure 3-9 shows the required waveforms. To plot this waveform, the 7-bit ASCII binary pattern is reversed so that the LSB follows the start bit. As noted

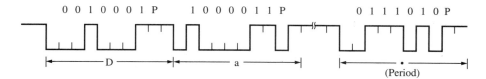

**Figure 3-9**   Waveform for Example 3-4

earlier, asynchronous transmission is character framed by start and stop bits. These bits as well as the parity bit are added to the ASCII pattern not by the computer, but by the UART.

## 3-3   Practical Considerations

So far, only ideal asynchronous waveforms have been shown, without regard to how the communication line, equipment, and external noise could distort the wave. Not yet discussed either is when the receiving equipment should sample the incoming wave to determine the logic state of each bit. Both conditions will now be studied.

### 3-3.1   Waveform Distortion

The distorted waveform of Figure 3-10 shows what can result from a combination of practical problems such as line impedance, transmitting and receiving equipment, the speed at which the data is being sent, external noise, and the bandwidth of the communication equipment. The resistance and capacitance effects of the line as well as the transmitting drive and receive circuitry cause the voltage to rise and fall exponentially as shown in Figure 3-10a. If the speed of the data is increased or the bandwidth is decreased, the wave will become even more distorted as shown in Figure 3-10b. Figure 3-10a and b shows how noise signals may appear on the wave. Another problem that may occur is that the duration of a mark and space interval may be different. This condition can happen if the output resistance of the drive circuitry and the input resistance of the receive circuitry are different for a mark-to-space transition than it is for a space-to-mark transition. This type of distortion is called **bias distortion.** In particular, if the mark bit duration is longer than the space bit duration, it is called **marking distortion.** Similarly, if the duration of space bits is longer than the duration of mark bits, it is called **space distortion.** Figure 3-10c is an example of marking distortion.

Although the incoming wave may be quite distorted, it is still possible to recover the data. But first, the receiving equipment must square-up the wave before it samples the logic state of each bit.

### 3-3.2   Need for Hysteresis

The input circuitry of the simplest receiving unit is designed to produce a mark condition when the input voltage is above a reference level and a space condition when the input voltage is below the reference. Figure 3-11 shows the relationship

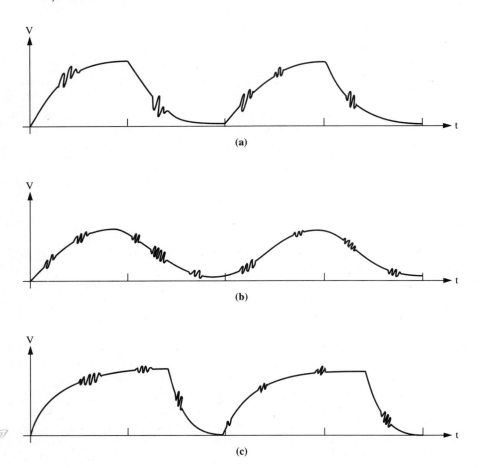

**Figure 3-10**    **Examples of Waveform Distortion**

*marking distortion*

between an input wave without noise and a squared-up wave. If external noise is not present, then the input wave may appear as shown in Figure 3-11a and the receiving unit squares-up the wave as shown in Figure 3-11b.

However, there is always a very good chance of noise being present and it may occur around the reference level as shown in Figure 3-12a. Every time the input voltage crosses the reference level, the receiver's circuitry will respond and its output will change as shown in Figure 3-12b. These extra pulses may produce errors in the receiving unit by being interpreted as bits that have been transmitted.

A way to solve this problem is to design the receiving unit's circuitry so that it does not respond to noise pulses. This is done by adding **hysteresis** to the receiver. Hysteresis is the principle whereby the output changes from one state to another state at one level and back at a different level. This principle is best shown by Figure 3-13. Figure 3-13a is similar to Figure 3-12a but now the receiving unit has two threshold voltage levels: one above the original reference voltage called

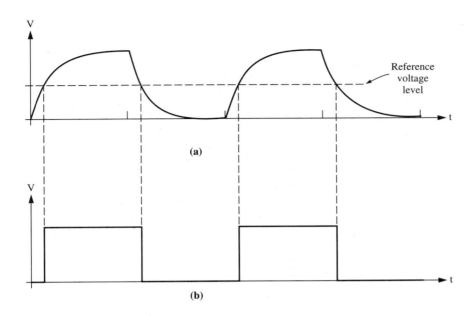

**Figure 3-11**   (a) Input Wave to a Receiver and (b) Squared-up Wave

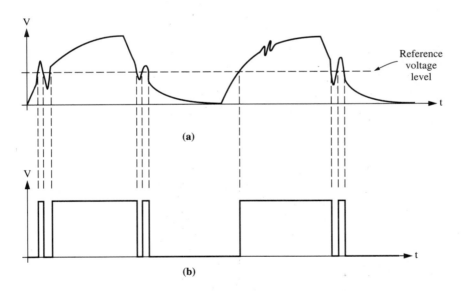

**Figure 3-12**   (a) External Noise Added to the Input Wave of a Receiver Causes False Logic State Changes in Waveform (b)

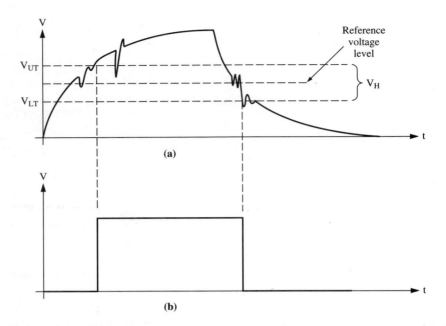

**Figure 3-13   The Receiving Unit is Less Susceptible to Noise Signals if the Receiver is Designed with Hysteresis Voltage**

the **upper threshold voltage, $V_{UT}$,** and one below the reference level called the **lower threshold voltage, $V_{LT}$.** The difference is the **hysteresis voltage, $V_H$.**

$$V_H = V_{UT} - V_{LT} \tag{3-6}$$

The input wave must cross $V_{UT}$ for the receiving unit to record a mark condition. Noise pulses may cause the input wave to hover about $V_{UT}$ or the reference level but the receiving unit will not record a space condition until the input wave drops below $V_{LT}$. See Figure 3-13b. In most applications, the threshold voltages are centered about the reference level.

Chapter 5 will cover an integrated circuit that is designed to be used at the front end of a receiving unit because it has a built-in hysteresis voltage and it is capable of transforming the different voltages that exist between a modem and a UART. Typical hysteresis voltages for such devices range either from 1.0 to 1.25 volts or from 0.8 to 1.95 volts. These integrated circuits are not part of the UART but rather are an interface device. Now let's turn our attention to when the receiving unit samples the new squared-up wave. This task is accomplished by the UART.

## 3-4   External Clock Requirements

The first task at the receiving unit is for the incoming unit to be squared-up so that it will not be susceptible to every noise pulse in the vicinity of the reference level. The second task is for the squared-up wave to be sampled near the center of each bit. In order to do this, an external clock signal operating at a frequency much faster than the incoming bit rate is applied to the UART. Typical external clock frequencies are 16, 32, or 64 times the bit rate. As an example, if the bit rate is 1200 bps and a multiplying rate of 16 is used, then the external clock frequency is 19,200 hertz (16 × 1200). Receiving units have internal divide networks to divide the external clock frequency and to use the result to sample the incoming asynchronous wave as close to the center of each bit as possible. The reason for sampling near the center of the wave is that this point should be the most stable.

Figure 3-14 shows the start and first data bit along with the receiver's external and internal clock waveforms. The transition of mark to space condition signifying the start bit causes the receiver's internal circuitry to use each of the first eight clock pulses (some UARTs use nine clock pulses) and to sample the line to see if it remains in the space condition. If it has, the receiver accepts this bit as a "true" start bit. After the receiver detects a valid start bit the receiver uses another internal counter to produce a pulse at the end of 16 clock pulses. This internal clock pulse should be near the center of each bit following the start bit.

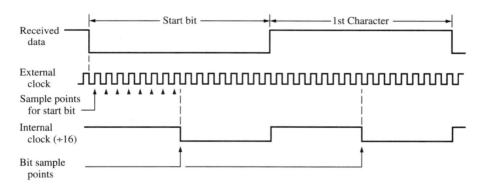

**Figure 3-14  Receiver Start Bit Detection. The Beginning of the Start Bit and the Negative Going Edge of the External Clock Pulse Occur at the Same Time**

In theory, the sampling of a bit can vary by 50% of a bit time before an error occurs. The 50% comes from the fact that there is one-half a bit time from the sampling point to the next bit. Although the ideal case is 50%, usually there is less time than that because of different types of sampling distortion. Consider some of the reasons.

## 3-4.1  Receiver Distortion Tolerance

In Figure 3-14, the start bit and the external clock pulse began at the same time. In practice, however, the incoming asynchronous waveform could occur at any time. Figure 3-15 shows the start bit occurring at a time other than at the beginning of an external pulse. If the UART needs a full clock pulse before the line can be sampled, almost one complete clock pulse is wasted before the first sample takes

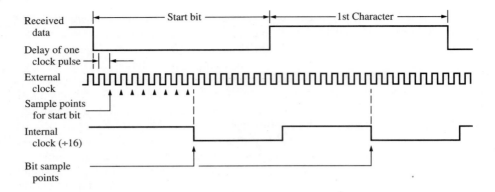

**Figure 3-15   Sampling of the Start Bit May Be Delayed by One Clock Pulse Whenever the Start Bit's Transition from Mark to Space Does Not Provide Enough Set Up Time for a UART's First Sample Point**

place. If the external clock is operating at a rate of 16 times the bit time, then the loss of one clock pulse causes an error of 6.25% (1/16 of a bit time = 6.25%). This loss of 6.25% reduces the time the receiving unit has to sample the bits from 50% to 43.75% (50% − 6.25% = 43.75%). This value may be seen on UART data sheets under the heading ''Receiver Distortion Tolerance, RDT.''

In equation form this tolerance factor can be expressed as

$$RDT = 50\% - \frac{1}{\text{external clock rate multiplier}} \times 100\% \qquad (3\text{-}7)$$

**E  X  A  M  P  L  E     3 - 5**

If a receiving unit's external frequency is set at a rate of 32 times the asynchronous line speed, (a) what is the receiver distortion tolerance and (b) if the bit rate is 600 bps what is the actual time the receiving unit has to sample the line?

**Solution**

**(a)** Applying Equation (3-7) yields

$$RDT = 50\% - \frac{1}{32} \times 100\% = 46.875\%$$

**(b)** From Figure 3-8 or from Equation (3-2) a bit rate of 600 bps results in a bit time of 1.666 ms. The amount of time the receiving unit has to sample the line is found by multiplying the bit time × the RDT:

$$1.666 \text{ ms} \times 0.46875 = 0.781 \text{ ms}$$

This answer also may be checked by the following procedure. For this example, the maximum sampling time the receiving unit has is one-half a bit time or 0.833 ms. The delay caused by the receiving unit's inability to sample the start bit on the first external clock pulse may be calculated from

$$\frac{1}{32} \times 1.666 \text{ ms} \simeq 0.052 \text{ ms}$$

and the final time duration for sampling is

$$0.833 - 0.052 \text{ ms} = 0.781 \text{ ms}$$

### 3-4.2  Clock Speed Distortion

The UART within the receiving unit uses an external clock signal in order to "know" when to sample each bit. Any variation in the clock frequency will cause a condition known as **clock speed distortion.** This results in a further reduction of the amount of time the receiving unit has to sample the communication line. Unlike other errors due to distortion, a clock distortion error is cumulative. This means that the amount of time for sampling a bit decreases nearer the end of each character. Remember that for asynchronous transmission everything starts anew at the beginning of the next start bit. Therefore, a clock speed distortion error will not continue to be cumulative into the next character. A variation of only 0.15% of the external clock causes a 2.4% error at the end of 16 pulses ($0.15\% \times 16 = 2.4\%$). Since this error is cumulative, the amount of time the receiving unit has to sample the stop bit may be quite small as shown in the following example.

E  X  A  M  P  L  E     3 - 6

Assume that the receiver's external clock frequency is 16 times the line speed. If the clock frequency increases by 0.15% per cycle, determine the percent of a bit time to sample the (a) start bit and (b) stop bit. The asynchronous character contains 1 start bit, 7 data bits, I parity bit, and 1 stop bit for a total of 10 bits.

**Solution**

**(a)** The maximum percent of a bit time for sampling is 50% and this may be reduced to 43.75% due to the start bit and the external clock pulse not starting at the same time. If the start bit is sampled at the end of eight clock pulses, then a clock error of 0.15% per cycle causes an error of 1.2% at the end of the eighth pulse. At this time the worst possible percent of a bit time to sample the start bit is

$$43.75\% - 1.2\% = 42.55\%$$

**(b)** In the ideal situation, the center of the stop bit occurs $9\frac{1}{2}$ bit times after the beginning of the start bit. Since each bit time has 16 clock pulses and each pulse increases the error by 0.15%, the clock speed error at the stop bit is

$$9.5 \times 16 \times 0.15\% = 22.8\%$$

Therefore, the percent of the bit time for the UART to sample the stop bit is

$$43.75\% - 22.8\% = 20.95\%$$

This small percent value shows how a small clock frequency error is cumulative, leaving approximately one-fifth of the stop bit for the receiver to do its work. This time may be further reduced if other distortion factors occur.

### 3-4.3   Bias Distortion

When the duration of the mark and space signals of the receiving unit is not equal, the condition is known as **bias distortion.** If the mark interval is longer than the space interval, the situation is known as **marking bias** or **marking distortion.** A space interval longer than the mark interval is known as **spacing bias** or **spacing distortion.** Figure 3-16 gives examples of both types.

Bias distortion is caused by a lack of symmetry in the driver and/or receiver circuitry as well as the line's resistance and capacitance effects. Another cause of bias distortion is within asynchronous modems. These devices have an inherent bias distortion. This section will investigate how the lack of symmetry in the

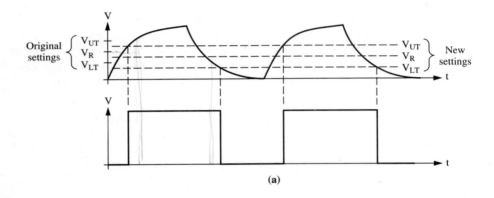

(a)

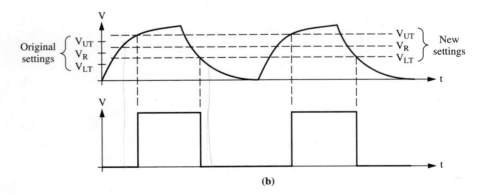

(b)

**Figure 3-16   Examples of Bias Distortion (a) Marking Distortion and (b) Space Distortion**

receiver results in bias distortion. Bias distortion within an asynchronous modem is covered in Chapter 9.

The ideal receiver circuitry has the hysteresis voltage centered about the reference voltage as shown in Figure 3-13. The reference voltage is centered at the midpoint between the mark and space condition. If the reference voltage is not at the midpoint and/or if the hysteresis voltage is not symmetrical about the reference voltage, then bias distortion will result. Figure 3-16a and b shows the hysteresis voltage symmetrical about the reference voltage, but with the reference voltage not at the normal midpoint position. Figure 3-16a shows that marking bias results when the reference and hysteresis voltages are lower than their normal positions. If the reference and hysteresis voltages are adjusted so that they are higher than the normal position, as shown in Figure 3-16b, then spacing bias results.

For small variations (less than 10%) in reference and hysteresis voltage, this percent change may cause the same percent change at the bit boundaries of the squared-up wave as shown in Figure 3-17. This is because although the incoming wave increases and decreases exponentially, it is assumed that it is linear over this small range.

E X A M P L E   3 - 7
_____

The reference and hysteresis voltages decrease by 5%.

(a) What type of bias distortion results?

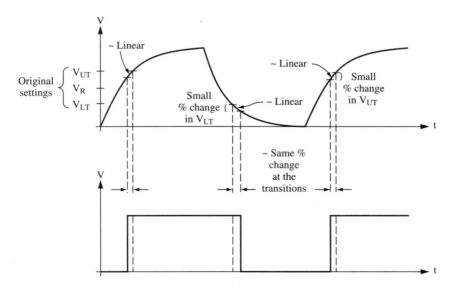

**Figure 3-17   Small Percent Change in $V_{UT}$, $V_R$, and $V_{LT}$ Causes Approximately the Same Percent Change at the Transitions of the Squared-up Waveform**

**(b)** For a bit rate of 1200 bps, calculate the time duration for a mark and space condition.

**(c)** If this bias distortion occurs at the same time the external clock speed variation of Example 3-6 is happening, what is the total distortion in percent at the start bit and at the stop bit?

**Solution**

**(a)** In Figure 3-17, the time duration for a mark is longer than a space. Therefore, marking distortion is occurring.

**(b)** A 5% change in hysteresis voltage causes approximately 5% change at each bit boundary of a mark-to-space or space-to-mark transition. At 1200 bps, the time interval is

$$0.05 \times 0.833 \text{ ms} \simeq 0.042 \text{ ms}$$

Therefore, a transition from space to mark causes the mark state to be increased by 5% or 0.042 ms. Similarly, a transition from mark to space causes the space duration to be decreased by 5% or 0.042 ms. As an exercise, the student should plot out an alternating sequence of mark, space, mark, space, etc., to see what happens for such a pattern.

**(c)** Bias distortion further reduces the time available to sample the line. Using the results of Example 3-6, the following is obtained at the start bit:

$$42.55\% - 5\% = 37.55\%$$

and at the stop bit:

$$20.95\% - 5\% = 15.95\%$$

---

As the different types of distortion add together, the receiving unit may not be able to sample each bit. This should eventually cause a framing error (a topic covered in Chapter 4).

Bias distortion has been examined from the receiving end and what happens if the reference and hysteresis voltage varies. Bias distortion may also occur because of a problem at the transmitting end. A mark condition may be transmitted for a longer (or shorter) period of time than a space condition, thus causing marking (or space) distortion, respectively. Whether bias distortion occurs because of a situation at the transmitting or receiving end or both, the time the receiving unit has to sample the line is reduced.

## Summary

Asynchronous transmission is widely used for personal computers and for many time sharing applications. It is a convenient way of transferring data because the time between each character may be different. Thus, large memory buffers at the transmitting and receiving units are usually not needed, reducing the system cost. The disadvantage of this method of communication is the overhead of the start and stop bit for each character. This chapter showed several examples of how ASCII characters with parity are transmitted using the asynchronous format. This method of transmission is used for many applications with bit rates less than 19,200 bps. At any bit rate, distortion occurs and several causes were examined, including an exponential rise and fall of voltage, external noise, variations of clock frequencies, and bias distortion.

## Problems

* **3.1** Asynchronous transmission begins when the line is brought from _____ to _____ .

**3.2** What is the function of the start bit?

* **3.3** Is parity a method of error detection?

**3.4** If parity is used, does the receiving circuitry count the total number of logic 1s in the data plus the parity bit?

**3.5** What are the two types of parity check characters?

* **3.6** For the following binary patterns, determine the logic state of the parity bit if the data is being sent using (a) odd parity and (b) even parity.
   1. 0000000    2. 1010011    3. 1111111
   4. 0111001    5. 1000111

* **3.7** Determine the binary sequence for the message "Check #38742." Use the ASCII character set and odd parity.

**3.8** The following binary sequence is transmitted. Answer questions (a) through (e), checking to see if parity is still correct for each case.

| P | $b_7$ | $b_6$ | $b_5$ | $b_4$ | $b_3$ | $b_2$ | $b_1$ |
|---|---|---|---|---|---|---|---|
| 1 | 0 | 0 | 1 | 0 | 1 | 0 | 1 |

Note: even parity is being used by the transmitter.
   **(a)** Bit $b_7$ changes from 0 to 1.
   **(b)** Bits $b_1$ and $b_5$ change from 1 to 0s.
   **(c)** Bit $b_1$ changes from 1 to 0 and bit $b_2$ changes from 0 to 1.
   **(d)** Parity bit changes from 1 to 0.
   **(e)** Bits $b_1$, $b_3$, and $b_5$ change from 1 to 0s.

* **3.9** From the results of Problem 3.8, is a parity checking scheme foolproof? Explain your answer.

---

* *See* Answers to Selected Problems.

**3.10** The following message is being received by a UART. The ASCII character set is being used along with the start bit, odd parity, and 1 stop bit. The character format for each 10 bits is

start bit    $b_1$ $b_2$ $b_3$ $b_4$ $b_5$ $b_6$ $b_7$    parity bit    stop bit

The first character is the leftmost binary pattern. Determine:
(a) Is there a parity error?
(b) Translate the message into English.

1st character

0100001101011001110101001111010011101101
0110001111000010110100100111110111101111
0011101101011110111101010111010110011101
0000001001000101111100100111110100001101
0011101101011001110101011011010100101111
0110011101011001110101001011110111101111
0011101101

Last character

**\*3.11** For asynchronous transmission (a) is the presence of a start bit optional? (b) Is the presence of a stop bit optional?

**3.12** List three causes of waveform distortion.

**\*3.13** What are the two types of bias distortion?

**3.14** A receiving unit's lower and upper threshold voltages are set at 0.8 and 1.95 volts, respectively. Calculate the hysteresis and reference voltages. Assume the threshold voltages are symmetrical about the reference voltage.

**\*3.15** A UART has its external clock frequency set at 76,800 hertz. What rate will it transmit and receive data if its internal divider is set at (a) 16 or (b) 64?

**3.16** Refer to Problem 3.15 and determine the (a) receiver distortion tolerance and (b) the actual time delay of the RDT.

# *Universal Asynchronous Receiver/Transmitter*

# 4

*Use NS16450*

O B J E C T I V E S

Upon completion of this chapter on UARTs, the student will be able to

- Understand the reason for using a UART in a computer system.
- Describe the operation of the external pins on a UART.
- Describe the function of the internal registers within a UART.
- Know the reason for double buffering.
- Learn how to use Motorola's asynchronous I/O device.
- Know the function of each bit or group of bits of a control register.
- Know the function of each bit of a status register.
- Show how a programmer can use certain bits in the status register to detect a variety of errors.
- Show how Motorola's ACIA can be connected to a MC68000 μP.
- Learn the function of a bit rate generator IC and how to connect it to an ACIA.

## Introduction

A universal asynchronous receiver/transmitter (UART) is the general acronym to describe an I/O device that is used in a computer system to transmit and receive serial asynchronous data. Manufacturers often refer to their device by a particular name. For example, one of Intel Corporation's 8-bit serial I/O devices is a programmable communication interface (PCI). This device is capable of transmitting and receiving both asynchronous and synchronous data and is known as a Universal Synchronous/Asynchronous Receiver/Transmitter (USART). Because of the different protocols associated with synchronous communication (see Chapters 11 and 12), the PCI device is used most often with asynchronous communication and other I/O devices are used for synchronous communication. Motorola's 8-bit UART is known as an asynchronous communication interface adapter (ACIA). It is only for asynchronous communication; Motorola has other products for synchronous communication. The first part of this chapter introduces many of the functions found in all UARTs, regardless of the manufacturer. Sections 4-3 to 4-5 show how many of these functions have been incorporated into Motorola's ACIA.

Like other peripheral devices, UARTs are programmable and their internal registers are addressable. The students will study how the UART's internal registers operate and what programming steps are necessary to send and receive data between a UART and a $\mu$P. Originally, UARTs were designed to operate with 8-bit microprocessor chips. However, many of these devices are also being used with 16- and 32-bit microprocessor chips. Since most first-time data communication users have microprocessor-based equipment, Section 4-8 shows how a UART, in particular Motorola's ACIA, may be connected to an MC68000 $\mu$P.

## 4-1   External Connections of a UART

Like other I/O devices, a UART can be thought of as having a $\mu$P (or CPU) side and a peripheral side. The pins connected directly to the $\mu$P or through interface chips to the $\mu$P are considered on the processor side and the pins connected to external equipment are on the peripheral side, as shown in Figure 4-1.

The UART, like any other I/O device, also has chip select or chip enable pin(s) that are used by the $\mu$P to select the device, that is, to enable the data bus buffers. These pins are usually connected to the $\mu$P's address lines through decoder chips, as shown in Figure 4-2. A more complete circuit schematic is shown in Section 4-8. In order to select a particular register within the UART, a register select pin or pins are used by the $\mu$P. This pin(s) is connected to the $\mu$P's lowest numbered address line such as $A_0$ or $A_1$.

Data is transferred between the $\mu$P and a UART over an 8-bit bidirectional data bus. All of these data transfers are synchronized from a clock signal that drives the $\mu$P or is derived from the $\mu$P's internal circuitry. The read-write line is used by the $\mu$P to read or write data to the UART over the data bus. UARTs also have an interrupt request ($\overline{\text{IRQ}}$) line to signal the $\mu$P that it is time to send more data or to receive data or to signal the $\mu$P that data should not be sent or received because of a situation at the modem.

On the peripheral side, UARTs have a transmit data (Tx Data) line, a receive data (Rx Data) line, and peripheral control lines, as shown in Figure 4-1. Serial data is transmitted and received on the Tx Data and Rx Data lines, respectively. Thus, a UART receives parallel data from the $\mu$P over the data bus and transmits it serially on the Tx Data line. Similarly, a UART receives serial data on the Rx Data line and transfers it to the $\mu$P in a parallel format over the data bus. Hence, the basic functions of UARTs are as a parallel-to-serial and serial-to-parallel converter. To transmit serial data, UARTs automatically insert the start, parity (if any), and stop bits before transmitting the data serially. After a UART receives a

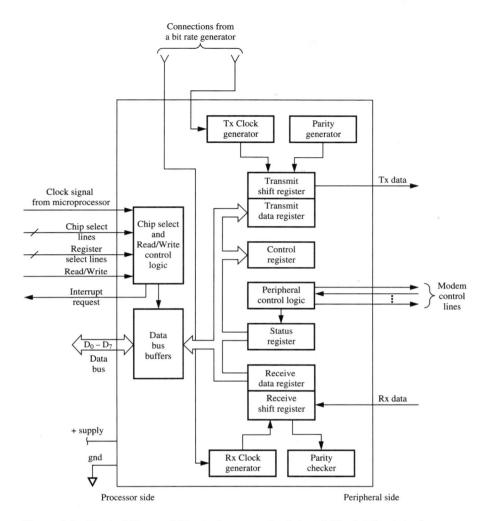

**Figure 4-1** Typical External Pin Assignments for Internal Block Diagram of a UART

character on the Rx Data line, it "strips away" the start, parity, and stop bits before the μP reads the data.

UARTs are often connected to modems, and so manufacturers have included a number of peripheral control (handshaking) lines to ensure an orderly flow of data between the UART and modem. These handshaking lines are covered in Chapters 5 and 6.

The rate at which data is transmitted and received is set by an external clock signal. In some UARTs an external crystal can be connected directly to the device.

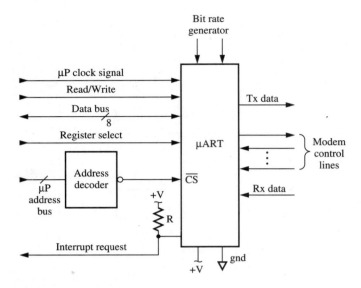

**Figure 4-2**   **Typical Wiring Connections for a UART**

For other UARTs the external clock signal is obtained from a bit rate or baud rate generator. Section 4-9 will introduce such a device.

## 4-2  Internal Block Diagram of a UART

Figure 4-1 shows the basic internal blocks of a UART. The registers associated with transmission of serial data are the transmit shift register and the transmit data register. The receive shift register and the receive data register are the registers associated with receiving serial data. The μP sends characters to be transmitted only to the transmit data register and receives characters only from the receive data register. It does not directly communicate with either the transmit shift register or receive shift register. A UART's internal circuitry automatically transfers the next character to be sent from the transmit data to the transmit shift register whenever the shift register is empty. Similarly, on the receive side, a UART automatically transfers received characters from the shift register to the data register when the data register is empty. The character is held in the receive data register until the μP reads it. Two registers working together is known as **double buffering.** This feature, on the transmit side, allows the μP to send data to the transmit data register and not be concerned about immediately sending another character to the UART or about when will it be transmitted. Double buffering on the receive side allows a character to be received by a UART and the μP does not have to move the data immediately from the receive shift register at the end of a stop bit so the next character can be received. The UART will automatically transfer data from the receive shift register to the receive data register and hold it there until the μP has time to move it to a CPU register or memory. Remember that the μP is able to move data to and from a UART in microseconds, while it takes milliseconds for serial data to be sent and received. Thus, a UART, like any other I/O device, "frees" the μP from mundane tasks that are necessary but time consuming.

A binary pattern stored in the control register programs the operation of a UART. The binary pattern, known as a control word, is sent from the μP to the UART, usually as an initial line of code in an application program. The binary pattern programs the UART for a particular system or application. For example, it sets the data rate, the number of data bits to be sent and received for each character, the type of parity (if any), the number of stop bits, and whether or not the UART will send an interrupt request to the μP when the transmit data register is empty or the receive data register is full. Section 4-4 shows how to program a control register within Motorola's ACIA for different applications.

The 8-bit status register is a "record keeper" of what has happened within the UART. Each bit indicates the logic state for a particular function. For example, bits are used to indicate the condition of the peripheral control lines, whether or not the transmit and receive data registers are full or empty, and the condition of the received data, for example, whether a parity error, an overrun error, or a framing error has occurred. A parity error occurs if the parity of the received data does not agree with the condition set up in the UART's control register. An overrun error occurs if the UART tries to transfer a character into the receive data register and the μP has not read the previous character from the register. A framing error occurs if the UART does not receive the correct number of stop bit(s).

Typically, the μP communicates only with four UART registers: the transmit data register, control register, status register, and receive data register. The transmit data register and control registers are write-only registers, while the receive data register and status register are read-only registers. The microprocessor usually does not communicate directly with the other UART registers. Like other I/O devices, a UART contains control logic circuitry and data bus buffers to interface as shown in Figure 4-1.

In order to show how some of these functions are incorporated into a particular UART device, Sections 4-3–4-9 cover the ACIA device.

## 4-3  MC6850 ACIA

Motorola's UART device is known as an asynchronous communication interface adapter (ACIA) and its part number is MC6850. It is housed in a 24-pin dual-in-line package as shown in Figure 4-3a and its internal block diagram is shown in Figure 4-3b. Its internal and external structure is similar to most general purpose UARTs.

For example, pins 8, 9, and 10 are the chip select pins that are used by the microprocessor to select the device. Once the device is selected, data is transferred between the μP and the ACIA over a bidirectional data bus. All of these transfers are synchronized with a clock signal on the enable line (pin 14). The read/write line (pin 13) is used by the μP to receive or send data to the ACIA over the data

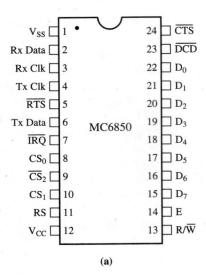

**(a)**

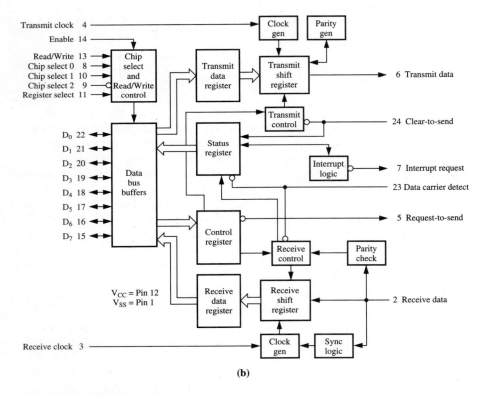

**(b)**

**Figure 4-3    The MC6850 ACIA Pin Assignments in (a) and Internal Block Diagram as Given in (b)** *(Courtesy of Motorola, Inc. Used by permission)* bus lines. Pin 11, the register select pin, is used by the μP to address the ACIA's internal registers.

A μP can access four of the ACIA's registers; they are: transmit data register, receive data register, control register, and status register. The reason four internal ACIA registers can be accessed with only one register select line is that two registers are read-only (status and receive data) and two are write-only (control and transmit data). The logic state of the register select line is used in conjunction with the logic state of the read/write line to provide the necessary information to the ACIA for decoding. Table 4-1 shows the different logic states for both lines, the registers selected, and the direction of data flow for each condition.

**Table 4-1**  The MC6850 Uses the Logic State on Both the RS and R/W Pins to Select an Internal ACIA Register

| RS | R/W | Direction of Data Between Microprocessor and ACIA |
| --- | --- | --- |
| L | L | From microprocessor to control register |
| L | H | From status register to microprocessor |
| H | L | From microprocessor to transmit data register |
| H | H | From receive data register to microprocessor |

The ACIA's transmit shift and data registers as well as its receive shift and data registers operate as described for any general purpose UART in Section 4-2. The μP and hence the programmer has no direct control of the operation.

If the ACIA wants to send an interrupt request to the μP, this is done using pin 7. The ACIA only has three peripheral control line $\overline{\text{RTS}}$ (pin 5), $\overline{\text{DCD}}$ (pin 23), and $\overline{\text{CTS}}$ (pin 24).

## 4-4  ACIA's Control Register

Like other UART devices, Motorola's ACIA's control register is an 8-bit write-only register. The binary pattern written into this register programs how the ACIA will operate for both transmitting and receiving serial data. Figure 4-4 shows how the bits of the control register are grouped and the function of each group.

### 4-4.1  Control Bits 0 and 1

These two bits are referred to as the clock divide and master reset bits. As the names imply, these bits have two functions: a master reset and to help set the bit rate of the transmitted and received serial data. Let's consider how these bits are used.

After power is applied to the ACIA, its internal circuitry senses the power-on and holds the chip in a reset condition. This prevents erroneous data from being outputted on the Tx Data line. In order to use the device, two lines of code are necessary. The first line of code releases the ACIA's reset circuitry and the second line of code programs the device for the application. The reset circuitry is released

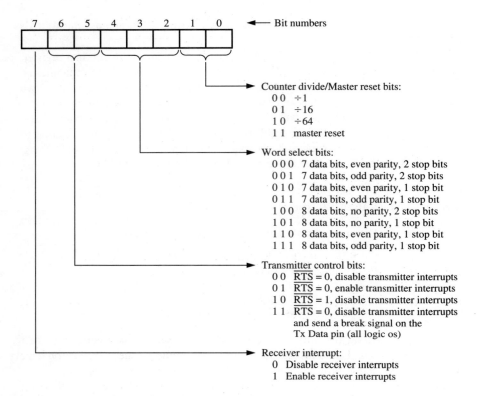

**Figure 4-4    The Format for the MC6850 Control Register** *(Copyright of Motorola, Inc. Used by permission)*

by writing logic 1s to bits 0 and 1 of the control register, and then the ACIA is programmed when the control register receives the second line of code. Assume that an ACIA is connected to a μP so that the control register is at address $10040. Using MC68000 μP assembly language, we could clear the internal power-on reset logic by the following instruction:

MOVE.B #$03,$10040

Now, bits 0 and 1 of the control register are ready to be used for their second function as a divide ratio. The ACIA has three divide ratios: 1, 16, and 64. The binary pattern for each ratio is shown in Figure 4-4. A divide ratio means that the transmit and receive clock frequencies from an external bit rate generator are divided by this number and the result sets the rate at which the serial data is transmitted and received. Section 3-4 of the previous chapter discussed the relationship between these pulses. In equation form

$$\text{Serial Data Rate} = \frac{\text{External Bit Rate Frequency}}{\text{ACIA's divide ratio}} \qquad (4\text{-}1)$$

E X A M P L E    4 - 1

An external bit rate generator is set at 76,800 pulses per second. If a 0,1 binary pattern is stored in the control register of an ACIA, what is the transmitted and received data rate?

**Solution**

From Figure 4-4, a 0,1 binary pattern is a divide by 16 ratio. Applying Equation (4-1), the data rate is

$$\frac{76,800}{16} = 4800 \text{ bps}$$

In some applications, you may see the control register bits referred to as multiplier bits instead of a divide ratio. This is because if the serial data rate and the value stored in control register are known, then a multiplication of the two numbers results in the frequency needed by the external bit rate generator. This is just a rearrangement of Equation 4-1.

E X A M P L E    4 - 2

Assume that the first two bits of an ACIA's control register contain a 0,1 binary pattern and the serial data rate is 2400 bps. What is the frequency of the external bit rate generator?

**Solution**

From Figure 4-4, a 0,1 binary pattern is a factor of 16. Rearranging Equation (4-1) yields the frequency of the bit rate generator as

$$16 \times 2400 = 38,400 \text{ pulses per second}$$

In Examples 4-1 and 4-2, the data rate is the same for transmitting and receiving. Section 4-9 shows how they may be set differently.

## 4-4.2   Control Bits 2, 3, and 4

Control bits 2, 3, and 4 are known as the word select bits and determine the number of data bits, the type of parity, and the number of stop bits for both transmitting and receiving data. These three bits produce 8 ($2^3 = 8$) possible combinations, as shown in Figure 4-4. Remember that the ACIA, like any UART device, automatically inserts the start bit before transmitting any serial data.

E X A M P L E    4 - 3

Assume that your application requires the serial data to be transmitted and received as 8 data bits, no parity, and 1 stop bit. What binary pattern must be stored in the word select bits of the control register?

**Solution**

From Figure 4-4, the binary pattern is

$$4 \ 3 \ 2 \ \leftarrow \text{Bit number}$$
$$1 \ 0 \ 1 \ \leftarrow \text{Binary pattern}$$

---

**E X A M P L E     4 - 4**

If the binary pattern contained in bits 4, 3, and 2 of an ACIA's control register is 1 1 0 respectively, describe how the device is programmed.

**Solution**

The format that the ACIA will transmit data and expects to receive data is found from Figure 4-4 as 8 data bits, even parity, and 1 stop bit.

---

### 4-4.3   Control Bits 5 and 6

These bits in the control register of an ACIA are known as the transmitter control bits and provide for three functions which deal with transmitting data:

1. Enable or disable an interrupt request signal to the microprocessor when the ACIA's transmit data register is empty.

2. Set the logic state of a modem's control line known as request to send (the function of this $\overline{\text{RTS}}$ line will be studied in Chapter 6).

3. Signal a break condition which is a transmission of a series of spaces.

**E X A M P L E     4 - 5**

Assume an application requires an ACIA to send an interrupt request to the microprocessor when the transmit data register is empty and the ACIA is to keep its $\overline{\text{RTS}}$ pin at a low logic level. What binary pattern must be stored in bits 5 and 6?

**Solution**

From Figure 4-4 the only binary pattern that programs the ACIA for these conditions are

$$6 \ 5 \ \leftarrow \text{Bit number}$$
$$0 \ 1 \ \leftarrow \text{Binary pattern}$$

---

### 4-4.4   Control Register Bit 7

This bit is known as the receive interrupt enable bit. It determines whether or not the ACIA will send an interrupt request signal to the microprocessor whenever the receive data register is full or if the data carrier detect line (pin 23) goes high. A logic 0 in this bit programs the ACIA not to send an interrupt request to the microprocessor from the receiver side of the ACIA. *Note:* A logic 0 in this bit does not stop the ACIA from sending an interrupt request from the transmitter side as set up in control bits 5 and 6.

After the application is specified and Figure 4-4 is used, the entire binary pattern for the control register can be determined and then the assembly language line of code can be written.

E X A M P L E    4 - 6

Determine the binary pattern that must be stored in the control register so that the ACIA will be programmed to transmit and receive data to satisfy the following conditions: (a) a serial data rate of 1200 bps if the external frequency from a bit rate generator is 19,200 pulses per second; (b) a word select format of 7 data bits, odd parity, and 1 stop bit; (c) the ACIA is to send an interrupt request whenever the transmit data register is empty or the receive data register is full.

**Solution**

To obtain the binary pattern for bits 0 and 1, use Equation 4-1, $19,200/1200 = 16$ and then from Figure 4-4 a 0,1 combination is required for this divide ratio. From Figure 4-4, the word select bits must be 0 1 1. Control bits 6 and 5 enable and disable an interrupt request signal for the transmitter side of the ACIA. For this application they must be set at 0 and 1, respectively. Control bit 7 must be a logic 1 for the receiver side of the ACIA to also send an interrupt request to the microprocessor. Therefore the entire binary pattern that must be stored in the control register is

$$7\ 6\ 5\ 4\ 3\ 2\ 1\ 0 \leftarrow \text{Bit number}$$
$$1\ 0\ 1\ 0\ 1\ 1\ 0\ 1 \leftarrow \text{Binary pattern}$$

E X A M P L E    4 - 7

Write the two lines of code necessary to (1) release the ACIA's reset circuitry and (2) program the ACIA for the conditions given in Example 4-6. Use assembly language code for the MC68000 microprocessor.

**Solution**

From Example 4-6, the control word 10101101 = $AD. Therefore, the lines of code are

```
MOVE.B #$03,$10040     Releases the reset logic
                       (see Section 4-4.1)
MOVE.B #$AD,$10040     Programs the ACIA
```

### 4-5   ACIA's Status Register

As previously mentioned, the status register is a "record keeper" of conditions that have occurred at the UART. As shown in Figure 4-5, the status register for an ACIA is an 8-bit read-only register. Each bit of the register indicates the status of a different function.

#### 4-5.1   Status Register Bit 0

This bit is the receive data register full (RDRF) bit. When new data is transferred from the receive shift register to the receive data register, this bit goes to a logic 1. It is cleared to a logic 0 when the microprocessor reads the receive data register or if a power on condition occurs or if the $\overline{\text{DCD}}$ line goes high.

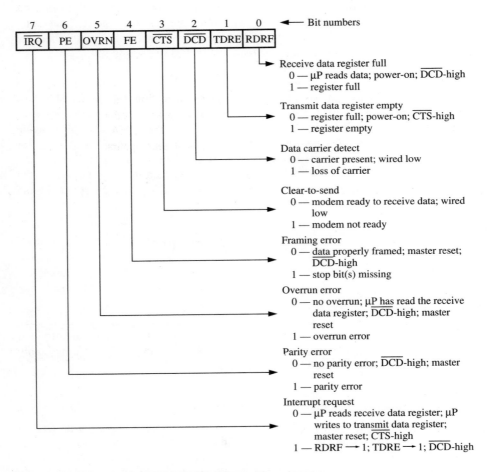

**Figure 4-5   Format for the MC6850 ACIA's Status Register** *(Copyright of Motorola, Inc. Used by permission)*

### 4-5.2   Status Register Bit 1

This bit is known as the transmit data register empty (TDRE) bit. The ACIA sets this bit to a logic 1 when the transmit data register is empty. *Note:* The transmit shift register may contain data that the ACIA is transmitting but the transmit data register is capable of receiving new data from the microprocessor. The TDRE bit is cleared to a logic 0 if the transmit data register is full or if a power on condition occurs or if the ACIA's $\overline{\text{CTS}}$ line goes high.

### 4-5.3   Status Register Bit 2

This bit is the data carrier detect bit and it indicates the logic state of the $\overline{\text{DCD}}$ (data carrier detect) line. The $\overline{\text{DCD}}$ line (pin 23) is used by a modem to signal the ACIA if a communication carrier has been lost. This topic will be discussed in Chapter 6. If a modem is not connected to the ACIA then the $\overline{\text{DCD}}$ pin must be wired to a low logic level.

### 4-5.4   Status Register Bit 3

This bit is known as the clear to send ($\overline{\text{CTS}}$) status bit, and it reflects the logic state of the clear-to-send input line (pin 24). The ACIA uses this bit to inhibit the transfer of serial data when peripheral equipment such as a modem is not ready to receive the data. As long as the $\overline{\text{CTS}}$ bit is a logic 1, the ACIA will not transmit data. When the $\overline{\text{CTS}}$ line goes high, a sequence of events occurs:

**1.** The $\overline{\text{CTS}}$ status bit goes high.

**2.** The TDRE bit goes to a logic 0.

**3.** The interrupt request bit of the status register (bit 7) goes to a logic 0.

If your application is not using the $\overline{\text{CTS}}$ line, it must be wired to a low logic level. A master reset does not affect the $\overline{\text{CTS}}$ status bit.

### 4-5.5   Status Register Bit 4

This bit is the framing error (FE) bit. In asynchronous communication, each character is framed by a start and stop bit. If these bits do not appear correctly on received data, the ACIA sets the framing error bit to a logic 1. This bit is cleared to a logic 0 when the received character is properly framed. It is also cleared for two other conditions: (1) a master reset and (2) the $\overline{\text{DCD}}$ input line goes high.

### 4-5.6   Status Register Bit 5

Bit 5 in the status register is the overrun error (OVRN) bit. If the $\mu$P has not read the receive data register before the ACIA tries to transfer a new character to it, then bit 5 is set to a logic 1. *Note:* If the new character is not transferred the old character remains in the receive data register. The new character will be lost if another character is received by the ACIA. This bit is cleared to a logic 0 if no overrun error occurs, if the μP reads the receive data register, if the $\overline{DCD}$ line goes high, or if a master reset occurs.

### 4-5.7   Status Register Bit 6

This status register bit is the parity error (PE) bit. It is set to a logic 1 when a parity error occurs. Remember parity is set by bits 2, 3, and 4 of the control register. If the receive character's parity does not agree with what has been programmed into the control register, a parity error occurs and bit 6 will be set to a logic 1. This bit is cleared to a logic 0 when the next character is received without a parity error, the DCD line goes high, or a master reset occurs.

### 4-5.8   Status Register Bit 7

This status bit is the interrupt request ($\overline{IRQ}$) bit. It is set to a logic 1 when there is an interrupt request pending at the ACIA. An interrupt request can occur from a loss of carrier ($\overline{DCD}$ line goes high), or from the transmitter side (transmitter interrupt enable is active from control bits 5 and 6), or from the receiver side (receiver interrupt is active from control bit 7). This bit is cleared to a logic 0 if the μP reads data from the receive data register or writes data to the transmit data register, a master reset occurs, or the CTS line goes high.

  *Note:* The logic state on the interrupt request line (pin 7) is the complement of the logic state of the $\overline{IRQ}$ status bit.

## 4-6   Transmit Routine

Figure 4-6 shows a flow chart that enables a μP to determine if the transmit data register is empty so that another character may be sent to it. As seen from Figure 4-6, the μP reads the status register to check the TDRE bit. If this bit is a logic 1, the μP will move the next character from a memory buffer location to the transmit data register. If the TDRE bit is a logic 0, the $\overline{CTS}$ bit must be checked to be sure the ACIA has not received a signal from a modem indicating no further transmission at this time.

### E  X  A  M  P  L  E    4 - 8

Use MC68000 μP assembly language and write a program to satisfy the flow chart of Figure 4-6. Assume the memory buffer for stored characters begins at location $2000, and the ACIA's status register and transmit data registers are at locations $10040 and $10042, respectively.

### Solution

```
         LEA      $2000,A1        Load memory buffer address.
READST:  MOVE.B   $10040,D0       Read the status register.
         LSR      #02,D0          Shift TDRE bit into C flag.
         BCS      TXDATA          Test the TDRE bit; if C = 1, branch to
                                     TXDATA.
```

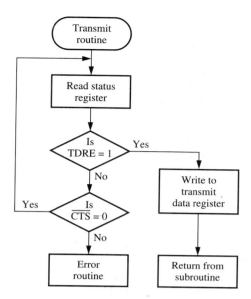

**Figure 4-6  A Flowchart Illustrating the Steps Involved for the Microprocessor to Write a Character to the ACIA's Transmit Data Register** *(Courtesy of Motorola, Inc. Used by permission)*

## Solution

|         | LSR    | #02,D0        | Shift $\overline{\text{CTS}}$ bit into C flag. |
|---------|--------|---------------|------------------------------------------------|
|         | BCC    | READST        | Test $\overline{\text{CTS}}$ bit; if C=0, branch back to READST. |
|         | BRA    | ERROR         | Branch to an error program (not shown). |
| TXDATA: | MOVE.B | (A1)+,$10042  | Move the next character to ACIA. |
|         | RTS    |               | Return from the subroutine. |

## 4-7  Receive Routine

Figure 4-7 shows a flow chart for a μP to read the status register and check to find out if the receive data register is full and if the data is valid. If the RDRF bit is a logic 0, the $\overline{\text{DCD}}$ bit is checked to be sure there has not been a loss of carrier. The flow chart shows that the framing error, overrun, and parity error bits are first checked to be sure the receive data register holds valid data.

### E X A M P L E   4 - 9

Use the flow chart of Figure 4-7 as a guide and write a program for the μP to read the receive data register. Assume the status and receive data registers are at locations $10040 and $10042, respectively. A memory buffer beginning at location $2500 may be used to store the received characters.

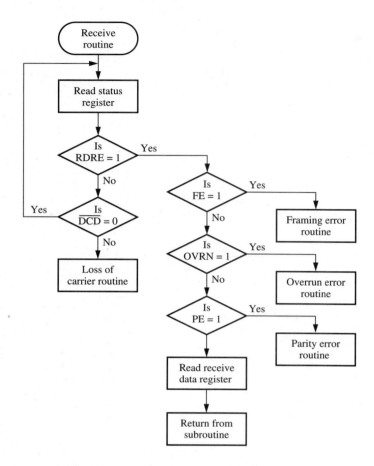

**Figure 4-7   A Flowchart Illustrating the Steps Involved for the Microprocessor to Read a Character from the Receive Data Register** *(Courtesy of Motorola, Inc. Used by permission)*

## Solution

| | | | |
|---|---|---|---|
| | LEA | $2500,A2 | Load the memory buffer address. |
| READSR: | MOVE.B | $10040,D0 | Read the status register. |
| | LSR | #01,D0 | Shift RDRE bit into the C flag. |
| | BCS | FEBIT | If C = 1, branch to check FE bit. |
| | LSR | #02,D0 | Shift $\overline{DCD}$ bit into C flag. |
| | BCC | READSR | If C = 0, branch back to READSR. |
| | BRA | LOSTCA | If C = 1, branch to lost carrier routine (not shown). |
| FEBIT: | LSR | #04,D0 | Shift FE bit into C flag. |
| | BCC | OVBIT | If C = 0, branch to check OV bit. |
| | BRA | ERROR1 | Branch to framing error routine (not shown). |

**Solution**

| OVBIT: | LSR | #01,D0 | Shift OV bit into C flag. |
| | BCC | PEBIT | If C = 0, branch to check PE bit. |
| | BRA | ERROR2 | Branch to overrun error routine (not shown). |
| PEBIT: | LSR | #01,D0 | Shift PE bit into C flag. |
| | BCC | RXDATA | Branch to RXDATA. |
| | BRA | ERROR3 | Branch to a parity error routine (not shown). |
| RXDATA: | MOVE.B | $10042,(A2)+ | Move the received character into the memory buffer. |
| | RTS | | Return from subroutine. |

## 4-8  Interconnecting ACIAs to a MC68000 μP

Section 4-1 introduced the principles of how to connect a UART to a μP. This section shows a more detailed schematic of connecting two ACIAs to a 68000 μP. Motorola designed an MC68000 Education Computer Board ((ECB) system that has two serial ports each using an ACIA. The MC68000 has a 16-bit data bus ($D_{15}$–$D_0$). Since an ACIA has an 8-bit data bus, one ACIA is connected to the upper data byte ($D_{15}$–$D_8$) and another ACIA is connected to the lower data byte ($D_7$–$D_0$). (They both could have been connected to the upper or lower 8 bits of the data bus but the ECB system was not designed that way.) Figure 4-8 shows the memory map scheme for these ACIAs. Remember each ACIA requires only two locations to address the four internal registers. This is because two registers are read only and two are write only.

ACIA #1 is wired to the 68000's upper data lines and ACIA #2 is wired to the lower data lines. Both chips use the same output from an address decoder

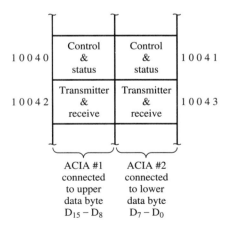

**Figure 4-8   A Memory Map Scheme to Visualize the Locations of the ACIA's Internal Registers**

connected to $CS_1$ and the µP address line $A_6$ connected to $CS_0$. The MC68000 µP uses its data strobe lines to select one of the ACIAs. The µP $\overline{UDS}$ line is wired to $\overline{CS_2}$ of ACIA $^\#1$ while the $\overline{LDS}$ line is wired to $\overline{CS_2}$ of ACIA $^\#2$. Now when the µP puts out on the address bus \$10040 or \$10042, $\overline{UDS}$ goes low and $\overline{LDS}$ goes high. Hence, ACIA $^\#1$ is selected. $\overline{UDS}$ is high and $\overline{LDS}$ is low for addresses \$10041 and \$10043, thereby selecting ACIA $^\#2$. This wiring diagram is shown in Figure 4-9.

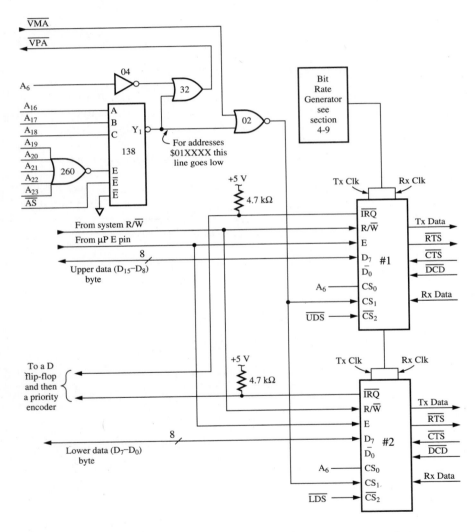

**Figure 4-9    A Typical Interconnection for Two ACIAs Connected to an MC68000 Microprocessor System**

## 4-9 MC14411 Bit Rate Generator

The ACIA has two clock lines—Tx Clk (pin 4) and Rx Clk (pin 3)—for setting the data rate for transmitting and receiving serial data. In many applications, these lines are tied together and connected to a single pin on a bit rate generator as shown in Figure 4-10a. When the lines are tied together, the serial data is sent and received at the same on rate. This type of application was studied in Examples 4-1 and 4-2. Remember from Section 4-4.1 that the external clock signal set

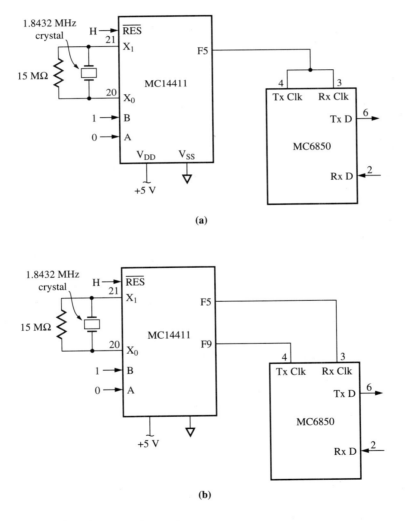

(a)

(b)

**Figure 4-10** The ACIA's Tx Clk and Rx Clk Lines Can be Tied Together and Connected to One Pin on the MC14411 as in (a) or Connected Separately as in (b).

by the bit rate generator is divided by ratios set up in the control register (bits 0 and 1).

In order to provide the external frequencies that are needed by an ACIA, bit rate generators such as Motorola's MC14411 or MC145411 ICs can be used. The MC14411 provides 16 clock signals from different pins as shown in Figure 4-11a. The MC145411 is housed in only a 16-pin package and provides 8 clock signals. For either device, the clock signals are derived from a 1.8432MHz crystal. Figure 4-10a and b shows the crystal connected between pins 20 and 21 of the MC14411. The following examples show how this device is used with an ACIA.

### E  X  A  M  P  L  E    4 - 10

An ACIA is being used to transmit and receive data at a rate of 2400 bps. If its divide ratio is set at 16 and the MC14411 is also set at rate of 16, what pin on the bit rate generator should be wired to the ACIA's Tx Clk and Rx Clk pins?

**Solution**

The external clock frequency is found by rearranging Eq. 4-1:

$$2400 \times 16 = 38,400 \text{ pulses per second}$$

Use Figure 4-11b and in the $\times 16$ column find 38.4k. This corresponds to the output pin labeled F5, which is pin 3 on the MC14411. A wiring schematic is shown in Figure 4-10a. Figure 4-10b shows how two jumpers can be used to set different baud rates for the Tx Data and Rx Data lines.

### E  X  A  M  P  L  E    4 - 11

Refer to Figure 4-10b and determine the ACIA's serial data rate if its divide ratio is set at 16.

**Solution**

From Figure 4-10b, $A = 0$ $B = 1$. Knowing this, now use the $\times 16$ column in Figure 4-11b to obtain 38.4k for the F5 output and 4800 for the F9 output. For transmitting data

$$\frac{4800}{16} = 300 \text{ bps}$$

For receiving data

$$\frac{38400}{16} = 2400 \text{ bps}$$

This application shows that an ACIA can receive data, possibly from a terminal, at 2400 bps and transmit data at 300 bps, possibly to a printer.

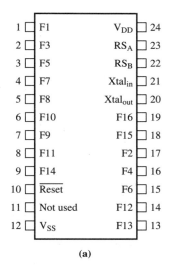

**(a)**

*Rate Select*

| B | A | Rate |
|---|---|------|
| 0 | 0 | × 1 |
| 0 | 1 | × 8 |
| 1 | 0 | × 16 |
| 1 | 1 | × 64 |

| Output Number | Output Rates (Hz) | | | |
|---------------|-------|-------|-------|-------|
|               | × 64 | × 16 | × 8 | × 1 |
| F1  | 614.4 k | 153.6 k | 76.8 k  | 9600   |
| F2  | 460.8 k | 115.2 k | 57.6 k  | 7200   |
| F3  | 307.2 k | 76.8 k  | 38.4 k  | 4800   |
| F4  | 230.4 k | 57.6 k  | 28.8 k  | 3600   |
| F5  | 153.6 k | 38.4 k  | 19.2 k  | 2400   |
| F6  | 115.2 k | 28.8 k  | 14.4 k  | 1800   |
| F7  | 76.8 k  | 19.2 k  | 9600    | 1200   |
| F8  | 38.4 k  | 9600    | 4800    | 600    |
| F9  | 19.2 k  | 4800    | 2400    | 300    |
| F10 | 12.8 k  | 3200    | 1600    | 200    |
| F11 | 9600    | 2400    | 1200    | 150    |
| F12 | 8613.2  | 2153.3  | 1076.6  | 134.5  |
| F13 | 7035.5  | 1758.8  | 879.4   | 109.9  |
| F14 | 4800    | 1200    | 600     | 75     |
| F15 | 921.6 k | 921.6 k | 921.6 k | 921.6 k |
| F16* | 1.843 M | 1.843 M | 1.843 M | 1.843 M |

*F16 is buffered oscillator output.

*Source:* Reprinted with permission of Motorola Incorporated.

**(b)**

**Figure 4-11   The MC14411 Bit Rate Generator's Pin Assignments are Given in (a) and Output Frequencies are Given in (b)**

Motorola includes the MC14411 bit rate generator along with two ACIA devices on their MC68000 Educational Computer Board (ECB), a portion of which was shown in the previous section. Figure 4-12 shows one ACIA and a modified version of what is on the ECB to set the serial data rates. *Note:* Although different frequencies are available, the ACIA in Figure 4-12 has the same data rates for transmitting and receiving data because the Tx Clk and Rx Clk pins are tied together.

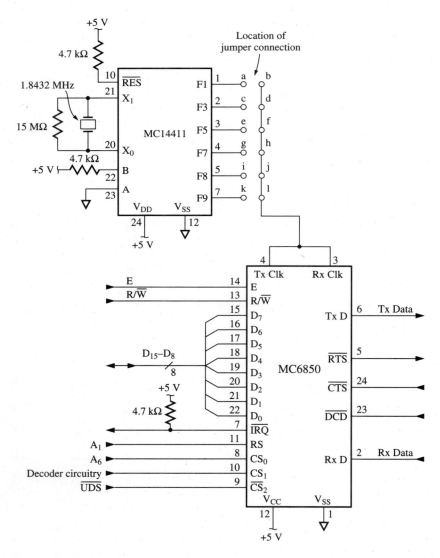

**Figure 4-12   Different External Frequencies Can be Applied to the MC6850 ACIA by Using a Jumper Connection Arrangement of Output Pins of the MC14411**

E X A M P L E   4 - 12

If a jumper is connected between a and b in Figure 4-12, determine the ACIA's data rate if its divide ratio is set at (a) 16 and (b) 64.

**Solution**

From Figure 4-12 A = 0 and B = 1 and from Figure 4-11b the output at F1 = 153.6k.

**(a)** A divide by 16 ratio yields

$$\frac{153.6k}{16} = 9600 \text{ bps}$$

**(b)** A divide by 64 ratio yields

$$\frac{153.6k}{64} = 2400 \text{ bps}$$

The ECB system provides similar jumper pairs for ACIA $^\#2$ from the same bit rate generator. There are also a few more outputs available from the MC14411 on the ECB.

## Summary

I/O devices are an important part of a microcomputer system. There are general purpose and specific I/O devices. A specific I/O device, such as a UART, has been designed to make the interfacing between a CPU and peripheral equipment as easily as possible and off-load several mundane tasks from the CPU. The term UART is the generic term for any I/O device that transmits and receives asynchronous data. A control word written to the control register of a UART programs how the device will operate. In order for the μP to know what has happened, UARTs have a status register and each bit indicates the status of a particular function. A character to be transmitted is sent by the CPU to the UART's transmit data register. A character received by the UART on its Rx Data line is read from the receive data register by the CPU.

Sections 4-4 and 4-5 show how the MC6850 control and status register operates. Section 4-6 shows how the μP uses the status register bits to determine if another character should be sent to the transmit data register. Section 4-7 gives an example of how the μP uses the status register bits to determine if the receive data is full and if the data is valid. An example of how two ACIAs are connected to a 68000 μP is given in Section 4-8. In order to generate the ACIA's timing and counting pulses needed for serial transmitting and receiving of data, an external bit rate generator is required. Motorola's MC14411 bit rate generator is such a device and is given in Section 4-9.

## Problems

**\*4.1** Name the read-only registers in a UART.

**4.2** Does the μP read data from the receive data register or the receive shift register?

**\*4.3** Do most UARTs have the double buffering capability?

**4.4** What bits are "stripped away" by a UART when it transfers data from its receive shift register to its receive data register?

**\*4.5** Is the bit rate generator's frequency used as a clock signal to synchronize the transfers between the μP and the ACIA?

**4.6** What is the function of the UART's status register?

**\*4.7** Why is it recommended to wire the lowest numbered address bus line to the UART's register select line?

**4.8** If the RS and R/$\overline{\text{W}}$ pins are at logic 0, what ACIA register is accessed?

**\*4.9** Assume an ACIA's control register bits 2, 3, and 4 contain logic states 001, respectively. What is the format for transmitting and receiving serial data?

**4.10** What must be the control word's binary pattern to program an ACIA for the following conditions: (a) divide by 16 ratio; (b) 7 data bits, even parity, 1 stop bit; (c) RTS low and transmitter interrupt disabled; (d) received interrupt disabled.

**\*4.11** Which ACIA peripheral control pins must be wired low if they are not used?

**4.12** Name each bit of the status register.

**\*4.13** What conditions clear the $\overline{\text{DCD}}$ status bit?

**4.14** What conditions clear the OVRN status bit?

**\*4.15** Refer to Figure 4-12 and determine the data rate for each of the following jumper connections: (a) e-f; (b) g-h; (c) k-l. Assume the ACIA's divide ratio is 16.

**4.16** Repeat Problem 4-15 with the ACIA's divide ratio set at 64.

*See Answers to Selected Problems.

# RS-232-C Mechanical and Electrical Characteristics

5

**OBJECTIVES**

Upon completion of this chapter on the RS-232-C mechanical and electrical characteristics, the student will be able to

- Define the terms "data terminal equipment" and "data communication equipment."
- Specify the standard's mechanical characteristics.
- Know the standard's electrical characteristics. *voltage range only for topic 3*
- Draw the standard's equivalent circuit of an interface line.
- Use an integrated circuit line driver and receiver.
- Describe the standard's signal limitations.
- Understand the principle of slew rate and solve a line driver's maximum rate of change.
- Learn how to protect a line driver circuit from power supply failure.

## Introduction

Chapter 1 introduced many terms that are used in the field of data communications. Two terms that have been left until now to be covered in more detail are **data terminal equipment** (DTE) and **data communication equipment** (DCE). DTE is any digital device that transmits and/or receives data and uses communication equipment for the data transfer. Most often DTE devices are thought of only as computers but CRT displays, printers, teletypes, and front-end processors for mainframes are all examples of DTE. DCE devices are connected to a communication line (usually the telephone line) for the purpose of transferring data from one point to another. In addition to transferring the data, DCE devices are designed to establish, maintain, and terminate the connection. They do not process data but transfer it without regard to the contents. The data may be transferred in either analog or digital form depending on the communication link. The most commonly used DCE device is the modem. Another example is a digital line driver. Modems, which were introduced in Chapter 1 (review Section 1-4), will be studied in more detail in Chapters 8 and 9. Digital line drivers are studied in Chapter 13.

DTE and DCE products are often designed by different manufacturers; therefore, it is necessary to have an interface standard so that these devices may be interconnected easily. One of the most commonly used interface standards, the RS-232-C, will be covered here and in Chapter 6. See Figure 5-1. The prefix "RS" stands for recommended standard, the 232 is the committee number, and the C designates the version. This standard is published by the Electronics Industries Association (EIA). The EIA is an industry group which helps form and publicize standards related to many different areas of the electronic industry such as components, equipment, systems, packaging, and communications. The newest version of this standard is known as the EIA-232-D. However, the term RS-232-C, or simply RS-232, will probably be encountered more often because data communication manufacturers still use it. Therefore, the term RS-232-C will be used and the differences between the versions highlighted where necessary.

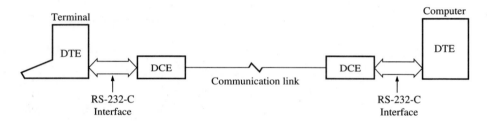

**Figure 5-1    Interconnection between DTE and DCE**

There are many ways to design and implement a standard for transferring data serially. The RS-232-C is one standard being used by many manufacturers. The EIA cannot legally force a manufacturer to use this interface standard because use of the standard is voluntary. Since the RS-232-C interface does not cover every possible application, some manufacturers modify it for their particular situation. However, the standard does provide a framework allowing terminal and communication equipment to be connected together easily. The formal name for the RS-232-C interface is **Interface Between Data Terminal Equipment and Data Communication Equipment Employing Serial Binary Data Interchange.** Although the RS-232-C is widely used, it does have its limitations. Many of these inherent drawbacks are overcome by other standards that will be introduced in Chapter 7.

The RS-232-C standard describes mechanical, electrical, and functional characteristics. In this chapter the mechanical and electrical characteristics along with two integrated circuits (ICs) that implement the electrical characteristics will be studied. The functional characteristics, along with some common applications and some nonstandard applications, are covered in Chapter 6. The RS-232-C interface can be used for full- and half-duplex operations, point-to-point or multipoint systems, as well as asynchronous and synchronous communication. Therefore, it is quite flexible and is used in a variety of applications.

## 5-1 Mechanical Characteristics

As previously mentioned, the RS-232-C standard is a reference for equipment designers. It specifies most, but not all, characteristics. One characteristic _not_ specified in the C version is the shape of the connector. However, the most commonly used one was the DB-25 connector. This connector is described in the D version. Figure 5-2 shows a mechanical drawing of this type of connector. The male portion of the connector is a plug type (such as DB-25P) and is associated with the DTE. The female portion of the connector is a socket type (such as DB-25S) and is associated with the DCE. Figure 5-2 shows the front view and pin numbering for each portion of the connector. When the connectors are put together (front views together) the pin numbers align. Figure 5-3 lists the name of each pin connection. Note that in this standard everything is in reference to the DTE; therefore, the name for pin 2 is Transmit Data. It is used to transmit data from the DTE to the DCE. Similarly, the name for pin 3 is Receive Data. It is used by the DTE to receive data from the DCE. The use of each pin will be covered in Chapter 6.

The standard recommends a maximum cable length of 50 feet (or 15 meters) between DTE and DCE. However, many companies use longer cable lengths with satisfactory results. This is accomplished by operating at less than the maximum

*EIA-232D* [handwritten margin note]

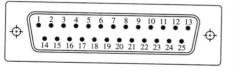

(a) Front view DB-25P connector

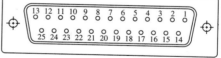

(b) Front view DB-25S connector

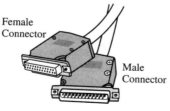

(c) 3 dimensional view
of 25 pin connectors

**Figure 5-2  (a) Front Face View of a Male (DB-25P) Connector, (b) Female (DB-25S) Connector, and (c) Three-Dimensional View of a 25-Pin Connectors**

| Pin Number | EIA Circuit | CCITT V.24 Circuit | Signal Description | To DCE | From DCE |
|---|---|---|---|---|---|
| 1 | AA | 101 | Protective ground (chassis)[1] | X | |
| 2 | BA | 103 | Transmitted data | | X |
| 3 | BB | 104 | Received data | X | |
| 4 | CA | 105 | Request-to-send | | X |
| 5 | CB | 106 | Clear-to-send | | X |
| 6 | CC | 107 | DCE ready (also known as Data Set Ready) | X | X |
| 7 | AB | 102 | Signal ground (common return) | | X |
| 8 | CF | 109 | Received line signal detector | | X |
| 9 | — | | (Reserved for data set testing) | | |
| 10 | — | | (Reserved for data set testing) | | |
| 11 | | | Unassigned | | X |
| 12 | SCF | 122 | Secondary received line signal detector | | X |
| 13 | SCB | 121 | Secondary Clear-to-Send | | |
| 14 | SBA | 118 | Secondary transmitted data | X | |
| 15 | DB | 114 | Transmitter signal element timing (DCE source) | | X |
| 16 | SBB | 119 | Secondary received data | | X |
| 17 | DD | 115 | Receiver signal element timing (DCE source) | | X |
| 18 | LL | 141 | Local loopback[2] | X | |
| 19 | SCA | 120 | Secondary request-to-send | X | |
| 20 | CD | 108/2 | Data terminal ready | X | |
| 21 | RL/CG | 110 | Remote loopback/Signal quality detector | | X |
| 22 | CE | 125 | Ring/calling indicator | | X |
| 23 | CH | 111 | Data signal rate selector (DTE source) | X | |
| 23 | CI | 112 | Data signal rate selector (DCE source) | | X |
| 24 | DA | 113 | Transmitter signal element timing (DTE) | X | |
| 25 | TM | 142 | Test mode[2] | | X |

[1]Not defined as part of the D version.    [2]Unassigned in the C version.

**Figure 5-3  Pin Assignments for EIA's 232 Interface and the Corresponding International Telegraph and Telephone Consultative Committee (CCITT) V.24 Equivalent Circuit Number** *(Permission granted by Electronic Industries Association.)*

data rate (which is 20,000 bits per second [bps]) and/or using cable with lower capacitance. The effect of cable capacitance will be studied in this chapter.

## 5-2  Electrical Characteristics

The electrical portion of the standard covers the voltage and current specifications for each pin. Table 5-1 lists the RS-232-C voltage range along with commonly used terminology.

Up to this point in the text, data has been expressed as transistor-transistor logic (TTL) levels. These levels are positive logic; that is, a logic 1 is a more positive voltage than a voltage value for a logic 0. The RS-232-C standard uses

**Table 5-1  Voltage Range of the Receiver**

|  | $-15V < V_1 < -3V$ | $3V < V_1 < 15V$ |
|---|---|---|
| Logic state | 1 | 0 |
| Signal | mark | space |
| Control | off | on |

negative logic; that is, a logic 1 voltage level is negative with respect to a logic 0 voltage level as shown in Table 5-1 and Figure 5-4. The voltage range between +3 volts and −3 volts is a transition region and the signal is not defined within it. Figure 5-4 illustrates the voltage range for the driver and termination ends. A transmitted mark condition is between −5 volts and −15 volts relative to signal ground. If the received voltage is more negative than −3 volts with respect to signal ground, the signal will be considered as the mark condition. A transmitted space condition is between +5 volts and +15 volts relative to signal ground. If the received voltage is more positive than +3 volts with respect to signal ground, then the signal will be considered as a space condition. This standard allows for a 2-volt noise margin for each condition.

Normally it is assumed that the interface is being used to transmit data between the DTE and DCE and vice versa. However, most of the lines in the standard are for timing and control signals so that the data is transferred in an orderly fashion. The timing and control lines use ON and OFF terminology instead of mark and space terminology. Table 5-1 and Figure 5-4 give the voltage ranges for the ON and OFF conditions.

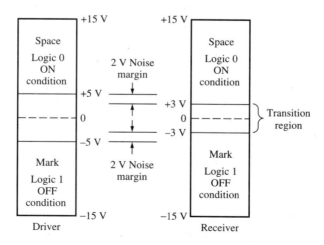

**Figure 5-4  RS-232-C Voltage Range**

### 5-2.1  Equivalent Circuit

Figure 5-5 shows the equivalent circuit as given in the standard for each line in the RS-232-C interface, regardless of whether the driver is DTE and the terminator is DCE or vice versa. Each term in the equivalent circuit will be defined and some commercially available devices will be analyzed.

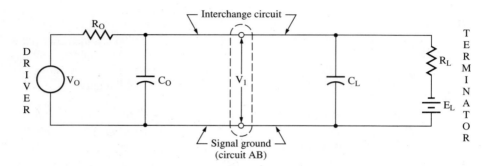

**Figure 5-5    Equivalent Circuit for Each RS-232-C Cable Except the Grounds**

$V_O$ is the open-circuit driver voltage with respect to signal ground (pin 7) and shall not exceed 25 volts in magnitude.

$R_O$ is the driver internal dc resistance. Although the value of $R_O$ is not specified in the standard, it must limit any short circuit current not to exceed 0.5 amperes.

$C_O$ is the total effective capacitance associated with the driver. It is measured at the interface point looking back toward the driver and therefore includes the capacitance of the driver circuitry plus any cable capacitance on the driver side of the interface point. The value of $C_O$ is not specified in the standard but equipment designers must build a circuit capable of driving $C_O$ plus the maximum value of $C_L$, which is 2500 pF.

$C_L$ is the total effective capacitance associated with the terminator. It is measured at the interface point looking toward the terminating end and therefore includes the cable capacitance plus the capacitance associated with the load. The standard does specify that $C_L$ shall not exceed 2500 pF.

$R_L$ is the terminator load dc resistance. The range is between 3000 and 7000 ohms. The standard specifies in more detail that $R_L$ shall not be less than 3000 ohms with an applied voltage not greater than 25 volts in magnitude and $R_L$ shall not be greater than 7000 ohms with an applied voltage of 3 to 25 volts in magnitude.

$E_L$ is the open circuit terminator voltage and shall not exceed 2 volts in magnitude.

$V_1$ is the voltage at the interface point.

The RS-232-C specifications show the equivalent circuit with only passive components of resistors and capacitors and voltage sources. However, when systems are going to be built, designers use ICs that conform to the RS-232-C and EIA-232-D specifications. Two such devices are the MC1488 line driver and the MC1489 line receiver. These devices will be examined in more detail.

### 5-2.2  Integrated Circuit Line Driver

As shown in Figure 5-6, the MC1488 houses four RS-232-C line drivers while the MC1489 or MC1489A contains four RS-232-C line receivers. IC packages such as these and other data communication ICs have allowed manufacturers to reduce the size, cost, and power consumption of their equipment and yet increase the versatility and reliability of their product. These ICs have been designed to meet or exceed the RS-232-C specifications. As with all ICs, normal precautions should be taken when handling and using them in systems where they could be subjected to loss of system power. Such an example is studied in Section 5-2.8.

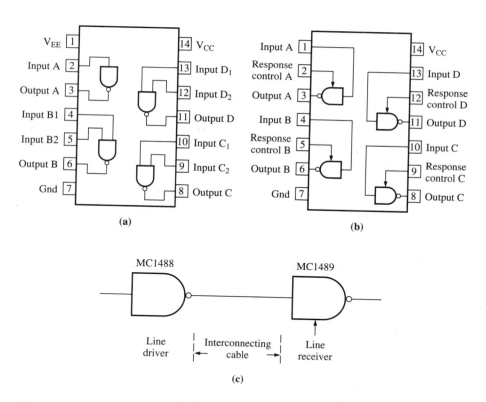

**Figure 5-6**   (a) MC1488 Line Driver Pin Assignments. (b) MC1489 Line Receiver Pin Assignments. (c) Typical Interconnection Application *(Courtesy of Motorola Incorporated, Austin, Texas)*

The MC1488 is a versatile line driver, and although we are using it to drive RS-232-C lines, it can be used as a voltage translator between different logic families. For our present application, it is being used to translate the TTL output levels of a universal asynchronous receiver/transmitter (UART) to RS-232-C voltage levels. For example, if the MC1488 package is operating from a power supply of $\pm 9$ volts, then a TTL logic 0 ($<0.8$ volts) results in a line driver voltage of approximately $+7$ volts, which is an RS-232-C space. Similarly, a TTL logic 1 ($>2.4$ volts) results in a line driver voltage of approximately $-7$ volts, which is an RS-232-C mark. Although this example used power supply voltages of $\pm 9$ volts, the MC1488 package can operate from other supply voltages up to a maximum of $\pm 15$ volts. It can even operate from unsymmetrical supply voltages. The driver circuitry has been designed so that the output voltage will be within 2 volts of the supply voltage as long as the output current limit is not exceeded. Each line driver has short circuit protection of 10 mA. The driver circuitry also has been designed to deliver the RS-232-C voltage levels when the output of the circuit is terminated with a resistor between 3000 and 7000 ohms as specified in the standard. More information is given on the MC1488 in Sections 5-2.6 through 5-2.8. These sections will show how this device conforms to the RS-232-C specifications.

### 5-2.3   IC Line Receivers

IC line receivers such as Motorola's MC1489 or MC1489A devices are used to simplify the design of DTE and DCE and meet the RS-232-C specifications. Figure 5-6b shows the package configuration. The primary purpose of line receivers is to translate incoming RS-232-C voltage levels to TTL levels. For example, an input voltage of $+3$ volts or greater (a space condition) results in an output voltage of approximately 0.4 volts (a TTL logic 0). Similarly, an input voltage of $-3$ volts or less (a mark condition) results in an output voltage of approximately $+5$ volts (a TTL logic 1). Each line receiver has an input resistance between 3000 and 7000 ohms for input voltages between 3 and 25 volts in magnitude. These values conform to the RS-232-C specifications. The line receiver's open-circuit voltage is only one diode drop, which is much less than the 2 volts given in the specification for the open-circuit voltage at the terminator.

Each line receiver in the MC1489 package has a reference control that may or may not be used. If not used, the pin is left open and the MC1489 line receiver is designed to have 250 mV of hysteresis voltage centered around a reference of 1.125 volts. If used, a resistor-voltage circuit is applied to this pin as shown in Figure 5-7a. This combination allows the user to vary the input hysteresis voltage and the center reference voltage as shown in Figure 5-7b.

### 5-2.4   Signal Limitations

The RS-232-C standard specifies that the signals transmitted across the interface point shall not exceed certain limits. Two of these limits, for data and control signals, are

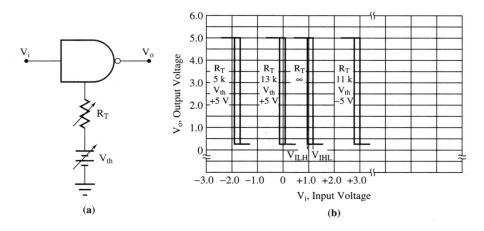

**Figure 5-7    The $R_T$—$V_{th}$ Circuit May be Used to Vary the Hysteresis and Center Voltage** *(Courtesy of Motorola Incorporated, Austin, Texas)*

1. The maximum rate of change of voltage with respect to time shall not exceed 30 V/μs.

2. The time required to pass through the transition period ($-3$ to $+3$ volts or vice versa) shall not exceed 1 ms or 4% of the nominal bit time, whichever is less.

Both of these limitations are shown in Figure 5-8. RS-232-C control signals must conform to the first limitation but only the 1-ms limitation of part 2. Since control signals do not occur as a sequence of bits, then the 4% limit does not apply to them. Both types of limitations and how well the MC1488 line drivers conform to these limitations will be examined.

### 5-2.5  Maximum Rate of Voltage Change

Except for an unpredictable noise spike, the maximum rate of change of a signal should occur at the bit boundaries when there are transitions, that is, the times when the driver circuitry is beginning to change the signal from a mark-to-space or space-to-mark condition. The dotted lines in Figure 5-8 show the initial slope at the bit boundaries. This initial slope is the maximum **rate of voltage change.** In order to conform to the standard, the driver circuit cannot force this voltage change at a rate faster than 30 volts in 1 μs. Hence, the slope of the dotted lines in Figure 5-8 is $\Delta V/\Delta t$ and is expressed as

$$\text{Rate of voltage change} = \frac{\Delta V}{\Delta t} \leq \frac{30\text{ V}}{\mu s} \qquad (5\text{-}1)$$

IC line drivers such as the MC1488 easily can exceed the 30 V/μs rating if a low value of capacitance is connected to its output terminal. Therefore to use IC

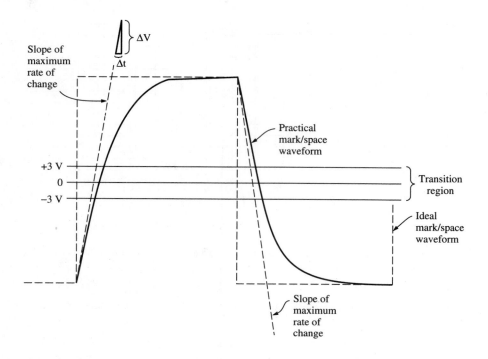

**Figure 5-8   Comparison of an Ideal and Practical Mark/Space Waveform**

line drivers and to conform to the RS-232-C standard, we must understand the driver's data sheet because IC manufacturers use a term called **slew rate** instead of rate of voltage change.

Rate of voltage change, also referred to as **change of voltage with respect to time,** is a general term that applies to any voltage wave. The term **slew rate** applies to ICs and is a measurement of how fast the device's output voltage can change with respect to time. A device's slew rate varies for different load capacitances. Therefore, manufacturers often give a graph of slew rate versus load capacitance. Figure 5-9a shows such a plot for the MC1488 line drivers. Equation (5-1) can be rewritten in terms of slew rate as

$$\text{Slew rate} = \frac{\Delta V}{\Delta t} \le \frac{30\ V}{\mu s} \tag{5-2}$$

Hence, the units for slew rate are volts per microsecond. The cause of slew rate limiting and the use of information provided by the IC manufacturer will be examined next.

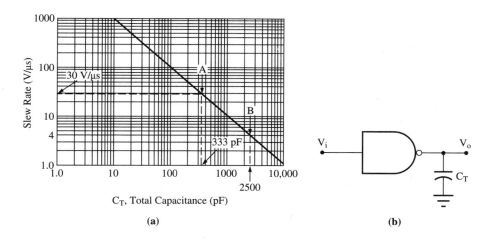

**Figure 5-9**   **(a) Output Slew Rate versus Total Line Capacitance, $C_T$ and (b) Circuit Symbol of an MC1488 Line Driver and $C_T$** *(Courtesy of Motorola Incorporated, Austin, Texas)*

### 5-2.6   Cause of Slew Rate Limiting

Figure 5-9b shows a single capacitor, $C_T$, connected to an MC1488 line driver. $C_T$ represents the total capacitance as "seen" from the driver's output. It includes all cable and terminator capacitance as discussed in Section 5-2.1. In Equation form,

$$C_T = C_O + C_L \qquad (5\text{-}3)$$

The internal circuitry of the line driver furnishes a current to charge $C_T$. It is this current charging $C_T$ that causes the voltage across $C_T$ to change with respect to time. Hence the output of the driver circuit is said to be slew rate limited. The range of current, $I_{OS}$, is from 6 to 12 mA with a typical value of 10 mA. Equation (5-2) can be rewritten as

$$\text{Slew rate} = \frac{\Delta V_O}{\Delta t} = \frac{I_{OS}}{C_T} = \frac{10\,\text{mA}}{C_T} \qquad (5\text{-}4)$$

If $C_T$ is controlled, then the slew rate can be limited to meet the RS-232-C specifications. Equation (5-4) is the expression used to plot slew rate versus load capacitance as shown in Figure 5-9a.

E  X  A  M  P  L  E     5 - 1
_____

If $I_{OS}$ = 10 mA, calculate the minimum value of $C_T$ to limit the slew rate to 30 V/$\mu$s.

**Solution**

Rearranging Equation (5-4) yields

$$C_T = \frac{10 \text{ mA}}{\Delta V_O / \Delta t} = \frac{10 \text{ mA}}{30 \text{ V}/\mu s} = 333 \text{ pF}$$

This value can also be found by using Figure 5-9a. Obtain the intersection of the 30 V/$\mu$s line and the $I_{OS} = 10$ mA line, which is point A. Below this intersection on the $C_T$ axis, read 333 pF.

---

E  X  A  M  P  L  E     5 - 2

---

If the total capacitance as "seen" from an MC1488 line driver is 2500 pF, determine the slew rate if $I_{OS} = 10$ mA.

**Solution**

Use Figure 5-9a and enter the graph at 2500 pF and obtain the intersection with the $I_{OS} = 10$ mA line, which is point B. From the vertical axis, obtain a slew rate of 4 V/$\mu$s. This answer can be checked by using Equation (5-4).

$$\text{Slew rate} = \frac{I_{OS}}{C_T} = \frac{10 \text{ mA}}{2500 \text{ pF}} = 4 \text{ V}/\mu s$$

---

From these examples, we now know that the slew rate of these IC line drivers is controlled by $C_T$. Therefore, if the line capacitance and terminator capacitance do not produce a slew rate less than 30 V/$\mu$s, then an external capacitor should be connected to the driver's output terminal.

---

E  X  A  M  P  L  E     5 - 3

---

The line capacitance and terminator capacitance on an interface circuit are 400 pF. Calculate an external capacitor that must be connected to an MC1488 line driver to obtain a slew rate of 20 V/$\mu$s. $I_{OS} = 10$ mA.

**Solution**

Rearranging Equation (5-4) yields

$$C_T = \frac{10 \text{ mA}}{\text{slew rate}} = \frac{10 \text{ mA}}{20 \text{ V}/\mu s} = 500 \text{ pF}$$

Since the fixed capacitance on the interface circuit is 400 pF, then an external capacitor of 100 pF (500 − 400 pF) is needed to maintain a slew rate that is not greater than 20 V/$\mu$s.

---

### 5-2.7   Transition Period Time Limitation

The second limitation given in Section 5-2.4 dealt with time duration to pass through the transition period. For data and timing signals, this time duration shall not exceed 1 ms or 4% of a nominal bit time. As previously mentioned, for control signals, only the 1-ms requirement is applicable. Figure 5-10a illustrates that an

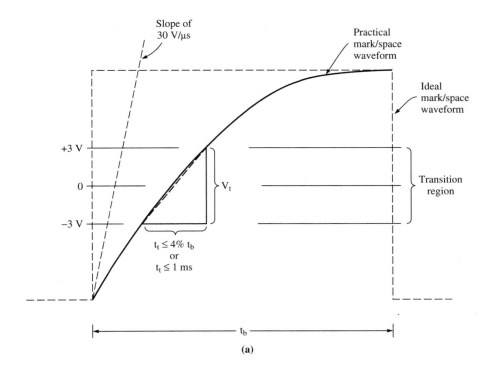

| Bit rate | Bit time ($t_b$) milliseconds | $t_t = 4\% \ t_b$ microseconds |
|---|---|---|
| 110 | 9.09 | 364 |
| 150 | 6.99 | 280 |
| 300 | 3.33 | 133 |
| 600 | 1.666 | 66.6 |
| 1200 | 0.833 | 33.3 |
| 2400 | 0.416 | 16.6 |
| 4800 | 0.208 | 8.32 |
| 9600 | 0.104 | 4.16 |
| 19.2K | 0.052 | 2.08 |

(b)

**Figure 5-10   The Line Voltage Must Pass Through the Transistion Region at a Rate Not to Exceed 4% of $t_b$ or 1 ms**

initial slope of 30 V/μs is not necessarily 30 V/μs through the transition period for a practical waveform. Figure 5-10b lists the bit time and 4% of a bit time for many commonly used bit rates. The transmitter must be capable of driving the line impedance so that the 4% limit is not exceeded but not so fast as to exceed the 30 V/μs specification. Both of these limits depend on the total line capacitance. From the solution to Example 5-1, the minimum value of line capacitance was calculated to be 333 pF to limit the slew rate to 30 V/μs. The maximum value of total line capacitance needs to be determined. Although the RS-232-C standard specifies $C_L$ shall not exceed 2500 pF, this capacitance value is on the terminator side of the interface point (*see* Fig. 5-5) and may not be the total capacitance as ''seen'' by the driver circuitry. Since total capacitance affects slew rate, it should be possible to determine a minimum slew rate to ensure that the signal passes through the transition period in the time allotted. Remember the maximum slew rate is still 30 V/μs. For the small values of $t_t$, we can assume the line voltage increases linearly. The following example shows how this assumption is applied.

**E X A M P L E     5 - 4**

For a bit rate of 19,200 bps, calculate (a) the minimum rate of change of voltage and (b) the total line capacitance that causes this minimum rate of change.

**Solution**

**(a)** From Equation (3-2)

$$t_b = \frac{1}{19,200 \text{ bps}} = 0.052 \text{ ms}$$

and

$$t_t \leq (0.04)(0.052 \text{ ms}) \cong 2.08 \text{ μs}$$

If we assume the voltage increases linearly through the transition period, the following is obtained:

$$\frac{V_t}{t_t} = \frac{6 \text{ V}}{2.08 \text{ μs}} = 2.88 \text{ V/μs}$$

In order to meet the RS-232-C specification, this value of 2.88 V/μs is the minimum voltage rate of change that is permissible for a bit rate of 19,200 bps.

**(b)** If a line is being driven by an MC1488 line driver, assume $I_{OS} = 10$ mA. Then Equation (5-4) yields

$$C_T = I_{OS} \times \frac{t_t}{V_t} = 10 \text{ mA} \times \frac{1}{2.88 \text{ V/μs}} \cong 3472 \text{ pF}$$

This value of $C_T$ does exceed the maximum recommended value, which is 2500 pF.

## 5-2.8   Power Supply Failure and Package Protection

The standard specifies that the driver circuit shall be designed to withstand either an open circuit or a short circuit from any other conductor in that cable or any other passive noninductive load without sustaining damage to itself or its associated equipment. If a short circuit does occur, the short circuit current shall not exceed 0.5 amperes. The worst possible condition would be another driver capable of delivering $\pm 15$ volt and 500 mA being applied to the output of your driver circuit. ICs that are used for line drivers can withstand a lot of abuse but some precautions should be taken. For example, the MC1488 houses four line drivers in a 14-pin dual-in-line package as shown in Figure 5-6a. This package has been designed to withstand indefinitely a short circuit to all four outputs as long as the power supply voltages are equal to or greater than $\pm 9$ volts. If, however, an accident occurs when there is a loss of supply power and all four outputs are shorted to $\pm 15$ volts from the other active drivers, the power dissipation rating of the package would surely be exceeded. The reason is that a loss of supply power results in a very low impedance to ground and the current at each output pin is limited only by the driver's output resistance (300 ohms for the MC1488). Figure 5-11 shows the effect of this type of accident—one end of the 300 ohms is at ground potential and the other end is at the external driver's voltage, $\pm 15$ volts. **Note:** This type of accident with this line driver package does not result in exceeding the RS-232-C specification of 500 mA but rather the total excess current causes too much heat to build up within the package, thus destroying the IC.

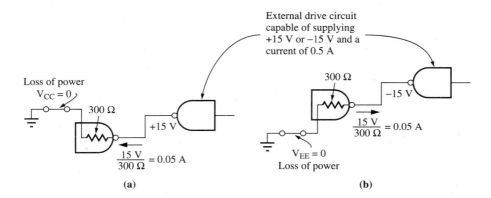

**Figure 5-11   An External Drive Circuit May Destroy the MC1488 IC**

E X A M P L E    5 - 5

Refer to Figure 5-12 and calculate the total power that the MC1488 package would try to dissipate.

### Solution

Regardless of the direction of current, heat is being generated within the package. From circuit fundamentals, $P = I^2R$ or $P = V^2/R$. Therefore, the power dissipated by each line driver within the MC1488 package is $P = (15 \text{ volts})^2/300\Omega = 0.75$ watts.

Since all four outputs are shorted to an active line drive, the total power would be 3 watts ($4 \times 0.75$ watts). This value far exceeds the package limitation of 1 watt at an ambient temperature of 25°C. Now that it is known that such an accident could occur and the overheating can destroy the device, how can the IC package be protected?

A diode in each power supply lead as shown in Figure 5-13a prevents excess current from flowing when there is a power supply failure, thereby guaranteeing protection for the package. Figure 5-13b shows that the same two diodes can protect several line driver packages.

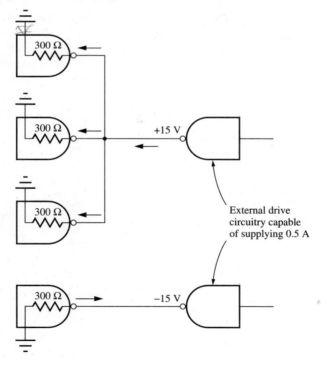

**Figure 5-12   Circuit Diagram for Example 5-5**

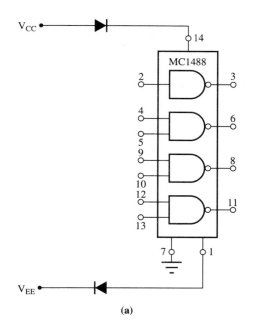

(a)

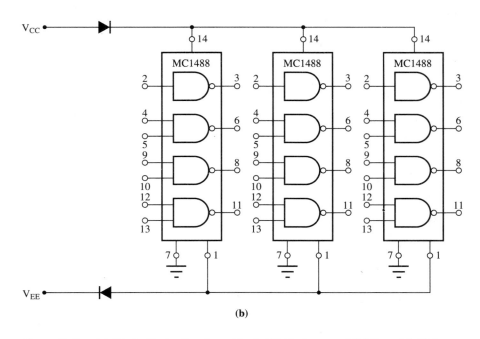

(b)

**Figure 5-13   (a) Diode Protection for a Single IC Package and (b) for a Multiple Package** *(Courtesy of Motorola, Inc.)*

## Summary

This chapter introduced the terms "data terminal equipment" (DTE) and "data communication equipment" (DCE). Often DTE is thought of only as a keyboard/ monitor combination or a computer, but some other DTE devices are printers, plotters, and teletypes. Most DTE devices are designed to communicate with DCE such as modems and line drivers. It is the DCE units that establish, maintain, and terminate the connection to the communication link. Since DTE and DCE devices are often purchased from different vendors, a standardized interface is needed so the equipment can be installed, operated, and maintained easily. One of the most commonly used interface standards is the RS-232-C. This standard describes the mechanical, electrical, and functional characteristics to be followed. The mechanical and electrical characteristics were described in this chapter while Chapter 6 will cover the functional characteristics.

Two ICs that designers use to meet the RS-232-C specification are the MC1488 line drivers and the MC1489 line receivers. Other line drivers and receivers are available from Motorola and other manufacturers. Many of these newer versions draw less power supply current. The line drivers translate TTL voltages to the RS-232-C voltage levels. At the other end of an interface cable is a line receiver. These devices translate the voltages from the RS-232-C levels to TTL voltages. Line receivers also square-up an incoming wave and provide a hysteresis voltage against noise signals that are superimposed on the input wave.

The RS-232-C standard specifies a maximum rate of voltage change and the time required to pass through the transition period. Both of these limits were introduced and the way the MC1488 line drivers conform to meet these specifications was discussed.

The E-version of the 232 standard will be released shortly and it will provide for asynchronous communication of 38.4 k bps and for synchronous communication in conjunction with lower voltage requirements.

## Problems

* **5.1** Define and give examples of DTE and DCE.

 **5.2** What is the formal name for the RS-232-C interface?

* **5.3** What are the three general characteristics of the RS-232-C standard?

 **5.4** Can the RS-232-C interface be used for both asynchronous and synchronous communication?

* **5.5** Does the RS-232-C standard specify the DB-25 connector?

* *See* Answers to Selected Problems.

**5.6** If a DB-25 connector is used, which part is associated with the (a) DTE (b) DCE?

* **5.7** When using the RS-232-C interface, is the reference point the DTE or the DCE?

**5.8** At the receiver end, what is the voltage range for (a) mark condition, (b) space condition, (c) a control OFF condition?

* **5.9** Define $C_L$.

**5.10** Can the total effective capacitance as "seen" by the driver "looking" toward the terminator be greater than 2500 pF?

*__5.11__ Determine the total line capacitance, $C_T$, connected to the output of an MC1488 line driver for the following slew rates: (a) 20 V/$\mu$s, (b) 10 V/$\mu$s, and (c) 8 V/$\mu$s. $I_{OS} = 10$ mA.

**5.12** An RS-232-C line has a total effective capacitance of 1500 pF. If the driver is an MC1488, calculate the rate of voltage change for the following $I_{OS}$ values: (a) 10 mA, (b) 6 mA, (c) 12 mA.

*__5.13__ The line capacitance and terminator capacitance on an interface circuit are 350 pF. Is it necessary to add additional capacitance to limit the driver's slew rate to less than (a) 25 V/$\mu$s, (b) 15 V/$\mu$s? Assume $I_{OS} = 6$ mA.

**5.14** What value of line capacitance would cause the 4% of $t_b$ to be exceeded if the transmission rate is 9600 bps? Assume $I_{OS} = 10$ mA.

# 6 | *RS-232-C Functional Characteristics*

O B J E C T I V E S

Upon completion of this chapter on the functional characteristics of the RS-232-C standard, the student will be able to

- List the functional characteristics and general categories, and know which interface circuits belong to each category.

- Describe how data is transferred between data terminal equipment (DTE) and data communication equipment (DCE).

- Know what a null modem is and when it is needed.

- Know which control circuits are needed for half- or full-duplex operation and if a dial-up or leased line is used.

- Understand how the control circuits are used in a variety of applications.

- Understand when RS-232-C circuits are trying to be used for nonstandard applications.

- Use the timing interface circuits in conjunction with other control circuits for synchronous transmission of data.

- Know the purpose of secondary control circuits and when to use them.

- Define the terms ''backward channel,'' ''auxiliary channel,'' and ''reverse channel.''

## Introduction

The previous chapter introduced the electrical and mechanical characteristics of the RS-232-C standard. Remember, the newest version of the standard is the D version. However, the term ''RS-232-C'' will probably be encountered more often, at least for the next several years. Therefore, the term ''RS-232'' will be used to refer to both standards, and the difference where necessary will be indicated.

In this chapter, how the interface circuits are used to transfer data between DTE and DCE and vice versa will be studied. These properties are known as the functional characteristics of the standard. Figure 5-3 listed the interface circuits.

However, the standard has been designed to cover many different applications including asynchronous or synchronous communication using half-duplex or full-duplex transmission over private or switched (dial-up) communication channels. Since no one application requires all the interface circuits, the function of the most commonly used interface circuits for a variety of different applications will be examined. Figure 6-1 arranges the RS-232 circuits according to similar functions. The first letter designates the category and the second letter represents a particular interface circuit within the category. The categories are

A—Ground or common return

B—Data circuits

C—Control circuits

D—Timing circuits

S—Secondary circuits

The function of each interface circuit will be studied.

| | Interchange circuit | Direction | |
|---|---|---|---|
| | | DTE | DCE |
| AA | Protective ground (Does not exist in Version D) | — — | — — |
| AB | Signal ground | — — | — — |
| BA | Transmitted Data | | → |
| BB | Received data | ← | |
| CA | RTS | | → |
| CB | CTS | ← | |
| CC | DCE Ready (also known as Data Set Ready) | ← | |
| CD | DTR | | → |
| CE | Ring/calling Indicator | ← | |
| CF | Received Line Signal Detector (Data Carrier Detect) | ← | |
| RL/CG | Remote Loop Back/Signal Quality Dectector | ← | |
| CH | Data Signal Rate Selector (DTE source) | | → |
| CI | Data Signal Rate Selector (DCE source) | ← | |
| DA | Transmitter Signal Element Timing (DTE source) | | → |
| DB | Transmitter Signal Element Timing (DCE source) | ← | |
| DD | Receiver Signal Element Timing (DCE source) | ← | |
| SBA | Secondary Transmitted Data | | → |
| SBB | Secondary Received Data | ← | |
| SCA | Secondary RTS | | → |
| SCB | Secondary CTS | ← | |
| SCF | Secondary Received Line Signal Detector | ← | |
| LL | Local Loop back (D version only) | | |
| TM | Test mode (D version only) | | |

**Figure 6-1   RS-232 Interchange Circuits** *(Permission granted by Electronic Industries Association.)*

## 6-1    Grounds

Earlier versions of the standard, such as the RS-232-C, included Circuit AA (pin 1) for a protective ground conductor, also referred to as the frame or chassis ground. These versions of the standard allowed this conductor to be optional. The EIA-232-D version no longer includes Circuit AA and the definition of protective ground because it is included in the definition of signal ground (Circuit AB). In some applications, pin 1s are connected. This use of pin 1 is allowed by the standard.

---

**Circuit AB Signal Ground (pin 7)**    This conductor is the reference for all other interface circuits. The signal ground is also referred to as the reference or common return line. The signal ground conductor must always be used and connected at both the DTE and DCE. Within the DCE, this conductor should be brought to one point. If a protective ground is used, the signal ground may be connected to it by means of a ground strap within the DCE equipment. The ground strap can be removed to conform to local regulations or to minimize the introduction of noise.

---

## 6-2    Data Circuits

---

**Circuit BA Transmitted Data (pin 2) DTE → DCE**    Data is transferred from the DTE to the local DCE on this circuit. Between characters or when no data is being transferred, the DTE holds this circuit in the marking condition. Data can be transferred only when certain control circuits are in the ON condition. The control circuits most often used are Request-to-Send (RTS), Clear-to-Send (CTS), DCE Ready, and DTE Ready. If these control circuits are being used and are in the ON condition, then the data transmitted across Circuit BA is transmitted over the communication channel by the DCE.

**Circuit BB Received Data (pin 3) DTE ← DCE**    The DTE receives data from the local DCE over this circuit. The data is generated originally at a remote site, sent over the communication channel, and received by the local DCE. The local DCE then sends the data to the local DTE via Circuit BB.

---

**Note:** *All signals are viewed with respect to the DTE. Therefore, the terms "transmit" and "receive" refer to what happens at the DTE. The DTE transmits data on pin 2 and receives data on pin 3. The DCE transmits data on pin 3 and receives data on pin 2.*

Figure 6-2a shows the minimum connections needed to transmit data across the interface. This application does not have any control circuits, which most microcomputer systems use. For example, the DCE holds the received data line in the marking condition whenever the Received Line Signal Detector (Circuit CF)

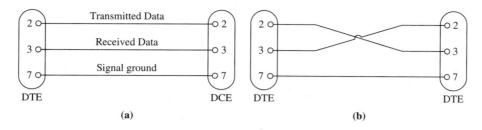

**Figure 6-2** (a) Minimum Connection Needed to Transmit Full-Duplex and (b) Null Modem

is in the OFF condition. Another example is if the application uses a half-duplex channel, then the DCE holds the received data line in the marking condition whenever the RTS (Circuit CA) is in the ON condition and for a brief interval following its ON to OFF transition. This allows for the transmission to be completed and the line to be "turned around." The definition and use of these and other control circuits are studied in Sections 6-3 and 6-4.

Although the RS-232 standard was designed to interface DTE to DCE, nonstandard applications, such as trying to connect DTE to DTE, may be encountered. This requires connecting the Transmitted Data pin (pin 2) to the Received Data pin (pin 3) as shown in Figure 6-2b. This arrangement is known as a **null modem.** This and other nonstandard applications are covered in Section 6-5.

## 6-3 Control Circuits

As mentioned in the introduction of this chapter, not all control lines are used for every application. The ones used depend on the type of transmission channel: simplex, half-duplex, or full-duplex, and whether switched (dial-up) or private lines are used. This section defines the nine control circuits while the next section describes their applications and use.

---

**Circuit CA Request to Send (pin 4) DTE → DCE** The RTS circuit is used to send a signal from the DTE to the DCE. This signal, along with the type of transmission, controls the local DCE for transmission to and reception from the communication channel.

---

For simplex and full-duplex channels, an ON condition of circuit CA RTS (pin 4) DTE → DCE keeps the DCE in the **transmit mode,** which means that the DCE accepts data from the DTE and passes it to the communication's channel. An OFF condition for simplex and full-duplex operation keeps the DCE in the **nontransmit mode.** This means that the local DCE will not pass data to the communication channel.

For half-duplex channels, the ON condition maintains the DCE in the transmit mode and inhibits the DCE from receiving data from the communication channel. The OFF condition for half-duplex communication allows the DCE to receive data from the communication channel and pass it on to the DTE. This condition is referred to as the **receive mode** and inhibits the DCE from transmitting data it receives from the DTE to the communication channel. These conditions are summarized in Table 6-1.

**Table 6-1    Summary of RTS Signals**

| Condition | Mode | Simplex and Full-Duplex | Half-Duplex |
|-----------|------|------------------------|-------------|
| ON        |      | transmit mode          | transmit mode |
| OFF       |      | nontransmit mode       | receive mode |

The transition from OFF to ON indicates to the DCE that it should enter its transmit mode and begin any actions that are necessary to initiate transmission on the communication channel. As soon as the communication link is established, the DCE sends a CTS signal (Circuit CB) to the DTE as shown in Figure 6-3. The time delay between the RTS ON condition and the CTS ON condition depends on the type of equipment used; a delay of 200 ms is not uncommon but 8 to 50 ms is more typical.

The transition from ON to OFF on the RTS line instructs the DCE to complete the transmission of any previously held data that it received from the DTE before assuming a nontransmit mode (*see* Fig. 6-3). Note that although the DCE is in the

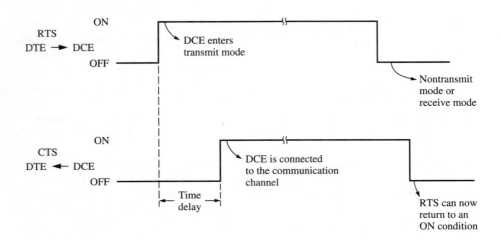

**Figure 6-3    Handshake Waveform between the DTE and DCE Using the RTS and CTS Interface Circuits. DCE Ready is in the ON Condition**

nontransmit mode if half-duplex communication is being used, the DCE is in the receive mode and can pass data it receives from the communication channel to the DTE.

When the RTS line is turned OFF, it cannot be turned ON again until the CTS line has been turned OFF by the DCE.

---

**Circuit CB Clear to Send (pin 5) DTE ← DCE**   This circuit is used for simplex (transmit only), half-, and full-duplex transmissions. The DCE generates a signal on this circuit and sends it to the DTE. The ON condition indicates to the DTE that data sent to the DCE will be transmitted over the communication channel. An OFF condition is an indication to the DTE that it should not send data to the local DCE on the transmitted data line (Circuit BA).

---

The OFF to ON transition of a CTS signal is a response to an ON condition on Circuit CA (RTS) and Circuit CC (DCE Ready). The CTS signal is not an immediate response to an RTS signal; rather it is delayed by a time interval (typically 8 to 50 ms but may be as long as 200 ms) that is set within the DCE (*see* Fig. 6-3). The CTS signal indicates to the local DTE that there is a high probability that a remote modem is ready to receive data.

---

**Circuit CC DCE Ready (pin 6) DTE ← DCE**   An ON condition on this circuit indicates that the DCE is connected to the communication channel (the equivalent to an ''off hook'' condition in a switched telephone network) and is not in a test, talk, or dial mode. It also indicates that the local DCE has completed any timing functions required by the switching system to establish a call and, if used, any special answering tone signals. **Note:** The ON condition is not an indication that the local DCE has established a communication channel to a remote DCE but rather that the local DCE is powered up and ready to be used. The OFF condition is an indication to the DTE to disregard any other signals except the Ring Indicator (RI) (Circuit CF). In the RS-232-C standard, this interface circuit is known as Data Set Ready (DSR) and in the EIA-232-D version Circuit CC is known as DCE Ready.

**Circuit CD Data Terminal Ready (pin 20) DTE → DCE**   This interface circuit, known as DTR, is used on switched (dial-up) systems. The ON condition prepares the local DCE to be connected to the communication channel and to maintain the connection once it is established. The channel connection may be made by manually dialing a remote station, manually answering an incoming call, or automatically dialing a remote station. The channel connection can also be made by using automatic answering equipment with the DCE in the automatic answering mode.

---

In some of these automatic answering applications, the DTR signal is left in the ON condition indicating that the DTE is always ready to transmit or receive data. For these applications, the DCE will be connected to the line whenever it receives a ringing signal as shown in Figure 6-4a. In other applications, the DTR is in the OFF condition. When the DCE receives a ringing signal, it must signal the DTE (using Circuit CE) and wait for an ON signal on the DTR circuit as shown in Figure 6-4b.

An OFF condition on the DTR circuit causes the DCE to be removed from the communication channel. **A note of caution:** If the station is transmitting data,

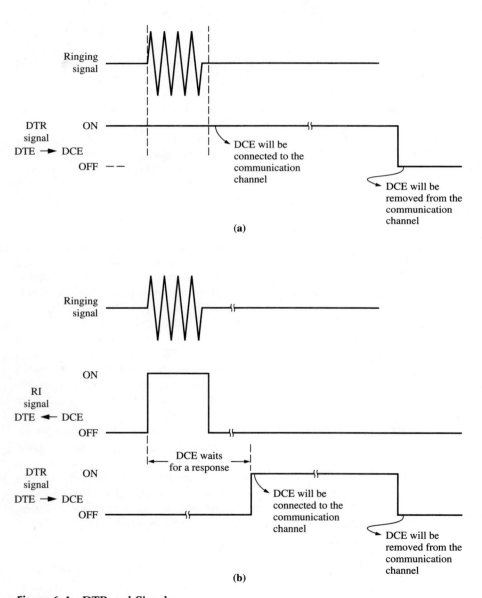

Figure 6-4   DTR and Signals

all the data must be transmitted before the DCE is removed from the channel. Remember that the DCE does not interrupt the data but only passes it along to the communication channel. Therefore, the DTE's software must keep track of when the end of transmission occurs and provide sufficient time for the DCE to transmit all the data.

In switched network applications, when the DTR circuit is turned OFF it is not to be turned ON again until the DCE Ready circuit (Circuit CC) is turned OFF by the DCE. **Note:** An OFF condition on the DTR circuit does not disable the RI (Circuit CE).

**Circuit CE Ring Indicator (pin 22) DTE ← DCE**   This circuit is used in switched (dial-up) network applications. An ON condition indicates to the DTE that the local DCE is receiving a ringing signal from a remote DCE. Between rings and at all other times when there is no ringing signal, the local DCE holds this circuit in the OFF condition as shown in Figure 6-5. The RI circuit allows DCE units to use automatic answering equipment and signal the DTE when a ringing signal occurs. As previously mentioned, this circuit is not disabled by an OFF condition on the DTR circuit (Circuit CD).

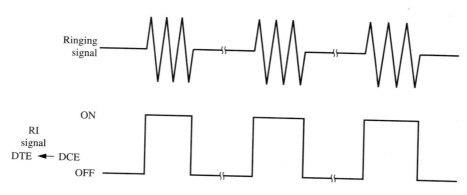

**Figure 6-5   RI Signal**

**Circuit CF Received Line Signal Detector (pin 8) DTE ← DCE**   This circuit is also known as Data Carrier Detect (DCD). An ON condition on this circuit means the local DCE is receiving a suitable carrier signal from a remote DCE. The OFF condition indicates either that no signal is being received or that the received signal cannot be demodulated. Whether or not a signal is suitable for demodulation is a criterion set by manufacturers of the DCE and will be discussed in Chapter 9. The OFF condition on this circuit causes the DCE to clamp the Received Data line (Circuit BB) to the mark condition (*see* Fig. 6-6).

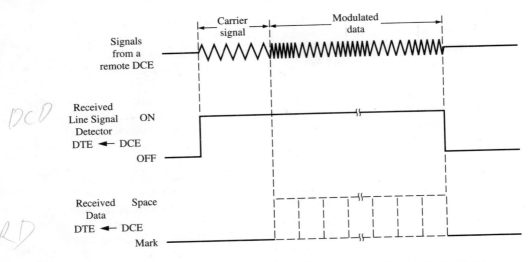

Figure 6-6   Received Line Signal Detector Waveform for Full-Duplex Operation

On half-duplex channels, the Received Line Signal Detector circuit is held in the OFF condition when the RTS circuit (Circuit CA) is in the ON condition and for a time interval after the RTS line goes from the ON to OFF condition. This is because in half-duplex operation the channel must be "turned around" so that the remote DCE can send data. A typical turn around time is 200 ms. Figure 6-7 shows the control signals for a half-duplex operation on a nonswitched system. If a switched system is used, then the DTR circuit (Circuit CD) and the RI circuit (Circuit CE) would also be used as was shown in Figure 6-4b.

**Circuit CG Signal Quality Detector (pin 21) DTE ← DCE**   This interface circuit is not recommended for new designs. It is, however, still part of the standard to cover any previous designs. The Signal Quality Detector signal is used to indicate whether or not there is a high probability that an error has occurred on the Received Data line (Circuit BB). An ON condition indicates there is no reason to believe that an error has occurred. An OFF condition indicates that there is a high probability an error has occurred. In some applications, the OFF condition may trigger an automatic retransmission of data.

**Circuit CH Data Signal Rate Selector (pin 23) DTE → DCE or Circuit CI Data Signal Rate Selector (pin 23) DTE ← DCE**   This interchange circuit may be used either with the DTE as the source and referred to as Circuit CH or with the DCE as the source and referred to as Circuit CI. This interface circuit is used to select between different data signaling rates for synchronous DCEs or between two ranges for asynchronous DCEs. In either case the ON condition selects the higher rate.

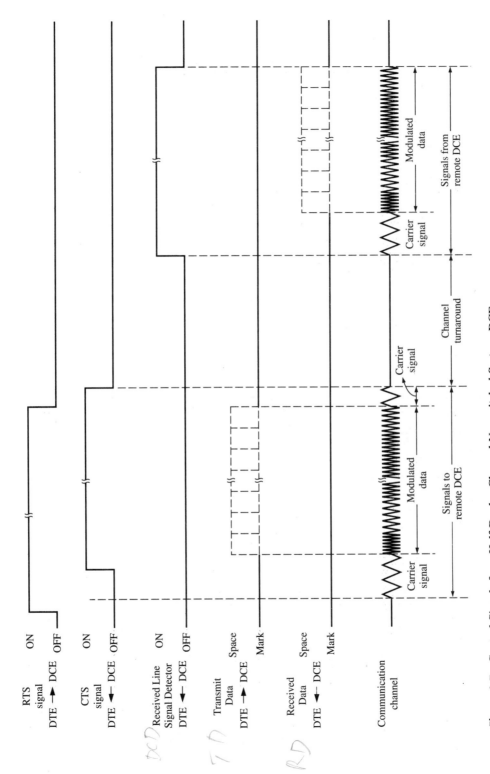

**Figure 6-7** Control Signals for a Half-Duplex Channel Nonswitched System. DCE Ready Signal is Assumed to be in the ON Condition

107

## 6-4  Common Applications Using the Control Circuits

Between telephone offices a conversation is carried over a four-wire circuit. Two wires are used for talking and two wires for listening. However, between the telephone office and the customer's site there are usually only two wires. These two wires must carry both parts of the conversation. For an additional charge, the customer can have the telephone company extend the four-wire circuit from the telephone office to the customer's site. This will allow the customer to have a four-wire leased line connection from one site to another. Such a system allows point-to-point or multipoint full-duplex systems to be used over leased lines. If a four-wire leased line system is installed, the customer eliminates the dependency on a dial-up line and its inherent problems. However, both leased and dial-up systems are used for data communications. In the following examples, the modems used to send and receive data over the telephone channel are simply a piece of DCE. Of primary concern are the RS-232 connections between the DTE and DCE. The following examples illustrate how the control circuits are used for handshaking.

### 6-4.1  Full-Duplex Leased Line System

Figure 6-8 shows a point-to-point full-duplex system using a four-wire system. In addition to the transmit, receive, and signal ground circuits, this application always requires the DCD circuit (pin 8). Remember, in the standard's specification the DCD line is known as the Received Line Signal Detector. However, the DCD terminology will probably be encountered most often; therefore, it will be used in these applications. The DCD circuit provides the minimum control signal required by the DTE and DCE for this application. Usually additional control signals such as RTS (pin 4), CTS (pin 5), DCE Ready (pin 6), and sometimes DTR (pin 20) are needed. For the system using only the DCD line, the modem brings the DCD to the ON condition whenever a carrier signal is detected. As soon as the carrier frequency is lost or the modulated data signal can no longer be demodulated, the

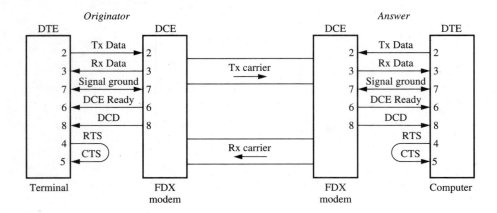

**Figure 6-8   Full-Duplex Four-Wire System**

modem brings the DCD line to the OFF condition. This signal would be used by the DTE to stop the transmission and reception of data.

As previously mentioned, in most full-duplex applications, other RS-232 control signals are used as shown in Figures 6-8 and 6-9. Figure 6-9 shows the steps involved in establishing the link for a leased four-wire system using DCE Ready, RTS, CTS, and DCD control signals. The signal ground (Circuit AB, pin 7) between the DCE and DTE must always be connected.

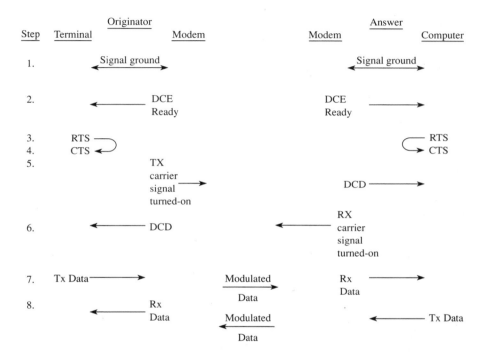

**Figure 6-9   Full-Duplex Handshaking on Leased Four-Wire Line**

The DCE Ready signal indicates the modem is ready to operate. Usually this occurs when power is applied. This signal also indicates the modem is not in its test, talk, or dial mode, and thus is ready to transmit and receive data.

When the DTE is ready to send data, it asserts (ON condition) the RTS line. In leased line applications, the RTS line is often wired back to the CTS pin as shown in Figures 6-8 and 6-9. In half-duplex operation, the modem's response to an RTS signal is to activate the CTS line if the communication channel is clear to send data. For leased line applications, however, the carrier should always be on but the DTE may need to receive a CTS signal; thus, the loop back connection between RTS and CTS. Another loop back condition that may be encountered is at the modem. If the modem requires an RTS signal, the CTS line may be wired back to the RTS pin at the modem end. This condition is not shown in Figure 6-8 or 6-9.

The modem at the originating end now turns on its transmitting carrier (Tx) signal. After the answering end receives the Tx carrier signal, the answering modem activates its DCD line and after a short delay turns on the receiver carrier (Rx) signal. Upon receiving the Rx signal, the modem at the originating end activates its DCD line. Thus, the link is established and data can be sent. **Note:** The words "transmit" and "receive" refer to the originating end (*see* Figs. 6-8 and 6-9).

### 6-4.2   Half-Duplex Dial-Up System

Dial-up applications are usually half-duplex. The variations that may be encountered deal with whether or not the calls are manually or automatically dialed and answered. Although the RS-232 standard does not specify auto dial, some manufacturers do provide this capability. In this and the next subsection, two applications will be studied—manual dial/manual answer and manual dial/auto answer.

If the call is manually dialed and answered, then the RS-232 interconnections are similar to Figure 6-8. However, the RTS line would not be looped back to CTS. Instead, it would be connected as shown in Figure 6-10. In this system, the originator dials the number and when the call is answered both parties transfer control to the modem. This is done by pressing a switch on the modem from voice to data.

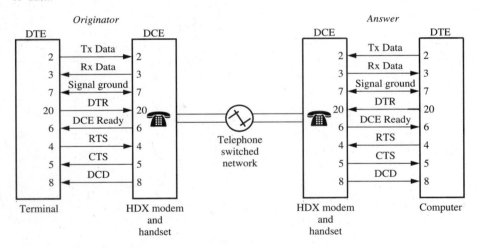

**Figure 6-10   Half-Duplex Manual Dial-Up Connections**

Remember, every system requires the signal ground. The RTS and CTS circuits determine the direction of transmission as shown in Figure 6-7. At the originating end, the DTE brings the RTS line to the ON condition. This signal initiates the DCE to send a carrier signal and after a short delay returns a CTS signal. Now the originating end can send data across the communication channel. After the last message is transmitted, the originating DTE turns off its RTS signal. This causes the DCE to turn off the carrier signal and the CTS signal. At the answering end, the DCD line is turned off as shown in Figure 6-11. Now DTE at the answering

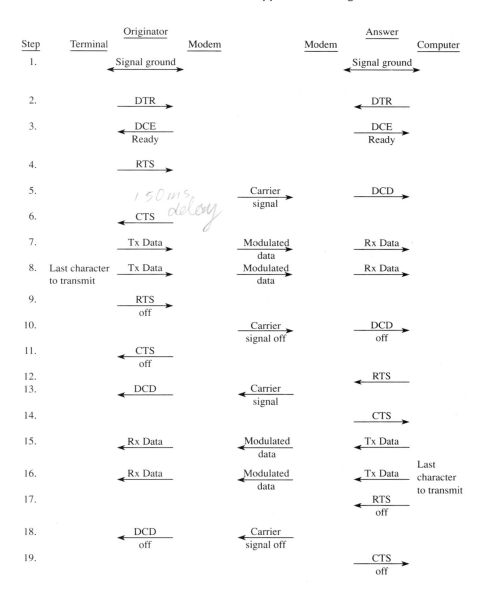

**Figure 6-11   Handshaking Sequence for a Half-Duplex Manual Dial-Up/Manual Answer. The Link is Established and then the Switch on the Modem is Pressed from Voice to Data**

end can use the communication channel to send data. This reverses the channel's direction. This condition is known as ''turnaround.'' Steps 12–19 of Figure 6-11 show what is involved for the answering end to transmit data. When the call is terminated, the link is disconnected. Between making the call and terminating it, Figure 6-11 shows a typical handshaking sequence.

Consider a half-duplex application in which data is transferred from the originator end to the answer end in blocks of 128 characters and each character is 8 bits. At the end of each block the communication channel is "turned around" and the answer end replies with a 6-character acknowledgment. Calculate the percentage of time that is spent on "turnaround" if the data rate is 600 bits per second (bps) and the "turnaround" time is 200 ms.

**Solution**

From Equation (3-2) the bit time is

$$t_b = \frac{1}{600 \text{ bps}} = 1.66 \text{ ms/b}$$

The time to transmit 128 characters is

$$128 \text{ characters} \times \frac{8 \text{ bits}}{\text{characters}} \times \frac{1.66 \text{ ms}}{\text{bit}} = 1,700 \text{ ms}$$

The time to transmit the 6-character acknowledgment is

$$6 \text{ characters} \times \frac{8 \text{ bits}}{\text{characters}} \times \frac{1.66 \text{ ms}}{\text{bit}} = 80 \text{ ms}$$

For each 128-character block and reply, the line is "turned around" twice for a total "turnaround" time of 400 ms before the next block can be transferred. Therefore, the percentage of time lost on "turnaround" is

$$\frac{400 \text{ ms}}{1700 \text{ ms} + 400 \text{ ms} + 80 \text{ ms}} \times 100\% = 18.3\%$$

### 6-4.3   Half-Duplex Auto Answer

In an auto answer application, the modem at the receiving end must answer and hang-up automatically. The computer usually has the auto answering capability and, as seen in Figure 6-12, the RI (pin 22) circuit is needed at the answer end.

Assume that a call is manually dialed and the answering modem detects the ring and generates an RI signal to the computer. The computer's response is to activate its DTR line. The answering modem then connects itself to the communication channel and sends an answering tone to the originating end. This action is the equivalent of an answering party lifting the handset on a telephone. If the DSR signal is not already in the ON condition, the answering modem would now turn on this signal, thus indicating to the computer that the modem is connected to the channel. The computer is now ready to receive or send data. Figure 6-13 shows the sequence of RS-232 handshake signals for the computer first to receive data and then to send data. In this application, the DTR at the originator end is in the ON condition but the DTR signal at the answer end is OFF until the modem receives a ringing signal. Then the computer brings the DTR circuit to the ON

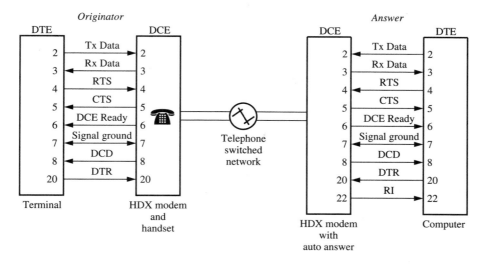

**Figure 6-12  Half-Duplex Connections for Manual Dial-Up and Auto Answer**

condition and waits to receive a DCE Ready signal. In some systems, the DTR signal may always be in the ON condition such as shown in Figure 6-14. This figure also shows the handshaking sequence if the computer first wants to send data. The communication channel is "turned around" at step 16 so that the computer now receives data.

### 6-4.4  Full-Duplex Dial-Up System

This type of application uses the same control lines as a half-duplex dial-up system. The exception is the RTS line. It is required in a half-duplex system but not required in a full-duplex system. This is because once the channel is established, the DTE can begin transmitting and the communication channel does not have to be "turned around." Figure 6-15 shows the connections for this application without the RTS line. The computer end has auto answering. The handshaking sequence is shown in Figure 6-16. Although many full-duplex systems use a dedicated four-wire network, as was shown in Figure 6-8, it is possible at slower speeds to have full-duplex communication on a two-wire network. This is accomplished by a technique called frequency multiplexing (more on this topic in Chapters 8 and 9). Hence, if an application requires full-duplex operation on a dial-up network, it surely will be using a two-wire system as shown in Figure 6-15.

## 6-5  Nonstandard Applications

The purpose of EIA-232-D or the earlier version RS-232-C is to provide a standard for connecting DTE to DCE. However, with the wide acceptance of microcomputers, more is seen and heard about devices that are EIA-232-D or RS-232-C compatible or equipment with RS-232 ports. Examples are computers, video dis-

*(Text continued on page 117.)*

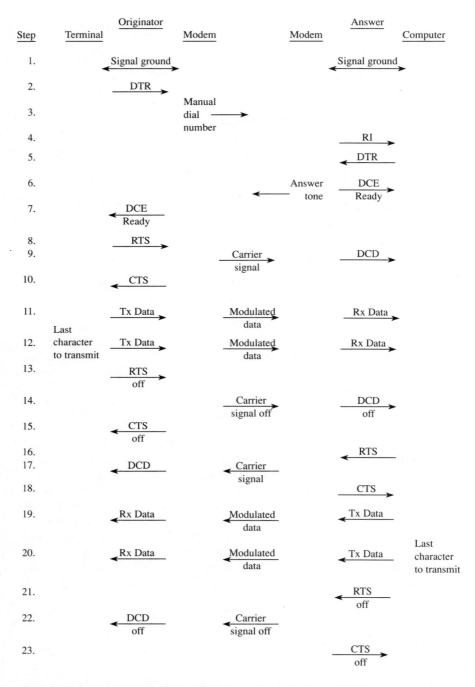

**Figure 6-13 Handshaking Sequence for a Half-Duplex Manual Dial-Up Auto Answer System**

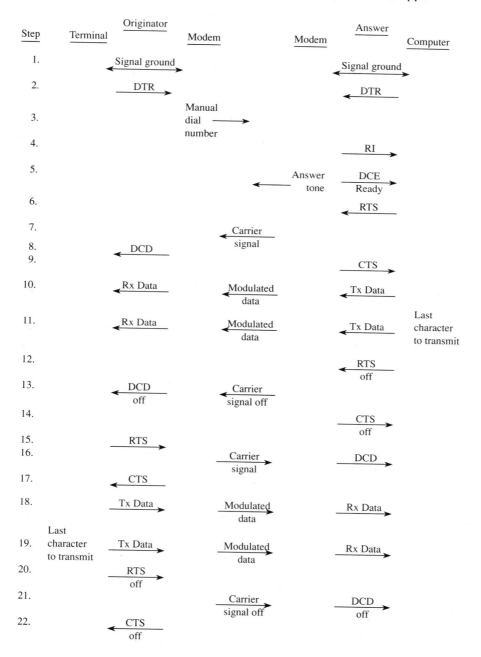

**Figure 6-14  Handshaking Sequence for a Half-Duplex System. The Computer is the First DTE Unit to Send Data**

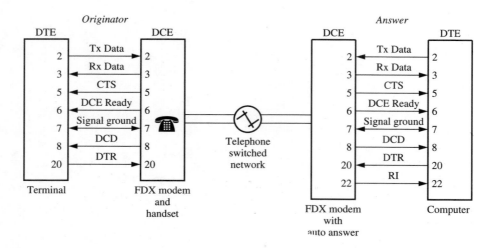

**Figure 6-15   Full-Duplex Connections for Manual Dial-Up and Auto Answer**

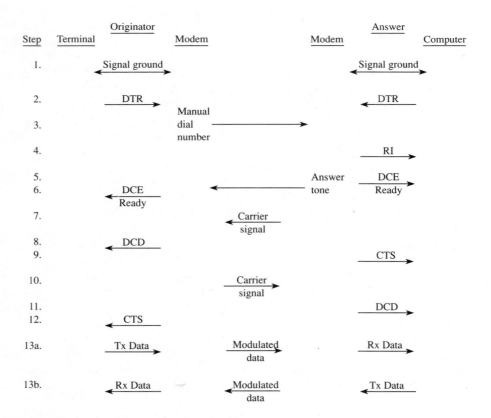

**Figure 6-16   Handshake Sequence for a Full-Duplex System on a Dial-Up Network**

play terminals (monitors), printers, plotters, and scientific equipment. None of this equipment has been designed to be connected to telephone lines; therefore, it certainly is not DCE. Therefore, one could easily purchase a computer and monitor and be faced with connecting two pieces of equipment together, both of which have DTE connectors. In this situation, pins 2 and 3 must be interchanged in the cable as was shown in Figure 6-2b. Otherwise, both the computer and monitor would be expecting to transmit and receive data on a single line. The crossover connection can be wired as part of the cable adapter and is referred to as a null modem. Although adapters for male-to-male and female-to-female can be purchased, they are easy to wire.

Often a microcomputer and monitor are purchased from the same manufacturer and a cable comes as part of the system. Therefore, the user never needs to consider these interconnections. A more common problem can occur when a microcomputer owner decides to expand the system by purchasing a serial printer. The printer is advertised as being RS-232-C or EIA-232-D compatible and, sure enough, a port and cable are available. Unless the printer and cable were designed specifically for the user's computer model, problems can occur because the interface standard was never intended to service this application. Consider some of the problems that could occur if the computer and printer are from different manufacturers. The computer is most likely wired as DTE but what about the printer? Does it have a DTE or DCE connector? If there is a DCE connector, a standard cable may work. If the printer comes with a DTE connector, a null modem may be the answer. In either case, identifying the type of cable does not ensure either that the printer will receive data or that there will be an orderly transfer of data.

These are some of the problems that may be encountered. After pressing the print key (or typing the print command), nothing happens. The computer may expect to receive some of the control signals that are not being sent by the printer. For example, the EIA-232-D (or RS-232-C) port on the computer may issue a DTR signal and expect it to receive a DCE Ready signal. The computer may then want to send an RTS signal and expect to receive a CTS signal. In other words, the computer port that is being used is designed to be connected to DCE such as a modem and expects to generate and receive the handshaking signals as discussed in the previous section. Since the printer was never designed to simulate a modem's handshaking signals, there is no data transfer from the computer to the printer. This problem can be solved at the computer end by looping back DTR to DCE Ready and RTS to CTS. This could be the solution but it is quite possible that the printer needs to receive certain signals in order to accept data. Obviously the manufacturer's specifications for both pieces of equipment will be needed to be sure of the connections. Figure 6-17 shows two loop back configurations that may be encountered.

Consider another potential problem. The printer's specification is that it can operate at 4800 bps and expects all data to be of the format of 7-bit American Standard Code for Information Interchange (ASCII), odd parity, and 1 stop bit for a total of 10 bits (remember to include the start bit) per character. If the computer is set up for this bit rate and data format, this should solve such problems, right? Maybe, but as so often happens, another problem presents itself. The printed

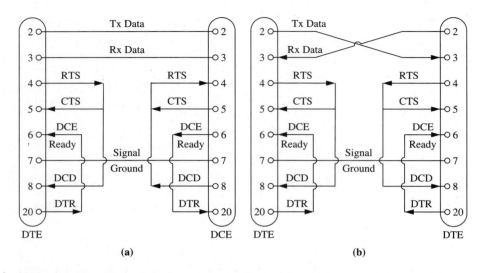

**Figure 6-17**  Loop Back Configuration with DTE to DCE Connections for (a) Tx
and Rx Data Lines and (b) with Null Modem Connections

message may look nothing like what was typed at the terminal. Words and large
sections of paragraphs may be missing. A lack of flow control between the
computer and printer caused this problem. The printer's specification of 4800 bps
converts to 480 (4800/10) characters per second. This is the rate at which the
printer can store characters in its memory buffer and not the rate at which the
mechanical printhead can operate. If the print mechanism can turn out text at a
rate of only 120 characters per second, then the computer is sending data four
times faster than the print mechanism, causing the memory buffer to fill and in
this situation to overflow, thus the missing words. What is needed is a method of
having the printer communicate with the computer so that it can indicate when its
memory buffer is nearly full (about 75%) and when it is nearly empty (about 25%).
This type of communication is referred to as flow control and was introduced in
Section 2-2.4. The EIA interface standard was never intended for this application.
Can the problem be solved by using a CTS signal? No, because the CTS signal is
not an appropriate handshake signal. The CTS signal was intended to be a response
to an RTS signal and it indicates that information by the DTE will be transmitted
over the communication channel. Remember from the examples in the previous
section, the CTS is turned ON and OFF as a response to RTS. Therefore, if the
computer was designed to respond to a CTS signal only after its own RTS signal,
then trying to use the CTS signal alone has no meaning for the computer. Instead
of using these or other control signals, a better method is to use control characters.
These control characters are usually labeled XON and XOFF. As shown in the
ASCII Table of Figure 2-1 they are DC1 and DC3, respectively (*see* Section
2-2.4). The printer would send an XOFF when its memory buffer is approximately
75% full and XON when its memory buffer is nearly empty (approximately 25%

full). For some systems, such problems may disappear; for others they may not. This is because the software driver program must be capable of recognizing the XON and XOFF binary patterns. If it doesn't, then the driver program will have to be modified. **A note of caution:** The EIA-232-D or RS-232-C standard is intended as an interface between DTE and DCE. Now that the terms EIA-232-D or RS-232-C compatible are being used quite often, users must be careful when trying to interconnect equipment from different vendors.

## 6-6  Timing Circuits

The interface standard was designed for both asynchronous and synchronous transmission. Up to this point in the chapter, examples have dealt only with the handshaking sequence for asynchronous transmission. In order to transmit and receive synchronous transmission over telephone lines, synchronous modems are used. These devices allow faster data rates, they cost more, and they require timing signals, in addition to control signls, between the DTE and DCE. Later chapters will discuss synchronous protocols, but this section deals with the interface standard's timing signals in order to synchronize the transfer of data between the DTE and DCE and vice versa. There are three signal lines designated for timing, they are

| Circuit | Pin No. | Name | Direction |
|---------|---------|------|-----------|
| DA | 24 | Transmitter signal element timing | DTE → DCE |
| DB | 15 | Transmitter signal element timing | DTE ← DCE |
| DD | 17 | Receiver signal element timing | DTE ← DCE |

The first two cases differ by having either the DTE or the DCE as the source of the timing signals for transmitted data on Circuit BA. In the third situation, the DCE establishes the timing signals for the data that is transferred from the DCE to the DTE on the Received Data line (Circuit BB). The function of each timing circuit will be studied in more detail.

**Circuit DA Transmitting Signal Element Timing (pin 24) DTE → DCE**   This circuit is used by the DTE to provide timing information for the transmitted data on Circuit BA. An ON to OFF transition of a timing signal indicates the center of each transmitted data signal element as shown in Figure 6-18. The standard specifies that the DTE should provide the timing signals whenever power is applied to the system. An exception may occur when the RTS (Circuit CA) signal is in the OFF condition. For this situation, the DTE may stop the timing signals for a short period of time. An example is when the DTE is performing maintenance tests.

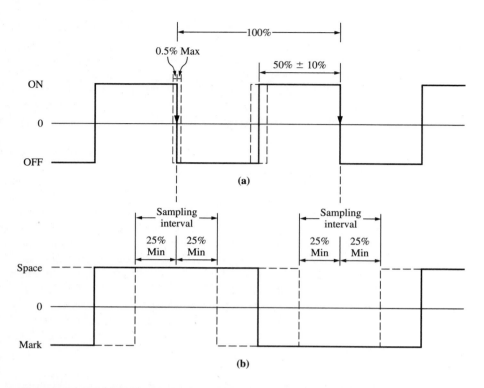

**Figure 6-18**   (a) Timing Waveform on Circuit DA, Pin 24. (b) Transmitted Data on Circuit BA, Pin 2

As shown in Figure 6-18a, the peak distortion at the ON to OFF transition of the timing signal is 0.5% maximum. Although the timing signal in Figure 6-18a is drawn with a 50% duty cycle, the range of duty cycle can be from 40% to 60% (50% ± 10% as shown in Figure 6-18a). In Figure 6-18b, the term ''25% min'' refers to the time duration from the ON to OFF transition of the timing signal to the transmitted data's bit boundary. This duration cannot be less than 25% of a nominal signal element interval. This specification ensures that the DTE transmits the data near the center of each signal element.

---

**Circuit DB Transmitting Signal Element Timing (pin 15) DTE ← DCE**   This timing signal is similar to the signal on Circuit DA except that the DCE is the source. When Circuit DB is used, the DTE sends a data signal on Circuit BA (Transmitted Data line) when the OFF to ON transitions of the timing signal occur as shown in Figure 6-19. This figure illustrates that the data is transmitted on the OFF to ON transition of the timing signal thereby allowing the DCE to sample Circuit BA on the ON to OFF transition.

---

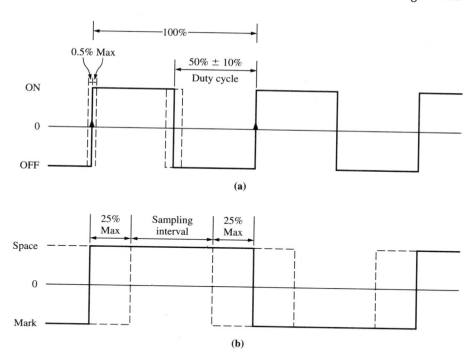

**Figure 6-19**   (a) Timing Signal on Circuit DB (Pin 15) is Generated by the DCE. (b) Transmitted Data on Circuit BA, Pin 2

Figure 6-19b shows that the maximum allowed distortion at a bit boundary is 25%. Even with this maximum distortion of the transmitted data and distortion in the timing signal's duty cycle, the DCE can still sample the data signal near the center of a bit.

The DCE provides the timing signal as long as power is applied to the unit. An exception to this provision are short periods of time but the DCE Ready signal must be in the OFF condition. This situation may occur when the DCE is performing maintenance tests.

---

**Circuit DD Receiver Signal Element Timing (pin 17) DTE ← DCE**   Circuit DD is used by the DCE to provide a timing signal to the DTE. The transition from ON to OFF indicates the center of a bit on the Received Data line (Circuit BB) as shown in Figure 6-20. When Circuit DD is used, the DCE provides a timing signal as long as the Received Line Signal Detector (Circuit CF) is in the ON condition. Remember, Circuit CF is also known as the DCD line. If the voltage level on Circuit CF goes to the OFF condition, the timing signal may not be present.

---

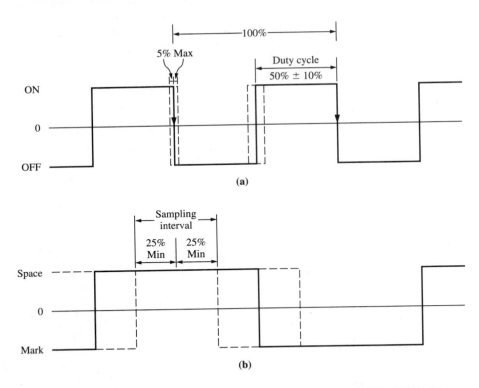

**Figure 6-20** (a) Timing Signal on Circuit DD (Pin 17) is Generated by DCE. (b) Received Data on Circuit BB, Pin 3

Figure 6-20a,b shows the amount of distortion that is tolerated for the timing signal and for the received data. The sampling interval must be at least 50% of a bit time and there must be at least 25% of a bit interval from the ON to OFF timing signal transition to a bit boundary.

### 6-6.1   Summary of Timing Signals

The local transmitting DCE device is the usual source of the timing signal. In this application, the timing signal is sent from the local transmitting DCE to the local transmitting DTE on pin 15. Signals on pin 15 provide the DTE with a timing pulse necessary to keep the data coming at the proper rate. The DTE then provides the mark to space transitions for the transmitted data when an OFF to ON condition occurs as shown in Figure 6-19. This local DCE unit also encodes timing information into the data before it is transmitted on the communication channel.

At the receiving station the DCE can extract this timing information from the received data to generate the timing signal waveform shown in Figure 6-20. This technique of encoding the timing information into the transmitted data ensures that a data communication system has only one source for all timing signals. For this application, the receiving DCE transmits the derived timing signal to the receiving DTE on pin 17 as shown in Figure 6-20. The transition from ON to OFF should indicate the center of each signal element that is being sent on the Received Data circuit (Circuit BB). Most synchronous modems are designed so that they can extract a timing signal from the received data.

If the local transmitting DCE is not the source of the timing signals but rather the local DTE unit, then an ON to OFF transition on pin 24 indicates the center of each data bit. The local DCE would still have to encode a timing signal into the data that is being transmitted onto the communication channel.

E X A M P L E    6 - 2

What interface circuits would you use if your application requires full-duplex synchronous transmission on a leased line?

**Solution**

For this application, consider that the DCE is the source of the timing signals and an RTS control signal is used. Therefore, the interchange circuits needed are

| Circuit | Pin | Function |
|---------|-----|----------|
| AB | 7 | Signal ground |
| BA | 2 | Transmitted data |
| BB | 3 | Receive data |
| CA | 4 | RTS |
| CB | 5 | CTS |
| CC | 6 | DCE ready |
| CF | 8 | Received line signal detector (DCD) |
| DB | 15 | Transmitter signal element timing |
| DD | 17 | Receiver signal element timing |

E X A M P L E    6 - 3

If the application in Example 6-2 is changed from a leased line to a switched network, which interchange circuits are needed?

**Solution**

All of the interchange circuits given in the solution of Example 6-2 plus two others. They are Circuit CD (pin 20), DTR, and Circuit CE (pin 22) RI.

E X A M P L E    6 - 4

If the application in Example 6-2 is changed to half-duplex synchronous transmission on switched service, what interface circuits are needed?

**Solution**

All of the interface circuits given in the solution to Example 6-2 and also those given in the solution to Example 6-3. Remember, for half-duplex operation the RTS and CTS circuits are in either the ON or OFF state, depending on which station is transmitting. They indicate when the line is "turned around."

## 6-7  Secondary Circuits

Up to this point, data, control, and timing interchange circuits have been used for transmitting and receiving data on what is known as the primary channel. However, the interface standard contains other circuits that are used as a secondary channel. In most applications, a secondary channel is not needed and therefore the circuits are not used. If they are used, the channel may be used for either simplex, half-duplex, or full-duplex modes of communication. The data rate on the secondary channel is much less than that on the primary channel. For example, the primary channel may be transmitting data at a rate of 1200 bps while the secondary channel is transmitting at 75 bps.

There are two classes of secondary channels: a **backward channel** and an **auxiliary channel.** The direction of transmission on a backward channel is always opposite to that on the primary channel. For this reason the backward channel is also referred to as a **reverse channel.** Figure 6-21 gives examples of the direction of transmission for a backward channel. The terms "primary and secondary channels" refer to circuits in the interface between the DTE and DCE. Figure 6-21 shows the communication channel carrying data in both directions (full-duplex operation). But unlike a true full-duplex channel which carries data at the same

*ACK/NAK protocol typical*

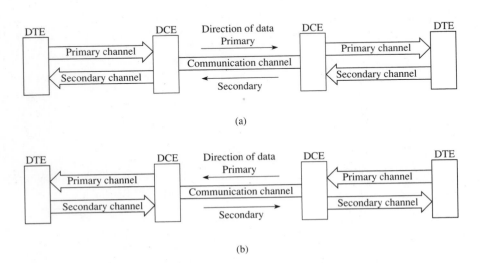

(a)

(b)

**Figure 6-21   Secondary Channel Used as a Backward Channel**

bit rate, this application transmits the data from the primary channel at one bit rate (e.g., 1200 bps) and the data from the secondary channel at a much slower bit rate (e.g., 75 bps). As seen in Chapters 8 and 9, it is not necessary to always have a four-wire communication channel for full-duplex operation. The data from the secondary channel can be carried on the communication channel at a frequency different from that used for the data from the primary channel.

In some systems, the backward channel is not used to transmit data but is used for circuit assurance or interrupt control. Circuit assurance is an indication that the receiving station is still there. An interrupt control signal can be used by the receiving station to signal the sending station to stop transmission on the primary channel.

The direction of transmission on an auxiliary channel does not depend on the direction of transmission on the primary channel. Therefore, in some applications the data on both the primary and secondary channels flow in the same direction. At other times, the primary and secondary data are in opposite directions similar to a backward channel.

There are five secondary channel circuits in the EIA standard. Two are for data transmission and three for control. They are

| Circuit | Pin No. | Name | Direction |
|---|---|---|---|
| SBA | 14 | Secondary transmitted data | DTE → DCE |
| SBB | 16 | Secondary received data | DTE ← DCE |
| SCA | 19 | Secondary RTS | DTE → DCE |
| SCB | 13 | Secondary CTS | DTE ← DCE |
| SCF | 12 | Secondary received line signal detector | DTE ← DCE |

The function of each secondary circuit will be investigated in more detail.

**Circuit SBA Secondary Transmitted Data (pin 14) DTE → DCE**   The use of this circuit is similar to Circuit BA (Transmitted Data). That is, data is transmitted from DTE to DCE. The difference is that Circuit BA is used to transmit data for the primary channel and Circuit SBA is used to transmit data for the secondary channel. The DTE holds Circuit SBA in the marking condition at all times when no data is being transmitted and during intervals between characters.

When the following four circuits are used

Circuit SCA Secondary RTS
Circuit SCB Secondary CTS
Circuit CC DCE Ready
Circuit CD DTR

they must be in the ON condition for the DTE to transmit on the secondary channel. If these control circuits are used and are in the ON condition, then all signals transmitted on Circuit SBA will be transmitted to the communication channel by the DCE.

As previously mentioned, the secondary channel may be used only for circuit assurance or interrupt control and not for transmitting data. If this is the application, Circuit SBA (Secondary Transmitted Data) is normally not used and the secondary channel carrier is turned ON or OFF by Circuit SCA (Secondary RTS). An ON carrier signal indicates circuit assurance or no interrupt. An OFF carrier signal is interpreted as circuit failure or an interrupt condition.

---

**Circuit SBB Secondary Received Data (pin 16) DTE ← DCE**   Circuit SBB is equivalent to Circuit BB (Received Data). The difference is that Circuit SBB is used by the DTE to receive data from the local DCE on the secondary channel. When the secondary channel is used only for circuit assurance or to interrupt the flow control of data in the primary channel, Circuit SBB is normally not used. What is used in this application is Circuit SCF (Secondary Received Line Signal Detector) as will be described in that section.

**Circuit SCA Secondary RTS (pin 19) DTE → DCE**   This circuit's function is similar to Circuit CA (RTS). The difference is that Circuit SCA requests the establishment of the secondary channel while Circuit CA requests the establishment of the primary channel.

---

If the secondary channel is being used as a backward channel, then an ON condition of Circuit CA (RTS) should disable Circuit SCA. Similarly, an OFF condition of Circuit CA (RTS) can be used to enable Circuit SCA. This ensures that the primary and secondary channels are not trying to transmit in the same direction.

When the secondary channel is used only for circuit assurance or to interrupt the flow of data in the primary channel, Circuit SCA controls the secondary unmodulated carrier signal. An ON condition of Circuit SCA turns on the carrier signal indicating a circuit assurance or a noninterrupt condition. An OFF condition on Circuit SCA indicates a circuit failure or an interrupt condition.

---

**Circuit SCB Secondary CTS (pin 13) DTE ← DCE**   This circuit is equivalent to Circuit CB (CTS). Circuit SCB, however, indicates that the secondary channel can be used while Circuit CB indicates the availability of the primary channel. Circuit SCB is not used if the secondary channel is needed only for circuit assurance or as an interrupt channel.

**Circuit SCF Secondary Received Line Signal Detector (pin 12) DTE ← DCE**   This circuit indicates the reception of a carrier signal on the secondary channel. Its function is similar to that of Circuit CF (Received Line Signal Detector also known as DCD), which indicates a carrier signal on the primary channel. An ON condition on Circuit SCF signifies a properly received secondary carrier signal, that is, a signal whose voltage and frequency are within the guidelines for a secondary carrier signal set by the manufacturer. The secondary channel can be used for circuit assurance or as an interrupt channel. If this is the application for the secondary channel, then Circuit SCF indicates the status at the remote station. An ON condition indicates circuit assurance or a noninterrupt condition. An OFF condition indicates circuit failure or the interrupt condition.

---

E X A M P L E    6 - 5

Which interface circuits are needed on a switched network for full-duplex asynchronous transmission for both the primary and secondary channels?

**Solution**

As previously mentioned for full-duplex transmission, the RTS circuit may or may not be used. Assume that an application requires it; the circuits used are the same as given in Example 6-2 with the following exceptions: Circuits DB and DD are not used because this is an asynchronous application and all five secondary circuits are used.

---

E X A M P L E    6 - 6

If the secondary channel in Example 6-5 is used only for circuit assurance, which secondary circuits are needed?

**Solution**

Only Circuit SCA (pin 19)—Secondary RTS and Circuit SCF (pin 12)—Secondary Received Line Signal Detector.

---

## 6-8   Miniature Connectors

Since most applications do not require all the interface circuits, there is a growing popularity to use smaller connectors with fewer pins. Two popular miniature connectors are the 8-pin modular plug-and-jack connector as found on many telephones and the DB9 connector found on the IBM PC. The 8-pin modular connector is described in the EIA-561 standard and the DB9 connector is described in the EIA-574 standard. The reason for their wide acceptance is that they are easy to use, do not require very much panel space, and provide all the necessary functions required by most microcomputer systems. Figure 6-22 shows the pin numbering and descriptions for each type of connector. It is possible to use other modular plugs and DB type connectors but they may not be standardized.

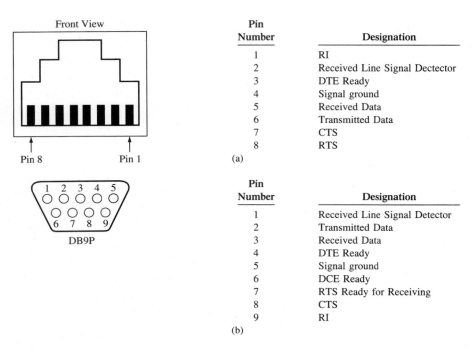

| Pin Number | Designation |
|---|---|
| 1 | RI |
| 2 | Received Line Signal Dectector |
| 3 | DTE Ready |
| 4 | Signal ground |
| 5 | Received Data |
| 6 | Transmitted Data |
| 7 | CTS |
| 8 | RTS |

(a)

| Pin Number | Designation |
|---|---|
| 1 | Received Line Signal Detector |
| 2 | Transmitted Data |
| 3 | Received Data |
| 4 | DTE Ready |
| 5 | Signal ground |
| 6 | DCE Ready |
| 7 | RTS Ready for Receiving |
| 8 | CTS |
| 9 | RI |

(b)

**Figure 6-22   Pin Numbering and Designations for (a) 8-Pin Modular Plug-and-Jack Connector and (b) 9-Pin DB9 Connector**

| Data transmission configuration | Interface type |
|---|---|
| Transmit only | A |
| Transmit only | B |
| Receive only | C |
| Half-duplex | D |
| Duplex | D |
| | |
| Duplex | E |
| Primary channel transmit only / secondary channel receive only | F |
| Primary channel transmit only / secondary channel receive only | H |
| Primary channel receive only / secondary channel transmit only | G |
| Primary channel receive only / secondary channel transmit only | I |
| | |
| Primary channel transmit only / half-duplex secondary channel | J |
| Primary channel receive only / half-duplex secondary channel | K |
| Half-duplex primary channel / half-duplex secondary channel | L |
| Duplex Primary Channel / duplex secondary channel | L |
| Duplex Primary Channel / duplex secondary channel | M |
| | |
| Special (circuits specified by supplier) | Z |

**Figure 6-23   Summary of Different Interface Applications as Specified in the RS-232-C Standard** *(Permission granted by Electronic Industries Association.)*

# Summary

In this chapter, the functional characteristics of the RS-232-C and EIA-232-D interface standards were studied. As previously mentioned, not all interface circuits are used in every application. Figure 6-23 summarizes the different configurations given in the RS-232-C and EIA-232-D standards. The term "duplex" refers to full-duplex operation. Figure 6-24 summarizes the interface circuits that are used for each application.

| Interchange circuit | | A | B | C | D | E | F | G | H | I | J | K | L | M | Z |
|---|---|---|---|---|---|---|---|---|---|---|---|---|---|---|---|
| | | — | — | — | — | — | — | — | — | — | — | — | — | — | — |
| AB | Signal ground | x | x | x | x | x | x | x | x | x | x | x | x | x | x |
| BA | Transmitted Data | x | x | | x | x | x | | x | | x | | x | x | ° |
| BB | Received Data | | | x | x | x | | x | | x | | x | x | x | ° |
| CA | RTS | | x | | x | | x | | | | x | | x | | ° |
| CB | CTS | x | x | | x | x | x | | x | | x | | x | x | ° |
| CC | DCE Ready | x | x | x | x | x | x | x | x | x | x | x | x | x | ° |
| CD | DTR | s | s | s | s | s | s | s | s | s | s | s | s | s | ° |
| CE | RI | s | s | s | s | s | s | s | s | s | s | s | s | s | ° |
| CF | Received Line Signal Detector | | | x | x | x | | x | | x | | x | x | x | ° |
| CG | Signal Quality Detector | | | | | | | | | | | | | | ° |
| CH/CI | Data Signal Rate Selector (DTE)/DCE) | | | | | | | | | | | | | | ° |
| DA/DB | Transmitter signal element timing (DTE)/DCE) | t | t | | t | t | t | | t | | t | t | t | t | ° |
| DD | Receiver signal element timing (DCE) | | | t | t | t | | t | | t | | t | t | t | ° |
| SBA | Secondary Transmitted Data | | | | | | | x | | x | x | x | x | x | ° |
| SBB | Secondary Received Data | | | | | | x | | x | | | x | x | x | ° |
| SCA | Secondary RTS | | | | | | | x | | | x | x | x | | ° |
| SCB | Secondary CTS | | | | | | | x | | x | x | x | x | x | ° |
| SCF | Secondary Received Line Signal Detector | | | | | | x | | x | | | x | x | x | ° |
| LL | Local loop back* | | | | | | | | | | | | | | ° |
| RL | Remote loop back* | | | | | | | | | | | | | | ° |
| TM | Test mode* | | | | | | | | | | | | | | ° |

Legend: °, to be specified by the supplier.
  −, optional.
  s, additional interchange circuits required for switched service.
  t, additional interchange circuits required for synchronous channel.
  x, basic interchange circuits, all systems.
  *, D version.

**Figure 6-24  Summary of the Interface Circuits Used for Different Applications as Given by the RS-232-C Standard** *(Permission granted by Electronic Industries Association.)*

## Problems

* **6.1** List the interface circuit categories in the RS-232-C standard.

  **6.2** (a) Is a chassis ground part of the RS-232-C or EIA-232-D standard? (b) Is a signal ground always required?

* **6.3** What is the function of a null modem?

  **6.4** For a half-duplex communication channel, what is the operating mode for DCE if the RTS signal is (a) ON? (b) OFF?

* **6.5** What signal does the DTE receive when the DCE has established a communication channel and is ready to transmit data?

  **6.6** Does an ON condition on DCE Ready circuit indicate that the DCE is connected to the communication channel?

* **6.7** For a full-duplex leased line application would you expect to find the DTR in an ON condition?

  **6.8** Consider a dial-up application, either full- or half-duplex. Is it possible to have the DTR circuit at the answering end in OFF condition and have the DTE still receive an RI ON signal?

* **6.9** By what name is the Received Line Signal Detector also known?

  **6.10** What is the function of the Received Line Signal Detector circuit?

* **6.11** Why was it necessary to provide the loop back connection in Figure 6-8?

  **6.12** What applications require the RI circuit?

* **6.13** How could you provide the DCE Ready signal in Figure 6-17a if the DTR signal is not available?

  **6.14** Consider the half-duplex application shown in Figure 6-10. The originator end is to transmit a large data file at a rate of 1200 bps. The data is divided into blocks of 256 characters and each character is 8 bits. At the end of each block, the communication channel is "turned around" and the originating end receives a 3-character acknowledgment. If the "turnaround" time is 120 ms, what percentage of the total time is spent on (a) "turnaround" and (b) transmission from the originating end to the answering end?

* **6.15** If the application in Problem 6.14 eliminated the "turnaround" time by using a 75 bps secondary channel, would the percentage rate of transmitting data from the originating end to the answering end improve? If so, by how much? Assume that the 3-character acknowledgment is still required at the end of each 256-character block.

---

* *See* Answers to Selected Problems.

**6.16** Why isn't a timing circuit(s) required for asynchronous modems?

**\*6.17** For most applications, identify the source of timing signals for synchronous communication: local DTE, local DCE, remote DCE, or remote DTE.

**6.18** What interface circuits are needed for asynchronous transmission on a switched network where the primary channel is used only for transmitting and the secondary channel is used only for receiving?

*brief*

# 7

# *Other Interface Standards*

**OBJECTIVES**

Upon completion of this chapter on other interface standards, the student will be able to

- Compare the RS-232-C standard with other standards.
- Know the difference between balanced and unbalanced interface circuits.
- Describe the electrical characteristics of RS-422 line drivers and receivers.
- Determine the maximum cable length for a particular data rate on an RS-422 line.
- Describe the electrical characteristics of an RS-423 line driver.
- Solve for and compare linear and exponential transition time on an interface circuit.
- Describe how data modulation rate varies as cable length increases for RS-423 lines.
- Understand the principles of the RS-449 standard.
- Interconnect equipment using RS-232 and RS-449 connectors.
- Know the advantages of the RS-530 interface over the RS-449.
- Know the advantages of current loops.
- Build the circuits necessary to implement a current loop for a variety of applications.

## Introduction

There are two electrical ways of interconnecting equipment to transmit serial voltage data signals: single-ended transmission and differential transmission. Single-ended transmission uses one signal line and a common return line. Differential transmission uses two signal lines.

Single-ended transmission, like the RS-232 standard, is a cost-effective solution for transmitting data over short distances at slow data rates. As line length

132

increases, and the need to transmit data at higher data rates is more common, it becomes difficult for the circuitry in single-ended receivers to distinguish between valid logic states in the presence of noise and voltage differences on the ground line. Differential transmission techniques overcome these problems but at the expense of providing two signal lines for each interface circuit requiring fast data transfer. Faster data rates can be accomplished by newer Electronics Industry Association (EIA) and International Telegraph and Telephone Consultative Committee (CCITT) standards. The electrical characteristics for single-ended transmission or unbalanced interface circuits are set forth in an RS-423 (or newer version RS-423-A) standard. The electrical characteristics for differential transmission or balanced interface circuits are given by the RS-422 (or newer version RS-422-A) standard. Their mechanical and functional characteristics are given by another standard, the RS-449. **Note:** The EIA-232-D is only the newest version of the RS-232 standard. It is not considered a new standard for the purposes of transferring data at a faster rate. Remember that although the EIA-232-D is the newest version, many microcomputer manufacturers still advertise their products as having RS-232-C ports, because this standard has been used for over 25 years and is widely known in the industry. The general expression RS-232 will be used for discussion in this chapter. To overcome a major disadvantage of the RS-449 standard, the RS-530 standard has been introduced.

Similar to RS-232, the RS-422, RS-423, RS-449, and RS-530 standards are based on a serial train of voltage signals. Applications that require transferring serial data in noisy environments may use a current loop interconnection standard. Current loops use the presence or absence of current to transmit binary data and these will be studied in Section 7-12.

## 7-1   Comparison of Interface Standards

Although the RS-232 standard is still widely used in microcomputer systems, its limitations are restrictive for many of today's systems that require faster data rates over longer distances. New standards try to incorporate new technologies and overcome the limitations of previous standards. Therefore, the objectives of the new standards are to increase the data rate and the maximum distance permitted by the RS-232 interface standard, which are 20,000 bits per second (bps) and 50 feet, respectively. To overcome these limitations the RS-423, RS-422, and RS-449 standards have emerged. The RS-423, like the RS-232, is designed for single-ended transmission. However, the RS-423 extends the maximum data rate to 100 kilobits per second (kbps) up to 300 feet. If the data rate is reduced to 1.0 kbps, the distance can be increased to 4000 feet (1200 meters). In addition to these improvements, RS-423 interface circuitry reduces cross talk between signal lines and improves the waveshapes. The RS-423 has a greater output impedance when power is off than the RS-232. This feature reduces the loading effect on the transmission line. Although the RS-423 has many improvements over the RS-232, it is still single-ended transmission and hence all interface circuits share a common return line.

The RS-422 interface standard uses differential transmission techniques to increase the maximum data rate over 100 kbps for line lengths up to 4000 feet. For distances up to 40 feet, the RS-422 allows data rates up to 10 megabits per second (Mbps). Differential transmission requires two interface lines so that a common return line is not used. Since control information does not require the faster data rate, both the RS-423 and RS-422 electrical characteristics are used together in the same RS-449 connector.

Although Section 7-7 gives many of the RS-449 specifications, one of the differences from the RS-232 standard is that the RS-449 standard uses a new set of names and mnemonics. This is to avoid confusion with the RS-232 mnemonics. Also, the RS-449 standard specifies a 37-pin connector for the signal, control, and timing interface circuits. The secondary channel circuits are carried by a separate 9-pin connector. It is the use of the longer size 37-pin connector and a second connector that has caused many users, in particular microcomputer manufacturers, not to incorporate an RS-449 port into their system despite its advantages. The RS-449 and RS-423 standards were designed to allow RS-232 equipment to be connected to RS-449 equipment without costly redesign. This interconnection is shown in Section 7-8.

## 7-2   Balanced and Unbalanced Interface Circuits

The RS-422 standard specifies the electrical characteristics for a balanced voltage digital interface circuit. The interface circuit consists of a generator and load interconnected by a balanced cable as shown in Figure 7-1a. The load may contain an optional termination resistor, $R_t$. The interface characteristics are specified in terms of measured values of voltage, current, and resistance at the generator and receiver, as will be studied in Section 7-3. The characteristics of the interconnecting cable are covered in Section 7-5. Balanced interface circuits are used for high speed data and timing signals. At the same time and within the same interconnection cable, unbalanced circuits are used for control and for other signals that do not require high speed data rates. This is one of the reasons for the RS-423 standard.

The RS-423 standard specifies the electrical characteristics for unbalanced voltage digital interface circuits. Figure 7-1b shows the generator, interconnection cable, and load for an unbalanced interface circuit. Although a different generator integrated circuit (IC) is needed, the same IC used as a receiver for RS-422 circuits also can be used for RS-423 circuits. Consider the important characteristics of these two standards and some ICs that may be used.

## 7-3   RS-422 Line Driver Electrical Characteristics

As previously noted, the RS-422 standard specifies the electrical characteristics for a balanced interface circuit. Figure 7-1a shows the interface circuit for a balanced line. As in any data communication system, this system consists of three parts:

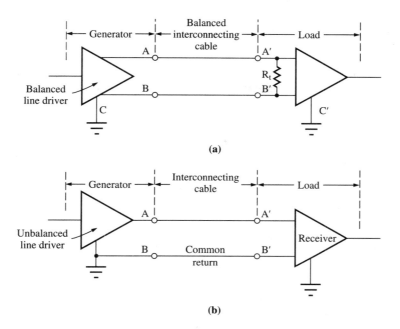

**Figure 7-1** **(a) Balanced Interface Circuit for the RS-422 Standard. (b) Unbalanced Interface Circuit for the RS-423 Standard.** *(Permission granted by Electronic Industries Association)*

**1.** A generating section, which is also known as the sending unit or line driver

**2.** A medium, which is the interconnecting cable in our system

**3.** The load section, which includes the line receiver and the optional resistor, $R_t$

The line driver is designed to have a low impedance (100 ohms or less) balanced voltage source. It produces a differential voltage in the range of 2 to 6 volts.

For a binary 0 (SPACE or ON state), the A terminal is positive with respect to the B terminal. For a binary 1 (MARK or OFF state), the A terminal is negative with respect to the B terminal. Figure 7-2 shows a transistor-transistor logic (TTL) input waveform and the corresponding output waveforms at the inverting and noninverting terminals. These waveforms are measured with respect to ground and propagation delays are ignored. Figure 7-3 shows a test circuit and the steady-state voltages for a binary 1 input. **Note:** The voltage at terminal A is negative with respect to the voltage at terminal B, which conforms to the standard (voltage at A is less than voltage at B for a binary 1). If a binary 0 is applied at the input, the voltage at A is greater than the voltage at B. **Note:** In the RS-422 standard, a small circle is shown at the B terminal. On manufacturers' data sheets, however, it is shown at the terminal whose output wave is inverted from the input wave;

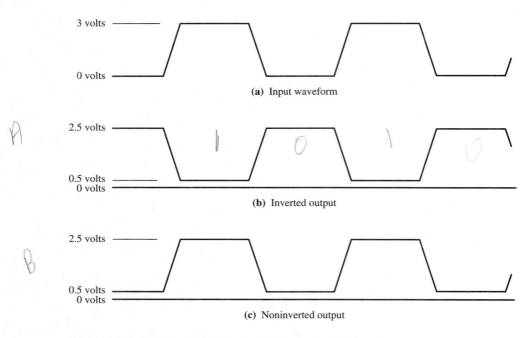

**Figure 7-2    Waveforms Measured with Respect to Ground for an RS-422 Driver Circuit.**

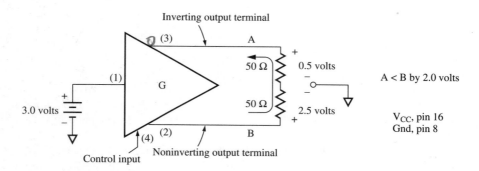

**Figure 7-3    Test Circuit to Determine the Voltages at A and B for a Binary 1 Input. Pin Numbers are for ¼ MC3487 RS-422 Line Driver**

this would be terminal A in Figure 7-3. The IC manufacturers' data sheet conforms to the digital logic notation. The circle at the B terminal in the standard signifies that the voltage at the B terminal is the complement of the voltage at the A terminal, not that the voltage at the B terminal is the input wave inverted.

The standard shows how to set-up and measure a driver circuit's performance for a variety of conditions and gives their maximum or minimum permissible values. These include the following:

1. The maximum magnitude output differential voltage for an open circuit load (6 volts).

2. The maximum magnitude of output voltage with respect to ground for an open circuit load (6 volts).

3. The maximum output current of each terminal under a short circuit condition (150 mA).

4. The maximum output leakage current at each terminal when the supply power is off (100 μA).

5. The minimum differential voltage with a 100-ohm load (2 volts).

6. The maximum output voltage from a center point of a 100-ohm load and ground (3 volts).

7. The maximum time for the output signal waveform to rise or fall from 0.1 to 0.9 of $V_O$ (20 ns or 0.1 of a unit interval, whichever is greater).

These specifications are met or exceeded by those manufacturers that design RS-422 driver circuits.

Motorola's MC3487 IC contains four RS-422 line drivers and each complies with the EIA electrical standards. Figure 7-4 shows the pin connections, block diagram, and truth table. The inputs are buffered to minimize input loading either for a logic 1 or logic 0. The control pin causes the outputs to be either at a logic level or a high impedance state.

## 7-4   RS-422 Line Receiver Electrical Characteristics

The load in an RS-422 interface circuit consists of a line receiver and an optional resistance, $R_t$, as shown in Figure 7-1a. The line receiver should have an input impedance greater than or equal to 4 kΩ, an input transition between −0.2 and +0.2 volts, and allowance for an internal bias voltage not to exceed 3.0 volts in magnitude.

Motorola's MC3486 line receiver can be used as a line receiver either for RS-422 or RS-423 interface circuits. The IC package houses four line receivers as shown in Figure 7-5. Each input has 30 mV of hysteresis to improve noise margin and ensure the output is stable when the input waveform changes slowly. The inputs are buffered to minimize loading and the output has three-state capability (logic 0, logic 1, or high impedance state). The three-state capability is controlled by the two control inputs (pins 4 and 12).

When the device is used for an RS-422 interface circuit, both input pins are used as shown in Figure 7-6a. If the device is used for an RS-423 interface circuit the ( − ) input is ground and the ( + ) input is connected to the interface circuit as shown in Figure 7-6b.

Like the RS-422 driver circuit, the standard sets forth test circuits and how to measure the maximum and minimum permissible values for an RS-422 line re-

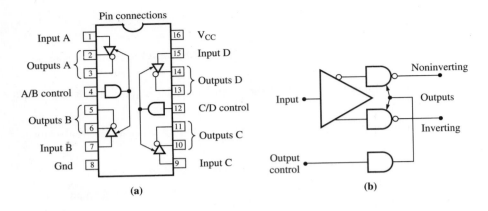

Figure 7-4   The MC3487 Quad Line Driver with Three-State Outputs: (a) Pin Assignments; (b) Block Diagram; and (c) Truth Table *(Courtesy of Motorola Inc.)*

ceiver. These measurements include a range for input current and voltage regardless of whether the supply power is on or off, input sensitivity, input balance, and fail safe operation. The standard also covers multiple receiver, load characteristics, and interconnecting cable characteristics. The MC3486 IC meets or exceeds the requirements set forth for either an RS-422 or RS-423 line receiver.

## 7-5   RS-422 Cable Characteristics

The maximum cable length between the generator and load depends on the data rate, the amount of noise and distortion that can be tolerated, and any cable imbalance that may exist. If the cable is lengthened, there is more likelihood of distortion. Hence, cable length should be kept as short as possible to minimize problems. Figure 7-7 is a plot of cable length versus data rate. This graph is given in the standard and is considered a conservative guide. It is based on 24 AWG

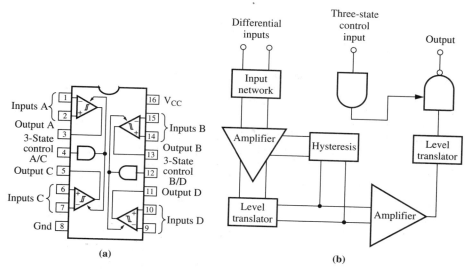

**Figure 7-5   The MC3486 Quad RS-422/423 Line Receiver with Three-State Outputs:
(a) Pin Assignments and (b) Internal Block Diagram.** *(Courtesy of Motorola Inc.)*

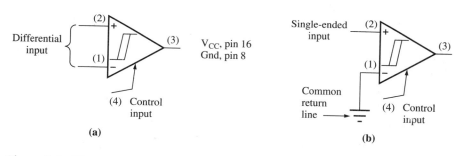

**Figure 7-6   The MC3486 Can be Used as Either an RS-422 Receiver in (a) or as an
RS-423 Line Receiver in (b)**

twisted pair with a 100-ohm termination load. The cable length restriction is based
on the following:

**(a)** The maximum voltage between the generator and load is 6 dbV. This restriction
is the dominant factor for data rates below 90 kilobauds and is the reason the
cable length is limited to 4000 feet (1200 meters).

**(b)** The signal's rise and fall time is equal to or less than 1/2 a unit interval at
that particular data rate. This restriction is the dominant factor for data rates
between 0.09 and 10 megabauds.

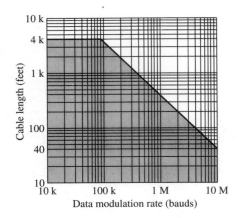

**Figure 7-7    Cable Length versus Data Modulation for Balanced Interface Lines.** *(Courtesy of the Electronic Industries Association)*

## 7-6    RS-423 Line Driver Electrical Characteristics

The RS-449 connector provides for the use of both balanced and unbalanced interface circuits. The RS-422 standard sets forth the guidelines for the electrical characteristics for the balanced circuits. The electrical characteristics for the unbalanced circuits are given in the RS-423 standard. The standard shows the following:

1. The test circuits and how to measure open circuit output voltage ($V_O$ = 4 to 6 volts).

2. Short circuit output current ($I_{SC} \leq 150$ mA).

3. Output leakage current with supply power turned off ($I_X \leq 100$ μA).

4. Output voltage with a test load of 450 ohms ($V_t \leq 0.9\ V_O$).

5. Signal waveforms.

Remember, all the voltages for RS-423 circuits are measured with respect to the common return line as shown in Figure 7-1b. The RS-423 interface circuits are single-ended.

Motorola's MC3488A or MC3488B ICs house two single-ended line drivers as shown in Figure 7-8a. The inputs of the A version are compatible with TTL or metal oxide semiconductor (NMOS) circuitry and the inputs of the B version are for use with complementary metal oxide semiconductor (CMOS) circuitry. Although this device is being used as an RS-423 line driver, it could also be used to drive RS-232 interface circuits because both devices use single-ended operation.

The output slew rate (dv/dt) of an MC3488 IC can be adjusted by a single resistor and not by a capacitor. Refer to Section 5-2.5 for review of slew rate. This resistor provides for linear waveshaping instead of exponential waveshaping and, as will be shown in the following examples, a higher baud rate by a factor

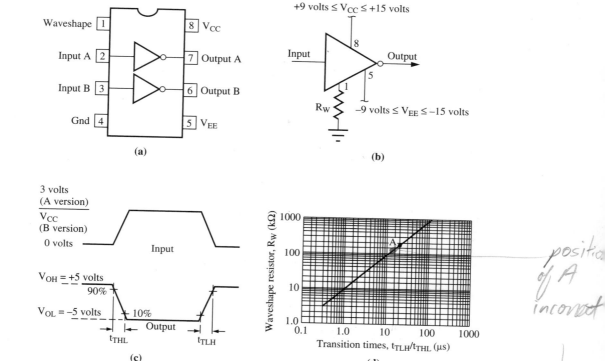

**Figure 7-8** (a) Pin Assignments for the MC3488A (or MC3488B) RS-423 Line Driver. (b) Resistor $R_W$ Adjusts the Rise and Fall Transition Times $t_{TLH}$ and $t_{THL}$ as Shown in (c). (d) Graph of $R_W$ versus Transition Time. *(Courtesy of Motorola Inc.)*

of 2.7. Figure 7-8d is a plot of waveshaping resistor, $R_W$, versus **transition time.** Transition time is defined as the time for the output voltage to change either from 10% to 90% or from 90% to 10% of its final value. Figure 7-9 compares ideal, linear, and exponential waves for an interface circuit.

E X A M P L E   7 - 1

The waveshaping resistor, $R_W$, for an MC3488A line driver is set at 180 kΩ. (a) What are the rise and fall transition times? (b) Refer to Figure 7-8c and calculate the rate of change of voltage with respect to time from 10% to 90% if $V_{OL}$ is $-5$ volts and $V_{OH}$ is $+5$ volts.

**Solution**

(a) From Figure 7-8d at point A, at 180 kΩ, read the x axis at 20 μs.

(b) The rate of change of voltage with respect to time is dv/dt. The voltage change from 10% to 90% is 8 volts. Therefore,

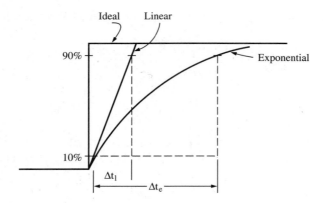

**Figure 7-9    Comparisons of Ideal, Linear, and Exponential Waves**

$$\frac{dv}{dt} = \frac{8 \text{ volts}}{20 \text{ μs}} = 0.4 \text{ V/μs}$$

The rate of change has been calculated with respect to time for a line driver with linear waveshaping. Now calculate the rise time for a line driver whose output voltage changes exponentially.

E  X  A  M  P  L  E    7 - 2

If the exponential wave of Figure 7-9 has the same maximum dv/dt as given in the solution of Example 7-1, determine the rise time for the exponential voltage to change from 10% to 90%.

**Solution**

The general equation for an exponential change of voltage across a capacitor is given by

$$v_C = V_{final} (1 - e^{-t/\tau}) + V_{initial}e^{-t/\tau} \qquad (7\text{-}1)$$

Equation (7-1) can be rearranged to yield a general expression for the change in time, $\Delta t$, for $v_C$ to change from 10% to 90%.

$$\Delta t_e = 2.2\tau \qquad (7\text{-}2)$$

where $t_e$ represents the time for the exponential waveform.

Time constant, $\tau$, can be obtained by knowing that if the capacitor could continue to charge at the initial dv/dt rate, then $v_C$ would equal the maximum value in one time constant. In equation form

$$\tau = \frac{\text{maximum voltage change}}{\text{maximum dv/dt}} \qquad (7\text{-}3)$$

For the waveform of Figure 7-9, $V_{final} = +5$ volts and $V_{initial} = -5$ volts or a maximum change of 10 volts. From the solution of Example 7-1b, then

$$\tau = \frac{10 \text{ volts}}{0.4 \text{ V/}\mu s} = 25 \text{ }\mu s$$

and

$$\Delta t_e = 2.2 \,(25 \text{ }\mu s) = 55 \text{ }\mu s$$

In order to prevent cross-talk near the end of unbalanced lines, a "rule of thumb" is to have the 10%-to-90% rise or fall times to be approximately 30% of a bit time. Therefore,

$$30\% \text{ } t_b = \Delta t \tag{7-4}$$

Equation (7-4) can be rearranged to solve for baud rate

$$max \quad \text{Baud rate} = \frac{1}{t_b} = \frac{0.3}{\Delta t} \tag{7-5}$$

The following example shows the advantage for a line driver with linear waveshaping.

## E X A M P L E   7 - 3

Calculate the baud rate for linear waveshaping in Example 7-1 and for exponential waveshaping in Example 7-2.

**Solution**

(a) In the linear waveshaping of Example 7-1, $\Delta t_l = 20$ $\mu s$. Then applying Equation (7-5) yields

$$\text{Baud rate} = \frac{0.3}{20 \text{ }\mu s} = 15 \text{ kilobaud}$$

(b) From Example 7-2, $\Delta t_e = 55$ $\mu s$, then

$$\text{Baud rate} = \frac{0.3}{55 \text{ }\mu s} = 5.5 \text{ kilobaud}$$

The ratio of these baud rates (15 k $\div$ 5.5 k = 2.7) shows that linear waveshaping increases the baud rate by a factor of almost 3.

## 7-6.1   RS-423 Cable Characteristics

Similar to the RS-422 standard, the RS-423 standard also gives a plot of cable length versus data modulation rate as given in Figure 7-10. The graph is for 24 AWG twisted pairs. In many applications the graph is conservative and for lower modulation rates the cable length may be extended to several miles.

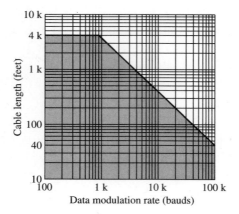

Figure 7-10   **Cable Length versus Data Modulation Rate for Unbalanced Interface
Lines** *(From EIA's RS-423 Standard)*

## 7-7   RS-449 Standard

The electrical standards for balanced and unbalanced interface circuits are set forth
in the RS-422 and RS-423 standards, respectively. If these standards are adopted,
then it is necessary to have standards for the mechanical and functional characteristics. These characteristics are given in the RS-449 standard. Unlike the RS-232
standard, the RS-449 gives specifications for the connector. The RS-449 uses two
connectors: a 37-pin connector and a 9-pin connector. The 37-pin connector contains the primary interface circuits while the 9-pin connector is used for the
secondary channel circuits. The connectors are "seen" by many data communication users as a major disadvantage with this standard. The data terminal
equipment (DTE) connector face for both the 37 and 9 position plug are shown in
Figure 7-11.

Figure 7-12 lists the RS-449 interface circuits along with their pin numbers,
mnemonic, signal direction, and circuit type. The pin numbers within the brackets
indicate those interface circuits contained in the 9-pin connector. Since balanced
circuits (RS-422 specifications) require two lines and hence two pins, both pin
numbers are shown separated by a slash. The first number is the A-A' line in
Figure 7-1a and the second number is the B-B' line. However, if the application
requires transmitting data at rates less than or equal to 20,000 bps, only unbalanced
circuits are needed (RS-423 specifications). In these applications, the number after
the slash would be connected to a common return, either SC (send common) or
RC (receive common). Which return line is used depends on the signal direction:
DTE to DCE (use SC) or DCE to DTE (use RC).

Those interface circuits that use only the RS-423 specification have one pin
connector number and use a common return line. For example, interface circuits
IS, NS, SF/SR, LL, RL, SS, SRD, and SRS use the SC line for their return path.

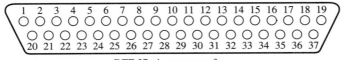

DTE 37-pin connector face

(a)

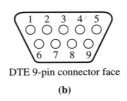

DTE 9-pin connector face

(b)

**Figure 7-11   The 37- and 9-Pin Male Connector Face as Shown are Used on DTE. The Compatible Data Communication Equipment (DCE) Connectors are Numbered from Right to Left**

Interface circuits IC, SQ, SI, TM, SB, SRD, SCS, and SRR use the RC line for their return path. Figure 7-13 shows the four possible interconnections between DTE and DCE and how the send and return common lines are used. Figure 7-13a,b shows balanced interchange circuits while Figure 7-13c,d shows unbalanced interchange circuits. The actual devices used could be the MC3487 for the balanced line driver and the MC3488 for the unbalanced line driver. The MC3486 could be used as the line receiver for both types of interchange circuits; however, the B' terminal is wired differently (*see* Fig. 7-6).

The RS-449 interface circuits are divided into two categories—category I circuits and category II circuits. Figure 7-12 shows the circuits in each category. If an application requires data to be sent at less than 20,000 bps, then category I circuits may be wired either as balanced circuits or as unbalanced circuits. For data rates greater than 20,000 bps, category I circuits are to be wired as balanced circuits, as given by the RS-422 standard.

All interchange circuits not classified as category I circuits are classified as category II circuits, as shown in Figure 7-12. Category II circuits are wired as unbalanced interchange circuits according to the RS-423 standard. These circuits use the two common returns depending on the direction of transmission (*see* Fig. 7-13). **Note:** The terms "send" and "receive" are in relationship to the DTE.

Space does not permit a detailed examination of the functional characteristics of each RS-449 interchange circuit. If a copy of the standard has been obtained, the student should not have difficulty understanding them if the functional characteristics of RS-232-C and EIA-232-D have been studied. Figure 7-14 lists the nearest equivalent circuit for the RS-449, RS-232-C, and CCITT's V.24. It should be noted that the nearest equivalent circuit does not infer exactly the same functional definitions.

| Category | Pin number(s) | Circuit mnemonic | Circuit name | Direction | | Circuit type | |
|---|---|---|---|---|---|---|---|
| | | | | DTE | DCE | | |
| II | 19, [5] | SG | Signal ground | — | — | Common | |
| II | 37, [9] | SC | Send common | → | | | |
| II | 20, [6] | RC | Receive common | ← | | | |
| II | 28 | IS | Terminal in service | → | | Control | |
| II | 15 | IC | Incoming call | ← | | | |
| I | 12/30 | TR | Terminal ready | → | | | |
| I | 11/29 | DM | Data mode | ← | | | |
| I | 4/22 | SD | Send data | → | | Data | Primary channel |
| I | 6/24 | RD | Receive data | ← | | | |
| I | 17/35 | TT | Terminal timing | → | | Timing | |
| I | 5/23 | ST | Send timing | ← | | | |
| I | 8/26 | RT | Receive timing | ← | | | |
| I | 7/25 | RS | Request-to-send | → | | Control | |
| I | 9/27 | CS | Clear-to-send | ← | | | |
| I | 13/31 | RR | Receiver ready | ← | | | |
| II | 33 | SQ | Signal quality | ← | | | |
| II | 34 | NS | New signal | → | | | |
| II | 16 | SF | Select frequency | → | | | |
| II | 16 | SR | Signaling rate selector | → | | | |
| II | 2 | SI | Signaling rate indicator | ← | | | |
| II | [3] | SSD | Secondary send data | → | | Data | Secondary channel |
| II | [4] | SRD | Secondary receive data | ← | | | |
| II | [7] | SRS | Secondary request-to-send | → | | Control | |
| II | [8] | SCS | Secondary clear-to-send | ← | | | |
| II | [2] | SRR | Secondary receiver ready | ← | | | |
| II | 10 | LL | Local loopback | → | | Control | |
| II | 14 | RL | Remote loopback | → | | | |
| II | 18 | TM | Test mode | ← | | | |
| II | 32 | SS | Select standby | → | | Control | |
| II | 36 | SB | Standby indicator | ← | | | |

**Figure 7-12   RS-449 interface circuits. Pin connector numbers in brackets are those on the 9-pin connector. Pin numbers separated by a slash are for the differential lines.** *(Permission granted by Electronic Industries Association.)*

## 7-8   Interconnecting RS-232 and RS-449 Equipment

An application may require interconnecting RS-232 equipment with RS-449 equipment. It could be that the DTE has an RS-232 port and the DCE has an RS-449 port or vice versa. In either case an adapter is needed. Since one piece of equipment is the RS-232, then the maximum data rate is 20,000 bps. This means the RS-423 electrical characteristics are used within the RS-449 equipment. The interconnection with the older RS-232 standard was one of the features designed into the RS-

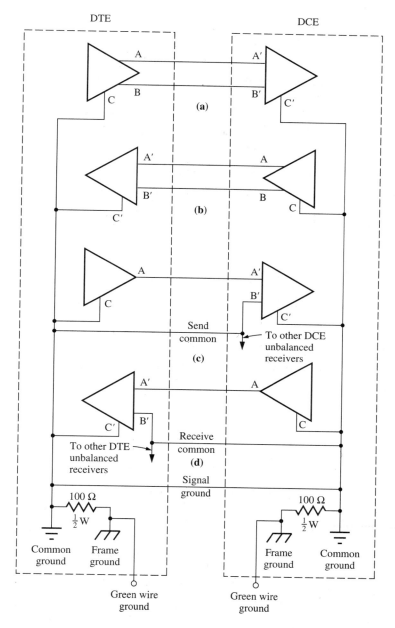

**Figure 7-13   Interconnection of two Balanced (a and b) and Two Unbalanced (c and d) Interchange Circuits.** *(Courtesy of Electronic Industries Association)*

| | RS-449 | | | RS-232-C | | CCITT Recommendation V.24 |
|---|---|---|---|---|---|---|
| SG | Signal ground | AB | Signal ground | 102 | Signal ground | |
| SC | Send common | | | 102a | DTE common | |
| RC | Receive common | | | 102b | DCE common | |
| IS | Terminal in service | | | | | |
| IC | Incoming call | CE | Ring indicator | 125 | Calling indicator | |
| TR | Terminal ready | CD | Data terminal ready | 108/2 | Data terminal ready | |
| DM | Data mode | CC | DCE ready | 107 | Data set ready | |
| SD | Send data | BA | Transmitted data | 103 | Transmitted data | |
| RD | Receive data | BB | Received data | 104 | Received data | |
| TT | Terminal timing | DA | Transmitter signal element timing (DTE source) | 113 | Transmitter signal element timing (DTE source) | |
| ST | Send timing | DB | Transmitter signal element timing (DCE source) | 114 | Transmitter signal element timing (DCE source) | |
| RT | Receive timing | DD | Receiver signal element timing (DCE source) | 115 | Receiver signal element timing (DCE source) | |
| RS | Request-to-send | CA | Request-to-send | 105 | Request-to-send | |
| CS | Clear-to-send | CB | Clear-to-send | 106 | Ready for sending | |
| RR | Receiver ready | CF | Received line signal detector | 109 | Data channel received line signal detector | |
| SQ | Signal quality | CG | Signal quality detector | 110 | Data signal quality detector | |
| NS | New signal | | | | | |
| SF | Select frequency | | | 126 | Select transmit frequency | |
| SR | Signaling rate selector | CH | Data signal rate selector (DTE source) | 111 | Data signaling rate selector (DTE source) | |
| SI | Signaling rate indicator | CI | Data signal rate selector (DCE source) | 112 | Data signaling rate selector (DCE source) | |
| SSD | Secondary send data | SBA | Secondary transmitted data | 118 | Transmitted backward channel data | |
| SRD | Secondary receive data | SBB | Secondary received data | 119 | Received backward channel data | |
| SRS | Secondary request-to-send | SCA | Secondary request-to-send | 120 | Transmit backward channel line signal | |
| SCS | Secondary clear-to-send | SCB | Secondary clear-to-send | 121 | Backward channel ready | |
| SRR | Secondary receiver ready | SCF | Secondary received line signal detector | 122 | Backward channel received line signal detector | |
| LL | Local loopback | LL | Local loopback* | 141 | Local loopback | |
| RL | Remote loopback | RL | Remote loopback* | 140 | Remote loopback | |
| TM | Test mode | TM | Test mode* | 142 | Test indicator | |
| SS | Select standby | | | 116 | Select standby | |
| SB | Standby indicator | | | 117 | Standby indicator | |

**Figure 7-14   An Equivalency Chart for RS-449, RS-232-C, and CCITT V.24 (*On the EIA-232-D Version Only)** *(Permission granted by Electronic Industries Association.)*

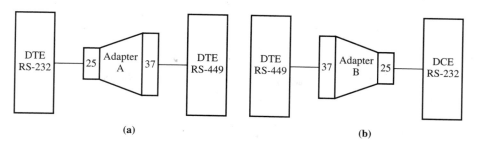

**Figure 7-15**   **Interconnection of RS-232 and RS-449 Equipment Requires an Adapter.** *(Courtesy of Electronic Industries Association)*

449 standard. Figure 7-15 shows two general interconnection diagrams for the RS-449 37-pin connector. If the secondary channel is also going to be used, a 9/25 or 25/9-pin adapter is needed. These interconnections are covered in EIA's Industrial Electronics Bulletin No. 12.

The RS-423 standard specifies that a line receiver need only to withstand 12 volts. However, RS-232 line drivers can exceed this limit. Therefore, in some applications, it may be necessary to insert a pad between an RS-232 driver and an RS-423 receiver as shown in Figure 7-16. These additional components are not necessary if you use IC receivers, such as the MC3486, which can withstand the RS-232 maximum voltage ratings. Figure 7-17a shows the A adapter connections without any L pads. If pads were needed, there would be five of them in the A adapter. They would be used on SD (pin 4), RS (pin 7), TR (pin 12), TT (pin 17), and SF/SR (pin 16) inputs. Figure 7-17b shows the B adapter connections without the use of L pads. If pads were needed to protect the RS-423 receivers, they would be used on nine lines. They are SI (pin 2), ST (pin 5), RD (pin 6), RT (pin 8), CS (pin 9), DM (pin 11), RR (pin 13), SQ (pin 33), and IC (pin 15). Every application would not require all the interconnections shown in Figure 7-17a,b. As studied in Chapter 6, half- or full-duplex operation on switched or private lines does not always require the same interchange circuits.

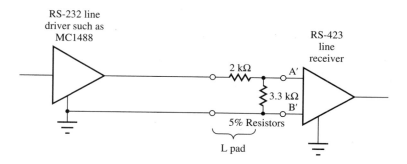

**Figure 7-16**   **An L-Pad Attenuator is Needed to Protect Some RS-423 Line Receivers**

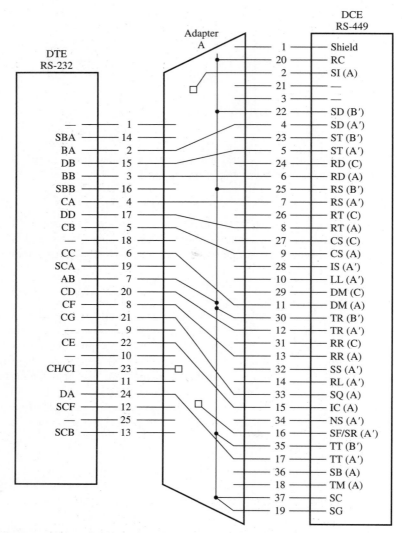

(a) RS-232 DTE to RS-449 DCE. Pin 28, IS, in the DCE is Strapped to a Positive Voltage. *(Courtesy of Electronic Industries Association)*

**Figure 7-17**  Interconnection of RS-449 37-Pin Connector to RS-232 25-Pin Connector. Some Applications Require CH to be Connected to SR or CI with SI. *(Courtesy of Electronic Industries Association)*

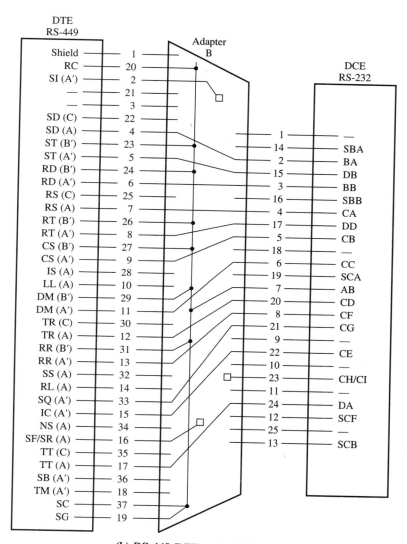

**(b) RS-449 DTE to RS-232 DCE**

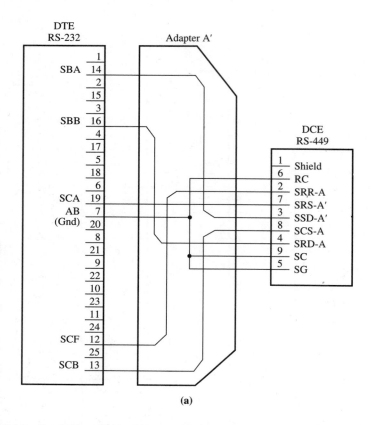

**Figure 7-18    Secondary Channel Connections between RS-232 and RS-449. (a) RS-232, DTE and RS-449, DCE and (b) RS-449, DTE and RS-232, DCE. The L-Pad Connections are Not Shown.** *(Courtesy of Electronic Industries Association)*

If the user's RS-449 equipment has a 9-pin connector for the secondary channel and it is to be used with RS-232 equipment, then Figure 7-18a,b shows how the interconnections are made.

## 7-9   RS-530 Standard

Remember that the RS-449 standard set forth functional and mechanical characteristics for interface circuits to connect DTE to DCE and provide for balanced and unbalanced circuits. This permitted higher data rates between the DTE and DCE. However, the major disadvantage of the RS-449 interface is that it requires two connectors—a 37-pin connector for the primary channel and most of the control interface circuits and a 9-pin connector for the secondary channel and its control interface circuits. Although the secondary may not be required in many applications, the 37-pin connector is still a major drawback in many situations. Many

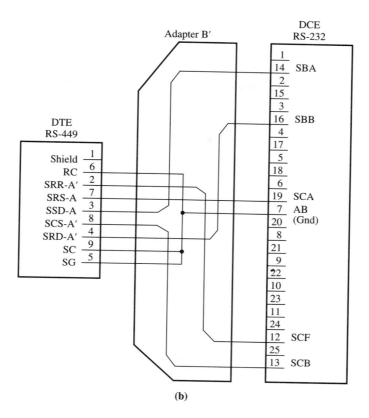

**(b)**

users desired a 25-pin connector, such as the DB-25, used in many RS-232 applications but which would provide for the higher data rates. The RS-530 interface standard has been introduced to supercede the RS-449. As shown in Figure 7-19a, it uses a 25-pin connector but it is not compatible with the RS-232. The RS-530 is designed to be used with the electrical interface standards of RS-422 (balanced interface circuits) and RS-423 (unbalanced interface circuits). The RS-530 standard permits data rates from 20 kbps to 2 Mbps provided that balanced circuits are used. It may be used for either asynchronous or synchronous transmission. A comparison between RS-530 and RS-232-C and the pins used and their functions are shown in Figure 7-19b.

## 7-10   RS-485 Standard

The RS-485 standard is similar to the RS-422 standard except that the output drivers are designed for three-state output and not two-state. This capability may be needed in a multipoint system. These devices are available in ICs such as Linear Technologies—LTC 485.

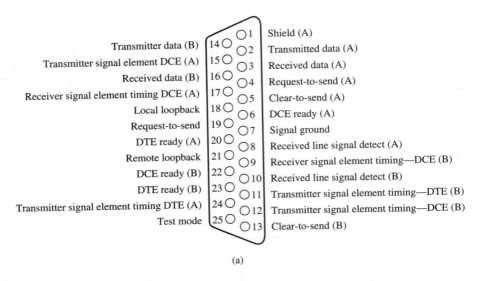

Figure 7-19   (a) Pin and Signal Descriptions for an RS-530 Male Connector.

## 7-11   CCITT V.35

CCITT V.35 is the international standard for data transmission at 48 kbps using 60–108 group-band circuits. It is used primarily in high speed digital data transmission such as AT&T's Dataphone® Digital Service (DDS). This topic is covered in more detail in Chapter 13. Figure 7-20 shows the pin and signal descriptions for the V.35 interface connector.

## 7-12   Current Loops

Up to this point, voltage signals have been used to transmit data between electronic equipment. The popular industry standards covered are the RS-232 (C and D versions), RS-422, RS-423, RS-485, RS-449, RS-530, and some of their international equivalents. In applications that require data to be transferred using a low cost interface, through a noisy environment over a distance of several thousand feet, a current signal may be a better solution than a voltage signal. Some of the reasons for this are that current signals are less susceptible to noise than voltage signals. Also, voltage signals decrease over distance whereas constant current signals do not. As studied in Chapter 5, the RS-232 standard specifies a maximum data rate of 20,000 bps for a distance of 50 feet. By using a current signal, the distance can be increased to over 3000 feet for the same data rate. Current signals are sent using a network known as a **current loop,** which is nothing more than an inexpensive twisted pair of wires connected between the transmitter and receiver as shown in Figure 7-21a,b. Current loops can be used in simplex, half-duplex,

| RS-530 interface | | | | RS-232 interface | | |
|---|---|---|---|---|---|---|
| 25-Pin | | EIA RS-530 circuit | RS-530 description | 25-Pin | EIA RS-232-C circuit | RS-232 description |
| A | B | | | | | |
| 1 | | | Shield | 1 | AA | Protective ground |
| 7 | | AB | Signal ground | 7 | AB | Signal ground common return |
| 2 | 14 | BA | Transmitted data | 2 | BA | Transmitted data |
| 3 | 16 | BB | Receive data | 3 | BB | Received data |
| 4 | 19 | CA | Request-to-send | 4 | CA | Request-to-send |
| 5 | | CB | Clear-to-send | 5 | CB | Clear-to-send |
| 6 | 22 | CC | DCE ready | 6 | CC | DCE ready |
| 20 | 23 | CD | DTE ready | 20 | CD | Data terminal ready |
| | | | | 22 | CE | Ring indicator |
| 8 | 10 | CF | Received line signal detector | 8 | CF | Received line signal detector |
| | | | | 21 | CG | Signal quality detector |
| | | | | 23 | CH | Data signal rate selector (DTE) |
| | | | | 23 | CI | Data signal rate selector (DCE) |
| 24 | 11 | DA | Transmitter signal element timing (DTE) | 24 | DA | Transmitter signal element timing (DTE) |
| 15 | 12 | DB | Transmitter signal element timing (DCE) | 15 | DB | Transmitter signal element timing (DCE) |
| 17 | 9 | DD | Receiver signal element timing (DCE) | 17 | DD | Receiver signal element timing (DCE) |
| | | BA | Transmitted data | 14 | SBA | Secondary transmitter data |
| | | BB | Receive data | 16 | SBB | Secondary receive data |
| | | | | 19 | SCA | Seconday request-to-send |
| | 13 | CB | Clear-to-send | 13 | SCB | Secondary clear-to-send |
| | | DB | Transmit signal element timing (DCE) | 12 | SCF | Secondary received line signal detector |
| 18 | | LL | Local loopback | 18 | LL | Local loopback* |
| 21 | | RL | Remote loopback | 21 | RM | Remote loopback* |
| 25 | | TM | Test mode | 25 | TM | Test mode* |

(b)

**Figure 7-19**  (b) A Comparison between the RS-232 and RS-530 Interface.
(* Interface Circuits that are Part of the D Version.)

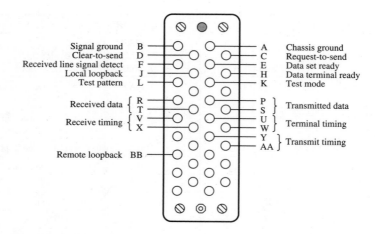

**Figure 7-20   Pin and Signal Designations for a V.35 Male Connector**

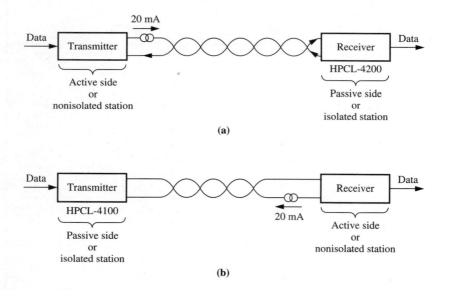

**Figure 7-21   Simplex Point-to-Point Current Loop Systems. (a) Active Transmitter and (b) Active Receiver.** *(Courtesy of Hewlett-Packard Company)*

and full-duplex configurations. Each of these configurations can be wired for point-to-point or multipoint systems.

Typical current loop values for digital circuitry are 0 to 20 mA or 0 to 60 mA. Since the range of 0 to 20 mA is used most often, this range will be used. For a data communication application a value 0 mA corresponds to a logic 0 or SPACE condition. A current value of 20 mA corresponds to logic 1 or MARK condition. Because of its high noise immunity property, current loops are also used in industrial applications to transfer analog information. The typical current range for these applications is 4 to 20 mA.

As shown in Figure 7-21, a current source is designed into the loop to provide the current. In Figure 7-21a, the transmitter is the active side, which means that its circuitry opens and closes the loop to correspond to the data that is being sent. The receiver senses the line and converts the presence or absence of current to a voltage signal, usually TTL levels. Since every loop needs a current source, it may be designed into the transmitter station as shown in Figure 7-21a or into the receiver station as shown in Figure 7-21b. The station that contains the current source is referred to as the active side and the other station is known as the passive station. Figure 7-21a shows a simplex configuration with an active transmitter while Figure 7-21b shows the same configuration with an active receiver. Although the design of current sources may range from a voltage source and resistor network to special purpose ICs, most often a transistor circuit is used, as will be shown shortly.

In many current loop applications, electrical isolation is needed to permit different ground references and to isolate a high voltage from TTL logic levels. This isolation can be obtained by using optocouplers. Only one optocoupler is needed in the loop either at the transmitting station or at the receiving station.

Although many general purpose optocouplers may be used for this application, devices manufactured by Hewlett Packard will be used because they are designed specifically for 20 mA current loops. The devices are HPCL-4100 and HPCL-4200. The HPCL-4100 (*see* Fig. 7-22) is designed to operate in the transmitting station and hence to isolate the transmitting station from the loop as shown in the simplex configuration of Figure 7-21b. The HPCL-4200 (*see* Fig. 7-23) is an optocoupler designed to operate in the receiving station and to isolate the receiver from the loop as shown in Figure 7-21a. Although both drawings in Figure 7-21 show simplex configurations, these optocouplers can be used in half-duplex and full-duplex applications as will be shown. In each circuit of Figure 7-21, the current source is at the active or nonisolated station (the side without the optocoupler). The optocoupler is at the isolated station or passive side.

## 7-12.1    Isolated Transmitter and Nonisolated Receiver

Figure 7-24 is a more complete version of Figure 7-21, and shows a simplex current loop circuit using an isolated transmitter and a nonisolated receiver. The one-stage transistor circuit provides the loop current. The transistor's supply voltage, $V_{CC}$, may have to be increased if line length is increased. $V_{CC} = 10$ volts allows the loop length to be approximately 2000 meters. If $V_{CC}$ is increased to 20

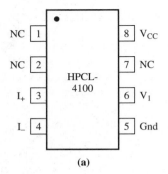

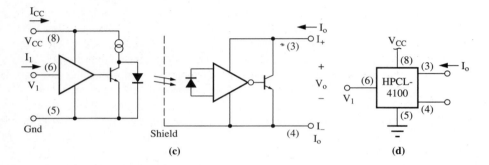

**Figure 7-22   The HPCL-4100 20 mA Current Loop Transmitter Pin Assignments in (a), Truth Table in (b), Schematic in (c), and Circuit Diagram in (d).** *(Courtesy of Hewlett-Packard Company)*

volts, the loop length can be increased to approximately 8000 meters. If an application is a multipoint system instead of a point-to-point system, then the $V_{CC}$ voltage also may have to be increased. As $V_{CC}$ is increased, the data rate will decrease for the same loop length. The reason for this is that it takes a longer time for the transistor to switch from cutoff to saturation and vice versa. A $V_{CC}$ voltage of 27 volts should not be exceeded because of the maximum breakdown voltage of the HPCL-4100. For the current source circuit in Figure 7-24, the loop current is given by

$$I_{loop} \simeq \frac{1.2 \text{ volts}}{R_1} \tag{7-6}$$

assuming $I_C \simeq I_E$ for a transistor.

The value of $R_2$ is found by

$$R_2 = \frac{V_{CC_2} - 1.8 \text{ volts}}{I_B + I_D} \tag{7-7}$$

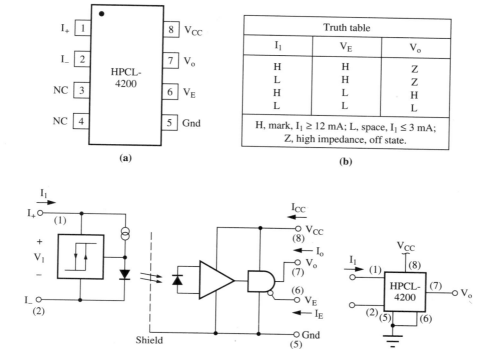

**(a)**

| Truth table | | |
|---|---|---|
| $I_1$ | $V_E$ | $V_o$ |
| H | H | Z |
| L | H | Z |
| H | L | H |
| L | L | L |
| H, mark, $I_1 \geq 12$ mA; L, space, $I_1 \leq 3$ mA; Z, high impedance, off state. | | |

**(b)**

**(c)**

**(d)**

**Figure 7-23   The HPCL-4200 20 mA Current Loop Receiver Pin Assignments (a), Truth Table in (b), Schematic in (c), and Circuit Diagram in (d).** *(Courtesy of Hewlett-Packard Company)*

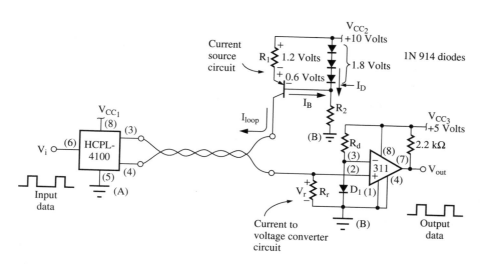

**Figure 7-24   Simplex Point-to-Point 20 mA Current Loop Using an Isolated Transmitter and a Non-isolated Receiver.** *(Courtesy of Hewlett-Packard Company)*

where

$$I_B = \frac{I_C}{\beta} \simeq \frac{I_{loop}}{\beta}$$

and $I_D \simeq 2.0$ mA for a 0.6 volt across a diode.

## E X A M P L E   7 - 4

Calculate the values for $R_1$ and $R_2$ in Figure 7-24 for a 20 mA current source. Assume the transistor's current gain equals 50 and $I_D$ is 2.0 mA.

### Solution

Rearranging Equation (7-6) yields

$$R_1 = \frac{1.2 \text{ volts}}{20 \text{ mA}} = 60 \text{ ohms}$$

The transistor's base current is 20 mA/50 = 0.4 mA. From Equation (7-7)

$$R_2 = \frac{(10 - 1.8) \text{ volts}}{2.4 \text{ mA}} = 3.4 \text{ k}\Omega$$

As shown in Figure 7-24, the receiver uses an LM311 comparator circuit to convert the presence or absence of loop current into TTL voltage levels. The principles of comparator circuits using the LM311 are covered in Chapter 9 and in the reference text *Operational Amplifiers and Linear Integrated Circuits* by Robert F. Coughlin and Frederick F. Driscoll.

The ($-$) input of the comparator is held at approximately $+0.6$ volts by the voltage drop across the diode, $D_1$. If the voltage at the comparator's ($+$) input is less than 0.6 volts, the output voltage is 0 volts. If the loop current causes $V_r$ to be greater than $+0.6$ volts, then $V_{out} = +5$ volts.

## E X A M P L E   7 - 5

In Figure 7-24, the LM311 comparator is used as a current loop to TTL converter circuit. (a) Show that the minimum value of $R_r$ is 50 ohms. (b) What is the value of $R_d$ if the current through diode $D_1$ is 2.0 mA?

### Solution

From Figure 7-22b, the minimum value of loop current for a MARK condition (logic 1) is 12 mA. All of this current flows through $R_r$ since the input circuitry of an op amp or comparator draws negligible current. This current must cause the voltage at the ($+$) input to be slightly greater (by a few microvolts) than the voltage at the ($-$) input, which is approximately 0.6 volts. Then

$$R_r = \frac{0.6 \text{ volts}}{12 \text{ mA}} = 50 \text{ ohms}$$

To account for differences in diode voltage, a typical value of 75 ohms should be used.

$$R_d = \frac{(5 - 0.6)\text{ volts}}{2.0\text{ mA}} = 2.2\text{ k}\Omega$$

Before leaving the circuit of Figure 7-24, note that the circuit common (A) on the transmitter side is not connected to the circuit common (B) on the receiver side. This is to ensure that there will be electrical isolation between the transmitter and receiver.

## 7-12.2   Nonisolated Transmitter and Isolated Receiver

The circuit of Figure 7-25 is also a simplex point-to-point 20 mA current loop network. Unlike the previous circuit, this network uses a nonisolated transmitter and an isolated receiver. Hewlett Packard's HPCL-4200 is used to isolate the receiver from the loop. The current source is similar to the one used in Figure 7-24, and Equations (7-6) and (7-7) can be used to solve for $R_1$ and $R_2$. The current source is controlled by the 7407 open collector buffer and current-limiting resistor $R_3$. When $V_i$ is a logic 1, the 7407's output saturates ($\sim$0.4 volts) and the current through $R_1$ should flow through $R_3$ to ground. For this condition, $I_{loop}$ should drop below 2.0 mA. When $V_i$ is a logic 0, the 7407's output is in cutoff and $I_3$ equals 0 mA. Supply voltages $V_{CC1}$, $V_{CC2}$, and $V_{CC3}$ do not have to be the same value. Circuit commons (A) and (B) should not be wired together.

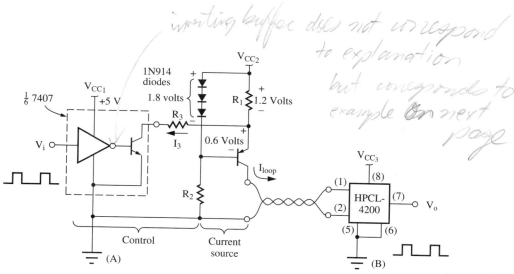

Figure 7-25   **Simplex Point-to-Point 20 mA Current Loop Using a Non-isolated Transmitter and an Isolated Receiver.** *(Courtesy of Hewlett-Packard Company)*

The maximum output current a 7407 can sink is 40 mA. Therefore, this device can easily handle the 20 mA loop current if it is diverted through $R_3$. If the 7407's output transistor saturates at 0.7 volts, calculate a maximum and minimum value for $R_3$. Assume $V_{CC2} = 10$ volts.

**Solution**

From Figure 7-25, the maximum value for $R_3$ is

$$R_{3max} = \frac{(10 - 1.2 - 0.7) \text{ volts}}{20 \text{ mA}} = 405 \text{ ohms}$$

A resistance value greater than 405 ohms may not divert all of the loop current through $R_3$ when $V_i$ is at a logic 0.

The minimum value for $R_3$ ensures that 7407 does not handle a current greater than 40 mA.

$$R_{3min} = \frac{(10 - 1.2 - 0.7) \text{ volts}}{40 \text{ mA}} = 202 \text{ ohms}$$

A typical value of 270 ohms would be a good choice to start a design. These simplex point-to-point circuits can be expanded to full- and half-duplex configurations.

### 7-12.3  Full-Duplex Point-to-Point Configurations

A full-duplex point-to-point configuration is shown in Figure 7-26a. It is a four-wire system that allows simultaneous transmission between local and remote stations. As shown, this system requires two current sources and is basically two simplex systems working together. In the system of Figure 7-26a, the remote station contains the optocouplers and is therefore the isolated station. A full-duplex system could be designed so that optocouplers are at the local station and the current sources are contained as part of the remote station as shown in Figure 7-26b. Both circuits of Figure 7-26 have the optocouplers at either the remote or the local station. Although it is possible to divide the optocouplers so that there is one at each end, a better design is to keep the optocouplers at one end as shown.

### 7-12.4  Half-Duplex Point-to-Point Configuration

Figure 7-27 shows a half-duplex point-to-point configuration. In this circuit, the remote station is the isolated station and hence the optocouplers are located at that end. As in any half-duplex configuration, data is transmitted over two wires. As studied in Chapter 6, a protocol procedure determines the station that is transmitting at a particular time. The HPCL-4100/4200 optocouplers can be wired together as

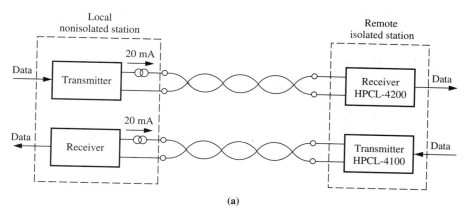

(a)

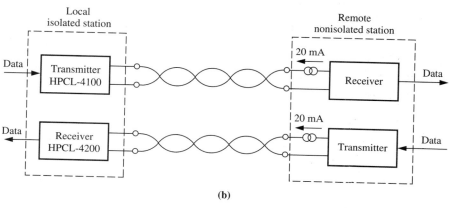

(b)

**Figure 7-26   Two Examples of a Four-Wire Full-Duplex Point-to-Point 20 mA Current Loop System.** *(Courtesy of Hewlett-Packard Company)*

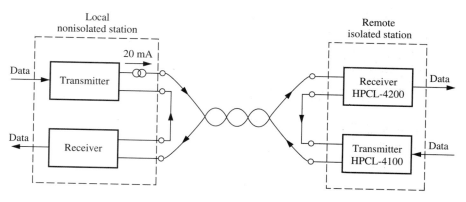

**Figure 7-27   Half-Duplex Point-to-Point 20 mA Current Loop System.** *(Courtesy of Hewlett-Packard Company)*

shown to create an isolated remote station. Similarly, an isolated local station could have been built. In a half-duplex system, only one 20 mA current source is needed. Additional information about the HPCL-4100/4200 optocouplers can be obtained from data sheets and Application Note 1018 furnished by Hewlett Packard.

## Summary

Chapters 5 and 6 introduced the most widely used interface standard for micro-computers, the RS-232-C and its latest version the EIA-232-D. However, other interface standards are used and this chapter introduced some of them. The RS-449 standard specified the mechanical and functional characteristics of an interface to replace the RS-232. It permits both balanced and unbalanced circuits within the same connector. The disadvantage with the RS-449 standard is that it requires a 37-pin connector and if a secondary channel is used another 9-pin connector is required. The RS-449 standard has been superceded for many applications by the RS-530 standard. The RS-530 also is designed for balanced and unbalanced circuits but uses a 25-pin connector. Whether the RS-449 or the RS-530 standard is being used, the electrical standards are set forth in the RS-422 standard for balanced circuits and the RS-423 standard for unbalanced circuits.

This chapter also covered IC devices that can be used for the drivers and receivers or balanced and unbalanced lines. The popular international standard for serial transmission is V.24. The standards mentioned thus far have used voltage signals to transmit the serial data. In noisy environments, current signals may be the best solution and current loops were covered in Section 7-12.

## Problems

* **7.1** Is the RS-422 interface standard designed for single-ended or differential configurations?

  **7.2** What is a major disadvantage of the RS-449 connector?

* **7.3** Does the RS-422 standard specify the electrical or mechanical characteristics?

  **7.4** In the test circuit of Figure 7-3, if the input signal is a logic 0 then A > B by 2.0 volts. Draw the output current direction and voltage polarities with respect to ground.

* **7.5** What is the purpose of having hysteresis voltage in a line receiver?

  **7.6** Use the MC3487, MC3486, and MC3488 chips. How would they be inter-connected for (a) single-ended and (b) differential-ended data communication links?

* *See* Answers to Selected Problems.

* **7.7** For a balanced configuration and a data modulation rate of 200 kilobauds, what would be the expected distance from driver to receiver?

**7.8** If $R_W$ in Figure 7-8b is set to 380 k$\Omega$, determine (a) rise and fall transition times and (b) the rate of change of voltage from 10% to 90%. Assume $V_{OL}$ = +5 volts, $V_{OH}$ = +5 volts.

* **7.9** For Problem 7.8, determine the baud rate for linear waveshaping.

**7.10** Calculate the baud rate for Problem 7.8 with exponential waveshaping circuitry.

* **7.11** For 24 gauge twisted wire, what is the difference (in feet) between using a balanced interface circuit and using an unbalanced interface circuit? The data modulation rate for both circuits is 100 kilobauds.

**7.12** If only the 37-pin RS-449 connector is being used, can both the balanced and unbalanced interface circuits be used?

* **7.13** What is the function of the 9-pin connection in the RS-449 standard?

**7.14** For those unbalanced lines that use only the RS-423 specification, which interface circuit in the RS-449 connector is used as the common return
(a) For signals from DTE to DCE?
(b) For signals from DCE to DTE?

* **7.15** For data rates greater than 20,000 bps, which group of circuits is wired as balanced circuits?

**7.16** Why is it necessary to use L pads on some interface circuits in the RS-449 connector?

* **7.17** In a 0–20 mA current loop, what value of current represents (a) mark condition, (b) space condition?

**7.18** If in Figure 7-24 $R_1$ is changed to a 100 ohm resistor, what is the value of loop current?

* **7.19** If the loop current values in Figure 7-24 are 0.5 mA and 15 mA and $R_r$ is 56 ohms, will the comparator sense the mark and space conditions?

**7.20** Determine a good design choice for $R_1$ and $R_2$ in Figure 7-25. The current gain of the transistor is 60.

# 8

# Modulation and Modems

OBJECTIVES

Upon completion of this chapter on modulation and modems, the student will be able to

- Define the basic types of modulation.
- Describe the basic modulation schemes used in data communication.
- Understand the principles used in frequency shift keying (FSK) modems.
- List the different types of FSK modems and identify their differences.
- Know the difference between an originate modem and an answer modem.
- Understand the principles of dial-up application.
- Describe the function of an acoustic coupler and its applications.
- Compare the differences of some of the international standards of modems with those of Bell Series.
- Describe the principles of quadrature phase shift keying (QPSK) and identify modems that use this modulation scheme.
- Understand why dibits are used and divide a bit stream into dibit combinations.
- Analyze a QPSK detector circuit.
- Describe quadrature amplitude modulation and the function of constellation patterns.
- Understand the differences in the international and Bell data communication standards.
- Know the types of standards used for fax transmission.

## Introduction

Up to now, data transmitted asynchronously from data terminal equipment (DTE) to data communication equipment (DCE), and vice versa, has been studied. One of the most commonly used pieces of DCE is a modem. The term "modem" was introduced in Chapter 1. The word "modem" is a contraction of two words, modulation and demodulation. Remember from Chapter 1 that modems are used because the telephone network is a convenient communication channel. However, it was designed for voice communication and not for today's high speed data transmission of digital information. Yet the convenience of the telephone system makes it necessary to design equipment such as modems to transmit data. A modem at the transmitter converts the digital data to an analog signal and transmits it. A modem at the receiver reconverts the analog signal to digital data. Either asynchronous or synchronous modems can be purchased. Whichever type of modem is used, the digital data is converted to an analog signal to be sent and the reverse process is done at the other end.

   This chapter introduces the basic principles of modulation and the characteristics of some of the available modems. Chapter 9 covers in more detail the principles of a low speed modem.

## 8-1   Basic Types of Modulation

A sine wave is characterized by its amplitude, frequency, and phase. Mathematically, a sine wave of voltage is expressed as $v = V_m\sin(2\pi ft + \theta)$ where $V_m$ is the peak amplitude in volts, f is the frequency in hertz, and $\theta$ is the phase angle in radians per second. Since these parameters can be modulated (changed), then a sine wave can be used as a carrier to transmit information from one modem to another. All modems are designed around the principles of either amplitude, frequency, or phase modulation or a combination of these.

   There are three basic methods of modulating a carrier wave: amplitude modulation, frequency modulation, and phase modulation. Amplitude and frequency modulation are similar to the principles used for radio transmission. Figure 8-1

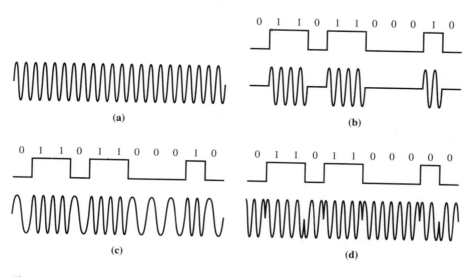

**Figure 8-1**   (a) Carrier Signal, (b) Amplitude Modulation, (c) Frequency Modulation, and (d) Phase Modulation

illustrates the three basic types of modulation. In amplitude modulation, the amplitude of the carrier changes in accordance with the binary pattern. In Figure 8-1b, a logic 0 causes the carrier's amplitude to go to zero and for a logic 1 the carrier is present. In frequency modulation, the carrier's frequency varies. A frequency lower than the carrier frequency represents a logic 0 and a frequency higher than the carrier frequency represents a logic 1. For example, if the carrier frequency is 1700 hertz, which is near the center of telephone bandwidth, a logic 0 can be represented by a frequency of 1200 hertz and a logic 1 by a frequency of 2200 hertz. A frequency modulated waveform is shown in Figure 8-1c. In phase modulation, the angle of the sine wave varies. Figure 8-1d illustrates an example of phase modulation where there is a phase angle change of 180° whenever there is a change in logic state. Section 8-4 will show a modified version of phase modulation that is used in modems. Phase modulation techniques also allow for a variety of phase angle changes and greater data carrying capacity than is presented in Figure 8-1d. Although the examples of Figure 8-1 illustrate the basic principles of modulation, this channel is not being used efficiently. The following sections will show how more bits can be packed together in the same time interval. Also, simple amplitude modulation (Fig. 8-1b) is not used in data communication because it is very susceptible to noise interference, causing errors in the received data. However, a combination of phase and amplitude modulation is used and this topic is discussed in Section 8-5. Low speed modems (0 to 1200 bits per second [bps]) use frequency modulation, medium speed modems (1200 to 4800 bps) use phase modulation, and the highest speed modems (9600 to 14,400 bps) use a combination of phase and amplitude modulation. These techniques allow the use of the voice band of the telephone network to transmit data. As seen, there is an overlap in the data rate of modems. An overlap also occurs between asynchronous and synchronous modems.

Transmission of digital data via the telephone network using analog signals will now be discussed. The frequency range of the telephone circuitry is 300 to 3300 hertz. This range is also referred to as the voice band. Modems, which are designed to produce analog signals in the voice band, are needed to convert the digital data to analog signals and vice versa.

When a carrier signal is modulated to transmit digital data, the terms "keying" and "shifting" are most often used, particularly with frequency and phase modulation. The term "amplitude modulation" is used, but instead of frequency modulation and phase modulation, the terms "frequency shift keying" (FSK) and "phase shift keying" (PSK) are used. Thus, the frequency or phase is shifted and the data is keyed onto the carrier signal. The term "amplitude shift keying" is used sometimes, but "amplitude modulation" is used more often.

## 8-2  Modulation Schemes

Modems for dial-up and leased line applications generally use one of the three modulation schemes to transmit data over telephone lines. They are

1. Frequency shift keying (FSK).

**2.** Quadrature phase shift keying (QPSK).

**3.** Quadrature amplitude modulation (QAM).

These schemes are based on the modulation principles previously discussed. FSK is the same as frequency modulation. QPSK is a modified version of phase modulation and QAM is a combination of phase and amplitude modulation. Before studying the circuitry contained within modems, FSK, QPSK, and QAM will be examined. In addition to these three modulation schemes, some high speed, limited distance modems (1200 to 19,200 bps) use other modulation techniques such as quadrature diphase modulation (QDM), differential diphase, and trellis coded modulation (TCM).

## 8-3   FSK Modems

FSK modems use frequency modulation. The transmitter sends an analog signal at a particular frequency to indicate a SPACE condition and it sends another at a different frequency to indicate a MARK condition. Modems that are designed for data rates not greater than 1200 bps use FSK. FSK can be used to transmit data either asynchronously or synchronously. Below 1200 bps, modems are designed only for asynchronous communication using FSK. At 1200 bps, modems are available for both asynchronous and synchronous communication using FSK.

Two of the most popular modems using FSK are the Bell 103 and the Bell 202 type modems. The international equivalents are the International Telegraph and Telephone Consultative Committee (CCITT) V.21 and the CCITT V.23, respectively. The international and Bell modems are not directly compatible, as will be discovered shortly.

Although the 103 is a low speed modem (0 to 300 bps) and its fundamental design has existed for many years, it is still available because of its low cost and because it is capable of full-duplex asynchronous communication on two-wire lines. It may be used on both dial-up and leased telephone networks. The Bell 202 type modem operates only in the half-duplex mode using a two-wire network. Therefore, if an application requires transmission at 1200 bps, full-duplex, using FSK, then a four-wire leased-line network is needed. The major disadvantage of FSK is the low data rate because only one bit per baud is transmitted. If QPSK is to be used (see Section 8-4), then a modem can be designed to transmit and receive at 1200 bps over a two-wire system.

### 8-3.1   Bell 103 Type Modems

There are a series of 103 type modems: 103, 101, 108, and 113. The most popular unit is the 103 model. This family of modems has many common features, the principal one being its full-duplex operation on either dial-up or leased two-wire telephone lines. Full-duplex operation is accomplished by dividing the telephone bandwidth into two channels—one channel for transmitting and the other for receiving. Both channels operate using FSK. Figure 8-2 shows the bandwidth of each channel. The lower band has a carrier (center frequency) of 1170 hertz. This

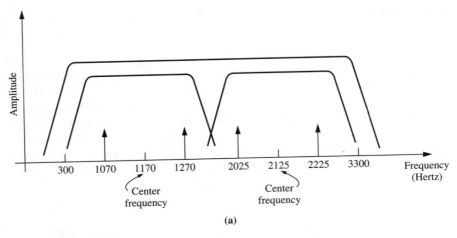

(a)

|  | | Originate End | Answer End |
|---|---|---|---|
| Transmit | SPACE | 1070 Hertz | 2025 Hertz |
| | MARK | 1270 Hertz | 2225 Hertz |
| Receive | SPACE | 2025 Hertz | 1070 Hertz |
| | MARK | 2225 Hertz | 1270 Hertz |

(b)

**Figure 8-2    (a) Bell 103 Channel Assignments and (b) Frequency Summary for the Bell 103 Modem**

frequency is varied ±100 hertz to generate a MARK and SPACE. In this band a MARK is 1170 + 100 hertz = 1270 hertz and a SPACE is 1170 − 100 hertz = 1070 hertz. In dial-up applications, the terms ''originate'' and ''answer'' are used. The unit that makes the call is called the **originate modem** and the other unit is called the **answer modem.** In the full-duplex system of Figure 8-2a, notice that the originate modem transmits data in the lower band and receives data in the upper band. The answering modem receives data using the lower band and transmits using the upper band. As an example, the originate modem transmits a SPACE condition as a 1070-hertz signal but receives a SPACE condition from the remote (answer) modem as a 2025-hertz signal. The answer modem transmits a SPACE as a 2025-hertz signal and receives a SPACE as a 1070-hertz signal. Figure 8-2b summarizes these points for the 103 type modem.

### 8-3.2  Dial-up Application

The Bell 103 modems are 300-baud asynchronous modems. These modems can be used at both ends of a switched network.

Assume that a call is dialed in the normal manner. When the answer tone is heard, the data/talk button is pressed. The modem at the calling end (now known as the originate modem) takes control of the line. A 103 type modem can be used with automatic calling units (ACU). Now when a call is made the modem automatically switches to the originate mode. In applications where calls always originate at a terminal and are always answered at the computer, the internal circuitry of the modem can be modified so that the transmitter, receiver, and filter networks do not have to switch from originate to answer. If calls are made to a computer, it is more convenient to have the incoming calls answered automatically. The auto answering capability is available in 103 type modems. However, not all 103 modems have auto answering capability. Those modems that do have this option automatically answer incoming calls whenever the RS-232 Data Terminal Ready line is asserted. After this modem receives an incoming ringing signal, it asserts its DCE Ready (also known as Data Set Ready) line if it has not already done so. After a short period of time (~200 ms), the answering modem sends a 2225-hertz MARK signal. This signal accomplishes two things: (1) it "tells" the originating modem that an answering modem has been reached and (2) it disables the communication channel's echo suppressor so full-duplex communication can occur.

When the originating modem receives the 2225-hertz signal, it sends out its own signal of 1270 hertz. After a wait of approximately 200 ms, the modem activates its CTS signal and DCD lines. These signals indicate to the DTE at the originating end that a communication link has been established and data can be sent and received.

### 8-3.3 Disconnect Procedure

A call may be terminated by a 103 type modem in one of the following ways:

1. Manually hang up at one end, which causes the other end to disconnect. This method uses the telephone network's dc holding current to cause the disconnect.

2. The carrier signal is lost for a time interval longer than 100 ms.

3. A DTE unit turns off its DTR line, thereby causing a loss of carrier.

4. Sending a break signal, which is a long sequence of SPACES without stop bits. The remote station disconnects after receiving the break signal, usually anywhere from several hundred milliseconds to 1.5 seconds.

5. Some modems are equipped with time out circuitry. This circuitry causes the modem to disconnect if it does not receive a carrier signal within a given number of seconds (typically 20 to 30 seconds) after a call is made. At the answer modem, the timer starts after a ringing signal is detected. At the originating modem, the timer begins after the modem's panel button is switched to the data mode.

### 8-3.4 Acoustic Couplers

A 103 modem can be used at the answer end of a telephone network and an **acoustic coupler** at the originate end. An acoustic coupler is a low speed modem that interfaces between DTE and a telephone. Similar to modems, acoustic couplers convert digital pulses into analog signals suitable for telephone transmission and vice versa. The telephone handset's mouthpiece is placed in the coupler's speaker cup and the handset's earpiece is placed in the coupler's microphone cup.

Although possible, acoustic couplers are not used at both ends of the communication link. A typical application is that of an individual in the field with portable equipment using an acoustic coupler to communicate with the home office. The DCE at the office would most likely be a hard-wired modem with auto answering capability as shown in Figure 8-3.

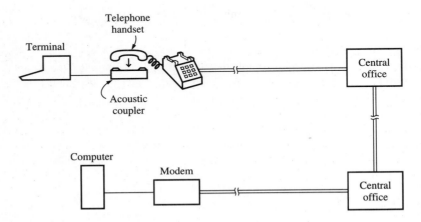

**Figure 8-3   An Acoustic Coupler in a Low Speed Modem which Allows any Telephone to be Used for Data Communications**

Acoustic couplers and modems perform similar functions, that is, they convert digital pulses to analog signals and vice versa. The difference is that a modem is connected directly to the telephone line and operates at a faster bit rate. Acoustic couplers are not connected directly to the telephone line and are suitable for portable equipment.

Acoustic couplers were introduced in the mid-1960s to solve the problem created by the telephone companies' refusal to allow equipment not manufactured by them to be directly connected to their lines; thus the need for a unit such as the acoustic coupler. Acoustic couplers solved problems over 25 years ago and are still used today with lap-top computers and portable diagnostic equipment.

### 8-3.5   CCITT V.21 Modems

The international standard CCITT V.21 modem also uses full-duplex operation over the telephone channel but it is incompatible with the 103 modem and has lower carrier frequencies; in addition, the MARK and SPACE frequencies are reversed. In the lower band, the center frequency is 1080 hertz and the MARK condition is sent as a 980-hertz signal (1080 − 100 hertz) and the SPACE condition is transmitted as a 1180-hertz signal (1080 + 100 hertz). In the upper band, the center frequency is 1750 and a MARK condition is transmitted as 1650 hertz (1750 − 100 hertz) and a SPACE condition is transmitted as 1850 hertz (1750 + 100 hertz). A V.21 modem is also limited to 200 baud, as opposed to 300 baud for the 103 type modems. Thus the same type of modem with the same options must be used at both ends of a communication link. **Note:** Modems come with many "strappable" options which must be set the same in both units to avoid major headaches.

### 8-3.6   Bell 202 and CCITT V.23 Modems

These modems are designed to transmit and receive data in half-duplex mode at a rate of 1200 bps using FSK. They have a primary and a secondary (backward) channel. The V.23 modem is a 600/1200 baud modem. The channel assignments are shown in Figure 8-4. Note that the channel assignments for a Bell 202 modem differ from a Bell 103 modem because the MARK condition is at a lower frequency (1200 hertz) than the SPACE condition (2100 hertz).

These modems have reverse channel capability. The Bell 202 uses amplitude shift keying, also called ON/OFF keying, at 387 hertz. A MARK condition is 387 hertz and a SPACE condition is 0 hertz. This provides a 5-bps reverse channel. Although some information can be transferred at this low bit rate, the reverse channel on the 202 modems is normally used to indicate that the remote station is still operating (circuit assurance). The V.23 modems have a 75-bps FSK reverse channel. Although slow, this channel's rate is fast enough to be used for transmitting information. Figure 8-4b,c shows that a MARK condition is 390 hertz and a SPACE condition is 450 hertz. Some nonstandard 202 type modems using a reverse channel of 75 bps or 150 bps may be encountered.

Although the Bell 202 modem primary channel is specified as 1200 bps, a good conditioned line may allow the transfer of data at a rate up to 1800 bps. Also, if the system transfers data at 1200 bps using 202 modems, you should be able to transfer data at 600 bps without any modifications.

### 8-4   QPSK Modems

Some modems that operate at 1200 bps, and all those that operate at data rates above 1200 bps, use modulation techniques that encode several data bits in a baud. One of these techniques is a modified version of phase modulation, QPSK. QPSK actually accomplishes two things that the simple phase modulation of Figure 8-1d does not. The first significant point is that two bits (called a dibit) are encoded into one baud (one time interval). The Bell 212 modem changes the phase angle of the carrier wave into one of four different phase angles. One phase angle is located in each of the four quadrants; hence the name quadrature phase shift keying. Each phase angle indicates a dibit combination. Figure 8-5 gives the dibit combinations along with the phase angles for a Bell 212 modem. The CCITT V.22 uses different phase angles for the dibits, also shown in Figure 8-5.

The second significant difference between QPSK and the basic phase modulation wave is the degree of phase angle shifts at the baud boundaries. In Figure

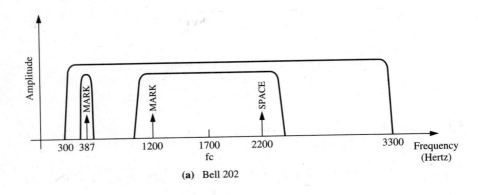

(a)  Bell 202

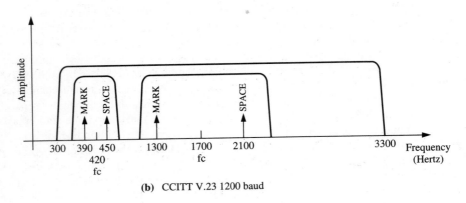

(b)  CCITT V.23 1200 baud

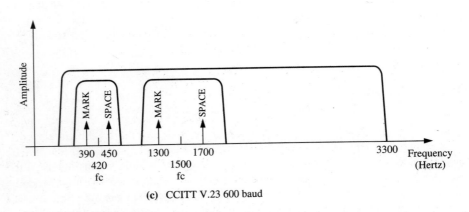

(c)  CCITT V.23 600 baud

Figure 8-4   Channel Assignments for the Bell 202 and CCITT V.23 Modem

| Dibit | Phase shift | |
| --- | --- | --- |
| | Bell 212 | CCITT V.22 |
| 0 0 | 45° | 0° |
| 0 1 | 135° | 90° |
| 1 1 | 225° | 180° |
| 1 0 | 315° | 270° |

**Figure 8-5** Phase Angle for Each Dibit Combination

8-1d, there was a phase shift of 180° for each logic state change. In QPSK, the phase shift for each new dibit combination is relative to the phase angle at the beginning of the preceding signal. This concept is known as differential. For example, if a dibit combination has a phase angle of 45° and the next dibit combination causes an additional +135°, then the carrier wave for the second dibit begins at 180° (45° + 135°).

To study how these phase shifts are calculated, begin with Figure 8-6 and the following procedures:

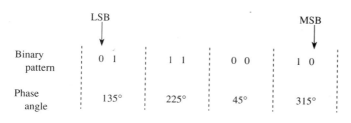

**Figure 8-6** An Example of Dividing a Binary Pattern to be Transmitted into Dibits and Assigning the Phase Angle to Each Pair. LSB, Least Significant Bit; MSB, Most Significant Bit

1. Divide the binary pattern that is to be transmitted into dibit combinations. This step is shown by the dashed lines in Figure 8-6. The least significant dibit combination is at the left and will be transmitted first.

2. Use Figure 8-6 and write down the phase shift for each dibit using Figure 8-5. For example, use the phase shifts for the 212 type modem. These phase shifts are in relation to the *beginning* phase angle of the preceding signal. To find the beginning phase angle of each dibit combination, start at the carrier signal which occurs before any data is sent.

   Assume that data at a rate of 2400 bps is to be sent. Using dibits, the baud rate is 1200. This type of modem has a carrier frequency of 1800 hertz, which results in 1.5 cycles (or 540°) of the carrier wave for each interval. Begin the analysis by drawing a carrier wave starting at 0° and ending at 540° (360° + 180°) later as shown in Figure 8-7. The first dibit 01 has a phase shift of 135°

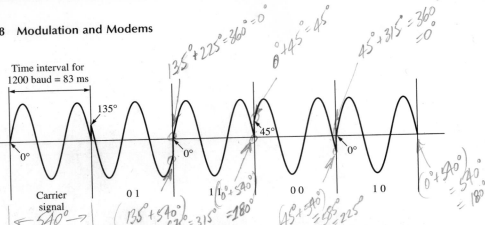

**Figure 8-7   An example of a QPSK Waveform for a 1200 Baud (2400 bps) Modem Using an 1800 Hertz Carrier Signal**

from the beginning phase of the carrier wave. Thus, the first dibit begins at 0° + 135° = 135° as shown in Figure 8-7. The ending phase angle of the first dibit is 135° + 540° = 675° = 315°. The second dibit 11 has a phase shift of 225° from the beginning phase of the first dibit. The wave for this dibit begins at 135° + 225° = 360° = 0° as shown in Figure 8-7. Figure 8-7 shows the waveform along with beginning phase angles for each dibit.

The rotating phaser and the sinusoidal waveform shown in Figure 8-8 are helpful for determining the beginning and ending phase angles for any dibit. If the beginning phase angle is known, enter the circle diagram at that point. The ending phase angle is 180° (which is the same as 540°) from the starting point. The sinusoidal waveform is a helpful aid in drawing the QPSK wave.

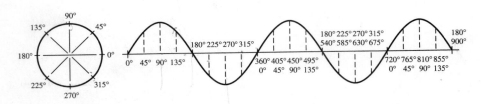

**Figure 8-8   Rotating Phaser and Sinusoidal Waveform Showing Different Phase Angles**

E X A M P L E   8 - 1
_____

From Figure 8-9, determine the binary pattern that is being transmitted. Assume that modems being used for the transmission and reception are the 212 type units.

**Solution**

From Figure 8-9 the carrier wave is a cosine wave. Compare the phase shift at each bit boundary with the phase shift from the preceding wave.

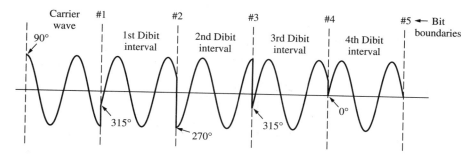

**Figure 8-9**  QPSK Waveform for Example 8-1

| Bit Boundary | Beginning Phase Shift of Previous Wave | Beginning Phase Shift at Bit Boundary | Positive Phase Shift Difference | Dibit |
|---|---|---|---|---|
| #1 | 90° | 315° | 225° | 11 |
| #2 | 315° | 270° | 315° | 10 |
| #3 | 270° | 315° | 45° | 00 |
| #4 | 315° | 0° or 360° | 45° | 00 |

Therefore the binary pattern is 11100000. **Note:** The phase shift difference is in the positive (or counter clockwise) direction when you use the phasor diagram in Figure 8-8.

## 8-4.1  QPSK Detection

One method of detecting the phase shift between QPSK signals is to compare the incoming wave with the previous wave. This is done by delaying the previous wave by one time interval and then comparing it with the new incoming wave in the next time interval. Figure 8-10 shows a block diagram of a circuit to detect QPSK signals using this method. The time delay for 1200 baud is 0.833 ms (1/1200 baud = 0.833 ms/baud).

To analyze this circuit, consider the waveform of Figure 8-11. The carrier wave is written as sin ωt and the first dibit combination as sin (ωt + θ). (For analysis purposes, assume the peak value is 1.) The time delay block delays the carrier and thus it reaches the multiplier blocks at the same time as the first dibit wave. From Figure 8-10, the input to multiplier #1 is sin (ωt + θ) and sin ωt. Using the trigonometric identity

$$\sin x \times \sin y = \frac{1}{2}[\cos(x - y) - \cos(x + y)] \tag{8-1}$$

the output of multiplier #1 yields

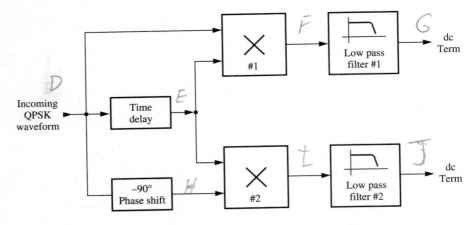

**Figure 8-10    Block Diagram of a QPSK Detection Circuit**

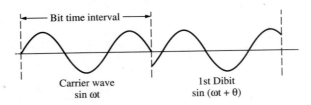

**Figure 8-11    A Carrier Wave and First Dibit Wave Used in the Analysis of Figure 8-10**

$$\sin(\omega t + \theta)\sin \omega t = \frac{1}{2}[\cos(\omega t + \theta - \omega t) - \cos(\omega t + \omega t + \theta)]$$

Combining terms yields

$$\sin(\omega t + \theta)\sin \omega t = \frac{1}{2}[\cos \theta - \cos(2\omega t + \theta)]$$

$$= \frac{1}{2}\cos \theta - \frac{1}{2}\cos(2\omega t + \theta) \qquad (8\text{-}2)$$

$$\underbrace{\phantom{\frac{1}{2}\cos\theta}}_{\text{dc term}} \quad \underbrace{\phantom{\frac{1}{2}\cos(2\omega t + \theta)}}_{\text{frequency term}}$$

The frequency term is removed by a low pass filter as shown in Figure 8-10. From multiplier #1, a positive dc term occurs for angles of 45° and 315°. A negative dc term occurs for angles of 135° and 225°. In order to distinguish one of the two possible answers in each group, a second multiplier chip is needed as shown in Figure 8-10. However, one of the inputs to this second multiplier chip first passes through a −90° phase shifter network. Using the trigonometric identity given in Equation (8-1), the output of multiplier #2 is

$$\sin(\omega t + \theta - 90°)\sin \omega t = \frac{1}{2}[\cos(\omega t + \theta - 90° - \omega t)$$

$$- \cos(\omega t + \theta - 90° + \omega t)] \quad (8\text{-}3)$$

$$= \frac{1}{2}\cos(\theta - 90°) - \frac{1}{2}\cos(2\omega t + \theta - 90°)$$

$$\underbrace{\phantom{= \frac{1}{2}\cos(\theta - 90°)}}_{\text{dc term}} \quad \underbrace{\phantom{\frac{1}{2}\cos(2\omega t + \theta - 90°)}}_{\text{frequency term}}$$

The frequency term is removed by a low pass filter, #2. This second multiplier unit produces a positive dc term for phase angles of 45° and 135° and a negative dc term for phase angles of 225° and 315°. These positive and negative dc voltages have to be converted to a dibit combination. Such a circuit is shown in Figure 8-12 along with a summary of each condition. The 311 is an integrated circuit (IC) comparator. The two devices are wired in a configuration called a *window detector*. Principles of comparator circuits are covered in the reference *Operational Amplifiers and Linear Integrated Circuits* and also in Chapter 9.

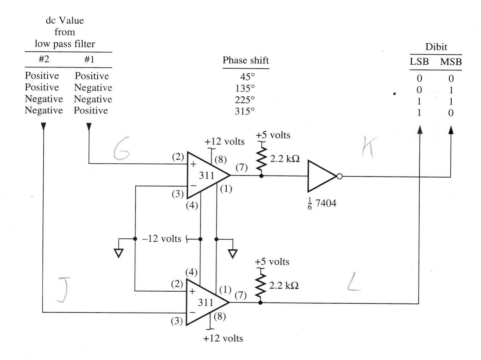

| dc Value from low pass filter | | Phase shift | Dibit | |
|---|---|---|---|---|
| #2 | #1 | | LSB | MSB |
| Positive | Positive | 45° | 0 | 0 |
| Positive | Negative | 135° | 0 | 1 |
| Negative | Negative | 225° | 1 | 1 |
| Negative | Positive | 315° | 1 | 0 |

**Figure 8-12  A Comparator Circuit that Converts the DC Values from the Low Pass Filter to a Dibit**

E X A M P L E   8 - 2
___

Refer to Figure 8-9 and show that the circuit of Figure 8-10 generates positive/positive dc terms for the third dibit time interval.

## Solution

For the third dibit time interval the incoming wave is $\sin(\omega t + 315°)$ and the preceding wave is $\sin(\omega t + 270°)$. Applying Equation (8-1), for multiplier #1 yields

$$\sin(\omega t + 315°) \sin(\omega t + 270°) = \frac{1}{2}[\cos(\omega t + 315° - \omega t - 270°)$$
$$- \cos(\omega t + 315° + \omega t + 270°)]$$
$$= \frac{1}{2}[\underbrace{\cos(45°)}_{\text{positive dc term}} - \cos(2\,\omega t + 585°)]$$

For multiplier #2, the incoming wave passes through the phase shift network yielding $\sin(\omega t + 315° - 90°) = \sin(\omega t + 225°)$. Now applying Equation (8-1), the following is obtained:

$$\sin(\omega t + 270°) \sin(\omega t + 225°) = \frac{1}{2}[\cos(\omega t + 270° - \omega t - 225°)$$
$$- \cos(\omega t + 270° + \omega t + 225°)]$$
$$= \frac{1}{2}[\underbrace{\cos(45°)}_{\text{positive dc term}} - \cos(2\,\omega t + 495°)]$$

From Figure 8-12 a positive dc term from each multiplier produces a 00 dibit.

## 8-5   QAM Modems

QAM is a combination of phase and amplitude modulation. The phase modulation techniques used are similar for the QPSK. That is, the phase shift of the new incoming wave is in relation to the phase angle of the preceding wave. Again, the term "quadrature" "tells" us that each of the four quadrants is to be used. As expected, the amplitude also varies. In QAM there are two carrier signals, a cosine wave and a sine wave. Since these waves are 90° apart, a resultant in any of the four quadrants can be obtained by varying the phase angle of the cosine and sine waves.

The Bell 209 modem was one of the earliest units in the United States to use QAM. These modems modulated a 1650-hertz carrier at a 2400-baud rate. Since 4 bits are encoded into each baud, the effective data rate is 9600 bps. Today, however, most 9600 bps modems conform to the CCITT V.29 standard. This standard specifies a carrier signal of 1700 hertz and 2400 baud. By encoding 4 bits per baud, this modem also operates at 9600 bps. However, it has fallback rates of 7200 and 4800 bps. In these modems, the data stream to be transmitted is scrambled and then divided into sets of 4 bits called **quadbits.** The first bit in each group of four determines the amplitude of the transmitted signal as shown in Figure 8-13a. The remaining 3 bits determine the phase shift as shown in Figure 8-13b.

| Phase Angle | $Q_1$ | Relative amplitude |
|---|---|---|
| 0°, 90°, 180°, 270° | 0 | 3 |
| | 1 | 5 |
| 45°, 135°, 225°, 315° | 0 | $\sqrt{2}$ |
| | 1 | $3\sqrt{2}$ |

(a)

| $Q_2$ | $Q_3$ | $Q_3$ | Phase angle |
|---|---|---|---|
| 0 | 0 | 1 | 0° |
| 0 | 0 | 0 | 45° |
| 0 | 1 | 0 | 90° |
| 0 | 1 | 1 | 135° |
| 1 | 1 | 1 | 180° |
| 1 | 1 | 0 | 225° |
| 1 | 0 | 0 | 270° |
| 1 | 0 | 1 | 315° |

(b)

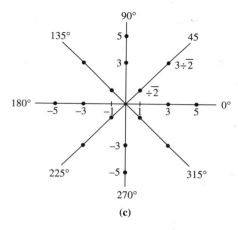

(c)

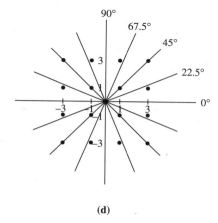

(d)

**Figure 8-13 QAM is a Combination of Phase and Amplitude Modulation to Encode 4 Bits. (a) The First Bit Designates the Amplitude. (b) Bits 2, 3, and 4 Encode the Phase Angle. (c) V.29 Constellation Pattern. (d) Bell 209 Constellation Pattern.**

A plot of these points is called a **constellation pattern.** The constellation pattern for V.29 is shown in Figure 8-13c. By varying the amplitude and phase shift, other constellation patterns are possible and Figure 8-13d shows the constellation for the 209 type modem. In order to transmit data, the originate and answer modems must have the same constellation pattern. The choice of the phase angles and amplitude variation represents a modem manufacturer's best guess as to the type and severity of different line errors that may be encountered. Since it is possible to design modems with a variety of phase angles and amplitude differences, standards are needed to allow vendors to interconnect equipment from different manufacturers. As has been previously stated, one standard that is most often used for 9600 bps modems is the CCITT V.29 specification.

## 8-6   Data and Fax Communication Standards

In Chapter 1 the need for standards in the field of data communications was discussed. The CCITT administers both data and fax standards in Europe and is also recognized as the worldwide administrator of standards. In the United States two committees of TIA (which was formerly part of Electronic Industries Association, EIA) handle the data and fax standards. These committees are TR-30 for data and TR-29 for fax. Both committees work closely with the corresponding CCITT committees. For transmitting data over telephone networks the international series code for modems is ''V'' and the ''T'' series is for terminal equipment including fax equipment. Some of the standards referred to in this text and others given below may be encountered.

### 8-6.1   Data Communication Standards

**V.21 and Bell 103**   These standards specify the requirements for a 300-bps modem using FSK modulation for full-duplex over a two-wire dial-up network. There are small differences between the Bell 103 and the international standard. Although the data rate (300 bps) is slow, asynchronous modems operating on a dial-up network have a large worldwide market and use one of these types of modems.

**V.22 and Bell 212A**   These standards specify the requirements for 1200 bps, full-duplex modem operating over a two-wire dial-up network. These modems use QPSK modulation techniques. By having a dibit combination in each quadrant, these modems operate at 600 baud (2 × 600 = 1200 bps). Although there are differences between the two standards, most 1200-bps modems support both standards.

**V.22 bis**   The term ''bis'' means ''second.'' This standard specifies the requirements for 2400-bps modems operating at full-duplex over a two-wire dial-up network. These modems transmit data at a rate of 600 baud but use QAM techniques to encode 4 data bits into each baud.

**V.23 and Bell 202**   The V.23 standard specifies a primary 1200-bps channel and a secondary (backward) 75-bps channel. Modems designed around this standard use FSK modulation. This type of modem is used more often in Europe than in the United States. Remember from Section 8-3.6 that the Bell 202 also has a 1200-bps primary channel but has only a 5-bps secondary channel. These modems have different MARK and SPACE frequencies and cannot be used together.

**V.27, V.27 bis, V.27 ter, and Bell 208**   The term ''ter'' stands for ''third.'' Modems designed around these standards operate at 4800 bps, half-duplex over two-wire or full-duplex over four-wires. The modems transmit at 1600 baud but use 3 bits and PSK techniques to achieve the 4800 bps. The V.27 and V.27 bis are both standards for leased circuits but the V.27 bis includes standards for automatic equalization. The V.27 ter standard is for switched telephone networks with a fallback data rate to 2400 bps. Each of the standards allows these modems to be designed with a secondary (backward) channel of 75 bps. V.27 ter is a requirement for fax transmission, which uses half-duplex two-wire networks. Bell 208 modems also operate at 4800 bps and use PSK but are not compatible with any of the V.27 modems because the constellation patterns are not the same.

**V.29 and Bell 209**  This standard is the specification for 9600-bps half-duplex communication over two wires and full-duplex communication over four wires on leased lines. The baud rate is 2400 and the modulation technique is QAM. Many fax transmissions use this standard although the fax equipment is normally designed with a fallback condition set to V.27 ter. Remember from Section 8-5 that Bell 209 modems have the same number of bits per second and use the same modulation technique but have a different constellation pattern than that of a V.29 modem.

**V.32**  This standard specifies the requirements for modems operating at 9600 bps, full-duplex over two wires. These modems operate at 2400 baud and use QAM techniques. Modems that operate using V.32 have a fallback operating mode to V.22. The fallback can be automatic when trying to operate on noisy lines that cannot handle 9600 bps.

**V.33**  This standard specifies the requirements for modems operating at 14,400 bps. Half-duplex communication takes place over two wires. Modems designed around this standard use trellis-coded modulation (TCM). Similar to QAM, TCM uses amplitude and phase to encode data. Unlike QAM, this modulation technique divides the data stream into 6-bit groups. The first 2 bits from each group are encoded with the first 2 encoded bits from the preceding group and the first 2 bits from the next group to generate a redundant bit. The new 7-bit group is mapped into a 128 ($2^7$) constellation pattern. TCM modems tolerate a poor signal-to-noise ratio better than other modems.

**V.42 and V.42 bis**  These units are classified as 9600-bps modems but they have additional features over other 9600-bps modems. The V.42 unit is an error-correcting type of modem. The V.42 bis uses data compression as well as error-correcting techniques of the V.42. Some modems use a data compression as high as 4 to 1. Under the best of conditions, this permits modem-to-modem data transfer rate of 38.4 k bps ($4 \times 9600$).

---

Table 8-1 summarizes many of the characteristics of modems that are available.

## 8-6.2  Fax Communication Standards

The CCITT standards for fax transmission are the T series.

---

**T.4**  This standard is pronounced "T dot 4." T.4 specifies fax transmission for 200 dots per inch (dpi), which is known as group 3. The T.4 standard refers to using V.27 ter or V.29 modems for such fax transmission, hence it is designed for dial-up (switched) networks.

**T.5**  T.5 specifies fax transmission for 400 dpi. It is designed to be used on switched networks, packet switched networks, and Integrated Service Digital Network (ISDN).

---

Table 8-1   Modem Characteristics

| Data Rate | Type of Modem | | Type of Transmission | Type of Modulation | Mode of Communication | Type of Line |
|---|---|---|---|---|---|---|
| | Bell | CCITT | | | | |
| 0–300 | 103 113 | V.21 | asynchronous | FSK | full | switched |
| 0–1200 | 202 | V.23 | asynchronous | FSK | half | switched |
| 1200 | 212A | V.22 | synchronous | QPSK | full | switched |
| 2400 | 201 B/C | | synchronous | QPSK | full | leased/switched |
| 2400 | | V.22 bis | synchronous | QAM | full | switched |
| 4800 | 208 | V.27 | synchronous | QPSK | full | leased |
| 9600 | 209 | V.29 | synchronous | QAM | full | leased |
| 9600 | | V.32 | synchronous | QAM | full | switched |
| 14.4k | | V.33 | synchronous | TCM | half | leased |

## 8-7   Modem ICs

ICs that contain most of the modem functions and conform to both U.S. and international standards are now available. The newest ICs have begun to include both data and fax functions. Some of the first modem chips were designed for 2400-bps and slower employed ICs with switch filters; the newest ICs, however, are designed using both analog and digital signal processing (DSP) techniques. This method allows for faster transmission of data and lower cost and smaller size per unit. The manufacturers have also reduced the power requirements, thereby making them suitable for portable and battery-powered equipment. Although the newest modem ICs can operate at 9600 bps, they are designed with fallback capabilities to 1200 bps and some devices even to 300 bps. This capability ensures that the newest ICs can be used with older equipment. Modem ICs that are designed with analog and DSP circuits use software algorithms to implement the modem functions that change from one modem to another. Therefore, to include the changes for different data rates requires only a change in an algorithm. If memory space is not a problem, the different data rates can easily be incorporated. This is easier than an all-analog modem because the analog circuit components have to be changed for each different data rate. Since fax modems use half-duplex communication techniques, they are simpler than full-duplex data modems.

## Summary

Modems are pieces of DCE and are used to convert digital signals to analog signals and vice versa. The analog signal is modulated to encode the digital data. There are three basic types of modulation: amplitude, frequency, and phase. Low speed modems use frequency modulation, FSK. Medium speed modems use phase modulation, the most common scheme known as QPSK. The highest speed modems use a combination of phase and amplitude modulation known as QAM.

The unit where the call is made is referred to as the originate modem. The unit at the other end is known as the answer modem. Modems can be used in dial-up and leased-line applications. There are also asynchronous and synchronous modems available. Low speed modems are for asynchronous applications and use FSK. There are medium speed modems for asynchronous and synchronous modems and they are designed using either FSK or QPSK. The highest speed modems are synchronous units. In some portable applications, acoustic couplers are used so that an ordinary handset can be used to transmit data.

The same type of modem has to be used at the originate and answer ends. Another way of stating this is that high speed synchronous modems must have the same constellation pattern. This topic is covered in Section 8-5.

Chapter 1 introduced the need for data communication standards. Section 8-6 introduced and compared modems designed around international standards and those designed around the Bell type standard. This section also described some of the standards for fax communication equipment.

## Problems

**\*8.1** For the following sinusoidal expressions of voltage, determine the peak amplitude, frequency in hertz, and phase angle in degrees.
  **(a)** $v = 3 \sin(4000t + \pi/4)$ volts
  **(b)** $v = 10 \sin(10,500t + \pi/3)$ volts
  **(c)** $v = -4 \sin(6280t - 1.57)$ volts.

**8.2** Would you expect to find low speed modems designed using FSK or PSK?

**\*8.3** Expand the following abbreviations:
  **(a)** QPSK
  **(b)** QAM
  **(c)** TCM
  **(d)** QDM

**8.4** Identify two low speed modems that use FSK.

**\*8.5** Can a Bell 202 type modem be used for full-duplex communication over a two-wire circuit?

**8.6** What name is used to describe the modem connected to the station that makes the call?

**\*8.7** For a Bell 103 type modem, what are the MARK and SPACE frequencies that the answer modem uses to transmit data?

**8.8** When a Bell 103 type modem is used for auto answering, does it send a

\* *See* Answers to Selected Problems.

MARK or a SPACE signal to the originating modem? What is the originating modem's reply?

**\*8.9** If a carrier signal greater than 100 ms occurs, would you expect a Bell 103 type modem to terminate the call?

**8.10** Why may it be necessary to use acoustic couplers?

**\*8.11** (a) Why can you not use a Bell 103 type modem at the originating end and a CCITT V.21 modem at the answer end? (b) Could you switch the modems and have the system work?

**8.12** Does the Bell 202 modem have a full secondary channel?

**\*8.13** Assign the phase angle to each dibit combination in the following binary stream:

LSB            MSB
1101101000011100

Use both standards.

**8.14** Plot the waveform for the first four dibit combinations of Problem 8.13 using the Bell 212 standard. The carrier signal is a sine wave of 1800 hertz and the data rate is 1200 baud.

**\*8.15** For the waveform in Figure 8-9 show that the dibit combination is (a) 10 in time interval #2 and (b) 00 in time interval #4.

**8.16** Assume that a manufacturer has a QAM modem with the following relative amplitudes and phase angles. Draw the corresponding constellation pattern.

| Phase angle | $Q_1$ | Relative amplitude |
|---|---|---|
| 22.5°, 157.5°, 202.5°, 337.5° | 0 | 2 |
| | 1 | 4 |
| 67.5°, 112.5°, 247.5°, 292.5° | 0 | 1 |
| | 1 | 3 |

| $Q_2$ | $Q_3$ | $Q_4$ | Phase angle |
|---|---|---|---|
| 0 | 0 | 1 | 22.5° |
| 0 | 0 | 0 | 67.5° |
| 0 | 1 | 0 | 112.5° |
| 0 | 1 | 1 | 157.5° |
| 1 | 1 | 1 | 202.5° |
| 1 | 1 | 0 | 247.5° |
| 1 | 0 | 0 | 292.5° |
| 1 | 0 | 1 | 337.5° |

**\*8.17** What do the terms (a) bis and (b) ter mean?

**8.18** For each of the international standards given in column A find the closest Bell equivalent from column B. (Some equivalent standards may be used more than once.)

| Column A | Column B |
|----------|----------|
| (1) V.23 | (a) Bell 212A |
| (2) V.27 | (b) Bell 203 |
| (3) V.21 | (c) Bell 209 |
| (4) V.29 | (d) Bell 202 |
| (5) V.22 | (e) Bell 208 |

# 9

# 300-Baud Modem Design

## OBJECTIVES

Upon completion of this chapter on 300-baud modem design, the student will be able to

- Describe the principles of operation and internal functions of a 300-baud modem using frequency shift keying (FSK).

- Know the frequency assignments for this type of modem.

- Determine whether a MARK or SPACE condition is being transmitted from the waveform on an oscilloscope.

- Analyze a modem's duplexer circuit.

- Understand why bandpass filters are needed and how they operate in a 300-baud modem.

- Use both an active filter using op amps and an integrated circuit (IC) switched capacitor filter.

- Design a threshold detector circuit and know why it is needed in a modem.

- Know the purpose of a limiter circuit and how to design it.

- Understand the types of distortion that can appear in the demodulator section of a modem,

- Describe the equipment called data access arrangement and know its function.

## Introduction

In Chapter 8, the fundamentals of modulation and modems used by data communication equipment (DCE) were examined. In this chapter, one of the modulation techniques, FSK, and the principles involved in the design of a 300-baud modem will be studied in detail. Figure 9-1 shows the block diagram of a data communication system. Remember from Chapter 1 that a modem is needed at both ends of the communication channel (telephone line). The end that establishes the link

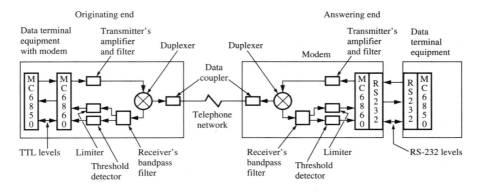

**Figure 9-1   A Data Communication System Using Modems. TTL, Transistor-Transistor Logic**

for data transmission is known as the originating modem; the other end is referred to as the answering modem. In Figures 9-1 and 9-2b the modem on the left has been chosen as the originating modem and the one on the right as the answering modem. In many computer systems, the modem either is built on a printed circuit board that plugs into a slot on the backplane (an add-on feature) or is an integral unit of the computer system. In either case, a serial interface such as the RS-232 is not required as shown at the originating end in Figure 9-1. However, in other systems, or in the same system at the other end where the modem may be separated from the data terminal equipment (DTE), a serial interface may be needed as shown at the answering end in Figure 9-1.

Since Chapters 5 to 7 dealt with serial interface standards, this chapter concentrates only on the modem. How the modem is connected into the system will determine if an interface standard is required. The devices covered in this chapter are the basic building blocks used to design 300-baud modems. As mentioned in Chapter 8, today's very large scale integration technology has allowed many of these blocks to be manufactured into a single-chip modem. However, the devices covered in this chapter are readily available, low in cost, easy to use in a laboratory experiment, and allow the study of fundamental principles in detail.

## 9-1   Frequency Assignments

As discussed in Chapter 1, the bandwidth of the telephone network is only 3000 hertz (from 300 to 3300 hertz). This limited bandwidth does restrict the data rate. However, it is still possible to have full-duplex operation even using FSK. But using this type of modulation, users are limited to slow speeds such as 300 bits per second (bps). For this application, the telephone's frequency range is divided into a lower and upper frequency channel as was shown in Figure 8-2a and repeated in Figure 9-2a. The originating modem transmits data on the lower channel and

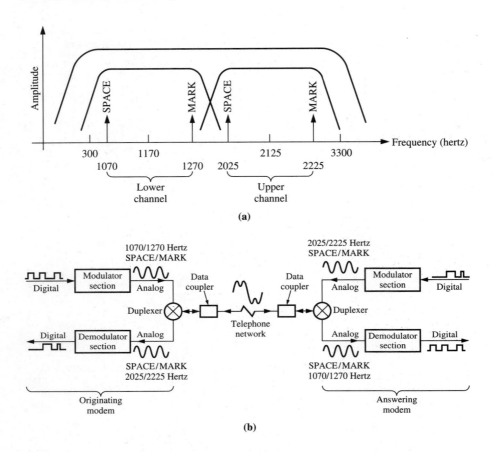

**Figure 9-2   (a) The Upper and Lower Frequency Bands for Full-Duplex Operation on a Telephone Network for a 300-Baud Modem. (b) Example of Analog and Digital Signals in Originating and Answering Modems. (c) Frequency Assignments.**

receives data on the upper channel. The answering modem transmits its data on the upper channel and receives data on the lower channel. This principle of dividing a frequency range into two or more subranges is known as **frequency multiplexing.** For Bell 103 type modems, the originating modem transmits a SPACE (logic 0) at a frequency of 1070 hertz and a MARK (logic 1) at a frequency of 1270 hertz.

This type of modem receives data from the answering modem at either 2025 hertz (SPACE condition, logic 0) or 2225 hertz (MARK condition, logic 1) (*see* Fig. 9-2b,c). Therefore, the modem's circuitry must be capable of keeping separate its transmit and received frequencies.

**Note:** The term "originating modem" refers to the DCE unit that established the link; the other end is known as the "answering modem." The terms do not mean that the originating modem is always transmitting and the answering modem is always receiving data.

## 9-2   Basic Principles of Operation

The MC6860 and the MC14412 have been designed and manufactured by Motorola as basic building blocks for slow speed (0 to 600 bps) modems. Modems can be designed for simplex, half-duplex, and full-duplex configurations. They can also be used in applications of originate only, answer only, or originate/answer. The auto answering and auto disconnect features are also included in the MC6860. Figure 9-1 shows the functional block diagram of a modem using the MC6860. Figure 9-3 shows the pin assignments and is a block diagram of the MC6860. The MC14412 is a CMOS device housed in only a 16-pin dual-in-line package. Although it has fewer functions than the MC6860, it is easy to use and can be used in a line-powered modem. The data sheet for the MC6850 is given in the Appendix. Both devices' modulator and demodulator sections are functional equivalents. Although the MC6860 will be discussed in this chapter, the operation of both devices will actually be shown.

As shown in Figure 9-1, the output of the MC6860's modulator is an input to a buffer/filter. The buffer is needed to isolate the modulator's low output impedance, which is less than 2 k$\Omega$ from the **duplexer.** A duplexer is an interface circuit between the modem and the communication channel. For applications used in this chapter, the communication channel is the telephone system. Section 9-3 describes how a duplexer operates. Although the buffer is required, the filter at the modulator's output is optional in some modems but is required in modems designed for full-duplex operation.

### 9-2.1   Modulator

The modulator circuitry of the MC6860 converts the incoming serial digital data on its transmit data line (pin 2) into an analog output signal. This output signal from the modulator appears on the transmit carrier line (pin 10) of the MC6860. The analog output signal is a digitally synthesized sine wave. Figure 9-4 shows such a sine wave as it would appear on an oscilloscope. The MC6860 uses FSK modulation. A logic 0 (SPACE condition) is the lower frequency and a logic 1 (MARK condition) is the higher frequency. The frequency that is generated depends not only on whether a MARK or SPACE is being transmitted but also on whether the originating or answering modem is sending the data. Figure 9-2c shows the four possible frequencies that can be generated by a modulator section.

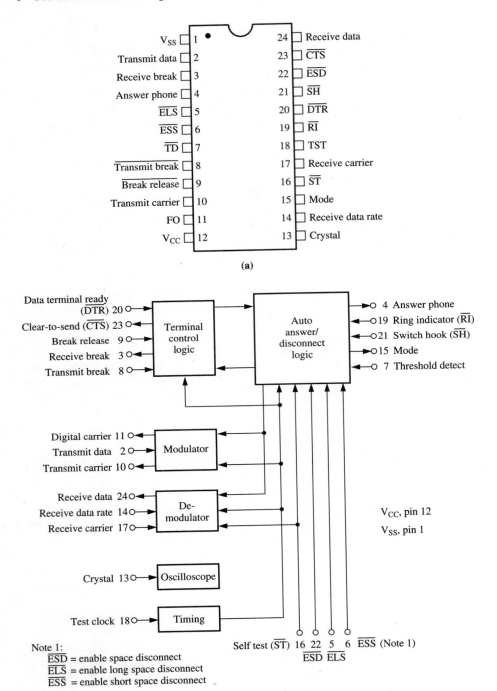

Figure 9-3    (a) Pin Assignments and (b) Internal Block Diagram of the
MC6860 *(Redrawn with permission of Motorola Incorporated, Austin, Texas)*

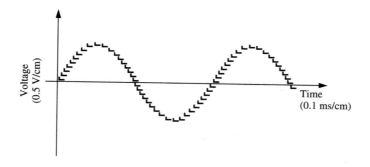

**Figure 9-4** A Digitally Synthesized Sine Wave Produced by the Modulator Section of the MC6860

The modulator's output voltage level is typically 0.35 Vrms into a 100-kΩ load. Since the input to the telephone network is 600 ohms, an interface circuit is needed. This interface circuit is the duplexer, as will be discussed in Section 9-3.

**E X A M P L E   9 - 1**

The time axis of an oscilloscope is set at 0.2 ms/cm. How many cycles of the digitally synthesized sine wave will appear on the screen for (a) an originating modem transmitting a SPACE condition, (b) an answering modem transmitting a MARK condition?

**Solution**

**(a)** From Figure 9-2c, a SPACE condition equals 1070 hertz.

$$T = \frac{1}{f} = \frac{1}{1070 \text{ hertz}} \simeq 0.935 \text{ ms/cycle}$$

Most scope screens have 10 centimeters in the horizontal axis. Therefore, the total time for the horizontal axis is

$$10 \text{ centimeters} \times 0.2 \text{ ms/cm} = 2 \text{ ms}$$

and the number of cycles is

$$\frac{2 \text{ ms}}{0.935 \text{ ms/cycle}} = 2.14 \text{ cycles}$$

**(b)**
$$T = \frac{1}{2225 \text{ hertz}} = 0.45 \text{ ms/cycle}$$

and thus

$$\frac{2 \text{ ms}}{0.45 \text{ ms/cycle}} = 4.44 \text{ cycles}$$

Consider that the waveform measured on an oscilloscope is similar to that in Figure 9-4. The scope's time base knob is set at 0.1 ms/cm and 1.27 cycles is displayed over 10 centimeters. Determine if the signal is generated from an originating or answering modem and whether a MARK or SPACE is being transmitted.

### Solution

Since the oscilloscope's time base generator is set at 0.1 ms/cm and 1.27 cycles are displayed over 10 centimeters, the frequency is

$$f = \frac{1.27 \text{ cycles}}{(10 \text{ centimeters})(0.1 \text{ ms/cm})} = 1270 \text{ hertz}$$

Thus, the signal is from an originating modem transmitting a MARK condition.

## 9-2.2  Demodulator

An incoming analog signal from the telephone line is filtered, amplified, and clipped before being received at pin 17 (Receive Carrier) of the MC6860. For the originating modem, the demodulator section receives the upper frequency pair (2025 and 2225 hertz). The demodulator of an answering modem receives the lower frequency pair (1070 and 1270 hertz). As might be expected, the component values of the receive filter for each type of modem are different. This topic is discussed in Section 9-4. The demodulator uses a technique called digital half-cycle detection to determine the difference between a MARK or SPACE frequency. As will be studied in Section 9-7, the limiter converts the analog signal to a digital waveform that is TTL compatible.

## 9-3  Duplexer

The duplexer is an interface circuit between the transmitting section, receiving section, and communication channel. In some applications the duplexer is connected between the transmitting and receiving sections to a data coupler, which is connected to the communication channel. These differences will be discussed in Section 9-9. The duplexer acts like a switch that connects the output of the modulating section to the communication channel and also allows the received modulated data to be connected to the receive filter and eventually to the demodulator section as shown in Figure 9-1.

Figure 9-5 shows that the duplexer is an op amp circuit wired as a basic differential amplifier. This circuit will be analyzed for three voltage signals:

1. Voltage $V_1$. This voltage is the signal transmitted on the telephone line. It is due to the modulator's output voltage, $V_m$ (see Fig. 9-5a).

2. Voltage $V_2$. This voltage is the voltage into the receiver's bandpass filter. It is due to the local modulator's voltage, $V_m$. Ideally, $V_2$ should be 0 volts. A

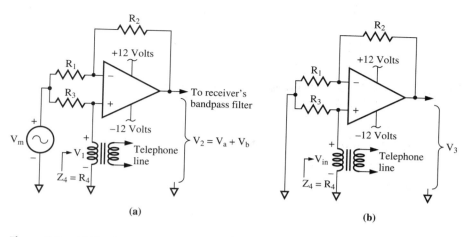

**Figure 9-5**   (a) Duplexer Circuit Showing $V_m$, $V_1$, and $V_2$. (b) Duplexer Circuit Showing $V_{in}$ and $V_3$

careful selection of resistor values can reduce $V_2$ approximately to 0 volts (*see* Fig. 9-5a).

3. Voltage $V_3$. This voltage is also an input voltage to the receiver's bandpass filter but it is due to the incoming voltage, $V_{in}$, from the telephone line (*see* Fig. 9-5b). Figure 9-5 will be analyzed for each condition.

**Voltage $V_1$**   From Figure 9-5a, the voltage $V_1$ is the voltage across $R_4$ and is equal to

$$V_1 = \frac{R_4}{R_3 + R_4} V_m \qquad (9\text{-}1a)$$

Since $R_4$ is the equivalent telephone line impedance, it equals 600 ohms. For maximum power transfer, $R_3$ must equal $R_4$ and Equation (9-1a) reduces to

$$V_1 = \frac{1}{2} V_m \qquad (9\text{-}1b)$$

**Voltage $V_2$**   To calculate $V_2$, superposition is used to determine that portion of $V_m$ at the op amp's output as a result of the gain generated by the noninverting amplifier, $V_a$, and that portion of $V_m$ at the op amp's output as a result of the gain generated by the inverting amplifier, $V_b$. As shown in Figure 9-5a

$$V_2 = V_a + V_b \qquad (9\text{-}2)$$

where

$$V_a = \underbrace{\frac{R_4}{R_3 + R_4} V_m}_{\substack{\text{Voltage at the} \\ (+) \text{ input}}} \underbrace{\left(1 + \frac{R_2}{R_1}\right)}_{\substack{\text{Gain of a non-} \\ \text{inverting amplifier}}} \qquad (9\text{-}3a)$$

if $R_4/(R_3 + R_4) = 1/2$, then Equation (9-3a) becomes

$$V_a = \left[\frac{1}{2}\right]\left[1 + \frac{R_2}{R_1}\right]V_m \tag{9-3b}$$

voltage $V_b$ is given by

$$V_b = -\left[\frac{R_2}{R_1}\right]V_m \tag{9-4}$$

Substituting Equations (9-3b) and (9-4) into Equation (9-2) produces

$$V_2 = \left[\frac{1}{2}\right]\left[1 + \frac{R_2}{R_1}\right]V_m - \left[\frac{R_2}{R_1}\right]V_m \tag{9-5a}$$

For the ideal condition $V_2 = 0$, therefore

$$0 = \left[\frac{1}{2}\right]\left[1 + \frac{R_2}{R_1}\right] - \frac{R_2}{R_1} \tag{9-5b}$$

which yields

$$R_1 = R_2 \tag{9-5c}$$

Thus, if $R_1 = R_2$ and $R_3 = R_4$, the local modulator's output voltage will be balanced by the duplexer and does not appear as an input voltage to the receiver's bandpass filter.

**Voltage $V_3$**   The modulating signal coming from a remote modem, $V_{in}$, is received across the equivalent impedance $R_4$. This signal "sees" the gain of a noninverting amplifier and thus the voltage at the duplexer's output as a result of $V_{in}$ is shown in Figure 9-5b as $V_3$ and is given by

$$V_3 = \left[1 + \frac{R_2}{R_1}\right]V_{in} \tag{9-6a}$$

if $R_1 = R_2$ then

$$V_3 = 2\,V_{in} \tag{9-6b}$$

E X A M P L E    9 - 3

For the duplexer circuit of Figure 9-5a, the resistor values are $R_1 = R_2 = 10\ \text{k}\Omega$ and $R_3 = R_4 = 600$ ohms. Calculate (a) $V_1$, (b) $V_2$, and (c) $V_3$. Assume $V_m = 0.35$ volts and $V_{in} = 0.20$ volts.

**Solution**

**(a)** Since $R_3 = R_4$, use Equation (9-1b)

$$V_1 = \frac{1}{2}(0.35\ \text{volts}) = 0.175\ \text{volts}$$

**(b)** With $R_1 = R_2$ and $R_3 = R_4$, then from Equation (9-5b)

$$V_2 = 0.$$

**(c)** Equation (9-6b) yields

$$V_3 = 2(0.2 \text{ volts}) = 0.4 \text{ volts}$$

---

E X A M P L E   9 - 4

Repeat Example 9-1 but with $R_2 = 10.5 \text{ k}\Omega$ and $R_3 = 560$ ohms.

**Solution**

**(a)** Applying Equation (9-1a)

$$V_1 = \frac{600}{560 + 600} (0.35 \text{ volts}) = 0.18 \text{ volts}$$

**(b)** Equation (9-3a) yields

$$V_a = \frac{600}{560 + 600} (0.35 \text{ volts}) \left[ 1 + \frac{10.5 \text{ k}}{10 \text{ k}} \right]$$

$$= 0.369 \text{ volts}$$

Equation (9-4) yields

$$V_b = -\frac{10.5 \text{ k}}{10 \text{ k}} (0.35 \text{ volts}) = -0.3675 \text{ volts}$$

Therefore,

$$V_2 = 0.369 \text{ volts} - 0.3675 \text{ volts} = 0.0015 \text{ volts}$$

**(c)** From Equation (9-6a)

$$V_3 = \left[ 1 + \frac{10.5 \text{ k}\Omega}{10 \text{ k}\Omega} \right] (0.2 \text{ volts}) = 0.41 \text{ volts}$$

Thus, if the resistors are carefully matched, $V_2$ can be reduced approximately to zero.

---

## 9-4  Bandpass Filters

Bandpass filters are an extremely important network within modems because they allow the transmitted or received signals to be accepted while rejecting interference signals. In answer only modems, the transmit filter is not required. In originate only modems, the receive filter is not required. Since many modems are designed to be used in either the originating or answering mode, both filters are included in the unit. In particular, if the modem is being used in a full-duplex application, then both filter networks are required and are discussed in this section. Modern filter networks are designed using active devices. In the recent past, several op amp stages have been used to design the filters and such circuits in units will be found in the field. Newer units are designed using IC filter networks. Both types will be studied for a full-duplex 300-baud modem application.

### 9-4.1  Discrete Op Amp Filter Stages

In the originating modem, the receive filter must pass the received frequencies from the remote station of 2025 and 2225 hertz but reject its local transmit frequencies of 1070 and 1270 hertz. In the answering modem, the receive filter must pass the incoming frequencies of 1070 and 1270 hertz and reject its local transmit frequencies of 2025 and 2225 hertz.

During full-duplex operation, the modulator within the originating modem generates second harmonic frequencies in the pass band of the received signals (2 × 1070 = 2140 hertz). Thus, the filter in the originating modem must be capable of rejecting its local carrier signal to an acceptable level usually less than −70 dB.

The design of the filter's bandwidth depends on the characteristics of the expected signal to be passed. Low speed modems operating in the full-duplex mode use the modulation technique of FSK. In this application, received data can be recovered by detecting the carrier signal and the first sidebands. For example, with a received data rate of 300 bps and an alternate MARK-SPACE combination, the first sidebands occur at ±150 hertz. Therefore, a bandwidth of 300 hertz is needed in the filter section. If the filter is able to pass this combination, it is capable of passing all other MARK-SPACE combinations at 300 bps.

Bessel, Butterworth, and Chebyshev are three types of filters commonly used in electronic systems. Each has advantages and disadvantages. Of the three, the Chebyshev filter has the steepest roll-off. However, it does have ripple in the pass band as shown in Figure 9-6. Since the ripple voltage is small and does not restrict the limiter and threshold detector from sensing the received signal, the Chebyshev filter is a good choice. However, a filter's ability to pass and reject certain fre-

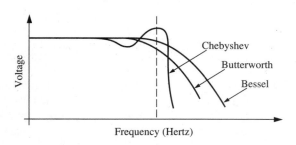

**Figure 9-6**  **Comparison of Voltage Versus Frequency for Three Types of Filters**

quencies is not the only criterion for choosing a particular type of filter. Another filter characteristic is its phase linearity. All filters change the phase angle of an incoming wave and, as frequency varies, the phase angle also varies. In some applications, a phase angle change is not a major concern. In modem design, phase linearity is important because all frequencies that pass through the filter should be delayed equally. Otherwise, the signals may be out of phase and the data will not be detected correctly. Although the Chebyshev filter does not have the best phase linearity, it is adequate for modem applications. The basic filter building block is shown in Figure 9-7a. This one stage does not provide a steep enough roll-off. For the transmit filter, two stages are usually required and for the receive filter either three or four stages are required. Figure 9-7b shows the interconnection of a three-stage receive filter. The component values depend on whether the receive filter is in the originate modem or in the answer modem. Figure 9-7c gives the values for each condition. However, modems that can be switched from originate to answer or vice versa are known as answer/originate modems and require circuitry to change some of the component values.

## 9-4.2 Filter Networks for Answer/Originate Modems

Answer and originate modems require different component values to design the bandpass filter for the different frequency ranges. It is easier to keep the capacitor values fixed and change resistors. Therefore, if a modem that can be used either for originate or answer is to be designed, then the ability to switch in and out resistors must exist. In addition, if the unit is designed to have auto answering capability then these resistor values must be changed automatically. As the following design shows, only four resistors have to be changed in the three-stage filter of Figure 9-7b. They are $R_2$, $R_5$, $R_6$, and $R_8$. Although the other resistor values for an originate and answer modem are not equal, they are close enough to build the filter network using their average value. Figure 9-8a lists the average values for the nonswitched resistors. Figure 9-8b lists the actual change in value for resistors $R_2$, $R_5$, $R_6$, and $R_8$. Figure 9-8c shows the bandpass filter built using the average values for the nonswitched resistors and manual switches to show how $R_2$, $R_5$, $R_6$, and $R_8$ can be changed. In an answer modem, the switches are open and total resistance in each branch is the sum of the two resistors $R_a$ and $R_b$. In an originate modem, the switches are closed and the resistance in each branch is decreased to the values given in Figure 9-8b.

Bipolar transistors such as 2N3904s provide low cost switches to short out $R_{2b}$, $R_{5b}$, and $R_{8b}$. An n-channel junction field effect transistor (JFET) is a better choice than a bipolar transistor as a semiconductor switch across $R_{6b}$. This is because $R_{6b}$ is in the feedback loop of an op amp and a high off resistance is needed so as to minimize the effect on the filter characteristics. Another choice for either type of switch is a CMOS analog switch such as a Siliconix DC412. This device contains four switches in a 16-pin dual-in-line package. Their ON resistance is less than 25 ohms and when the switch is open only nanoamperes of current flow. Therefore, this one device contains the four switches needed for Figure 9-8c.

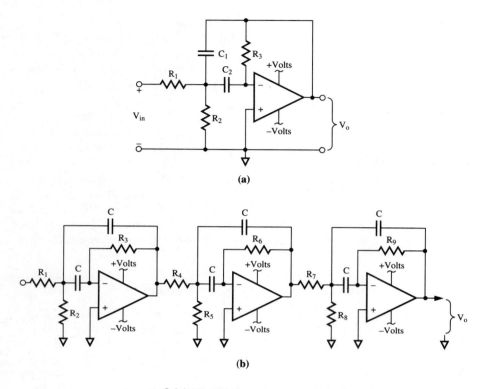

(a)

(b)

| | Originating Modem | Answering Modem |
|---|---|---|
| | 2025–2225 Hertz | 1070–1270 Hertz |
| $R_1$ | 24.26 KΩ | 23.89 KΩ |
| $R_2$ | 199.76 Ω | 632.2 Ω |
| $R_3$ | 217.26 KΩ | 211.7 KΩ |
| $R_4$ | 29.85 KΩ | 34.28 KΩ |
| $R_5$ | 242.36 Ω | 900.5 Ω |
| $R_6$ | 267.23 KΩ | 303.75 KΩ |
| $R_7$ | 13.88 KΩ | 14.24 KΩ |
| $R_8$ | 458.85 Ω | 1676.9 Ω |
| $R_9$ | 122.91 KΩ | 125.72 KΩ |

(c)

**Figure 9-7**   **(a) Single-Stage Bandpass Filter, (b) Three-Stage Bandpass Filter, and (c) Component Values for a Three-Stage Chebyshev Filter** *(Courtesy of Motorola Inc., Austin, Texas)*

The base of each bipolar transistor, the gate of the JFET, or the control pin of a CMOS switch is connected to circuitry that is controlled by the MC6860's mode control pin (pin 15). When the mode control line goes low, it indicates the unit is being used as an answer modem and the switches are open. A high condition on pin 15 indicates the modem is being used in the originate mode and the switches

| | Average value | | | Originate modem $R_a$ | Answer modem $R_a + R_b$ | Difference $R_b$ |
|---|---|---|---|---|---|---|
| $R_1$ | 24.1 K | | $R_2$ | 200 | 632 | 432 |
| $R_3$ | 214.5 K | | $R_5$ | 242 | 900 | 658 |
| $R_4$ | 32.1 K | | $R_6$ | 267K | 304K | 36K |
| $R_7$ | 14.1 K | | $R_8$ | 459 | 1677 | 1218 |
| $R_9$ | 124.3 K | | | | | |

(a)

(b)

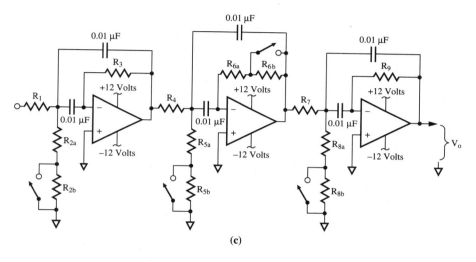

(c)

**Figure 9-8** **(a) Nonswitched Resistor Values. (b) Switched Resistor Values. (c) Three-Stage Bandpass Filter for an Answer/Originate Modem** *(Courtesy of Motorola, Inc.)*

are closed. Therefore, the MC6860 switches the modem from answer to originate and vice versa.

In either type of modem, the signal that passes through the received bandpass filter is applied to the limiter and threshold detector circuitry. Both of these circuits use a comparator IC as the basic building block. Principles of comparator circuits are covered in the next section but first the topic of filter networks used in modem design will be continued.

### 9-4.3 IC Modem Filters

Manufacturers have available ICs that house the bandpass filters for both the transmit and receive sides as well as an amplifier and buffer for the transmitting side. In addition to this circuitry, the IC package may contain an additional op amp so that the duplexer circuit can be designed. An IC that includes all these features is the MC145440 and is known as the 300-baud bandpass switched capacitor filter for Bell 103 type modems. A similar device for the International

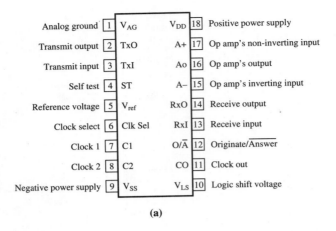

**(a)**

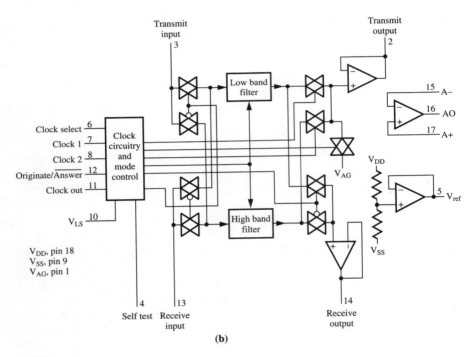

**(b)**

**Figure 9-9   (a) Pin Assignments, (b) Block Diagram, and (c) Frequency Response Plot for the MC145440 300-Baud Modem Switched Capacitor Filter** *(Courtesy of Motorola, Inc.)*

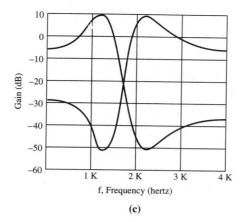

f, Frequency (hertz)

(c)

**Figure 9-9**   (continued)

Telegraph and Telephone Consultative Committee (CCITT) V.21 is the MC145441. Both devices are manufactured by Motorola. Figure 9-9 shows the pin assignments, internal block diagram, and frequency response curves for both the high and low pass filters.

The logic state applied to the originate/answer (O/$\overline{\text{A}}$) pin selects the mode of the device. A logic 1 selects the originate mode and the low pass filter is switched into the transmit path and the high pass filter is switched into the receive path. A logic 0 selects the answer mode. Now the low pass filter is switched into the receive path and the high pass filter is switched into the transmit path.

There are two pins on the MC145440 associated with the transmit data path—TxI and TxO. The TxI pin (transmit input—pin 3) receives the modulated analog data from the modem IC such as the MC6860 (pin 10) or from the MC14412 (pin 9). The signals received on the TxI pin are directed either to the low or high pass filter depending on the logic state of the O/$\overline{\text{A}}$ pin. The output on the TxO pin (transmit output—pin 2) is an amplified signal from the transmit amplifier and is the input signal ($V_m$ in Figure 9-5a) to the duplexer.

There are two pins associated with the receive data path; they are RxI (receive input—pin 13) and RxO (receive output—pin 14). The RxI pin is connected to the duplexer's output. If the additional op amp within the MC145440 is used for the duplexer, pin 13 is wired to pin 16, AO (op amp output). The analog signal that is received on the RxI pin is routed to either the low or high pass filters depending on the logic state at the O/$\overline{\text{A}}$ pin. The analog signal that passes through the receive bandpass filter, either low or high band, is the signal at the RxO pin. This signal is capacitively coupled to the limited and threshold detectors. The capacitor blocks any dc offset from the receive filter. The MC145440 is a self-contained and easy to use device using switched capacitor filter design, and the same principles are in many of the newest single-chip modems.

## 9-5  Comparators

A comparator circuit compares a signal voltage at one input with a reference voltage at the other input. The output voltage of the comparator indicates whether the signal voltage is more or less positive than the reference voltage. Many general purpose op amps are not suitable for comparator applications because the op amp's output voltage does not change fast enough with respect to time (the slew rate is too slow). Also the op amp's output voltages are fixed by its saturation voltages, $+V_{sat}$ and $-V_{sat}$, which are typically $\pm13$ volts. Since these voltages greatly exceed the TTL levels of the MC6860, a general purpose op amp is not suitable for this application. However, the 311 comparator is designed for voltage-level-detection applications, has a fast slew rate, and can be wired so that its output voltage switches between $+5$ volts and ground, making this device ideal for this modem application.

Figure 9-10a shows the basic 311 comparator. TTL output voltage levels are obtained by connecting pin 7 to $+5$ volts ($V^{++} = +5$ volts) via a 2-k$\Omega$ resistor and pin 1 to ground. The output voltage, $V_O$, is measured between the comparator's output pin (pin 7) and ground as shown.

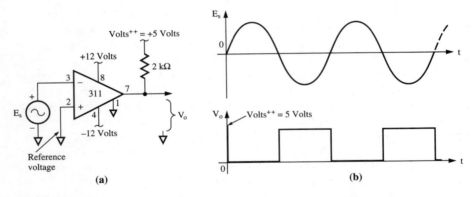

**(a)**                                    **(b)**

**Figure 9-10   (a) Basic Comparator Circuit and (b) Input and Output Voltage Waveforms for a Zero-Crossing Detector**

When the comparator's ($+$) input pin 2 is more positive than its ($-$) input pin 3, $V_O$ equals $V^{++}$. When the voltage at the ($+$) input is less than the voltage at the ($-$) input, the 311's output voltage equals 0V. Although voltage $V^{++}$ can range up to 40 volts more positive than the $-V$ supply voltage, for our application $V^{++}$ is set at $+5$ volts because of the need to interface between the analog output voltage from the bandpass filter and the TTL levels required at input pins of the MC6860. The reference voltage may be either positive, negative, or zero. Although the reference voltage in Figure 9-10a is applied to the ($+$) input, there are some applications in which it is applied to the ($-$) input. Figure 9-10b shows a sinusoidal input voltage and the corresponding output voltage. A 0V reference is applied to the ($+$) input. The limiter circuit uses a 0V reference while the threshold detector has a positive reference voltage. Although positive feedback can be added to make the comparator circuit less susceptible to noise, for this application high frequency signals are filtered out by the bandpass filter and therefore positive feedback should not be needed.

## 9-6   Threshold Detector

The purpose of the threshold detector is to determine if the signal from the bandpass filter is at an acceptable level. As shown in Figure 9-11, a threshold detector is a comparator circuit with a positive reference voltage at the (+) input. This voltage sets the minimum detectable level. If the output voltage from the bandpass filter is below this minimum level, the comparator's output goes high, indicating the received signal is unacceptable, and the MC6860 will stop demodulating. When the received signal coming through the filter is above the minimum level, the comparator's output goes low, indicating an acceptable signal. The minimum level is set by $R_1$ and $R_2$ and is given by

$$V_{min} = \frac{R_2}{R_1 + R_2}(+V) \tag{9-7}$$

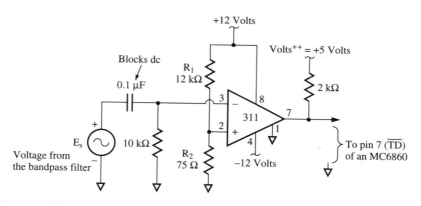

**Figure 9-11**   **Threshold Detector Circuit**

E  X  A  M  P  L  E     9 - 5

Calculate the minimum threshold voltage if $R_1 = 12$ k$\Omega$, $R_2 = 75$ ohms, and $+V = +12$ volts. Draw the output voltage of the detector for a received MARK signal at an originate modem. Assume $E_s = 250$ mV peak.

**Solution**

**(a)** From Equation (9-3)

$$V_{min} = \frac{75 \text{ ohms}}{12,075 \text{ ohms}}(12 \text{ volts}) = 74.5 \text{ mV}$$

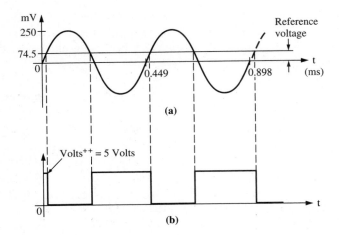

**Figure 9-12    Waveforms for Example 9-5**

**(b)** Figure 9-12a shows two cycles of a 2225-hertz sine wave that is a received MARK signal at the originate modem. Superimposed on Figure 9-12a is the reference voltage. Figure 9-12b shows the output waveform of the threshold detector, which is TTL compatible.

---

The output voltage of the threshold detector circuit is applied to the threshold detect (TD) pin (pin 7) of the MC6860. The MC6860 requires that the $\overline{TD}$ input be low for 20 μs at least once every 32 ms to maintain normal operation. This condition is easily met as long as the received signal is "strong" enough. An insufficient signal indicates a loss of carrier or modulated data from the remote station. If the $\overline{TD}$ line goes high for 51 ms or longer, the MC6860 brings the Clear-to-Send line high.

## 9-7   Limiter

The purpose of the limiter is to produce equal half-cycle periods. Each half-cycle is measured in reference to a time base to determine if a MARK or SPACE is being received. The output of the limiter must be symmetrical; otherwise errors will be produced in the demodulating process. The basic comparator circuit with a zero reference voltage as shown in Figure 9-13 is a limiter circuit. The coupling capacitor blocks any dc bias current coming from the bandpass filter. The limiter's output is applied to the receive carrier pin (pin 17) of the MC6860.

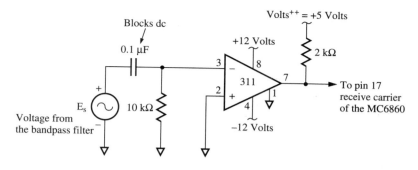

**Figure 9-13**  Limiter Circuit

E  X  A  M  P  L  E    9 - 6

Consider that an originate modem receives a MARK and then a SPACE signal at 300 bps. Draw the input and output voltage waveforms for the limiter circuit.

**Solution**

The time interval for each MARK and SPACE condition is found by Equation (3-2). For 300 bps, this equation yields

$$t_b = \frac{1}{300 \text{ bps}} = 3.33 \text{ ms}$$

and is shown in Figure 9-14a. From Figure 9-2c, an originate modem receives a MARK condition at 2225 hertz and a SPACE condition at 2025 hertz. The reciprocal of each frequency yields the period of wave.

$$T_M = \frac{1}{2225 \text{ hertz}} = 0.449 \text{ ms}$$

$$T_S = \frac{1}{2025 \text{ hertz}} = 0.494 \text{ ms}$$

For the MARK condition, there are 7.4 cycles (3.33 ms/0.449 ms) in one bit time and 6.7 cycles (3.33 ms/0.494 ms) for the SPACE condition as shown in Figure 9-14b.

The output of the limiter is shown in Figure 9-14c.

During the time interval when a MARK condition is being received, the pulse width from the limiter is 0.2245 ms (224.5 μs). The pulse width increases to 0.247 ms (247 μs) when a SPACE condition is being received. Both of these times are shown in Figure 9-14c. The average of these times is

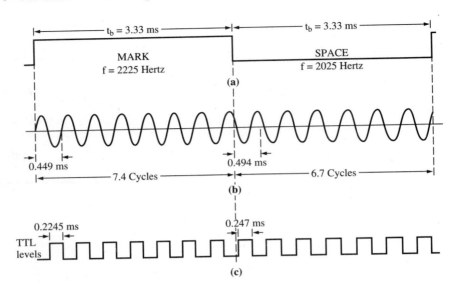

**Figure 9-14** **(a) Input MARK/SPACE Conditions to the Modulating Section for Example 9-6. (b) Input FSK Signal to the Limiter Circuit at the Originate Modem. (c) Output Waveform of the Limiter**

$$\frac{224.5 \ \mu s + 247 \ \mu s}{2} = 235.7 \ \mu s$$

The MC6860 uses this average time to demodulate the pulse wave coming from the limiter. This average time interval can easily be measured by digital counting circuits. A time interval less than 235 μs indicates a MARK condition is being received. If the time interval of an input pulse is greater than 235 μs, a SPACE condition is being received.

In an answer modem the received frequencies for the MARK and SPACE conditions are 1270 and 1070 hertz. The periods of these frequencies are 787.4 μs and 934.6 μs, respectively, and the corresponding pulse widths from a limiter are 393.7 μs and 467.3 μs. Therefore, the average time interval for an answer modem is 430 μs. Time intervals less than the average are demodulated as a MARK while time intervals greater than the average time interval indicate a SPACE.

## 9-8   Demodulator Distortion

The demodulator of the MC6860, and similar devices, uses half-cycle detection techniques to determine the presence of a MARK or SPACE condition. This technique leads to two inherent types of distortion, phase jitter and bias distortion.

## 9-8.1    Phase Jitter

In general, the term "phase jitter" describes a shift in phase for analog signals caused by power and/or communication equipment. This term, or simply jitter, is also used to describe the time difference between the ideal bit boundary and the actual bit boundary at the output of a demodulator (*see* Fig. 9-15a). Since demodulators similar to those used in the MC6860 use half-cycle measurement techniques, small errors can occur between MARK to SPACE and SPACE to MARK conditions. These errors can cause the bit intervals to vary slightly. View the condition on an oscilloscope and notice the lighter trace near the bit boundaries indicating that the transitions are not occurring at the same place each time (*see* Fig. 9-15b). Although jitter and noise are caused by different conditions, it is difficult to separate the effect of each at the output. Hence jitter may be described or identified as noise on the data output.

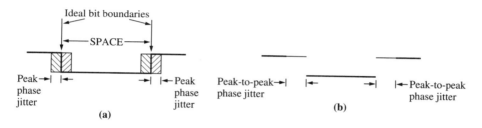

**Figure 9-15**    (a) Peak Phase Jitter at the Demodulator's Output. (b) An Oscilloscope Waveform Showing a Light Trace Indicating the Peak-to-Peak Phase Jitter

For the MC6860, the peak jitter is approximated by

$$\phi_J \simeq \frac{1/4 \text{ bit rate}}{\text{frequency}} \times 100\% \tag{9-8}$$

From Equation (9-8), a given bit rate phase jitter is indirectly proportional to frequency. Thus, the maximum phase jitter will occur during a SPACE condition.

**E  X  A  M  P  L  E      9 - 7**

(a) What is the maximum expected phase jitter in percent for a 300-baud answer modem? (b) How much time does this correspond to?

**Solution**

(a) For an answer modem the incoming SPACE frequency from an originating modem is 1070 hertz. Using Equation (9-8) yields

$$\phi_J \simeq \frac{1/4 \, (300)}{1070} \times 100\% = 7\%$$

**(b)** The peak phase jitter time is obtained by multiplying $\phi_J$ times the bit time. Bit time for 300 baud is 3.33 ms, thus

$$t_J = (0.07)(3.33 \text{ ms}) = 0.233 \text{ ms}$$

This time indicates that the MARK/SPACE transitions will occur within 0.233 ms of the ideal transition ignoring bias distortion.

## 9-8.2  Bias Distortion

The principles of bias distortion were introduced in Chapter 3. There are two types: marking and space bias distortion. The half-cycle demodulation process has an inherent marking bias distortion. That is, the interval for a MARK condition is greater than the interval for a SPACE condition. The percent of bias distortion for this type of demodulator is approximated by

$$\text{Bias distortion } \% \simeq \frac{T_S - T_M}{2t_b} \tag{9-9}$$

where $T_S$ and $T_M$ are the reciprocals of the SPACE and MARK frequencies, respectively, and $t_b$ is the bit time. As shown by Equation (9-9), bias distortion is given with respect to the bit time.

### E X A M P L E    9 - 8

What is the percent of bias distortion for a 300-baud answer modem?

**Solution**

The MARK and SPACE frequencies received at an answer modem are given in Figure 9-2c. Thus

$$T_S = \frac{1}{1070 \text{ hertz}} = 934.5 \text{ } \mu s$$

and

$$T_M = \frac{1}{1270 \text{ hertz}} = 787.4 \text{ } \mu s$$

From Equation (3-2)

$$t_b = \frac{1}{300 \text{ bps}} = 3.33 \text{ ms}$$

Applying Equation (9-9)

$$\text{Bias distortion } \% = \frac{(934.4 - 787.4)\mu s}{2(3.33 \text{ ms})} = 2.2\%$$

This percent means that the MARK condition is 2.2% greater than the ideal bit time of 3.33 ms.

### 9-8.3   Total Distortion

The maximum (or worst possible) percent distortion for the demodulator section is the percent of phase jitter plus the percent of bias distortion.

E X A M P L E   9 - 9

What is (a) the maximum total distortion and (b) the actual distortion time for a received signal at a 300-baud answer modem?

**Solution**

(a) From Example 9-7, the phase jitter is 7% and from Example 9-8 the bias distortion is 2.2%. Hence the maximum distortion could be

$$\text{Maximum distortion \%} = 7\% + 2.2\% = 9.2\%$$

(b) For a 300-baud modem $t_b = 3.33$ ms and the distortion time is

$$\text{Distortion time} = 9.2\% \times 3.33 \text{ ms} \simeq 0.31 \text{ ms}$$

This time indicates that MARK/SPACE transitions could occur with 0.31 ms of the ideal transitions.

## 9-9   Data Access Arrangement

All equipment that is to be connected to the telephone network (including modems), which was manufactured after June 1, 1977, must be registered with the Federal Communications Commission (FCC). This FCC regulation ensures that the equipment (such as new modem designs) will not damage any part of the telephone system. Prior to this FCC regulation, modems not manufactured by the telephone company had to be connected to a unit known as a **data access arrangement** (DAA). DAAs protected the telephone network from DCE manufactured by companies other than the telephone company. It is possible that the reader may encounter DAA units or at least the term. There are three types: a manual type, CDT, and two automatic types, CBS and CBT. Most of the time only the automatic types are mentioned. The manual type requires a telephone at both ends of the communication channel so that all calls are manually called and answered.

The CBS type unit uses RS-232 control signals; thus, it is referred to as a voltage type. The CBT type unit uses relay coils and hence is known as a contact closure type. The CBS and CBT units are also referred to as data couplers. For more information on these units refer to Bell System Data Communications: Technical Reference, *Data Couplers CBS and CBT for Automatic Terminals,* PUB 41802, August 1970, PUB 41802A, March 1971. Remember, however, that the modems today are registered units and can be connected directly to the communication channel and do not have to be connected to a DAA unit.

## Summary

Chapter 8 introduced the principles of modulation and modems. This chapter covered the parts that are needed in a low speed (300-baud) modem using FSK. Today's VLSI technology has incorporated many of these individual functions into one or a small set of ICs for both medium and high speed modems. The chips introduced in this chapter allow us to study the fundamentals.

The modulator circuitry in an FSK modem converts the digital serial data into a synthesized analog signal. This analog signal may have to be amplified and filtered to remove any harmonic frequencies so they are not "picked-up" by the local receiver's circuitry.

An incoming analog signal from the telephone line is filtered, amplified, and clipped before being received by the demodulator. The interface circuit connected between a modem's modulating section, demodulating section, and the telephone line circuitry is called a duplexer. If designed properly, a duplexer also eliminates the transmitter's analog signal from entering the receive circuitry of the same modem. This design is shown in Section 9-4.

Key blocks of modem design are the filter networks. Many modems in the field have been designed with active filters using either three or four stages. Newer modems are designed using switched filter networks either as a separate unit or as part of the IC modem chip. Both discrete op amp filter stages and IC modem filters are part of Section 9-4.

Comparators are used as the threshold detector and limiter circuits on the receive side of the modem. The purpose of the threshold detector is to "notify" the demodulator if the received signal is at an acceptable level. The limiter produces equal half-cycle periods. The operation and design of both of these circuits are the topics of Sections 9-6 and 9-7.

Section 9–8 described some of the distortion that may occur within the demodulation such as phase jitter and bias distortion.

## Problems

**\*9-1** Does the answering modem in a 300-baud FSK communication system use the upper or lower channel for receiving data?

**9.2** How is the originating modem identified in a system?

**\*9.3** What is the function of a duplexer?

**9.4** Repeat Example 9-1 for (a) an originate modem's MARK condition and (b) an answer modem's SPACE condition.

**\*9.5** Suppose that 4.45 cycles of a waveform is measured on an oscilloscope whose time base is set at 0.2 ms/cm. Determine whether a MARK or

---

\* *See* Answers to Selected Problems.

SPACE is being transmitted and if it is being sent by an originate or answer modem.

**9.6** What are conditions for a balanced duplexer circuit shown in Figure 9-5?

**\*9.7** Let the resistance values in the duplexer circuit of Figure 9-5 be $R_1 = 10$ k$\Omega$, $R_2 = 9.5$ k$\Omega$, $R_3 = 620$ ohms, and $R_4 = 600$ ohms. Calculate $V_1$, $V_2$, and $V_3$ if $V_m = 0.3$ volts and $V_{in} = 0.15$ volts.

**9.8** What is the function of a bandpass filter in the receiving side of an originate modem?

**9.9** Refer to Figure 9-10. If $Es = 1$ volt peak sinusoidal wave and the voltage applied to the comparator's $(+)$ input is 0.25 volts, draw the output waveform.

**9.10** What is the function of the threshold detector?

**\*9.11** What is the minimum threshold voltage set by the circuit of Figure 9-11 if $R_1 = 10$ k$\Omega$, $R_2 = 50$ ohms, and $+V = +12$ volts?

**9.12** Consider that a threshold detector circuit similar to Figure 9-11 is to be designed for a minimum voltage of 50 mV. Assume the supply voltages are $\pm 12$ volts and $R_1 = 10$ k$\Omega$ is chosen, determine $R_2$.

**\*9.13** What is the function of the limiter circuit?

**9.14** Show that the average time interval for the limiter circuit of a 300-baud answer modem is 430 $\mu$s.

**\*9.15** How much phase jitter could you expect in a 300-baud originate modem for a (a) MARK condition and (b) SPACE condition?

**9.16** Determine the approximate value of bias distortion for a 300-baud originate modem.

**\*9.17** What is the total percent distortion that you could expect from a 300-baud originate modem?

# 10 | *Error Detection*

OBJECTIVES

Upon completion of this chapter on error detection, the student will be able to

- Understand how bit errors can occur in data transmission.
- Know how to use parity bit checking and understand its limitations.
- Define what the abbreviation VRC represents.
- Detect bit errors using longitudinal redundancy checking.
- Know what a block check character is and how it is determined.
- Use cyclic redundancy checking to check for bit errors.
- Know what a generating polynomial is and how it is used.
- Determine the cyclic redundancy checking using a long division procedure and know how it is obtained in hardware.
- Write a generating polynomial in terms of powers of x given a binary pattern and vice versa.
- Describe how an integrated circuit (IC) polynomial generator checker is used in conjunction with a microprocessor to generate cyclic redundancy checking and detect bit errors.

## Introduction

The ideal data communication system is error free, that is, the received data is exactly the same as the information that was sent. This ideal situation requires that every received bit be at the same logic state as when it was sent. Since no system can guarantee zero errors, the receiving end must have a method of knowing if an error has occurred. Three of the most common error detection schemes used in data communication systems are

1. Parity bit checking.

2. Longitudinal redundancy checking.

3. Cyclic redundancy checking.

Knowledge that an error has occurred leads to the next logical step—what to do about it. The most common procedure is for the receiver to request a retransmission of the data. In some cases, a request for a retransmission is impossible. In these situations, a method of error detection and correction may be necessary. This method permits a certain number of errors to be detected and corrected at the receiver end. Since the error correction technique is limited, this chapter discusses only the basic principles of error detection along with some available ICs. Chapters 11 and 12 introduce the rules used by the receiving end in synchronous communication to notify the sending end if the data is error free or not.

## 10-1   Error Bits

A major concern of any user of data communication equipment (DCE) is that the data received was the actual data sent. In normal conversation, the listener may miss one, two, or even several words and still obtain the meaning of what was said. A similar situation is intolerable in the transmission of digital data. Not only is the loss of a byte unacceptable, but the change of logic state of a single bit is an error and may have catastrophic results.

A major cause of errors in data transmission is noise. Often a noise burst is of short duration but can cause a considerable number of bits to change logic state. For example, consider a data transmission rate of 2400 bits per second (bps). As reviewed in Chapter 3, 2400 bps converts to 0.416 ms per bit. If a 0.02-second noise burst occurs on the line, it is possible that 48 bits (0.02 s/0.416 ms) could change logic state. Table 10-1 lists the different bit rates and the possible number of error bits that could occur with a 0.02-second noise burst.

**Table 10-1   Comparison of the Possible Number of Error Bits for a Noise Burst of 0.02 Seconds**

| Bit Rate | Bit Time (ms) | Possible Number of Error Bits |
|----------|---------------|-------------------------------|
| 110 | 9.09 | 3 |
| 150 | 6.66 | 3 |
| 300 | 3.33 | 6 |
| 600 | 1.66 | 12 |
| 1200 | 0.833 | 24 |
| 2400 | 0.416 | 48 |
| 4800 | 0.208 | 96 |
| 9600 | 0.104 | 192 |
| 19.2k | 0.052 | 385 |
| 38.4k | 0.026 | 769 |

A data communication system is transmitting information at a rate of 9600 bps. If a noise burst on the line lasts for 10 ms, how many bits could possibly change state?

**Solution**

At 9600 bps the bit time is 0.104 ms. Therefore, the possible number of damaged bits = 10 ms/0.104 ms = 96 bits.

## 10-2    Parity

In Chapter 3, asynchronous communication was discussed and it was discovered that a universal asynchronous receiver-transmitter (UART) is capable of transmitting and detecting a character with parity. Parity enables the receiver to detect errors in data transmission. Parity is the simplest form of error detection and primarily detects only single bit errors; it does not detect double bit errors. For example, consider that odd parity is being used (the number of logic 1s including the parity bit is odd) and the binary pattern (letter D in ASCII) being transmitted is

P 7 6 5 4 3 2 1      Bit number

1 1 0 0 0 1 0 0      Binary pattern

If the bit stream is received and bits 3 and 4 have changed state, then the pattern is

P 7 6 5 |4 3 |2 1      Bit number

1 1 0 0 |1 0 |0 0      Binary pattern

There are still an odd number of logic 1s (including the parity bit). The conclusion would be that the received data is correct. Note, however, the binary pattern is H in ASCII. For another example, again consider the original binary pattern. This time, however, both bits 5 and 6 change logic state during transmission so that the received bit stream is

P 7 |6 5 |4 3 2 1      Bit number

1 1 |1 1 |0 1 0 0      Binary pattern

There is still an odd number of logic 1s including the parity bit but now the bit pattern would be interpreted as the letter t in ASCII. These examples show that a parity bit attached to each character does not guarantee that all bit errors will be detected. In fact, if there is an even number of bit errors, parity cannot detect that an error has occurred. Therefore, there is a definite need for a more sophisticated technique of error detection.

A bit parity added to each character is referred to as **vertical redundance check** or VRC. The idea of VRC may be seen better if the ASCII pattern is written as a column.

| Bit Position | D |
|:---:|:---:|
| 1 | 0 |
| 2 | 0 |
| 3 | 1 |
| 4 | 0 |
| 5 | 0 |
| 6 | 0 |
| 7 | 1 |
| P | 1 |

The reason for writing the binary pattern in a column will be clearer as the next type of error checking is reviewed.

Double bit errors in a character yield correct parity, thereby tricking the reader into believing that the correct character has been received; therefore, a more sophisticated technique of error detection is needed.

## 10-3   Longitudinal Redundancy Checking

An improvement over using a single parity bit for each character is to add a check character at the end of a block of characters. This additional character is known as the **block check character** (BCC). The technique of error checking described in this section is known as **longitudinal redundancy checking** (LRC). The name LRC comes from the way the BCC is determined. Each bit of the BCC is a parity bit calculated for each row of bits. Both VRC and LRC give a two-dimensional parity check and allow detection of many more errors.

Suppose that the expression Data Comm. is to be transmitted. Figure 10-1 shows the binary pattern using the ASCII format and odd parity for each character. The reader should check each column of the message for VRC.

To determine the BCC pattern, calculate the parity bit at the end of each row (bit position 1 to bit position 7). For example, refer to row 1 of Figure 10-1 since odd parity is being used and there are six logic 1s in the message; the BCC bit for this row must then be a logic 1 to ensure odd parity. In comparison, row 2 has three logic 1s in the message. Therefore, the BCC bit for this row is a logic 0. Each bit of the BCC except the parity bit is calculated in this way. The parity bit of the BCC word is calculated as a VRC and not along the parity row.

Often the reader may see the information presented in Figure 10-1 rotated clockwise 90° as shown in Figure 10-2. The advantage that Figure 10-2 has over Figure 10-1 is that the binary pattern for each character is given on a line. That is

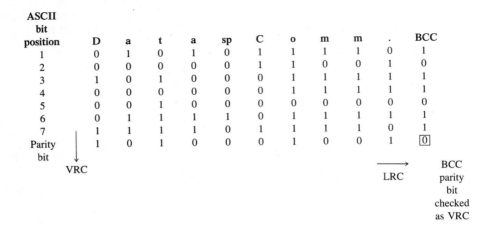

**Figure 10-1    Example of Determining VRC and LRC**

|        | Parity bit | 7 | 6 | 5 | 4 | 3 | 2 | 1 ← ASCII bit position |
|--------|:----------:|:-:|:-:|:-:|:-:|:-:|:-:|:-:|
| D      | 1 | 1 | 0 | 0 | 0 | 1 | 0 | 0 |
| a      | 0 | 1 | 1 | 0 | 0 | 0 | 0 | 1 |
| t      | 1 | 1 | 1 | 1 | 0 | 1 | 0 | 0 |
| a      | 0 | 1 | 1 | 0 | 0 | 0 | 0 | 1 |
| sp     | 0 | 0 | 1 | 0 | 0 | 0 | 0 | 0 |
| C      | 0 | 1 | 0 | 0 | 0 | 0 | 1 | 1 |
| o      | 1 | 1 | 1 | 0 | 1 | 1 | 1 | 1 |
| m      | 0 | 1 | 1 | 0 | 1 | 1 | 0 | 1 |
| m      | 0 | 1 | 1 | 0 | 1 | 1 | 0 | 1 |
|        | 1 | 0 | 1 | 0 | 1 | 1 | 1 | 0 | ↓ LRC |
| BCC    | [0] | 1 | 1 | 0 | 1 | 1 | 0 | 1 |

← VRC

**Figure 10-2    An Alternate Way of Presenting the Data Contained in Figure 10-1**

the way that it is more apt to be written. The BCC is the last character. Note the bits of the BCC word are still found by checking the logic 1s in each bit position. However, the bit positions for each character are in a column instead of a row. The parity bit of the BCC word is calculated by counting the logic 1s in the BCC word.

## 10-3.1   Error Detection Using LRC

It was determined from Section 10-2 that a double error in a character is not detected by a single parity bit. Suppose that the data in Figure 10-2 was transmitted but received as shown in Figure 10-3. The braces { } indicate where the errors occurred.

| | Parity bit | 7 | 6 | 5 | 4 | 3 | 2 | 1 | ASCII ← bit position |
|---|---|---|---|---|---|---|---|---|---|
| D | 1 | 1 | 0 | 0 | 0 | 1 | 0 | 0 | |
| a | 0 | 1 | 1 | 0 | 0 | 0 | 0 | 1 | |
| t | 1 | 1 | 1 | 1 | 0 | 1 | 0 | 0 | |
| a | 0 | 1 | 1 | { 1 | 1 } | 0 | 0 | 1 | ← Double error |
| sp | 0 | 0 | 1 | 0 | 0 | 0 | 0 | 0 | |
| C | 0 | 1 | 0 | 0 | 0 | 0 | 1 | 1 | |
| o | 1 | 1 | 1 | 0 | 1 | 1 | 1 | 1 | |
| m | 0 | 1 | 1 | 0 | 1 | 1 | 0 | 1 | |
| m | 0 | 1 | 1 | 0 | 1 | 1 | 0 | 1 | |
| . | 1 | 0 | 1 | 0 | 1 | 1 | 1 | 0 | |
| BCC | [0] | 1 | 1 | 0 | 1 | 1 | 0 | 1 | ↓ LRC |

VRC

Errors
detected

**Figure 10-3** Double Bit Errors in the Same Character Will Not be Detected by Checking the Parity Bit (VRC) But Will be Detected by Checking the BCC (LRC)

Note that there are still an odd number of logic 1s for the character row. A check of the character's parity does not indicate an error. The binary pattern would be interpreted as y, not a. As before, this double bit error would go undetected if it were not for the BCC. When a parity check is done for each bit position, an error is detected in both bit positions 4 and 5.

Is the technique of using both VRC and LRC together foolproof? The answer is no and Figure 10-4 shows how two double bit errors can go undetected.

A parity check of the characters does not reveal double bit errors. Now check the parity for bit positions 4 and 5. Since both positions have double bit errors,

| | Parity bit | 7 | 6 | 5 | 4 | 3 | 2 | 1 | ASCII ← bit position |
|---|---|---|---|---|---|---|---|---|---|
| D | 1 | 1 | 0 | 0 | 0 | 1 | 0 | 0 | |
| a | 0 | 1 | 1 | 0 | 0 | 0 | 0 | 1 | |
| t | 1 | 1 | 1 | 1 | 0 | 1 | 0 | 0 | |
| a | 0 | 1 | 1 | { 1 | 1 | 0 | 0 | 1 | ← Location |
| sp | 0 | 0 | 1 | { 1 | 1 } | 0 | 0 | 0 | ← of bit errors |
| C | 0 | 1 | 0 | 0 | 0 | 0 | 1 | 1 | |
| o | 1 | 1 | 1 | 0 | 1 | 1 | 1 | 1 | |
| m | 0 | 1 | 1 | 0 | 1 | 1 | 0 | 1 | |
| m | 0 | 1 | 1 | 0 | 1 | 1 | 0 | 1 | |
| . | 1 | 0 | 1 | 0 | 1 | 1 | 1 | 0 | |
| BCC | [0] | 1 | 1 | 0 | 1 | 1 | 0 | 1 | ↓ LRC |

VRC

Errors go
undetected

**Figure 10-4** Double Errors in the Same Bit Position Are Not Detected by LRC the parity check does not reveal an error. Since the parity for each character and the parity for each bit position have been checked, the conclusion would be that the received message is error free, which is clearly wrong. Although the VRC/LRC method is capable of detecting more errors than just a parity check of each character, this technique does fail if double bit errors occur in two characters and in the same bit positions. The likelihood of this problem occurring may be small but it should be considered. A more sophisticated method of error checking will now be examined.

## 10-4   Cyclic Redundancy Checking

Cyclic redundancy checking (CRC) is much more involved than parity checking. In this scheme, the data or message at the transmitter is considered to be one long binary number and it is divided by a binary constant called the **generating polynomial** or **CRC polynomial.** The remainder from the division operation becomes the BCC and is transmitted at the end of the original message. At the receiving end, the data and the BCC are divided by the same CRC polynomial. If there is a zero remainder, there is a very high probability the data has been received without any transmission errors. Note that the CRC polynomial is the same at the transmitter and receiver.

When using this procedure, the rules for determining the CRC polynomial are (1) it must contain one more bit than the BCC and (2) its least significant bit (LSB) must be a logic 1. Also in the division, binary subtraction is not performed; rather, an Exclusive-OR operation is done. Since a key Boolean operation for determining the BCC is the Exclusive-OR function, a review may be in order. The Exclusive-OR truth table is

| Inputs | | Output |
| A | B | $A \oplus B$ |
| --- | --- | --- |
| 0 | 0 | 0 |
| 0 | 1 | 1 |
| 1 | 0 | 1 |
| 1 | 1 | 0 |

Remember from a digital logic course that the output is a logic 1 when the inputs are different and the output is a logic 0 when the inputs are the same. The following examples show the Exclusive-OR result of each binary pattern combination:

(a)  A          1 0 1 0 0        (b)   A         1 1 0 1 1
     B          1 1 0 0 1              B         1 1 0 0 1
   $A \oplus B$   0 1 1 0 1          $A \oplus B$   0 0 0 1 0

(c)    A      1 0 1 1 0       (d)    A      1 1 1 1 0
       B      1 1 0 0 0              B      1 1 0 0 1
  A ⊕ B      0 1 1 1 0         A ⊕ B      0 0 1 1 1

## 10-4.1  CRC Long Division Procedure

The following example shows the long division steps involved in determining the BCC at the transmitter and then checking the total message including the BCC at the receiver end.

At the transmitter

1. Assume the following original message is given:

$$M = 1\ 0\ 1\ 0\ 0\ 1\ 1\ 1\ 0\ 0 \quad \text{(10 bits)}$$

and the generating polynomial

$$P = 1\ 1\ 0\ 0\ 1 \quad \text{(5 bits)}.$$

Then the size of the BCC will be 4 bits since the CRC polynomial has 5 bits.

2. When determining the BCC, the original message is modified by adding to the right hand end of the message as many logic 0s as there are bits in the BCC. The original message now appears as

$$M_m = 1\ 0\ 1\ 0\ 0\ 1\ 1\ 1\ 0\ 0\ \underbrace{0\ 0\ 0\ 0}$$

Additional 0s

3. The result of step 2 is divided by the CRC polynomial.

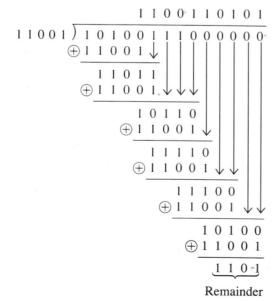

Remainder

**4.** The remainder, R, is considered to be the BCC and is attached to the original message, yielding the total message, $T_S$, that is sent.

$$T_S = 1\ 0\ 1\ 0\ 0\ 1\ 1\ 1\ 0\ 0\ \underbrace{1\ 1\ 0\ 1}$$

The remainder is the BCC.

At the receiver

The total received message, $T_r$, is divided by the same generating polynomial, P. If there is a zero remainder, the BCCs are removed and remaining bits are the original message.

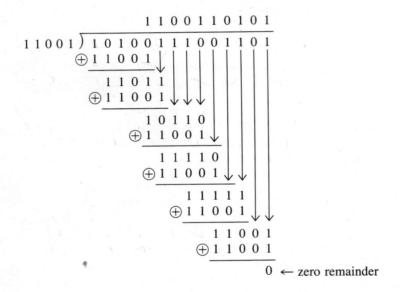

$$0 \leftarrow \text{zero remainder}$$

Since the remainder equals zero, the BCC bits of $T_r$ are removed and the original message, M, is recovered error free, hence

$$M = 1\ 0\ 1\ 0\ 0\ 1\ 1\ 1\ 0\ 0$$

Consider that noise on the line causes 2 bits to change state. The result is that the total message received, $T_r$, is not the same message that was sent, $T_S$.

$$T_S = 1\ 0\ 1\ 0\ 0\ 1\ 1\ 1\ 0\ 0\ 1\ 1\ 0\ 1$$
$$T_r = 1\ 0\ 1\ 0\ 0\ 1\ \underline{1\ 0\ 1\ 0}\ 1\ 1\ 0\ 1$$

Error bits

Now when $T_r$ is divided by P, the operation will generate a nonzero remainder.

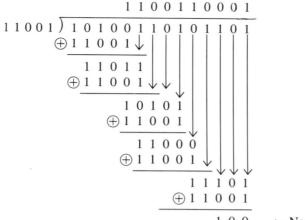

$$1\ 0\ 0 \quad \leftarrow \text{Nonzero remainder}$$

A nonzero remainder normally causes the receiving terminal equipment to request a retransmission. Chapters 11 and 12 show how different synchronous protocols accomplish this task.

   CRC error detection techniques are capable of detecting (1) all single bit errors, (2) all double bit errors as long as the generating polynomial, P, has at least three terms, (3) burst errors as long as the burst causes less errors than is in the BCC, and (4) most bursts that cause more errors than is in the BCC.

## 10-4.2  CRC Generating Polynomials

In the previous examples, the generating polynomial was written as the binary pattern 11001. However, generating polynomials are often written as a polynomial in terms of powers of x. This can be done by adding the powers of x wherever there is a logic 1. For example

$$\begin{array}{ccccc} 1 & 1 & 0 & 0 & 1 \end{array}$$

Powers of x
$$1x^4 + 1x^3 + 0x^2 + 0x^1 + 1x^0 = x^4 + x^3 + 1$$

**Note:** The powers of x increase from right to left beginning at $x^0 = 1$. Remember the rightmost term for a CRC generating polynomial will always be 1.

E  X  A  M  P  L  E      10 - 2

Write each of the following binary patterns as a CRC generating polynomial in terms of powers of x.

**(a)**  110101

**(b)**  1011001

**(c)**  1100001

**Solution**

(a) $1x^5 + 1x^4 + 0x^3 + 1x^2 + 0x^1 + 1x^0 = x^5 + x^4 + x^2 + 1$

(b) $1x^6 + 0x^5 + 1x^4 + 1x^3 + 0x^2 + 0x^1 + 1x^0 = x^6 + x^4 + x^3 + 1$

(c) $1x^6 + 1x^5 + 0x^4 + 0x^3 + 0x^2 + 0x^1 + 1x^0 = x^6 + x^5 + 1$

---

E  X  A  M  P  L  E     10 - 3

Write the binary pattern for each of the following CRC generating polynomials:

(a) $x^5 + x^3 + 1$

(b) $x^7 + x^5 + x^2 + 1$

(c) $x^4 + x^3 + 1$

**Solution**

The coefficient for each power of x given in the expression is 1; otherwise, it is a logic 0.

(a)  $x^5 + \quad 0x^4 + \quad x^3 \quad + \quad 0x^2 + \quad 0x^1 + \quad 1$
      1    0    1    0    0    1

(b)  $x^7 + 0x^6 + x^5 + 0x^4 + 0x^3 + x^2 + 0x^1 + 1$
      1   0   1   0   0   1   0   1

(c)  $x^4 + x^3 + 0x^2 + 0x^1 + 1$
      1   1   0   0   1

---

E  X  A  M  P  L  E     10 - 4

For each of the CRC generating polynomials of Example 10-3, what would be the size of the BCC?

**Solution**

The BCC size is 1 bit less than the number of bits in the CRC generating polynomial. Another way of stating this point is the BCC size equals the highest power of x.

(a) For $x^5 + x^3 + 1$, the highest power of x is 5. Therefore the number of bits in the BCC is 5.

(b) For $x^7 + x^5 + x^2 + 1$, the BCC size equals 7.

(c) For $x^4 + x^3 + 1$, the BCC size equals 4.

---

The four most often used versions of the generating polynomial are

CRC-12: $x^{12} + x^{11} + x^3 + x^2 + x + 1$

CRC-16: $x^{16} + x^{15} + x^2 + 1$

CRC-CCITT: $x^{16} + x^{12} + x^5 + 1$

CRC-32: $x^{32} + x^{26} + x^{23} + x^{22} + x^{16} + x^{12} + x^{11} + x^{10} + x^9 + x^7 + x^5 + x^4 + x + 1$

The CRC-12 polynomial is used in data communication applications where 6-bit characters are transmitted. This polynomial generates a 12-bit BCC. The CRC-16 polynomial is most popular in the United States and it generates a 16-bit BCC. These applications transmit data using 8-bit characters. The CRC-CCITT polynomial is similar to the CRC-16 except it is used for European applications. The CRC-32 polynomial is used in some local area networks and many military applications; it generates a 32-bit BCC.

**E X A M P L E   10 - 5**

Write the binary pattern for the CRC-16 polynomial.

**Solution**

Similar to the solution of Example 10-3

$$x^{16} + x^{15} + x^2 + 1 = 1 1 0 0 0 0 0 0 0 0 0 0 0 1 0 1$$

## 10-5  BCC Circuitry

Section 10-4 described how a BCC is determined using a modified version of long division. In data communication systems a BCC is not generated by software but rather by hardware. As will be shown in the next section, a programmable polynomial generator (PPG) IC is used in conjunction with a serial I/O device to generate the BCC and transmit it at the end of the original message. At the receiver end, another PPG IC is used to check for a zero remainder. Before studying how these ICs are connected into a system, a simplified version of their internal equivalent circuit will be reviewed.

A BCC generator equivalent circuit is made up of a shift register and Exclusive-OR gates. The circuit is composed as follows:

**1.** The number of bits in the shift register equals the BCC size.

**2.** The number of Exclusive-OR gates is one less than the number of logic 1s in the binary pattern of the generating polynomial.

As an example, consider the generating polynomial $x^4 + x^3 + 1$ and learn how to draw a BCC equivalent circuit.

**1.** Use the procedure described in Example 10-3 and write the binary pattern for the generating polynomial. This step is shown in Figure 10-5a.

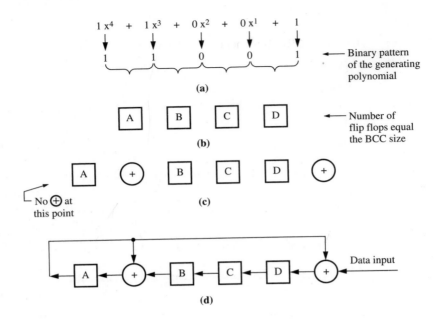

**Figure 10-5    The Steps Involved to Draw an Equivalent BCC Circuit When the Generating Polynomial is $x^4 + x^3 + 1$**

2. Between each pair of bits in the generating polynomial, draw a block to represent a flip-flop in the shift register. Label the flip-flops A, B, C, etc. as shown in Figure 10-5b. **Note:** There will be as many flip-flops as there are bits in the BCC.

3. Except for the leftmost logic 1 (the highest power of x), draw an Exclusive-OR gate wherever a logic 1 exists. For example, a logic 1 exists between flip-flops A and B and to the right of flip-flop D (*see* Fig. 10-5c).

4. Data will flow through the shift register from right to left and the output of flip-flop A is fed back to all the Exclusive-OR gates. *See* Figure 10-5d for a simplified circuit that can generate a BCC for the polynomial $x^4 + x^3 + 1$.

The way the BCC is generated using this circuit is that each bit of the message, $M_m$ (the message that contains the additional logic 0s), is clocked in on the data input line 1 bit at a time. After the last logic 0 is clocked in, the flip-flops will contain the BCC. The most significant bit (MSB) of the BCC is contained in the A flip-flop. The least significant bit (LSB), which is transmitted last, is contained in the D flip-flop of Figure 10-5d. This step-by-step procedure is shown in Figure 10-7.

E  X  A  M  P  L  E    10 - 6

Draw a circuit to generate a BCC for the CRC-16 polynomial.

**Solution**

The binary pattern for a CRC-16 generating polynomial is given in Example 10-5 as

1 1 0 0 0 0 0 0 0 0 0 0 0 1 0 1

Figure 10-6 shows the equivalent circuit by using the four-step procedure previously outlined.

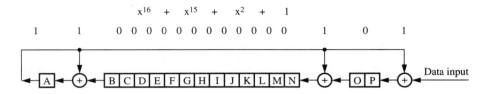

**Figure 10-6**   **Equivalent BCC for the CRC-16 Generating Polynomial**

These BCC equivalent circuits are simplified: they do not show the shift register clock line, preclear lines, or parallel output lines. In addition, manufacturers wire their interconnections differently. Therefore, this type of circuit may be wired differently in other textbooks.

How the circuit of Figure 10-5 generates the same BCC as shown in the CRC long division procedure will be examined next. As shown in Figure 10-7 the register is cleared to all logic 0s and then the data is shifted in 1 bit at a time. At each clock pulse, the data into each flip-flop of the shift register is given by

$$A \oplus B \rightarrow A$$
$$C \rightarrow B$$
$$D \rightarrow C$$
$$\text{Data in} \oplus A \rightarrow D$$

As shown in Figure 10-7, after the 14 clock pulses, register ABCD contains the BCC. It is in the same form as in the long division example of Section 10-4.1. The rightmost flip-flop (flip-flop D in this example) contains the last bit that will be transmitted.

## 10-6   Polynomial Generator Checker

IC chips, which are known as polynomial generator checkers (PGC), are capable of determining character parity (VRC), block parity (LRC), and BCC accumulation using a CRC generating polynomial. These devices compliment a serial I/O device because they are wired into the system so that it monitors the microcomputer's data bus. These ICs perform parity and/or BCC generation at the transmitter or detection at the receiver as the data is moved from the microprocessor to the serial I/O port or vice versa. These devices can be programmed for different CRC

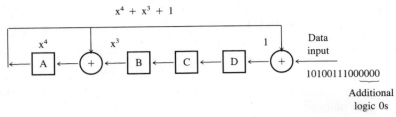

| Clock pulse | A | B | C | D | Data input |
|---|---|---|---|---|---|
|  | 0 | 0 | 0 | 0 | — |
| 1 | 0 | 0 | 0 | 1 | 1 |
| 2 | 0 | 0 | 1 | 0 | 0 |
| 3 | 0 | 1 | 0 | 1 | 1 |
| 4 | 1 | 0 | 1 | 0 | 0 |
| 5 | 1 | 1 | 0 | 1 | 0 |
| 6 | 0 | 0 | 1 | 0 | 1 |
| 7 | 0 | 1 | 0 | 1 | 1 |
| 8 | 1 | 0 | 1 | 1 | 1 |
| 9 | 1 | 1 | 1 | 1 | 0 |
| 10 | 0 | 1 | 1 | 1 | 0 |
| 11 | 1 | 1 | 1 | 0 | 0 |
| 12 | 0 | 1 | 0 | 1 | 0 |
| 13 | 1 | 0 | 1 | 0 | 0 |
| 14 | 1 | 1 | 0 | 1 | 0 |

**Figure 10-7   Generating the BCC Using the Equivalent Circuit of a Shift Register and Exclusive-OR Gates**

generating polynomials and to search for a particular character or characters. Although these devices can be used for either asynchronous or synchronous transmission, they are more often used in synchronous applications. The reason being that most serial I/O ports used in asynchronous communication use UARTs, which are capable of generating and detecting character parity (VRC). If an asynchronous application also required the generation and detection of LRC, a PGC chip would be needed because UARTs do not include this feature.

Figure 10-8a shows the pin configuration for the Signetics SCN2653 PGC. Figure 10-8b shows how this device could be wired into a microcomputer system. The microprocessor reads and writes data to the PGC by activating the chip enable #1 (CE1) line. The PGC chip enable #0 (CE0) line is tied to the serial I/O device's chip enable pin. When this line is activated by the microprocessor, the microprocessor can read or write to both devices simultaneously. This is how the PGC monitors the data bus. At the transmitting station, the PGC reads the data going from the microprocessor to the serial I/O device for generating a BCC. After the last character has been sent to the serial I/O device and the PGC has accumulated the BCC, the microprocessor transfers the BCC to the serial device. At the receiving station, the PGC reads the data going from the serial I/O device to the microprocessor for detection purposes. The PGC can be programmed to continue to accu-

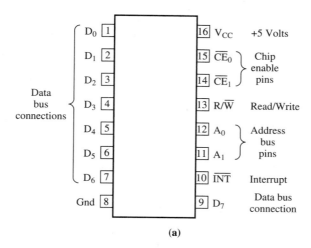

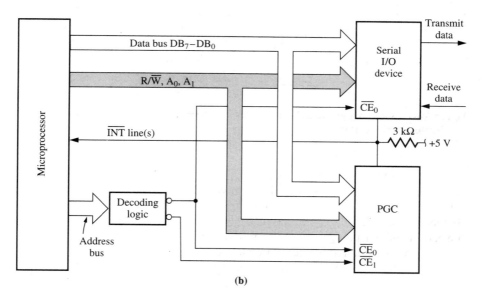

**Figure 10-8**   (a) Pin Assignments for the SCN2653 PGC. (b) A Typical System Configuration

mulate a BCC while searching for an ending character (*see* Chapter 11). After the last character has been accumulated, the microprocessor checks a bit in the PGC's status register to determine if the BCC was zero. If the BCC was not zero, we know an error in transmission has occurred and the receiving station may send a message to the original sending station for retransmission of data.

This device contains all the necessary circuitry to generate and detect BCC on a character-by-character basis and select from three generating polynomials, CRC-

16, CRC-12, and LRC-8. It can also be used to generate and check VRC parity either odd or even. This device does not require an external system clock but uses internal circuitry for the accumulation of the BCC.

## Summary

This chapter introduced the three most common error detection schemes used in data communications. They are parity bit checking, LRC, and CRC. Parity bit checking is the simplest technique and primarily detects only single bit errors (although it does detect an odd number of errors). LRC detects multiple bit errors but is not foolproof. LRC also introduced how to determine a BCC. A more sophisticated error detection scheme is CRC. This method uses a generating polynomial to create the BCC at the transmitter and the same generating polynomial is used at the receiver to detect transmission errors.

Section 10-4 illustrated how the BCC is generated at the transmitter and used at the receiver by a long division procedure. Section 10-5 illustrated the same procedure using an equivalent circuit. The use of a PGC IC was shown in Section 10-6, and how it can be connected to a microprocessor was also illustrated.

## Problems

**\*10.1** For the following bit rates, calculate the number of bits that could change state during a 12-ms noise burst.
**(a)** 300 bps      **(b)** 1200 bps      **(c)** 9600 bps

**10.2** Does parity (VRC) detect an even number of bit errors?

**\*10.3** For each of the following pairs of binary patterns, identify if a parity checker circuit testing for odd parity at the receiver would indicate a parity error.

| Data Sent | | Data Received | |
|---|---|---|---|
| P | LSB | P | LSB |
| **(a)** 1110 | 1100 | 1111 | 0010 |
| **(b)** 1011 | 0101 | 0011 | 0101 |
| **(c)** 0000 | 0111 | 0000 | 0100 |
| **(d)** 1011 | 1100 | 1011 | 1000 |
| **(e)** 0001 | 0011 | 1101 | 0011 |

**10.4** Is VRC a one-dimensional or two-dimensional parity checking scheme?

\**See* Answers to Selected Problems.

**\*10.5** Refer to Figure 10-2. If the binary pattern for the space (sp) row is received as

$$
\begin{array}{c}
\text{P 7 6 5 4 3 2 1} \quad \text{Bit position} \\
\hline
\text{0 0 1 1 1 0 0 0}
\end{array}
$$

would the error be detected during (a) VRC?   (b) LRC?

**10.6** Without LRC, what character would the receiver interpret the binary pattern of Problem 10-5 to be?

**\*10.7** Refer to Figure 10-2. If the binary patterns for the first two rows are received as

$$
\begin{array}{c}
\text{P 7 6 5 4 3 2 1} \quad \text{Bit position} \\
\hline
\text{1 1 0 0 0 1 1 1} \\
\text{0 1 1 0 0 0 1 1}
\end{array}
$$

would VRC, LRC, or both types of parity checking detect the bit errors?

**10.8** Use Figure 10-2 as a guide and show how the word Micro would appear if even parity for VRC and LRC is used.

**\*10.9** Refer to Figure 10-4 and consider that the logic 0s in columns 4 and 5 for the letter C also are received as logic 1s. Would you expect the receiver's VRC or LRC circuitry to detect an error?

**10.10** Determine the Exclusive-OR result for each binary pattern combination:

(a)    11011011
$\oplus$01110001
_____

(c)    00010111
$\oplus$11000011
_____

(b)    01011100
$\oplus$11110000
_____

(d)    11101101
$\oplus$01101100
_____

**\*10.11** Assume that the binary pattern of a generating polynomial is 10111. Determine the BCC for each of the following messages:
(a) 1100011101
(b) 01101000
(c) 1111111010

**10.12** What is the total transmitted message for each part of Problem 10.11?

**10.13** If each message of Problem 10.12 is received error free, show that the remainder at the receiver is zero. The binary pattern of the generating polynomial is given in Problem 10.11.

**10.14** If the first message of Problem 10.13 is received as

$$T_r = 1\ 1\ 0\ 0\ 1\ 0\ 1\ 1\ 0\ 1\ 1\ 0\ 1\ 0$$

determine the remainder generated at the receiver.

**\*10.15** Match the generating polynomial in terms of powers of x from column A with the correct binary pattern from column B.

|  | Column A | Column B |
|---|---|---|
| (a) | $x^5 + x^4 + x^2 + 1$ | (1) 1001111 |
| (b) | $x^6 + x^3 + x^2 + x + 1$ | (2) 111001 |
| (c) | $x^5 + x^4 + x^3 + 1$ | (3) 1101011 |
| (d) | $x^4 + x^2 + 1$ | (4) 110101 |
| (e) | $x^6 + x^5 + x^3 + x + 1$ | (5) 10101 |

**10.16** Write the generating polynomial given as a binary pattern in Problem 10.11 in terms of powers of x.

**\*10.17** For each of the generating polynomials given in column A of Problem 10.15, what would be the size of the BCC?

**10.18** For each polynomial given in column A of Problem 10.15, draw a circuit using flip-flops and Exclusive-OR gates that would generate the BCC.

# *Character Oriented Protocol*  11

OBJECTIVES

Upon completion of this chapter on character oriented protocols, the student will be able to

- Give a general definition of protocols and the reason for needing them.
- Distinguish between the physical layer and the data link layer of the International Standards Organization (ISO) model.
- Give the two major classifications of data link controls.
- Distinguish between character oriented protocols (COPs) and bit oriented protocols (BOPs).
- Identify the function of each field of a Bisync protocol.
- Show the handshake procedure used in a Bisync protocol.
- Show the traffic that occurs on a communication channel in a point-to-point and a multipoint system.
- Give examples of needing a transparent mode of transmitting data and how it is accomplished in the Bisync protocol.
- List the types of timeout procedures.
- Give some of the disadvantages of the Bisync protocol.
- Describe the advantages of a byte count protocol (in particular Digital Equipment Corporation's Digital Data Communications Message Protocol [DDCMP]) over a byte control protocol.
- Explain the principles of operation of a Bisync I/O device.

## Introduction

So far the discussion has primarily concentrated on synchronous communication with only brief mentions of synchronous communication. Chapters 5 to 8 discussed the electrical, mechanical, and functional characteristics of data transmission for both types of communication. These characteristics are known as the physical

233

layer. As large blocks of data are sent using synchronous techniques, another layer is needed to control and manage the exchange of data. This new layer is referred to as data link control (DLC), data link protocol, or simply protocols. This chapter begins with a specific type of data link protocol, the character oriented protocol (COP). Chapter 12 covers another type, the bit oriented protocol (BOP).

## 11-1   Protocols

**Protocols** are the rules that ensure an orderly transfer of data between digital equipment. In asynchronous communication, the rule is that each character has to be framed with a start and stop bit. But most applications that use asynchronous communication do not require the receiving station to reply to the sending station before a new message is sent. An acknowledgment is an integral part of a data link protocol as will be studied in this and in Chapter 12. Applications that use synchronous communication use data link protocols.

Protocols play an important part as an increasing amount of data is transferred and in particular applications that use packet switching and satellite technologies. Data communication protocols are classified into levels, or layers. Each level has certain functions and is designed to be operated independently of the others. However, the operation of one level does depend on the correct operation of the previous level.

Many manufacturers and users of data communication equipment (DCE) use a layered protocol model developed by the ISO. This model consists of seven layers as shown in Figure 11-1. Each layer performs certain functions for the orderly transfer of data. However, the ISO model does not specify the exact details for each layer but does specify the overall function of each layer. For example, the physical layer in the ISO model does not specify that RS-232-C, Electronics Industries Association (EIA)-232-D, International Telegraph and Telephone Consultative Committee (CCITT) V.35, RS-449, or another standard has to be used but rather that the bits are converted to electrical signals at the sending end that can be recognized by the receiving station. The signal may be sent over a twisted pair, coaxial, fiberoptic cable or other medium. As shown, the levels range from a physical layer to an application layer. In other chapters the physical layer was studied. In this chapter and in Chapter 12, we shall study the principles of the next layer called the DLCs. In a course on local area networks, the functions of the other layers would be examined.

## 11-2   Data Link Controls

DLCs are not concerned with the mechanical, electrical, and functional characteristics of particular interface circuits. These characteristics are all part of the physical layer. DLCs are the rules for transferring data efficiently and accurately between data equipment over communication channels. Some of the functions of the DLCs are

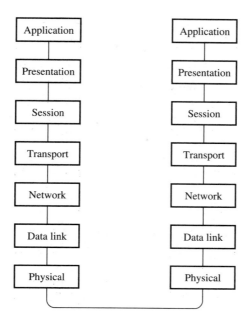

**Figure 11-1  ISO Layered Model for Protocols**

**1.** To establish and terminate connections between stations.

**2.** To identify the sending and receiving stations.

**3.** To monitor the message using error detection techniques.

**4.** To ensure that positive or negative acknowledgments are sent.

**5.** To request retransmission if an error is detected.

**6.** To handle special control functions such as status information, reset, and disconnect.

There are two classifications of DLCs: COPs and BOPs. COPs are subdivided into byte control and byte count protocols. Byte control protocols rely on the insertion of special control characters to separate the fields of the message. Byte count protocols rely on a count field to hold the number of bytes that will follow in the data field.

Bit control protocols use special opening and closing flags to identify the ends of the message but within the flags each bit has a function. This chapter covers the fundamental principles of both types of COPs and Chapter 12 will examine BOPs.

## 11-3   Character Oriented Protocol  ( COP )

The principles of COPs were introduced in the early 1960s by IBM and are still in use. IBM's protocol is known as Binary Synchronous Communication (BSC or Bisync) protocol. The international standards are American National Standards Institute (ANSI) 3.28 and ISO 1745.

Figure 11-2 shows the general format for a Bisync text message and it is evident where the control characters are used to separate the different fields. This separation provides for an orderly transfer of data. Synchronization at the receiver is accomplished by the detection of at least two synchronization characters (SYN) that precede the message. The sync characters are not part of the message and are not stored by the receiver and are not part of the block check character (BCC). In order to maintain synchronization for long text messages, the transmitter automatically inserts SYN characters once every second into the text portion. These characters are removed by the receiver and neither are they stored nor do they become part of the BCC.

| SYN | SYN | SOH | Header | STX | Text | ETX | BCC |
|-----|-----|-----|--------|-----|------|-----|-----|

**Figure 11-2   Bisync Text Message Format**

The header field in the Bisync protocol begins with start of header (SOH) control character and ends with start of text (STX) control character. The header is an optional field but if it is used its contents are user defined to carry auxiliary information that identifies the address of the message source or destination, the type of message (control or data), a job number, a positive or negative acknowledgment for a previous received message, or a control action. Some control actions reset or initialize a secondary station, abort a transfer sequence, or inquire why a response has not occurred.

The text block contains the data being transmitted. It may be divided into characters using a code set (such as American Standard Code for Information Interchange [ASCII] or Extended Binary Coded Decimal Information Code [EBCDIC]) or the data may be sent as a bit stream using a transparent mode. This topic is covered in Section 11-6. The text block begins after the start of text (STX) control character and ends with one of four ending control characters—ETB, ETX, EOT, or ITB. The function of each of these control characters is given in Table 11-1.

The BCC follows an ending control character. The BCC provides an error check field so that the receiver may determine if a transmission error has occurred. The BCC is generated and checked as discussed in Chapter 10. Although vertical redundancy check (VRC) along with longitudinal redundancy check (LRC) may be used, most systems use one of the cyclic redundancy checks (CRC) such as CRC-16.

If no error is detected, the receiver sends a positive acknowledgment (either ACK0 or ACK1). The receiver alternates the response—ACK0, ACK1, ACK0,

**Table 11-1  Bisync Control Characters**

| Control Character | Name | Description |
|---|---|---|
| ACK0 ACK1 | Positive acknowledgment | The previous message was received without an error. ACK0 is used for even-numbered messages and ACK1 is used for odd-numbered messages. |
| DLE | Data link escape | It is used to indicate transparent data. It is also used as the first control character in a two-control-character sequence (see Table 11-2). |
| ENQ | Enquiry | It is used to try to acquire the link in a point-to-point system. It is also used to request retransmission of an ACK or NAK response when the response is not received correctly. |
| EOT | End of transmission | It is used to indicate the end of transmission, which may have included a number of message blocks. |
| ETB | End of transmission block | It indicates the end of a block that began with SOH or STX. |
| ETX | End of text | This control character's function is similar to ETB but it also means there is no more data to be transmitted. |
| ITB | End of intermediate transmission block | A long message that is divided into sections may use the ITB control character so that the receiver may check for transmission errors. A response is not required. |
| NAK | Negative acknowledgment | The previous received message had a transmission error. |
| RVI | Reverse interrupt | It indicates a positive acknowledgment but it is also a request that the originating station terminate its transmission because the receiving station would like to transmit. |
| SOH | Start of header | It indicates the header portion of the message follows next. |
| STX | Start of text | It indicates the data field of message follows next. |
| TTD | Temporary time delay | It is used by the transmitting station to indicate that the station is not ready to transmit a message at this time but the station wishes to retain control of the link. |
| WACK | Wait before transmit Positive acknowledgment | It indicates a positive acknowledgment but the receiving station is not ready to receive another message at this time. |

etc. The first positive acknowledgment is ACK0, the next is ACK1, and so forth. This allows the station sending the messages to keep track of which message is being acknowledged by the receiver. The transmitting station then sends the next message. Note that Bisync is a half-duplex operation. If the receiving station detects an error, a negative acknowledgment (NAK) is sent back and the transmitting station retransmits the message.

After a line turnaround, the BCC logic circuitry is reset when a start of header (SOH) or start of text (STX) is received. For each data message sent, the generation of the BCC begins with the STX character and includes the ending delimiter (ETB, ETX, EOT, or ITB character).

One of the limitations with this type of protocol is that it is designed as a half-duplex protocol. After each message is transmitted, the sending station must wait until it receives an acknowledgment from the remote station before the next message may be sent. If the message is received error free (BCC = 0), a positive acknowledgment (ACK0 or ACK1) is returned from the remote station. If the BCC ≠ 0, a transmission error has occurred and the remote station sends a negative acknowledgment (NAK).

Bisync uses some control sequence pairs instead of a single control character. An example is ACK0: this is sent in ASCII as DLE 0 (the space is not included as part of the transmission). The other control sequence pairs are given in Table 11-2. Most Bisync applications use either ASCII or EBCDIC information codes. In this text, ASCII is used.

The Bisync protocol can be used for both point-to-point and multipoint systems.

**Table 11-2   Two-Control-Character Sequence**

| Control Character | ASCII Sequence |
| --- | --- |
| ACK0 | DLE0 |
| ACK1 | DLE1 |
| WACK | DLE; |
| RVI | DLE< |

## 11-4   Point-to-Point Communication

Bisync protocol was designed to provide an orderly transfer in point-to-point and multipoint systems. As with any DLC, Bisync provides the tools for establishing the connection, transferring the data, and terminating the connection. In a point-to-point system, either station may try to acquire control of the communication channel by transmitting

SYN SYN ENQ.

If both stations try to acquire the channel at the same time, and neither station is successful, then only the station that is designated as the primary station may retry. Once one station has acquired the channel and sent the above message, the other station has one of three responses:

**1.** It is ready (ACK0).

**2.** It is not ready (NAK).

**3.** It is temporarily not ready (WACK).

In the Bisync format these responses are transmitted as

| | |
|---|---|
| SYN SYN ACK0 | Ready to receive |
| SYN SYN NAK | Not ready to receive |
| SYN SYN WACK | Temporarily not ready to receive; try again later. |

(Remember from Table 11-2 that ACK0 and WACK are actually sent as a two-character sequence.) Now the sending station may transmit one or more blocks of data. After each block (except for blocks ending with ITB) the receiving station responds with one of the following acknowledgments:

| | |
|---|---|
| SYN SYN ACK0 | Positive reply for even-numbered blocks |
| SYN SYN ACK1 | Positive reply for odd-numbered blocks |
| SYN SYN NAK | Negative acknowledgment, last block was not accepted |
| SYN SYN WACK | Positive acknowledgment but receiving station is not ready for next block |
| SYN SYN RVI | Positive acknowledgment but receiving station needs the line |

E X A M P L E   11 - 1

Show an example of traffic on the communication channel in a point-to-point system to illustrate the following points: (1) the primary station acquires control of the communication channel after a collision; (2) the secondary station requests a temporary wait; and (3) the primary station tries again.

**Solution**

A collision happens when both stations try to acquire the line at the same time. The primary station is allowed to retry. Figure 11-3 shows the back and forth traffic that could occur on the channel for this example.

| Primary | | Secondary | Description |
|---|---|---|---|
| SYN SYN ENQ | ———→⁄←——— | SYN SYN ENQ | Both stations try to acquire the channel |
| SYN SYN ENQ | ————————→ | | Primary station retries |
| | ←———————— | SYN SYN WACK | Secondary acknowledges transmission but is temporarily busy (DLE; = WACK) |
| SYN SYN ENQ | ————————→ | | Primary tries again |
| | ←———————— | SYN SYN ACK0 | Secondary sends positive acknowledgment (DLE0 = ACK0) |

**Figure 11-3   Solution to Example 11-1.**

## E X A M P L E   11 - 2

Show an example of traffic on the communication channel in a point-to-point system to illustrate the following points: (1) the primary station establishes the connection; (2) the primary station wishes to send four message blocks but after the third block the secondary needs some additional time; and (3) the primary station terminates the connection after all four messages are sent and acknowledged.

**Solution**

Figure 11-4 shows the half-duplex communication that could take place on the communication channel. The first positive acknowledgment sent by the secondary begins with ACK0 and then the next positive acknowledgment is ACK1 and then they continue to alternate back and forth (ACK0, ACK1, ACK0, etc.).

| Primary | | Secondary | Description |
|---|---|---|---|
| SYN SYN ENQ | ————→ | | Primary wishes to send data |
| | ←———— | SYN SYN ACK0 | Positive reply |
| SYN SYN STX [Data] ETB BCC | ————→ | | First data block is sent |
| | ←———— | SYN SYN ACK1 | Positive reply |
| SYN SYN STX [Data] ETB BCC | ————→ | | Second data block is sent |
| | ←———— | SYN SYN ACK0 | Positive reply |
| SYN SYN STX [Data] ETB BCC | ————→ | | Third data block is sent |
| | ←———— | SYN SYN WACK | Positive acknowledgment but secondary is temporarily busy |
| SYN SYN ENQ | ————→ | | Primary is asking if it is okay to continue |
| | ←———— | SYN SYN ACK0 | It is okay to send data |
| SYN SYN STX [Data] ETX BCC | ————→ | | Fourth and last data block is sent |
| | ←———— | SYN SYN ACK0 | Positive reply |
| SYN SYN EOT | ————→ | | Primary terminates the connection |

**Figure 11-4   Solution to Example 11-2. (Remember DLE0 = ACK0; DLE1 = ACK1; and DLE; = WACK in ASCII)**

## 11-5    Multipoint Systems

The Bisync protocol also was designed to handle multipoint as well as point-to-point systems. In a multipoint system one station is designated as the primary station and the others as secondary stations. The primary can poll and select the secondaries. The format for polling is

SYN SYN EOT SYN SYN [ADDRESS] ENQ

and for selecting is

SYN SYN EOT SYN SYN [address] ENQ

The brackets are not part of the transmission but only indicate where in the message the secondary station's address belongs. An uppercase address indicates a polling procedure while an address in lowercase letters indicates that the primary station wishes to communicate with a particular secondary station.

The EOT control character resets the secondary stations from data mode to control mode so they can "search" for their address being sent by the primary. A polled station has three possible replies and a selected station has four possible replies. They are:

**Polled Station Replies**

| | |
|---|---|
| SYN SYN [Message] BCC | The secondary has information to send and communicates with the primary as in a point-to-point system. When all messages are sent the connection terminates with an EOT. |
| SYN SYN EOT | The secondary has nothing to send. |
| SYN SYN STX ENQ | The secondary is asking for a temporary delay. |

**Selected Station Replies**

| | |
|---|---|
| SYN SYN ACK0 | The secondary station is ready and enters the message transfer procedure as in a point-to-point system. |
| SYN SYN NAK | The secondary station is not ready. |
| SYN SYN WACK | The secondary station is temporarily not ready. |
| SYN SYN RVI | The secondary cannot receive because it is in a transmit mode and a polling sequence is required first. |

### E  X  A  M  P  L  E    11 - 3

Show the half-duplex communication in a multipoint system for the primary station, A, to poll secondary stations B and C to determine if they have anything to send. Assume the secondary stations have nothing to send.

**Solution**

Figure 11-5 shows the message traffic on the communication channel.

In COPs the secondary stations are referred to as tributary stations.

| Primary | | Secondary | Description |
|---|---|---|---|
| SYN SYN EOT SYN SYN B ENQ | ⟶ | | Primary polls station B |
| | ⟵ | SYN SYN EOT | Station B has nothing to send |
| SYN SYN EOT SYN SYN C ENQ | ⟶ | | Primary polls station C |
| | ⟵ | SYN SYN EOT | Station C has nothing to send |

**Figure 11-5   Solution to Example 11–3.**

E  X  A  M  P  L  E     11 - 4

Show the message traffic on the communication link in a multipoint system for the following situation: the primary station, A, tries to select secondary station B but it is not ready so the primary selects station C which is ready to receive data and A communicates with C. At the end of the transmission with C, primary A goes back to station B which is now ready.

**Solution**

Figure 11-6 shows the half-duplex communication that could take place at the link.

## 11-6   Transparent Mode

In some applications, someone may wish to transmit raw binary data, known as a bit stream. This application does not use an information code; therefore, each 8 bits does not represent an ASCII or EBCDIC character. However, the receiver's circuitry is constantly scanning each 8 bits for control characters, so care must be taken to ensure that the receiver does not mistake a certain binary sequence within the bit stream as a control character. Consider Figure 11-7, which is intended to be one long bit stream; however, the receiver detects an 8-bit binary sequence $17_{hex}$ as ETB. The receiver would automatically interpret this sequence as an end of transmission block and receive the next 16 bits as the BCC. This is not what should happen but rather the entire bit stream should pass (become transparent) to the receiver. To solve this problem Bisync protocol offers the transparent mode of transmission. The text filed for the transparent mode begins with DLE STX instead of STX. This two-character control sequence ''notifies'' the receiver that the following text block should be treated as a transparent bit stream. However, the receiver must be able to identify the end of the bit stream. This is done by using one of the following control character sequences: DLE ETB, DLE ETX, or DLE ITB as shown in Figure 11-8.

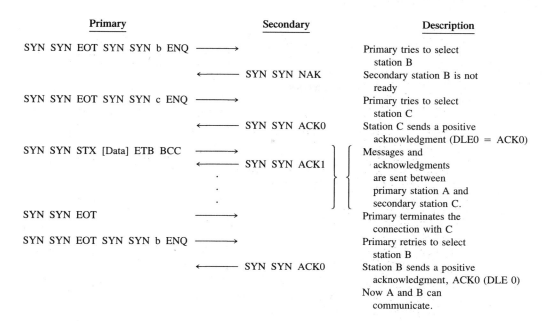

**Figure 11-6   Solution to Example 11-4.**

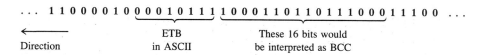

... 1 1 0 0 0 0 1 0 0 0 0 1 0 1 1 1 1 0 0 0 1 1 0 1 1 0 1 1 1 0 0 0 1 1 1 0 0 ...

| ← | ETB | These 16 bits would |
|---|---|---|
| Direction | in ASCII | be interpreted as BCC |

**Figure 11-7   Raw Binary Data Could Contain a Binary Sequence Identical to a Control Character**

| SYN | SYN | DLE | STX | Bit stream | DLE | ETB<br>ITB<br>ETX | BCC |
|---|---|---|---|---|---|---|---|

Transparent text

**Figure 11-8   Bisync Frame Format for Transparent Mode Transmission**

It is also possible that the bit stream may contain these control character pairs and the receiver must not interpret them as the ending of the block. The solution to this problem is that the transmitter automatically inserts a DLE character before any DLE that occurs within the transparent text block. Hence, a DLE ETB sequence in the transparent bit stream would be sent as DLE DLE ETB. Upon receiving a DLE DLE pair, the receiver removes the first DLE. The second DLE is considered as data within the bit stream and not as the first part of the ending control character pair. If the receiver removes a DLE character and the next character is ETB, ITB, or ETX, the receiver knows that the bit stream has ended.

As was mentioned in Section 11-3, the sequence of SYN SYN is inserted into a long block of text to maintain synchronization. The receiver discards them so they are not stored as data. In the transmit mode, the SYN SYN sequence is replaced by DLE SYN. As with SYN SYN sequence, the DLE SYN is not included as part of the BCC.

*really transmit DLE DLE SYN to distinguish between DLE SYN coincidence*

## 11-7   Timeout Procedure

The Bisync protocol contains four timeout procedures to handle exceptions. They are transmit timeout, receive timeout, disconnect timeout, and continue timeout.

---

**Transmit Timeout**   The sequence SYN SYN (or DLE SYN for transparent mode) is inserted into transmission blocks once per second. These sequences maintain synchronization.

**Receive Timeout**   If a station has not replied within 3 seconds, the transmitting station assumes the receiving station has failed and begins its recovery procedure.

**Disconnect Timeout**   If a station on a switched network (dial-up) is inactive for 20 seconds, it will disconnect itself from the network.

**Continue Timeout**   A 2-second timeout is obtained with either TTD or WACK. If a station wishes to extend the temporary timeout, it must send another TTD or WACK within 2 seconds.

---

## 11-8   Bisync Limitations

In today's high speed data communication applications, the Bisync protocol has severe limitations. Each message or portions of long messages has to be acknowledged by the receiving station before the next message can be sent. This prevents messages from being divided by sequence numbers to obtain the efficient use of high speed data lines. Half-duplex operation prevents full-duplex communication between stations. Control characters use up valuable time. The BCC applies only to the text block and not to the header block. Thus a transmission error in this block goes undetected. Although this protocol supports the transparent mode, you could see if the bit stream contained many patterns similar to DLE, and since each one has to be preceded by another DLE character, there could be a considerable waste of transmission time. These limitations are overcome by newer DLCs such as with the special case of COPs—the byte count protocols, Section 11-9, in particular with the BOPs that will be studied in Chapter 12.

## 11-9   Byte Count Protocol

Binary synchronous communications allow only one unacknowledged message and require special characters to be inserted in the transparent mode. These limitations can waste data communications resources as well as time. More efficient protocols have been designed such as the BOP given in Chapter 12. Another protocol that has some of the features of the BOP is a protocol based on a byte count. In some texts byte count protocols are considered a separate protocol but generally they are considered to be a subgroup of COPs similar to byte control protocols. (Bisync is a byte control protocol.)

One of the most commonly used byte count protocols is DDCMP. It is designed to operate on full- or half-duplex channels, dial-up or direct links, point-to-point or multipoint systems, asynchronous or synchronous communication, and serial or parallel transmission. Hence it is a protocol with many more communication features than Bisync.

The header, which is an optional block in the Bisync protocol, is required in DDCMP. The header contains information about the packed sequence number and character count. There are two types of messages—data and protocol. After the two synchronous characters (SYN SYN), the next character indicates whether a data or protocol message is being sent. An SOH (start of header) character signifies a data message while an ENQ (Enquiry) character indicates that a protocol message follows. Figure 11-9 shows the format for a data message. The count field contains 14 bits, which indicates the number of characters in the data field. This count is used by the receiver to determine the end of the data field. Since the receiver now knows the number of characters in the data field, it does not have to scan the data for special control characters. Therefore DDCMP is a fully transparent mode of transmission. The two flag bits designate control of the link. The response field indicates the last valid data message received. The sequence field contains the number of this message. The address field contains the address where this data message is being sent. The last part of the header is a 16-bit CRC block for detecting transmission errors in the header.

The reason for a CRC block at this point is that the header information is vital to the rest of the message. Remember, the information contained in the data field has no effect on the protocol's operation, so control characters may be inserted without causing unintentioned problems at the receiver. However, all characters in the data field must be in 8 bits. Additional zeros must be used to fill out any characters that do not contain 8 bits.

E  X  A  M  P  L  E     11 - 5

The count field in a DDCMP data message is 14 bits. What is the maximum number of 8-bit characters that may be in the data field?

**Solution**

Maximum data field size $= 2^{14} = 16,384$ characters.

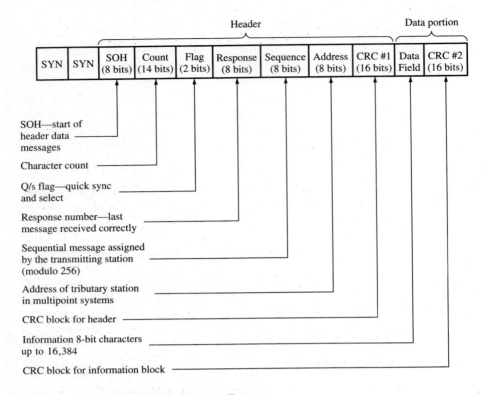

**Figure 11-9   DDCMP's Data Message Format**

E  X  A  M  P  L  E    11 - 6

How many data messages can be received by a station before it must acknowledge receipt of the message?

**Solution**

The size of the response field is 8 bits. Therefore, the maximum number of messages a station can receive without an acknowledgment receipt is $2^8 = 256$.

E  X  A  M  P  L  E    11 - 7

In a multipoint system using DDCMP, what would be the highest numbered address if all addresses are used?

**Solution**

There is an 8-bit address field. Therefore, the maximum number of stations on the link can be $2^8 = 256$ and the range is from 0–255 (the highest numbered address).

## 11-10   Bisync I/O Device (MC6852)

A number of manufacturers sell I/O devices that are designed for synchronous protocols. In this section, one such device will be introduced on Motorola's MC6852 Synchronous Serial Data Adapter (SSDA). It is a serial interface device for transmitting and receiving synchronous data simultaneously. The device contains chip select, read/write, interrupt, and bus interface circuitry to allow easy interconnection to an 8-bit microprocessor but it may also be used with 16-bit microprocessors. As with other I/O devices, the SSDA is programmable so that it may be used in a variety of applications and to transfer data at different rates.

The MC6852 can also be used for serial applications using floppy disk controllers, tape controllers, as well as DCE. Figure 11-10a shows pin assignments for the MC6852 and Figure 11-10b shows a simplified internal block. A more complete internal block diagram is shown in Figure 11-10c.

This I/O device appears as two addressable memory locations to the microprocessor. However, it has seven registers that the microprocessor can access (two read-only registers and five write-only registers). As shown by Table 11-3, it is the contents of bits 6 and 7 of Control Register 1 that allow the microprocessor to access the other registers when RS = 0 and R/W = 0.

The read-only registers are the status and the Receive Data FIFO (first in first out) register. The write-only registers are the Control $^\#$1, Control $^\#$2, Control $^\#$3, Sync Code, and Transfer Data FIFO registers.

Although space does not permit a complete description of this device, the basic principles of its operation will be covered.

### 11-10.1   Principles of Operation

Data to be transmitted over the communication link is sent from the microprocessor to the SSDA via the 8-bit data bus and into the 3-byte transmit data FIFO register. Once data enters the FIFO register, the SSDA's internal circuitry automatically moves the data to the last empty location and then eventually into the transmit shift register. The MC6852 can be programmed to generate either odd, even, or no parity. As with most other serial data transfer, the least significant bit (LSB) is transferred first. However, the MC6852 can be programmed to send the most significant bit (MSB) first. This feature allows the device to be used in an IBM system.

A condition known as "underflow" exists when both the Transmit Data Shift register and the Transmit Data FIFO registers are empty. In order to maintain character synchronization with the receiver, the SSDA device automatically inserts all logic 1s or the contents of the Sync Code register. The condition transmitted depends on how the device is programmed.

At the receiver side of the MC6852, serial data on the Receive Data line appears as one continuous bit stream. There are no start and stop bits as in asynchronous communications; therefore, it is necessary to achieve character synchronization. Once this is accomplished, it is assumed that character synchronization remains for the entire block.

*(Text continued on page 253.)*

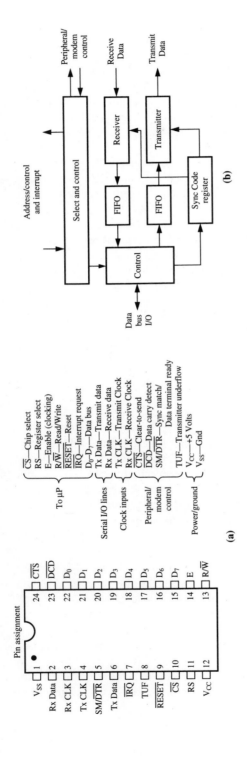

**Figure 11-10  a and b.  The MC6852 Synchronous Serial Data Adapter's Pin Assignments Are Shown in (a), Simplified Internal Block Diagram in (b).**  *(Courtesy of Motorola Incorporated, Austin, Texas)*

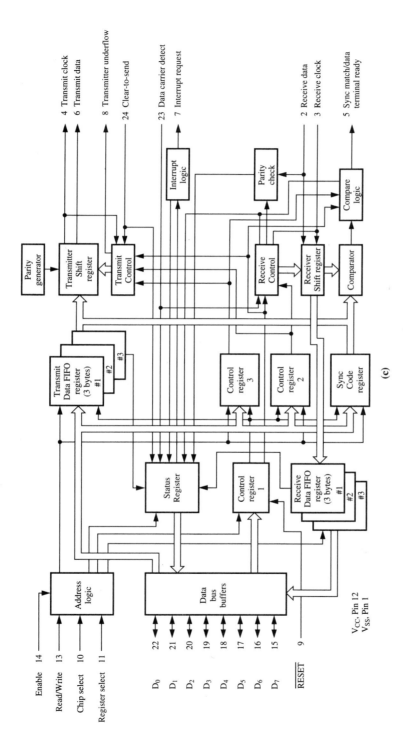

**Figure 11-10   c. An Expanded Internal Block Diagram.** *(Courtesy of Motorola Incorporated, Austin, Texas)*

**Table 11-3**   MC6852 Internal Registers (Copyright of Motorola, Inc. Used by permission.)

| Register | Control Inputs | | | | Register Content | | | | | | | |
|---|---|---|---|---|---|---|---|---|---|---|---|---|
| | RS | R/W | AC2 | AC1 | Bit 7 | Bit 6 | Bit 5 | Bit 4 | Bit 3 | Bit 2 | Bit 1 | Bit 0 |
| Status (S) | 0 | 1 | X | X | Interrupt Request (IRQ) | Receiver Parity Error (PE) | Receiver Overrun (Rx Ovrn) | Transmitter Underflow (TUF) | Clear-to-Send ($\overline{CTS}$) | Data Carrier Detect ($\overline{DCD}$) | Transmitter Data Register Available (TDRA) | Receiver Data Available (RDA) |
| Control 1 (C1) | 0 | 0 | X | X | Address Control 2 (AC2) | Address Control 1 (AC1) | Receiver Interrupt Enable (RIE) | Transmitter Interrupt Enable (TIE) | Clear Sync | Strip Sync Characters (Strip Sync) | Transmitter Reset (Tx Rs) | Receiver Reset (Rx Rs) |
| Receive Data FIFO | 1 | 1 | X | X | D7 | D6 | D5 | D4 | D3 | D2 | D1 | D0 |
| Control 2 (C2) | 1 | 0 | 0 | 0 | Error Interrupt Enable (EIE) | Transmit Sync Code on Underflow (Tx Sync) | Word Length Select 3 (WS3) | Word Length Select 2 (WS2) | Word Length Select 1 (WS1) | 1-Byte/2-Byte Transfer (1-Byte/2-Byte) | Peripheral Control 2 (PC2) | Peripheral Control 1 (PC1) |
| Control 3 (C3) | 1 | 0 | 0 | 1 | Not Used | Not Used | Not Used | Not Used | Clear Transmitter Underflow Status (CTUF) | Clear $\overline{CTS}$ Status (Clear $\overline{CTS}$) | One-Sync-Character/Two-Sync Character Mode Control (1 Sync/2-Sync) | External/Internal Sync Mode Control (E/I Sync) |
| Sync Code | 1 | 0 | 1 | 0 | D7 | D6 | D5 | D4 | D3 | D2 | D1 | D0 |
| Transmit Data FIFO | 1 | 0 | 1 | 1 | D7 | D6 | D5 | D4 | D3 | D2 | D1 | D0 |

X = Don't care

**Table 11-3**   *continued*

### STATUS REGISTER

| | | |
|---|---|---|
| IRQ | Bit 7 | The IRQ flag is cleared when the source of the IRQ is cleared. The source is determined by the enables in the Control Registers: TIE, RIE, EIE. |
| | Bits 6–0 | Indicate the SSDA status at a point in time and can be *reset* as follows: |
| PE | Bit 6 | Read Rx Data FIFO or a "1" into Rx Rs (C1 Bit 0). |
| Rx Ovrn | Bit 5 | Read Status and then Rx Data FIFO or a "1" into Rx Rs (C1 Bit 0). |
| TUF | Bit 4 | A "1" into CTUF (C3 Bit 3) or into Tx Rs (C1 Bit 1). |
| $\overline{CTS}$ | Bit 3 | A "1" into Clear $\overline{CTS}$ (C3 Bit 2) or a "1" into Tx Rs (C1 Bit 1). |
| $\overline{DCD}$ | Bit 2 | Read Status and then Rx Data FIFO or a "1" into Rx Rs (C1 Bit 0). |
| TDRA | Bit 1 | Write into Tx Data FIFO. |
| RDA | Bit 0 | Read Rx Data FIFO. |

### CONTROL REGISTER 1

| | | |
|---|---|---|
| AC2, AC1 | Bits 7, 6 | Used to access other registers, as shown above. |
| RIE | Bit 5 | When "1", enables interrupt on RDA (S Bit 0). |
| TIE | Bit 4 | When "1", enables interrupt on TDRA (S Bit 1). |
| Clear Sync | Bit 3 | When "1", clears receiver character synchronization. |
| Strip Sync | Bit 2 | When "1", strips sync codes from the received data stream. |
| Tx Rs | Bit 1 | When "1", resets and inhibits the transmitter section. |
| Rx Rs | Bit 0 | When "1", resets and inhibits the receiver section. |

### CONTROL REGISTER 3

| | | |
|---|---|---|
| CTUF | Bit 3 | When "1", clears TUF (S Bit 4), and IRQ if enabled. |
| Clear $\overline{CTS}$ | Bit 2 | When "1", clears $\overline{CTS}$ (S Bit 3), and IRQ if enabled. |
| 1 Sync/2 Sync | Bit 1 | When "1", selects the one-sync-character mode; when "0", selects the two-sync-character mode. |
| E/I Sync | Bit 0 | When "1", selects the external sync mode; when "0", selects the internal sync mode. |

### CONTROL REGISTER 2

| | | |
|---|---|---|
| EIE | Bit 7 | When "1", enables the PE, Rx Ovrn, TUF, $\overline{CTS}$, and DCD interrupt flags (S Bits 6 through 2). |
| Tx Sync | Bit 6 | When "1", allows sync code contents to be transferred on underflow, and enables the TUF Status bit and output. When "0", an all mark character is transmitted on underflow. |
| WS3, 2, 1 | Bits 5–3 | Word Length Select |

*continued*

**Table 11-3**  *continued*

| Bit 5 WS3 | Bit 4 WS2 | Bit 3 WS1 | Word Length |
|---|---|---|---|
| 0 | 0 | 0 | 6 Bits + Even Parity |
| 0 | 0 | 1 | 6 Bits + Odd Parity |
| 0 | 1 | 0 | 7 Bits |
| 0 | 1 | 1 | 8 Bits |
| 1 | 0 | 0 | 7 Bits + Even Parity |
| 1 | 0 | 1 | 7 Bits + Odd Parity |
| 1 | 1 | 0 | 8 Bits + Even Parity |
| 1 | 1 | 1 | 8 Bits + Odd Parity |

1-Byte/2-Byte

Bit 2   When "1", enables the TDRA and RDA bits to indicate when a 1-byte transfer can occur; when "0", the TDRA and RDA bits indicate when a 2-byte transfer can occur.

Bits 1-0   SM/$\overline{DTR}$ Output Control

PC2, PC1

| Bit 1 PC2 | Bit 0 PC1 | SM/$\overline{DTR}$ Output at Pin 5 |
|---|---|---|
| 0 | 0 | 1 |
| 0 | 1 | Pulse ⎍ , 1 Bit Wide, on SM |
| 1 | 0 | 0 |
| 1 | 1 | SM Inhibited, 0 |

NOTE: When the SSDA is used in applications requiring the MSB of data to be received and transmitted first, the data bus inputs to the SSDA may be reversed (D0 to D7, etc.). Caution must be used when this is done since the bit positions in this table will be reversed, and the parity should not be selected.

The MC6852 has three modes for character synchronization: one-sync character mode; two-sync character mode; and external sync mode. The one-sync and two-sync character modes are referred to as the internal sync modes.

Tape cassettes normally use one-sync character. The Bisync and DDCMP protocols require at least two synchronization characters (SYN SYN). When the MC6852 is programmed for the two-sync character mode, the device searches on a bit-by-bit basis for the first character and then "looks" at the next character for a match before establishing synchronization. If synchronization is not established, the SSDA goes back to a bit-by-bit search.

Any sync codes that are received before the completion of synchronization are not transferred to the Receive Data FIFO. Also, any sync codes that are used as "fill characters" can be automatically "stripped away" from the data. In order to accomplish the stripping away, bit 2 of Control Register #1 must be set to a logic 1.

After synchronization is achieved, any received character is automatically transferred from the Received Shift register into the Received Data FIFO #1. Similar to the transmit side, the SSDA transfers the data to the last empty receive FIFO register. In the one-byte transfer mode, bit 0 of Control Register 1 indicates when data is available in FIFO #3 Register for the microprocessor to read. In the two-byte transfer mode, bit 0 indicates when FIFO Registers #2 and #3 contain data for the microprocessor to read. FIFO Register #3 is read first. Bit 0 of Control Register #3 selects whether external or internal synchronization is used (*see* Table 11-3). An internal transfer mode is selected by the contents of bit 2 of Control Register #2 (logic 1-1 byte, logic 0-2 bytes).

The Sync Code register is an 8-bit register that is programmable and stores the synchronization code for received data as well as automatic insertion of fill characters in the transmitted data stream. Although the Sync Code register is only 8 bits, it can be used either for one or more bytes for sync detection by using software to check multiple bytes. Consider that an application requires detecting two sync codes. After there is a match with the first sync code, the SM (sync match) output line of the MC6852 can be used to send an interrupt request signal to the microprocessor. The microprocessor then changes the sync code before the next serial character is received by the SSDA. Remember that the microprocessor has quite a lot of time to change sync codes because it can read or write information to an I/O device in microseconds and serial data is received in the order of milliseconds.

An example of how this device can be wired to an 8-bit microprocessor is shown in Figure 11-11.

## Summary

Protocols are rules that ensure an orderly transfer of data between digital equipment. This chapter introduced one type of synchronous protocol—the COP. There are two types of COPs: byte control and byte count protocols. A popular byte control

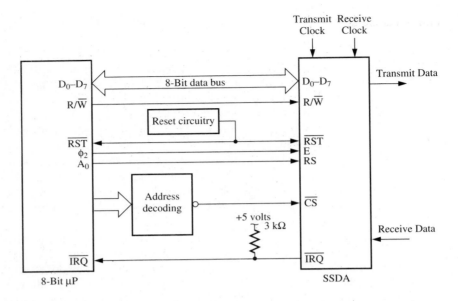

**Figure 11-11   Example of Interfacing the SSDA to an 8-Bit Microprocessor**

protocol is Bisync or BSC. This protocol was introduced in the early 1960s by IBM and has certain limitations, but it is still used. Two of its primary limitations are that it is only half-duplex and that an acknowledgment must be sent after every message. Thus it does not support a count sequence as newer protocols do. Bisync is a byte control protocol because special control characters are used within a frame to separate the fields. These control characters are covered in Sections 11-3 to 11-6. Although Bisync has its limitations, it does support point-to-point and multipoint communication as well as providing for transparent transmission.

Byte count protocol such as the DDCMP was introduced in Section 11-9. This protocol is more efficient than Bisync and some of its basic principles were introduced. Section 11-10 introduced a VLSI chip that is capable of supporting COPs.

## Problems

**11.1** Define the term "protocol."

**11.2** What is the protocol of synchronous communication?

**\*11.3** List three characteristics of the physical layer.

* *See* Answers to Selected Problems.

**11.4** What are the two classifications of DLCs?

**\*11.5** What type of protocol relies on the insertion of special control characters?

**11.6** Expand the abbreviation BSC.

**\*11.7** Is the header a required or optional field in the Bisync protocol?

**11.8** What is a major disadvantage of the Bisync protocol for today's high speed data communication needs?

**\*11.9** Assume in a point-to-point system that one station has acquired control of the link and has transmitted SYN SYN ENQ. What is the other station's reply if
(a) It is ready to receive data?
(b) It is temporarily not ready to receive data?

**11.10** Refer to Problem 11.9. What are the replies using the ASCII character set?

**\*11.11** If a transmitting station ends a block with an ITB control character, does the receiving station send an acknowledgment?

**11.12** Refer to Problem 11.11. Does the receiving station check for a bit error(s)?

**\*11.13** What is the receiver's reply if it wants the communication link?

**11.14** Refer to Example 11.1. If after step 3 the secondary station is still not ready to receive data, could it send another SYN SYN WACK control character sequence?

**11.15** Refer to Figure 11-4. If after the primary has sent the second SYN SYN ENQ sequence, trying to transmit block 4, the secondary is still not ready, what could be the traffic on the channel?

**11.16** If station C in Example 11.3 has a one-block message to send, how is the communication traffic modified in Figure 11.5?

**\*11.17** Assume that the following binary sequence is part of a longer sequence.

$$\ldots 0010110000010111011100 \ldots$$

$$\longleftarrow$$

Direction of data flow

If the transparent mode is off, would the receiver's circuitry detect an end of transmission control character?

**11.18** List the four types of timeout procedures contained in the Bisync protocol.

**\*11.19** Does the BCC in the Bisync protocol include the header?

**11.20** Is DDCMP a byte count or a byte control character?

**\*11.21** List at least two advantages of DDCMP over Bisync.

**11.22** What are the two types of DDCMP messages?

*11.23 The binary pattern in the count field of a DDCMP message is

MSB                        LSB
0 0 0 0 1 1 0 1 1 1 0 0 1 0

How many characters are in the message?

11.24 The binary pattern in the response field of a DDCMP message is

MSB              LSB
0 0 0 1 0 1 1 0

What is the last message to be received correctly?

*11.25 The address filed in a DDCMP message contains the following binary pattern:

MSB              LSB
0 0 0 1 1 0 0 1

What secondary station is being addressed by the primary station?

# Bit Oriented Protocols    12

O B J E C T I V E S

Upon completion of this chapter on bit oriented protocols, the student will be able to

- Explain the advantages of a bit oriented protocol (BOP) over a character oriented protocol (COP).

- List and explain the three types of message frames.

- Describe how the flag fields are used.

- Show how and why zero insertion and zero detection are used.

- Explain the need for the address field.

- Explain the function of each bit or group of bits in the control field for each type of message.

- Show how messages are transferred on the communication channel.

- Describe the basic operation of each type of unnumbered frame (U-frame).

- Show how a BOP is used in a loop configuration.

- Explain the difference between a block check character (BCC) and frame check sequence (FCS).

## Introduction

The tasks of any data link protocol are to establish a connection between stations, provide for an orderly flow, try to ensure error-free transmission of data, and then be able to terminate the connection. In addition to these requirements, today's data communication applications also require high-throughput, must support full-duplex operation, and must be capable of being used on point-to-point, multipoint, and loop configurations. The Bisync protocol studied in Chapter 11 has been widely used but has several limitations when trying to solve today's data communication problems. To overcome the Bisync limitations, IBM introduced in the mid 1970s a synchronous data link protocol (SDLC). Since then it has been slightly modified by other manufacturers as well as national and international organizations to include some additional features, but the basis for all of them is the SDLC.

Remember from Chapter 11 that Bisync is a COP, that is, special sync and control characters are needed to indicate the beginning and end of a frame as well as fields within the frame. SDLC, on the other hand, is a BOP. Although each SDLC frame begins and ends with a unique binary pattern, the fields within the frame are not separated by special binary patterns. Figure 12-1 shows the format for an SDLC frame. Since each frame has the same format, the receiver can identify the field that is being received. As seen in Figure 12-1, the information field is optional. The receiver "knows" whether or not it is included by data contained in the control field. The control field will be studied in more detail in Sections 12-5 to 12-8. The International Standards Organization (ISO) published a protocol that closely resembles the SDLC format. The ISO's protocol is called High-Level Data Link Control (HDLC).

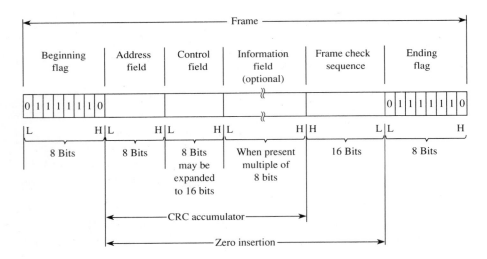

**Figure 12-1   Format of a Bit Oriented SDLC Frame. L is the Low Order Bit and H is the High Order Bit of Each Field. The High Order Bit is Sent First in the Frame Check Sequence.**

A BOP is bit positional. This name is used because the sequence of fields is always the same and the bit positions within the control field have special significance.

Most of the BOP functions are implemented by a peripheral chip such as Motorola's MC6854. This means that the functions are transparent to the user. Before analyzing each field of a bit oriented frame, some of the basic operating principles for exchanging messages will be discussed.

## 12-1 Principles of Operation

One station on the link is always designated as the primary station. It is usually a host computer, front-end processor, or data concentrator. All other stations on the link are designated as secondary stations. They receive commands and information from the primary station. Thus, the primary station retains control of the link at all times through a set of commands. Secondary stations respond to the primary command and may also send information to the primary when permitted to do so.

Figure 12-2 shows a multipoint system with primary station A and three secondary stations labeled B, C, and D. SDLC allows the primary station to transmit to one secondary while receiving messages from another secondary station. This is referred to as full/full-duplex operation. This system will be used for a number of examples in this chapter.

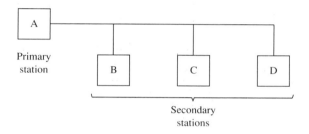

**Figure 12-2  A Multipoint System in a Nonswitched Application**

As previously mentioned, all message transfers between primary and secondary stations use the frame format given in Figure 12-1. There are three types of message frames:

1. Information frames (I-frames), which are used to carry user data.

2. Supervisory frames (S-frames), which are used to acknowledge and reject frames.

3. Unnumbered frames (U-frames), which are used for initializing and disconnecting stations on the link.

The type of frame transmitted depends on the intended task.

Multiple functions may be incorporated into a single frame. For example, if a primary station transmits an I-frame to a secondary station, part of the frame can be used to acknowledge receipt of previously received data from that secondary station. Another example could be when a secondary responds to the primary it can acknowledge that it has received one or more I-frames. If the frames have been received correctly (without errors), then the station that sent the frames can use that portion of its memory buffer for new data. If, however, an error has been detected, then a portion of the control field of an I- or S-frame can be used to identify how many frames have to be retransmitted. The examples in this chapter will show in more detail how these and other messages are transferred between the primary and secondary stations. The fields within each frame will now be studied.

The format of a message for BOPs is shown in Figure 12-1. The message, whether it is information or control, is transmitted and received in a format called a frame. Each frame begins and ends with a binary pattern called a flag. The opening flag is followed by an address field, control field, information field (optional), FCS, and closing flag.

## 12-2   Flag Field

The opening and closing flags have a unique binary pattern of 01111110. This pattern identifies the frame boundaries and is used as a reference for each field within the frame. For example, after the opening flag is identified by the receiver, the receiver knows that the address and control fields must follow. After the closing flag is detected, the receiver uses the two preceding bytes as the FCS.

In order to increase the number of message frames per unit time, two successive frames can share one flag: a closing flag for the first frame and an opening flag for the second frame. The generation, detection, sharing flags, and other routine tasks that will be studied have been incorporated as functions of peripheral I/O chips such as Motorola's MC6854. The receiver searches for a flag on a bit-by-bit basis and once the binary pattern 01111110 is detected the receiver interprets it as a frame boundary. It is quite possible that if an original message is perceived as a long sequence of bits, this binary pattern may occur. Therefore, another major function of the peripheral controller chips is **zero insertion and detection.**

## 12-3   Zero Insertion and Zero Detection

As previously mentioned, the receiver is constantly searching for a flag pattern to either open or close a frame. Since SDLC allows any sequence of binary digits, it is possible that the pattern 01111110 could occur within the message and not be intended as either the opening or closing flag. For example, consider the sequence of bits in Figure 12-3a as part of the information field that is being transmitted. It happens that the pattern 01111110 occurs and therefore the receiver will consider it a flag when actually it is only a portion of the I-field. To avoid this problem, a technique known as zero insertion (or bit-stuffing) is used. The way it works is the transmitter automatically inserts a bit 0 after each sequence of five 1s (of course the exception is the flag fields). Figure 12-3b shows how the binary sequence in Figure 12-3a would be transmitted using the zero insertion technique. The carets (∧) indicate the zero bits that have been inserted by the transmitter. The receiver automatically removes any 0 bit after the fifth 1. Therefore, if the sixth bit is a 0 it is deleted. If, however, the sixth bit is a 1, then the receiver checks the seventh bit. If it is a 0, then a flag pattern has been received. If bit 7 is a 1, then an abort condition has been received. See Figure 12-4 for an example of each condition.

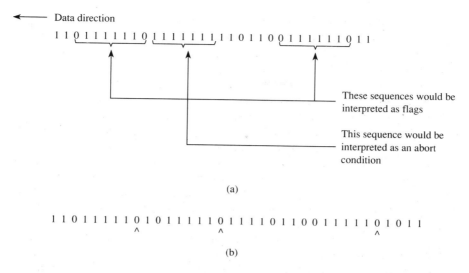

Figure 12-3 Original Binary Pattern in (a) and After Zero-Insertion in (b)

| Bit number → | Transmitted pattern | | | | | | | | Receiver's action | Final received pattern | | | | | | | |
|---|---|---|---|---|---|---|---|---|---|---|---|---|---|---|---|---|---|
| | 0 | 1 | 2 | 3 | 4 | 5 | 6 | 7 | | 0 | 1 | 2 | 3 | 4 | 5 | 6 | 7 |
| | 0 | 1 | 1 | 1 | 1 | 1 | 0 | 0 | Delete bit 6 | 0 | 1 | 1 | 1 | 1 | 1 | 0 | X |
| | 0 | 1 | 1 | 1 | 1 | 1 | 0 | 1 | Delete bit 6 | 0 | 1 | 1 | 1 | 1 | 1 | 1 | X |
| | 0 | 1 | 1 | 1 | 1 | 1 | 1 | 0 | Identifies flag pattern | 0 | 1 | 1 | 1 | 1 | 1 | 1 | 0 |
| | 0 | 1 | 1 | 1 | 1 | 1 | 1 | 1 | Identifies abort condition | 0 | 1 | 1 | 1 | 1 | 1 | 1 | 1 |

Figure 12-4 Action Taken by the Receiver After Checking Bits 6 and 7

The zero insertion technique allows any arbitrary binary sequence to be transmitted within the frame as well as guaranteeing that flag and abort conditions can exist. An abort condition is when the transmitting station prematurely terminates the transmission.

## 12-4  Address Field

The address field follows the opening flag. The purpose of the address field is to identify a secondary station in a multipoint system. Hence the primary station can address a secondary station that is to receive the frame. It is also used by a secondary station to identify itself when it is transmitting.

For most applications, an 8-bit address field is sufficient. However the HDLC format allows this field to be expanded in multiples of 8 bits. For HDLC, bit 1 in the address field is a control bit that indicates whether or not the address field is extended. If bit 1 is a logic 0, then the field is extended by 8 bits. If bit 1 is a logic 1, then the address field is not extended.

| Logic State of Bit 1 | Address Field Extended |
|:---:|:---:|
| 0 | Yes |
| 1 | No |

Since bit 1 of the address field is actually a control bit, the remaining 7 bits are the address. Figure 12-5 illustrates how the control bit is used and how a secondary station's address is calculated. Address field extension is not used in SDLC, only in HDLC and other modified versions of SDLC.

An address of all logic 1s (11111111) is a signal by the primary that this frame is intended for all secondary stations. Thus the primary has a way of getting the attention of all secondaries at once.

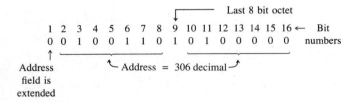

Figure 12-5   Example of Extending the Address Field to 16 Bits

## 12-5   Control Field

The control field identifies whether an I-frame, S-frame, or U-frame is being transmitted. Figure 12-6 shows the format for each type of control field. Each type will be examined.

## 12-6   Control Field for I-Frames

Most operations are the exchange of user data or information. Figure 12-6a shows the format for an 8-bit control field that identifies an I-frame. The bit numbers for the control field are numbered 1 to 8 with the least significant bit (LSB) (bit 1) at

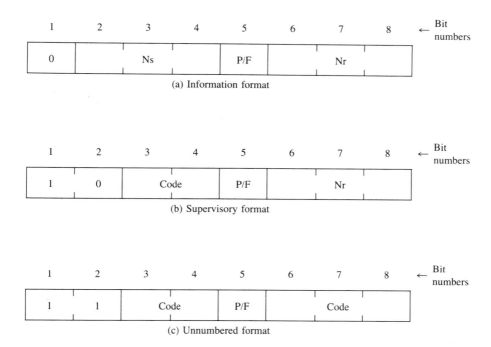

(a) Information format

(b) Supervisory format

(c) Unnumbered format

**Figure 12-6   Control Field Formats**

the left. If bit 1 is a logic 0, then an I-frame is being transmitted and the control field is divided as shown in Figure 12-6a. Bits 2, 3, and 4 identify Ns, the number of the frame sequence being sent. Each time an I-frame is transmitted, this number is incremented by one. The Ns value ensures that the frames are received in the correct order. In an 8-bit control field when the Ns count reaches 7 (111 in binary), the next count is 0 (000 in binary). This count operation is known as modulo 8.

The Nr count (identified by bits 6, 7, and 8) is known as the receive sequence number. Its value indicates the next I-frame to be received by the station that is transmitting the Nr count. Another way of stating the function of the Nr count is that the station that is transmitting has received error free all I-frames equal to $Nr - 1$.

The P/F bit is known as the Poll/Final bit. For the primary station transmission, this bit is referred to as the poll bit and for secondary station transmission it is referred to as the final bit. Primary stations transmit commands and the P/F bit is normally 0. However, when the primary wishes to give permission to a secondary station to transmit, the primary sets the poll bit to 1. As long as the secondary is transmitting a sequence of I-frames, the final bit is a 0. When the secondary transmits its last I-frame in the sequence, it sets the final bit to 1.

Before studying Examples 12-1 and 12-2, refer to Figure 12-7 to see the notation that is used for the I-frames.

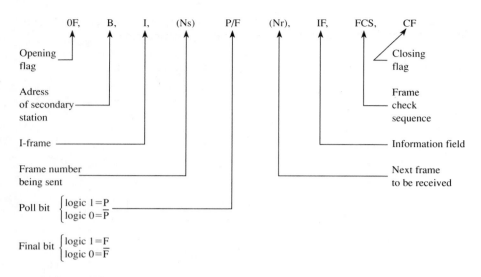

**Figure 12-7   I-Frame Notation**

E  X  A  M  P  L  E    12 - 1

Consider that primary station A has six I-frames (labeled 0 to 5) to transmit to secondary station B. After station B receives I-frame $^\#5$, it sends an acknowledgment that all the frames have been received correctly and sends two of its own I-frames (labeled 0 and 1). Show the communication traffic that would occur on the link.

**Solution**

The following eight steps show how the information is transferred.

| Step | Station A | Station B | Description |
|------|-----------|-----------|-------------|
| 1 | OF,B,I(0)$\overline{\text{P}}$(0),IF,FCS,CF  → | | A sends I-frame $^\#0$ |
| 2 | OF,B,I(1)$\overline{\text{P}}$(0),IF,FCS,CF  → | | A sends I-frame $^\#1$ |
| 3 | OF,B,I(2)$\overline{\text{P}}$(0),IF,FCS,CF  → | | A sends I-frame $^\#2$ |
| 4 | OF,B,I(3)$\overline{\text{P}}$(0),IF,FCS,CF  → | | A sends I-frame $^\#3$ |
| 5 | OF,B,I(4)$\overline{\text{P}}$(0),IF,FCS,CF  → | | A sends I-frame $^\#4$ |
| 6 | OF,B,I(5)P(0),IF,FCS,CF  → | | A sends $^\#5$ and requests a reply |
| 7 | | ←  OF,B,I(0)$\overline{\text{F}}$(6),IF,FCS,CF | B acknowledges all I-frames 0–5 and sends its own I-frame $^\#0$ |
| 8 | | ←  OF,B,I(1)F(6),IF,FCS,CF | B sends I-frame $^\#1$ |

At step 6, the primary station (station A) sets the P/F bit to a logic 1 (P). This logic state signals the secondary station B to begin transmission.

Note that at the end of step 8, the primary station has not acknowledged the I-frames received from the secondary. It will the next time it sends an I-frame to station B or it could send an S-frame, which will be covered in the next section.

This example is a demonstration of half-duplex operation since the transmission from station A was complete before the transmission from station B began. The next example demonstrates full-duplex operation between the primary station and one secondary station (a point-to-point system).

---

**E X A M P L E    12 - 2**

---

Reconsider Example 12-1 but now for full-duplex operation. Station B has another I-frame ($^{\#}2$) to transmit and the I-frames are not the same length. Show the traffic on the communication link.

**Solution**

Consider that station B transmits its I-frames $^{\#}0$ and $^{\#}1$ while station A is sending its I-frames $^{\#}1$, 2, 3, 4, and 5.

The following steps show how stations A and B exchange data for this application. As shown, the I-frames do not have to be the same length.

| Step | Station A | | Station B | Description |
|---|---|---|---|---|
| 1 | OF,B,I(0)P(0),IF,FCS,CF | $\rightarrow$ | | A sends I-frame $^{\#}0$ and signals B to transmit |
| 2 | OF,B,I(1)$\overline{P}$(0),IF,FCS,CF | $\rightarrow\leftarrow$ | OF,B,I(0)$\overline{F}$(1),IF,FCS,CF | A sends I-frame $^{\#}1$ and B sends I-frame $^{\#}0$ and confirms A's 0 frame |
| 3 | OF,B,I(2)$\overline{P}$(0),IF,FCS,CF | $\rightarrow$ | | A sends I-frame $^{\#}2$ |
| 4 | OF,B,I(3)$\overline{P}$(0),IF,FCS,CF | $\rightarrow$ | | A sends $^{\#}3$ |
| 5 | | $\leftarrow$ | OF,B,I(1)$\overline{F}$(3),IF,FCS,CF | B sends $^{\#}1$ and acknowledges frames $^{\#}1$ and $^{\#}2$ from A |
| 6 | OF,B,I(4)$\overline{P}$(1),IF,FCS,CF | $\rightarrow$ | | A sends $^{\#}4$ and acknowledges B's $^{\#}0$ |
| 7 | OF,B,I(5)P(1),IF,FCS,CF | $\rightarrow$ | | A sends $^{\#}5$ and has nothing more to send at this time |
| 8 | | $\leftarrow$ | OF,B,I(2)F(6),IF,FCS,CF | B sends $^{\#}2$ and acknowledges A's $^{\#}4$ and 5 |

As shown, the I-frames do not have to be the same length. Steps 2 through 7 are full-duplex operation, both transmissions occurring at the same time. *Note:*

Primary station A has not acknowledged frames 1 and 2 from secondary station B but may by using an S frame.

---

## 12-7   Control Field for S-Frames

S-frames control the flow and acknowledge received frames. They do not carry information messages themselves. Flow control means that an S-frame can be used to indicate whether or not a station is ready to receive information. S-frames can also be used to reject a frame(s). Thus S-frames are used to provide an orderly transfer of information.

Like other types of frames, it is the bit pattern within the control field that indicates to the receiver the type of frame being transmitted. Figure 12-6 shows that if bits 1 and 2 are 1,0, respectively, then an S-frame is being sent. Bits 3 and 4 are known as the code bits and identify the type of S-frame being transmitted. There are three types of S-frames:

| Bits 3,4 | Abbreviation | Name |
|------|------|------|
| 00 | RR | Receiver Ready |
| 10 | RNR | Receiver Not Ready |
| 01 | REJ | Reject |

### 12-7.1   RR S-Frames

An RR supervisory frame may be issued either as a command (by the primary) or as a response (by the secondary). If the primary station wishes to poll the secondary, it may send an RR supervisory frame with the poll bit set (logic 1). Thus the primary is "asking" the secondary whether it is ready to receive I-frames and the primary is waiting for a response.

A secondary station may issue an RR supervisory frame (1) to indicate to the primary that it is ready to receive an I-frame(s) (the secondary will put in the Nr field the number of the I-frame that it expects to receive) and (2) to acknowledge to the primary that it has received previously transmitted I-frames. The last I-frame that was received error free is $Nr - 1$. In both cases, the secondary sets the final bit to indicate it is not sending any other frames at this time. Although secondary stations may use I-frames to acknowledge previously transmitted I-frames, an RR supervisory frame may be the most efficient way of accomplishing the task. In Examples 12-1 and 12-2, the secondary was sending I-frames to the primary and the acknowledgments were attached (also called piggy backing) to the control field.

If an I-frame is not being sent, the secondary needs a way of transmitting positive acknowledgments: an RR supervisory frame is the answer. The format for transmitting S-frames for the following examples is shown in Figure 12-8.

**E X A M P L E    12 - 3**

Consider that a primary station A is to poll three secondary stations B, C, and D. Use an RR supervisory frame as a command and response.

**Solution**

| Step | Primary Station | | Secondary Stations | Description |
|------|-----------------|---|---------------------|-------------|
| 1 | OF,B,RR-P(0),FCS,CF | → | | A polls B |
| 2 | | ← | OF,B,RR-F(0),FCS,CF | B responds it is ready |
| 3 | OF,C,RR-P(0),FCS,CF | → | | A polls C |
| 4 | | ← | OF,C,RR-F(0),FCS,CF | C responds it is ready |
| 5 | OF,D,RR-P(0),FCS,CF | → | | A polls D |
| | | ← | OF,D,RR-F(0),FCS,CF | D responds it is ready |

**E X A M P L E    12 - 4**

Primary station A and secondary station B are connected in a point-to-point link. Show the protocol exchange if station A has four I-frames (labeled 3, 4, 5, and 6) to transmit and station B responds using an RR supervisory frame after I-frames #5 and #6.

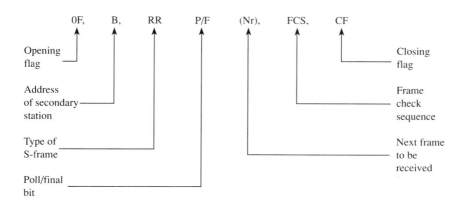

**Figure 12-8   An Example of an S-Frame Notation**

**Solution**

| Step | Station A | | Station B | Description |
|------|-----------|---|-----------|-------------|
| 1 | OF,B,I(3)$\overline{P}$(0),FCS,CF | → | | A sends I-frame [#]3 |
| 2 | OF,B,I(4)$\overline{P}$(0),FCS,CF | → | | A sends I-frame [#]4 |
| 3 | OF,B,I(5)P(0),FCS,CF | → | | A sends I-frame [#]5 |
| 4 | | ← | OF,B,RR-F(6),FCS,CF | B acknowledges I-frames [#]3 through [#]5 |
| 5 | OF,B,I(6)P(0),FCS,CF | → | | A sends I-frame [#]6 |
| 6 | | ← | OF,B,RR-F(7),FCS,CF | B acknowledges I-frame [#]6 |

## 12-7.2  RNR S-Frames

The second type of S-frame is the RNR. Either primary or secondary stations may issue RNR. This S-frame indicates that the receiver is temporarily unable to accept any more frames. Such a frame is issued when the memory buffer that is storing incoming data is filled. Therefore, the buffer must be cleared before any more data can be received. The station that sends an RNR S-frame can remove its busy status by transmitting an RR S-frame.

Figure 12-6b shows the control field for sending an RNR S-frame. Nr bits are also part of the control field. These bits can be used to acknowledge previously received I-frames. When a station issues an RNR frame, it does not mean that it has not accepted the I-frames already sent to it but rather that it cannot accept any more at this time.

### E X A M P L E    12 - 5

Consider again Example 12-4, but now after I-frame [#]5 is received, station B responds with an RNR S-frame. This requires primary station A to poll station B to determine if it is still busy. Consider that B requires another time frame before it is ready and show the protocol exchange.

**Solution**

| Step | Station A | | Station B | Description |
|------|-----------|---|-----------|-------------|
| 1 | OF,B,I(3)$\overline{P}$(0),IF,FCS,CF | → | | A sends I-frame [#]3 |
| 2 | OF,B,I(4)$\overline{P}$(0),IF,FCS,CF | → | | A sends I-frame [#]4 |
| 3 | OF,B,I(5)P(0),IF,FCS,CF | → | | A sends I-frame [#]5 and asks for a response |
| 4 | | ← | OF,B,RNR-F(6),FCS,CF | B is busy but acknowledges I-frames [#]3–[#]5 |
| 5 | OF,B,RR-P(0),FCS,CF | → | | A polls B and asks for a response |

**Solution** *(continued)*

| | | | |
|---|---|---|---|
| 6 | | ← OF,B,RNR-F(6),FCS,CF | B is still busy |
| 7 | OF,B,RR-P(0),FCS,CF → | | A polls B again |
| 8 | | ← OF,B,RR-F(6),FCS,CF | B is ready and expects I-frame #6 |
| 9 | OF,B,I(6)P(0),IF,FCS,CF → | | A sends I-frame #6 |
| 10 | | ← OF,B,RR-F(7),FCS,CF | B acknowledges I-frame #6 |

When the primary station polls the secondary station, the P/F bit is a logic 1.

## 12-7.3   REJ S-Frames

The third type of S-frame is the REJ. An REJ S-frame indicates that an error in transmission has occurred and the transmitting station must retransmit all I-frames starting with the number in the Nr bit position. This frame may be issued either from the primary or secondary station. If the primary station issues an REJ, the poll bit is set so that the secondary station knows the primary is expecting a response. An REJ can also be sent in reply to an RR S-frame because it is possible that even in an S-frame the FCS values may not agree. Consider an example using this type of S-frame.

**E X A M P L E   12 - 6**

Refer to Example 12-4. If a noise burst occurs causing errors in the transmission of I-frame #3 and station B still is not able to reply until step 4, show the protocol exchange.

**Solution**

| Step | Station A | Station B | Description |
|---|---|---|---|
| 1 | OF,B,I(3)$\overline{P}$(0),IF,FCS,CF —◊→ (noise) | | I-frame #3 is damaged |
| 2 | OF,B,I(4)$\overline{P}$(0),IF,FCS,CF → | | A sends I-frame #4 |
| 3 | OF,B,I(5)P(0),IF,FCS,CF → | | A sends I-frame #5 and requests a response |
| 4 | | ← OF,B,REJ-F(3),FCS,CF | B rejects I-frames #3, #4, and #5 |
| 5 | OF,B,I(3)$\overline{P}$(0),IF,FCS,CF → | | A retransmits #3 |
| 6 | OF,B,I(4)$\overline{P}$(0),IF,FCS,CF → | | A retransmits #4 |
| 7 | OF,B,I(5)P(0),IF,FCS,CF → | | A retransmits #5 and requests a response |
| 8 | | ← OF,B,RR-F(6),FCS,CF | B acknowledges #3, #4, and #5 |
| 9 | OF,B,I(6)P(0),IF,FCS,CF → | | A sends I-frame #6 and requests a response |
| 10 | | ← OF,B,RR-F(7),FCS,CF | B acknowledges I-frame #6 |

Sometimes a fourth S-frame called selective reject (SREJ) may be seen; however, it is not implemented often. Therefore continue by concentrating on U-frames.

## 12-8   U-Frames

The primary function of U-frames is to initialize and disconnect the link. They are also used for reporting certain procedural errors and transferring data that is not to be checked. If bits 1 and 2 of the control field are both 1s, then the receiver knows a U-frame is being transmitted. The general format for the control field within a U-frame is shown in Figure 12-6c. It can be seen that the control field for U-frames does not have Ns or Nr fields. Therefore, U-frames are not checked by a sequence count. The normal response to a U-frame is another U-frame.

A U-frame sent by a primary station is a command and a U-frame sent by a secondary station is a response. Some U-frames are only commands, others only responses, while some may be either commands or responses, depending on the station that is transmitting. Table 12-1 lists the U-frames in alphabetical order.

The binary pattern in bits 3, 4, 6, 7, and 8 identifies the U-frame. If the frame is a command, bit 5 is the poll bit. For a response, bit 5 is the final bit. Table 12-1 gives the abbreviation and binary pattern for each U-frame. For those frames that may be either a command or a response, bit 5 is shown as P/F.

**Table 12-1   Summary of U-Frame Commands and Responses**

| Acronym | Name | Binary Pattern |
|---------|------|----------------|
| BCN | Beacon | 1 1 1 1 F 1 1 1 |
| CFGR | Configure | 1 1 1 0 P / F 0 1 1 |
| DISC | Disconnect | 1 1 0 0 P 0 1 0 |
| DM | Disconnect mode | 1 1 1 1 F 0 0 0 |
| FRMR | Frame reject | 1 1 1 0 F 0 0 1 |
| RD | Request disconnect | 1 1 0 0 F 0 1 0 |
| RIM | Request initialization mode | 1 1 1 0 F 0 0 0 |
| SIM | Set initialization mode | 1 1 1 0 P 0 0 0 |
| SNRM | Set normal response mode | 1 1 0 0 P 0 0 1 |
| SNRME | Set normal response mode extended | 1 1 1 1 P 0 1 1 |
| TEST | Test | 1 1 0 0 P / F 1 1 1 |
| UA | Unnumbered acknowledgment | 1 1 0 0 F 1 1 0 |
| UI | Unnumbered information frame | 1 1 0 0 P / F 0 0 0 |
| UP | Unnumbered poll | 1 1 0 0 P 1 0 0 |
| XID | Exchange station identification | 1 1 1 1 P / F 1 0 1 |

NOTE: LSB is the leftmost bit.

## 12-8.1  U-Frame Descriptions

A short description of the U-frames is given in this section. The U-frames described in this section can be used on point-to-point and multipoint systems. Some U-frames (BCN, CRGR, and UP) are used for loop configurations and are grouped together in the next section.

---

**DISC (Disconnect)**   This U-frame is a command from the primary station. It terminates other modes and places the secondary station in a disconnect mode which means the secondary cannot send or receive I- or S-frames. The expected response to a DISC command is an unnumbered acknowledgment (UA).

**DM (Disconnect Mode)**   A secondary station sends this type of U-frame to notify the primary; it is the disconnect mode.

**FRMR (Frame Reject)**   This U-frame is a response by a secondary station when it receives an invalid frame, provided the secondary station is in the NRM or NRME mode.

Reasons that a received frame may be invalid are

1. The function(s) specified by the received control field are not performed at the secondary station.

2. A received I-field is too long for a secondary station's memory buffer.

3. The received control field does not specify that there is an I-field in the frame, though one is present.

4. The received Nr count is wrong.

After the secondary station sends an FRMR, it cannot release itself from this condition and will continue to send an FRMR response until it is reset. The secondary can be reset by the following commands: DISC, SIM, SNRM, or SNRME.

When a secondary station sends an FRMR type U-frame, it includes an I-field so that the primary can identify what has happened. The contents of the U-frame and, in particular, the I-field, are shown in Figure 12-9. This U-frame was formerly known as CMDR, Command Reject.

**RD (Request Disconnect)**   A secondary station wishing to be disconnected from the link would send this type of U-frame to the primary station. If the primary honors this request, it would send a DISC command. This U-frame was formerly known as RQD (Request Disconnect).

**RIM (Request Initialization Mode)**   When a secondary station wishes to receive an SIM command, it sends an RIM U-frame to the primary station. This U-frame was formerly known as RQI (Request for Initialization).

**SIM (Set Initialization Mode)**   This U-frame sent from the primary station is a command to the secondary station to initialize its link-level function. The expected response is UA. Both the primary and secondary stations reset to 0 their Ns and Nr counts.

**SNRM (Set Normal Response Mode)**   This U-frame command puts the secondary station in a normal response mode. This means that a maximum of seven I-frames can

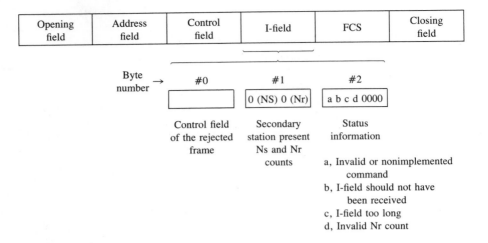

**Figure 12-9    An FRMR Type U-Frame and the Contents of its I-Field**

be sent without acknowledgment. The expected response is UA. The primary and secondary stations reset to 0 their Ns and Nr counts. A secondary station that has been put in the normal response mode remains in this mode until it receives a DISC or SIM command. Also the secondary is not allowed to send unsolicited transmissions.

**SNRME (Set Normal Response Mode Extended)**    This command is similar to SNRM except that the control field is 2 bytes long and the maximum number of I-frames that can be sent before an acknowledgment is 127.

**TEST (Test)**    This U-frame is either a command or a response depending on whether the primary or secondary station is transmitting. As a command, the primary is asking the secondary for a TEST response. The secondary responds by returning the frame. In some systems, the primary also sends an I-field. The secondary station's TEST response includes the information field if the secondary station has enough memory buffer to store the I-field. If the secondary station does not have enough memory buffer, the I-field will not be included in the response.

**UA (Unnumbered Acknowledgment)**    This U-frame is an affirmative response to the following commands: DISC, SIM, SNRM, or SNRME. This frame was formerly known as nonsequenced acknowledgment (NSA).

**UI (Unnumbered Information)**    This U-frame allows the primary station or secondary station(s) to transmit information without sequence numbers. This frame was formerly known as nonsequenced information frame (NSI).

**XID (Exchange Station Identification)**    This U-frame is either a command or a response. As a command, the primary is requesting the secondary to identify itself. The primary may include an I-field that provides its identification. The secondary responds with an XID U-frame. An I-field may be included in the response to identify the secondary.

E   X   A   M   P   L   E      12 - 7

Explain what happens at each of the following steps.

**1.** OF,B,SNRM-P,FCS,CF →

**2.**                              ← OF,B,UA-F,FCS,CF

**3.** OF,B,RR-P(0),FCS,CF →

**4.**                              ← OF,B,RNR-F(0),FCS,CF

**5.** OF,B,RR-P(0),FCS,CF →

**6.**                              ← OF,B,RR-F(0),FCS,CF

**Solution**

**1.** Primary station sets secondary station B's response mode and resets the Ns and Nr counts to 0.

**2.** Secondary station B sends an acknowledgment.

**3.** Primary station polls secondary station B for transmission.

**4.** Secondary station B is not ready at this time.

**5.** Primary station re-polls secondary station B.

**6.** Station B is ready but has nothing to transmit; it remains in the normal response mode.

E   X   A   M   P   L   E      12 - 8

Show the U-frame command that would be transmitted to a secondary station to disconnect it and the secondary's response.

**Solution**

| | | | |
|---|---|---|---|
| OF,B,DISC-P,FCS,CF | → | | Primary commands B to be disconnected (off line). |
| | ← | OF,B,UA-F,FCS,CF | B acknowledges the command |
| | ← | OF,B,DM-F,FCS,CF | B reports that it is disconnected. |

E   X   A   M   P   L   E      12 - 9

Continue Example 12-8 and show what U-frame command and response would be transmitted to reconnect station B to the line.

**Solution**

| | | |
|---|---|---|
| OF,B,SNRM-P,FCS,CF    → | | Primary commands B to be connected to the line. |
| | ←    OF,B,UA-F,FCS,CF | B acknowledges the command. Ns = Nr = 0. |

## 12-9   Loop Configuration

Up to this point applications have been either point-to-point or multipoint systems. A loop configuration as shown in Figure 12-10 may be a preferred solution than connecting several secondary stations in a multipoint system. Information flows around the loop in one direction (a simplex format) beginning at the transmit port of the primary station and ending at the receive port of the primary station. Only one station, either the primary or one of the secondaries, can transmit at a time.

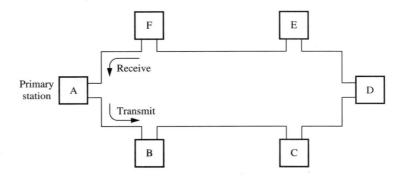

**Figure 12-10   A Loop Configuration with Primary Station A and Secondary Stations B, C, D, E, and F**

The primary transmits command frames to any or all of the secondaries by using the address field. Each secondary "reads" the address field to determine if it should accept the frame. Whether or not a secondary accepts a frame for processing, it sends all frames along the loop. As shown in Figure 12-11, eventually all frames return to the primary station. Thus a secondary station may accept a frame(s) but does not remove it from the string of frames. The primary station can monitor the received frames and know that the loop is in operation.

The way in which the primary station controls the loop amd permits secondary stations to transmit is with a turnaround sequence and a go-ahead sequence. When the primary finishes transmitting, it sends at least eight logic 0s following the last closing flag. A closing flag followed by eight logic 0s is the turnaround sequence. After the logic 0s, the primary station begins transmitting logic 1s. The pattern of 01111111 is the go-ahead sequence (*see* Fig. 12-12).

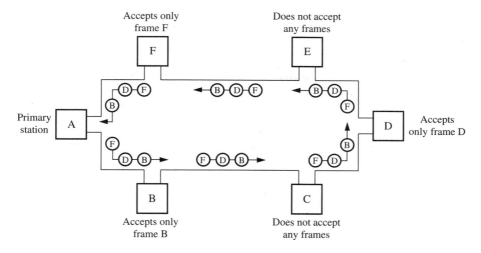

**Figure 12-11   A Secondary Station Accepts for Processing Only the Frames Addressed to It. All Frames are Passed Along the Loop**

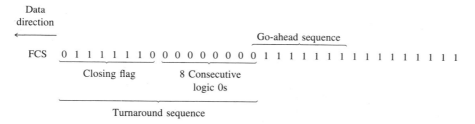

**Figure 12-12   Binary Pattern Showing Closing Flag, Turnaround Sequence, and Go-Ahead Sequence**

Now that the go-ahead sequence has been sent, the secondary stations may begin to transmit. The order is the way they are connected to the loop (B, C, D, E, and F). A secondary station does not transmit unless it has processed a frame with the poll bit set or unless it processed an unnumbered poll (UP) U-frame with the poll bit at logic 0; then transmission from the secondary is optional.

Refer to Figure 12-11 and assume that station B did not receive a UP frame and for any frame(s) it did process, the poll bit was a logic 0. Then station B does not transmit when it receives the go-ahead sequence. However consider station D did receive a frame with the poll bit set. Therefore when station D receives the go-ahead sequence, it converts the eighth bit (the seventh logic 1) to a logic 0. This creates an opening flag. Station D is now transmitting to the primary. When this station has completed its transmission, it sends the turnaround and go-ahead sequence and reverts to its previous state of monitoring the loop. If station F did not receive a UP frame or a frame with the poll bit set to a logic 1, it does not transmit. In this example, it is assumed that stations C and E never received a frame for processing.

The primary station always maintains control of the loop, even when a secondary station is transmitting. This is done by a shut-off sequence which is eight consecutive logic 0s. When a secondary station is transmitting and receives a shut-off sequence, it stops transmitting.

## 12-9.1  Loop Commands/Response

There are three U-frames that are used for loop exchanges. They are: BCN, CFGR, and UP. The binary pattern that appears in the control field is given in Table 12-1.

**BCN (Beacon)**  This U-frame is transmitted by a secondary station when it detects a loss of communication at its input. The purpose of this frame is to notify the primary station that a problem exists and its location. The secondary stops transmitting the BCN U-frame when the problem on the loop no longer exists.

**CFGR (Configure)**  This U-frame may be either a command or a response. As a command, the primary station uses this frame to cause a secondary station to perform diagnostic operations. A secondary station that receives a CFGR U-frame responds with a CFGR U-frame. There are six types of CFGR subcommands that may be sent by the primary station. These subcommands are sent as a single byte in the I-field. They are summarized in Table 12-2. Self test as a command and response is considered one command.

**UP (Unnumbered Poll)**  This U-frame command allows the primary to poll a station, a group of stations, or all the stations on a loop. If the poll bit is a logic 0, a response is optional.

The secondary will respond for any of the following conditions:

1. A confirming Nr count needs to be sent to the primary.

2. A response to an unnumbered command is required.

3. An exception condition has occurred and a response is required.

4. A change has occurred in the secondary, either from RR to RNR or vice versa.

5. The primary station has not acknowledged one or more I-frames sent by the secondary. Therefore the secondary retransmits the unacknowledged I-frames.

6. The secondary is in the DM and sends a DM U-frame. The secondary is expecting to receive an SNRM so that it can become operational.

If the poll bit is a logic 1, the secondary stations that receive this condition must respond. The response will be either

1. Frames the secondary has been waiting to transmit.

2. Retransmission of unacknowledged frames.

**Table 12-2   The Configure Subcommands**

| Name | Binary Pattern | Description |
|---|---|---|
| Clear | 0 0 0 0 0 0 0 0 | Secondary stops all previous functions |
| Beacon test | $\Bigl\{\begin{matrix}0\,0\,0\,0\,0\,0\,1\,1\\0\,0\,0\,0\,0\,0\,1\,0\end{matrix}$ | Secondary suppresses the carrier <br> Secondary resumes transmission of the carrier |
| Monitor mode | $\Bigl\{\begin{matrix}0\,0\,0\,0\,0\,1\,0\,1\\0\,0\,0\,0\,0\,1\,0\,0\end{matrix}$ | Secondary is put into a receive-only mode <br> Secondary can resume transmission |
| Wrap | 0 0 0 0 1 0 0 X | Secondary is off line but it does output whatever it receives |
| Self-test (as a command) | 0 0 0 0 1 0 1 X | Secondary begins a series of diagnostic tests |
| Self-test (as a response) | $\Bigl\{\begin{matrix}0\,0\,0\,0\,1\,0\,1\,1\\0\,0\,0\,0\,1\,0\,1\,0\end{matrix}$ | One or more of the tests failed <br> All diagnostic tests passed |
| Modified link test | $\Bigl\{\begin{matrix}0\,0\,0\,0\,1\,1\,0\,1\\0\,0\,0\,0\,1\,1\,0\,0\end{matrix}$ | Secondary responds to a TEST command with a TEST response that has an I-field <br> Secondary responds to a TEST command with a TEST response that has no I-field |

**3.** Transmission of S-frames—RR or RNR.

**4.** Transmission of U-frame—DM.

## 12-10   FCS

The FCS follows the I-field or the control field if there is no I-field. The FCS performs the same function as the cyclic redundancy check (CRC) block; that is, to allow the receiver to check for transmission errors. As shown in Figure 12-1, the FCS field is 16 bits. At the transmitter, the FCS is computed on the contents of the address, control, and I-field (if present). The generating polynomial is used at the transmitting and receiving stations and is $x^{16} + x^{12} + x^5 + 1$. An FCS is computed differently from the BCC studied in Chapter 10. For an FCS, the register is initially set to all logic 1s. The transmitter inverts the remainder and sends it at the end of the message. At the receiver, the register is preset to logic 1s and once again a division is carried out. For protocols using a BCC, a zero remainder indicates error-free transmission. For this protocol using an FCS, a remainder of $F0B8_{hex}$ indicates error-free transmission.

## Summary

This chapter introduced the principles of a BOP called SDLC. A BOP differs greatly from the Bisync COP covered in Chapter 11. For example, SDLC permits full-duplex operation, transparent mode transmission, and frame sequence numbering. BOP frames are composed of an opening flag, an address field, a control field, an optional I-field, an FCS, and the closing field. The control field identifies the type of frame and pertinent information about the frame. The control field for I-frames contains the number of the frame to be sent and received. For S-frames, the control field contains the number of the frame to be received and the type of S-frame. U-frames are unnumbered and therefore frame numbers are not part of the control field. But the control field does identify the type of U-frame being sent. Regardless of the type of frame, the control field includes a P/F bit. If the primary station sends this bit as a logic 1, it is "asking" for a response from a secondary station. If a secondary station sets the P/F bit to a logic 1, it is a signal to the primary station that this is the last frame of the message.

Transparent mode transmission is accomplished by using a technique called zero insertion and detection. Section 12-6 showed how information is transmitted between a primary and secondary station using I-frames. Sections 12-7 and 12-8 introduced the different types of S- and U-frames, respectively.

This BOP can also be used in a loop configuration. The U-frame commands needed for this type of application and how they are used are given in Section 12-9. A BOP error checking character is called an FCS. It is determined differently from a block check sequence. These differences are discussed in Section 12-10. The BOP can be implemented by an integrated circuit such as an MC6854 or MC145488.

## Problems

**12.1** List at least three functions of any data link protocol.

**12.2** What is the ISO's published protocol that closely resembles SDLC called?

**12.3** What does the term "bit positional" mean?

**12.4** What does the term "full/full-duplex operation" mean?

**\*12.5** Identify the type of message frames for each of the following conditions:
   **(a)** Used to acknowledge another frame without sending data.
   **(b)** Used to carry user data.
   **(c)** Used to initialize a station on the link.
   **(d)** Used to disconnect a station on the link.
   **(e)** Used to reject a frame without carrying any other user data.

* *See* Answers to Selected Problems.

**12.6** Can an I-frame sent by a secondary station be used both to acknowledge previously sent data and to transmit used data?

**\*12.7** **(a)** What field always follows the opening flag?
**(b)** What field always precedes the closing field?

**12.8** How do BOPs ensure transparent mode operation?

**12.9** If the following binary stream is part of the user data message being transmitted, indicate where logic 0s will be inserted.

. . .001111011111111100111111000 . . .

Direction of data flow ⟵

**12.10** After an opening flag has been detected by the receiver, assume that the following pattern is received. What happens?

. . . 01111110 . . .

**\*12.11** What is the binary pattern of an abort condition?

**12.12** **(a)** The following binary stream is received at a station. Remove any logic 0s that would have been inserted by the sending station.
**(b)** Has a closing or abort flag been transmitted?

. . . 00111110100111110011111100111 . . .

**\*12.13** Are logic 0s inserted into the address and control field if required?

**12.14** For each of the following control fields of an I-frame sent by the primary station, identify the frame being sent, the last frame that is accepted, and whether or not the primary station is requesting a reply.

| Bit Position 1 2 3 4 5 6 7 8 |
| --- |
| **(a)** 0 0 1 1 0 0 0 1 |
| **(b)** 0 1 0 1 1 1 0 0 |
| **(c)** 0 0 1 1 0 0 1 0 |
| **(d)** 0 1 1 1 0 0 1 1 |
| **(e)** 0 1 1 0 1 1 0 0 |

**\*12.15** Identify the type of frame being transmitted from each of the following control fields.

|   | Bit Position |
|---|---|
|   | 1 2 3 4 5 6 7 8 |
| (a) | 1 0 0 0 0 1 0 1 |
| (b) | 0 1 1 0 0 1 0 0 |
| (c) | 1 0 1 0 1 0 1 1 |
| (d) | 1 1 0 0 0 0 0 1 |
| (e) | 0 1 1 1 1 1 0 1 |

**12.16** Assume that each of the control fields in Problem 12.15 is being sent by the primary station. Which messages indicate a reply is being requested?

**12.17** Show the communication traffic that would occur on the link for the following conditions:
  **1.** Primary station A has two frames (labeled 3 and 4) to transmit to secondary station B.
  **2.** After station B receives I-frame $^\#4$ it sends a positive acknowledgment that all frames have been received correctly and it sends one I-frame (labeled $^\#0$).

**12.18** Refer to Problem 12.17. Now station B does not have an I-frame to send. Therefore, it sends an S-frame as an acknowledgment that it can receive more data. Show the communication traffic on the link.

**\*12.19** If the SDLC protocol is used in a full-duplex operation, do the I-frames transmitted between primary and secondary station have to be the same length?

**12.20** If a secondary station sends an RNR S-frame, does it mean that it has not accepted any previously received I-frames?

**\*12.21** Refer to the solution of Example 12-5. If at step 6 the secondary's reply was

OF,B,RR-F(6),FCS,CF,

what would be the communications traffic for the next two steps?

**12.22** What is the primary function of U-frames?

**\*12.23** How does a receiver station identify a U-frame?

**12.24** Identify the type of U-frame that would be sent for each of the following conditions:
  **(a)** A primary station wants to put a secondary station into a normal response mode.
  **(b)** A secondary's response if it receives an I-field that is too long for its communication memory buffer.
  **(c)** An expected response to an SIM U-frame.
  **(d)** A secondary station wishing to be disconnected from the link.

**12.25** Refer to Example 12-7 and assume that at step 6 the secondary station has one I-frame to transmit. Show the communication traffic on the link.

**12.26** Refer to Figure 12-11. Why do stations C and E not accept any frames?

*\*12.27* Refer to Figure 12-11. If station B has an I-frame to send, may it simply attach it after message F goes by?

**12.28** The generating polynomial for the FCS is the same as the generating polynomial for what type of CRC used with BCCs?

# 13 | *Multiplexing Techniques*

O B J E C T I V E S

Upon completing this chapter on multiplexing techniques, the student will be able to

- Describe the applications in which a multiplexer would be used and its advantages over other solutions.
- List the three basic types of multiplexing techniques and describe their operation.
- Describe the difference between fixed channel scanning and variable channel scanning used by time division multiplexers.
- Show applications that can use port concentrators and port selectors.
- Describe the advantages of using digital data service.
- Describe the basic principles of a T1 carrier system.
- Give examples of customers who would use fractional T1 carrier service.
- Give examples of customers who would need a fiber distributed data interface based network.
- Encode a bit stream using different line coding techniques such as non-return to zero, alternate mark inversion, and diphase.

## Introduction

A multiplexer is a piece of equipment that combines data from several inputs into one continuous serial data stream for transmission over a single communication channel. At the receiving end the unit demultiplexes the data stream and routes the data to the appropriate port. Although a multiplexer is part of the data terminal equipment (DTE), it is often combined with the circuitry of data communication equipment (DCE) and sold as a single unit. Therefore, multiplexers designed for data transmission will often be sold by DCE suppliers. Like modems, multiplexers are used in pairs: one for the sending end, the other for the receiving end. The units at both ends are known as multiplexers. Figure 13-1, like Figure 1-7, shows

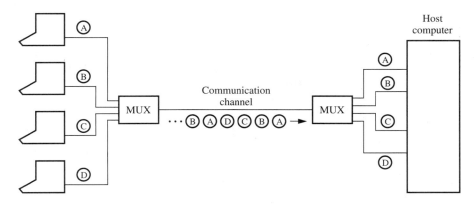

**Figure 13-1    An Example of a Data Communication System Using Multiplexers. A Portion of Each Terminal's Data is Sent in Sequence and the Process is Repeated to Send the Next Portion of Each Terminal's Message**

a typical multiplexer application. Four users share a single communication channel, which can be a considerable savings. To the individual users at the terminals, the multiplexer system is "transparent" because the users may act as if they each have a direct connection to the host computer. Thus, there is no interrupt in the flow of data between the terminals and host computer and vice versa.

Figure 13-2 shows another example of transparency. It is a modification of the direct connection shown in Figure 13-1. The telephone network in Figure 13-2 may be either dial-up or leased. In either case, the multiplexer system should not require either a hardware or software change in any other part of the system. **Note:**

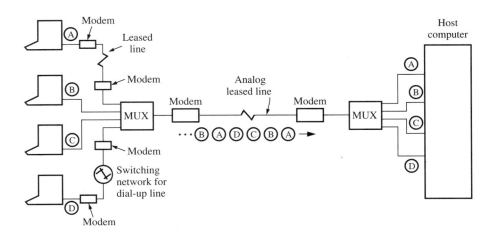

**Figure 13-2    Multiplexers May be Used with Modems to Transmit Data Using a Telephone Network**

In this multiplexer system the host computer still requires the same number of ports. The savings, therefore, is not in the DTE but in communication costs (telephone charges, etc.) and the fact that only one pair of modems is needed instead of a pair for each channel.

A multidrop system as shown in Figure 1-9 is another example of multiplexing. A number of terminals (remote stations) share a common communication channel to the host computer (primary station). In this application, only one I/O computer port is needed; however, additional software is required.

## 13-1    Multiplexing Techniques

There are three basic types of multiplexing techniques used in data communication. They are

**1.** Frequency division multiplexing (FDM).

**2.** Time division multiplexing (TDM).

**3.** Statistical multiplexing (STDM).

The oldest type of multiplexing is FDM. It is the type of multiplexing used in the Bell 103 modem (Chapters 8 and 9). From those chapters, we learned that for the 103 modem the frequency bandwidth of the telephone channel was divided into an upper and lower band. The use of these bands allowed the 103 modem to transmit and receive data simultaneously over a two-wire pair using frequency shift keying (FSK). FDMs are designed similar to a group of FSK modems that must use a single communication channel. Each modem, however, has a separate frequency band as will be shown in Section 13-2.

The fundamental principles of TDMs are that bits (bit TDM) or characters (character TDM) are interleaved, one from each channel, and then transmitted. The interleaved bits or characters are sent over a high speed communication channel. At the receiving end, the data is demultiplexed and then routed to the proper port (*see* Section 13-3).

STDMs are "intelligent" TDMs that use microcomputers to improve the line efficiency. STDMs are covered in Section 13-4.

## 13-2    Frequency Division Multiplexers

Although FDM is the oldest form of multiplexing, it is an inefficient method of transmitting data because the bands have to be separated from one another. This requires excellent filtering to keep the channels separated. Even the best filtering wastes bandwidth because some channel spacing must be maintained. For example, at 300 baud a channel of 480 hertz is required. Figure 13-3 summarizes some typical baud rates and their corresponding channel bandwidth and spacing. As learned in Chapter 1, the bandwidth of the telephone network is 3000 hertz (3300 to 300 hertz). This bandwidth limits the channel capacity, that is, the number of channels that can use the line at the same time for each data rate. As can be seen

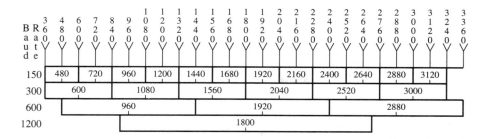

**Figure 13-3   Telephone Line Bandwidth Divided for Frequency Division Multiplexing for Commonly Used Baud Rates**

from Figure 13-3, at 300 baud there is a maximum of six channels. However, at 600 baud there are only three channels. At 1200 baud there is only one channel. Therefore, high speed data transmission is severely limited using FDM. Another disadvantage with FDM is the inability to make changes easily. For example, if the channel speed or the number of channels change, then the center frequency of each channel must change.

FDM does have the advantage that it can be used in multipoint applications. This is because each user has its own separate channel. This capability allows users to be added as needed as long as the maximum channel capacity is not exceeded. Since each user has its own channel, dumb asynchronous terminals may be used without either having individual addresses assigned to each station or requiring a specific communication protocol.

## 13-3   Time Division Multiplexing

Figure 13-4 shows a full-duplex TDM scheme. A constant stream of bits (bit TDM) of characters (character TDM) are transmitted from one multiplexer to the other. Each channel is designated a particular time slot in relation to the SYN characters. Each time slot contains a specific number of bits or characters. The receiving multiplexer knows which bits belong to which channel because of its relations to the SYN character. For example, the data from channel #1 always follows the SYN character. The data from channel #2 follows channel #1's data and so forth, as shown in Figure 13-4.

TDMs use synchronous transmission techniques. If a piece of DTE is sending asynchronous transmission to the multiplexer, the multiplexer strips away the start and stop pulse and sends the remaining bits synchronously. The receiver's multiplexer puts back the start and stop bits and sends the data along to the correct port.

Consider the case of a channel with no data to send. The time slot, however, is still allocated to that channel. Therefore, the channel transmits either an idle character, a break condition, status information, or some other command to fill the time slot.

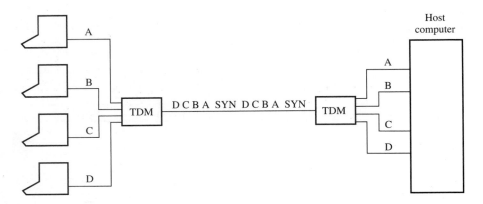

**Figure 13-4   A TDM System**

As shown in Figure 13-4, each channel's data is put into a high speed serial stream as each channel is scanned. This technique is known as **fixed scanning.** The disadvantage with this technique is that all channels occupy the same amount of bandwidth, which is based on the highest speed terminal. For example, if terminal D transmits at 1200 bits per second (bps) and this is the highest line speed, then all channel allocations are based on 1200 bps even if the other terminals have lower speeds. This disadvantage is overcome by a **variable channel scanning multiplexer.** These units have the ability to make additional samples for the higher speed terminals. For the systems shown in Figure 13-4, assume that the terminal data rates are A, 600 bps; B, 300 bps; C, 600 bps; and D, 1200 bps. The multiplexer at the terminal end will take four samples at terminal B for each sample taken at terminal D and two samples at terminals A and C for each sample taken at terminal D. This results in a much higher line efficiency.

However, in both fixed and variable scanning multiplexers, each time slot is fixed and the communication link is capable of supporting the channel transmitting continuously at maximum speed. In most systems, it is a rare case when even one channel is continuously transmitting at maximum speed. Therefore, the overall efficiency of the system may be low. A way to improve the efficiency is to use STDMs.

## 13-4   Statistical Multiplexing

In most applications, terminals do not communicate with the host computer continuously at their maximum data rate. Therefore, it is possible to design a multiplexer that takes advantage of this fact to incorporate more terminals to the system. This type of multiplexing is known as **STDM.** These devices allow more terminals to share a single line.

STDM is not a new type of multiplexing, but rather a more intelligent form of doing TDM. STDM has been used for years in large data communication networks with minicomputers serving as the multiplexing unit. Today, smaller systems can use STDM because of microprocessor technology and low cost, high density memory devices.

Some manufacturers refer to their STDMs as data concentrators. Other manufacturers use the term concentrator to mean those units that allow a larger number of terminals to be connected to fewer computer ports. These units are also known as port concentrators and are covered in the next section.

Figure 13-5 is similar to Figure 13-4; that is, four terminals are connected to a host computer using a multiplexer network. However, in Figure 13-5 assume that the four terminals are operating at 2400 bps and the communication link is operating at 4800 bps. If only TDM was being used, the communication link would have to be operating at $4 \times 2400$ bps = 9600 bps. The 9600-bps maximum is to ensure for the possibility that all the terminals may be trying to operate at their maximum speed. An STDM unit stores the data in its internal memory buffer, after which the data is divided into variable length blocks according to an individual terminal's needs. The data is blocked using one of the synchronous protocols and then transmitted. In Figure 13-5, if the terminal speeds were reduced to 1200 bps, it could be possible to connect eight 1200-bps terminals to an STDM and use a 4800-bps communication channel.

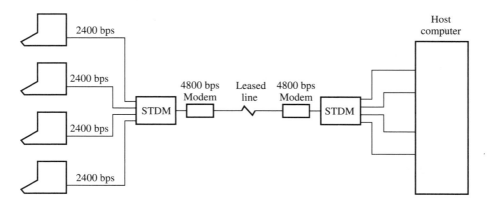

**Figure 13-5  STDMs Permit Lower Line Speed to Be Used**

## 13-5  Port Concentrators and Port Selectors

### 13-5.1  Port Concentrators

If the number of data ports on the host computer is limited, then a port-sharing unit, also called a port concentrator, as shown in Figure 13-6, may be the answer. At first glance, the configuration in Figure 13-6 appears similar to the multipoint system introduced in Chapter 1. Remember, however, in a multipoint system the host computer must have the polling software to handle the terminals, and execution of this software uses valuable central processing unit (CPU) time. A port concentrator offloads this problem from the host and it functions as a channel master. It

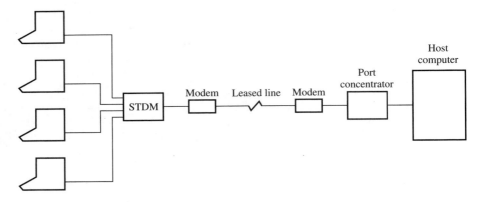

**Figure 13-6   A Port Concentrator Interfaces the Data Channel to One Port on the Host Computer**

interfaces between the computer and DCE. As shown in Figure 13-6, the terminals at the other end are connected to an STDM. A TDM could be used but an STDM will yield a higher line efficiency.

Communication between the host and port concentrator can be as simple as lines of text preceded by the terminal's address. The protocol between the host computer and port concentrator may be either asynchronous or synchronous. The primary function of the port concentrator is to offload tasks for the computer and send only error-free messages to it. Some of the tasks of the port concentrator are

1. Establishing and maintaining synchronization with the STDM.

2. Checking for transmission errors (using a 16-bit CRC character) from the STDM.

3. Maintaining backup messages for retransmission in the event an error is detected.

Messages are sent and received as numbered frames; therefore, the port concentrator must keep a record and buffer for each station at the receiving end.

Although the software requirements at the host computer are much less than they would be if the computer had to support a multipoint system without a port concentrator, the computer must have software to support the port concentrator.

## 13-5.2   Port Selectors

If an application requires users to have access to a computer facility, then a port selector may be needed. Figure 13-7 shows how a port selector can interface among a number of terminals using a variety of communication links and three computers. The terminals may be connected to the port selector by dial-up lines, private lines, leased lines, direct connected, multiplexer inputs, and even current loops. The port selector allows the users, on a first come, first serve basis, to be connected to the computer of their choice.

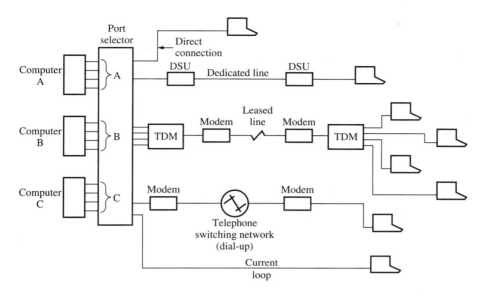

**Figure 13-7    A Port Selector Allows Users at Terminals in a Variety of Locations to Be Connected to the Computer of their Choice. DSU, Digital Service Unit**

The heart of the port selector is crossbar switching circuitry under control of a microcontroller. Once a connection is made it is transparent to the user. This is similar to the operation of the telephone dial-up system. A typical operation is that a user at a terminal initially accesses the port selector by pressing a key (except on a dial-up line, then a call first has to be made to the port selector), the port selector sends a prompt message asking which computer the user wants to access, and the user replies. If a port on that computer is available, the user's terminal will be connected to it and an acknowledgment message sent. If all lines to that computer are busy, the user will be notified and be told how many other terminals are awaiting access to that same computer. The user may then be asked to ''wait in line,'' use another computer, or terminate. If the user does nothing, the port selector will terminate the connection anyway because of inactivity on the line.

Thus port selectors provide a cost-effective solution for connecting a number of different terminals to a number of different computers. By interconnecting data communication units, Figure 13-8 shows that the computers do not have to be in the same location.

## 13-6    Other Data Communication Technologies

As data communication systems expand and an increasing amount of information must be transmitted, faster data rates can be obtained if the information is sent in digital form. The information may be voice, data, or video. This section introduces

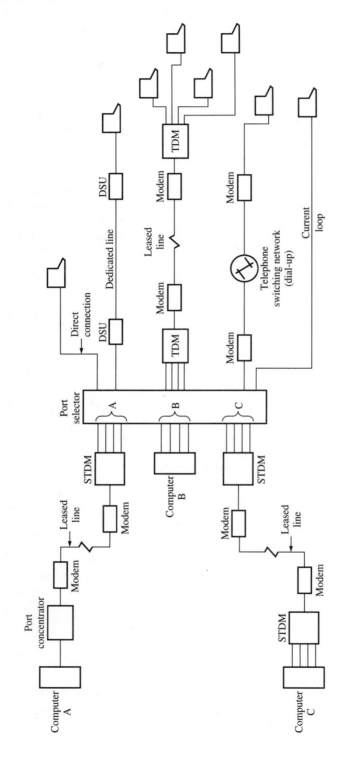

**Figure 13-8    An Expanded Application of Figure 13-7**

some of the communication technologies that may be encountered when sending data in digital form via a telephone carrier.

### 13-6.1 Digital Data Service

Digital data service (DDS) is a method of transmitting data in digital form instead of analog form. This method eliminates the need for a modem to convert the digital data to an analog signal at the transmitter and another modem to reconvert the analog signal to a digital signal at the receiver. The equipment used to interface DTE to DDS is called a digital service unit (DSU) or a customer service unit (CSU). There is a difference between DSU and CSU which will be addressed later in this chapter. Figure 13-9 shows a DDS line in a multipoint system that uses four DSUs. DSUs can also be used in point-to-point systems. Manufacturers sell different models of DSUs. The slower speed units (9600 bps) may use an RS-232 interface with either an asynchronous or synchronous protocol. However the real advantage of DDS can be obtained by using DSUs that have a V.35 interface. These units permit data rates of 56K bps but use only synchronous protocols. Although DSUs can be used for half-duplex operation, full-duplex operation over a four-wire circuit yields maximum performance.

Multiplexer type DSUs are also available. These units are designed using TDM. The maximum composite data rate of multiplexer/DSU equipment connected to DDS lines is 56K bps.

### 13-6.2 T1 Carrier

In the early 1960s, the Bell system introduced a telephone carrier system known as the T1 carrier. This system divides the telephone bandwidth into time divisions instead of frequency divisions. Hence the T1 system uses TDM and not FDM.

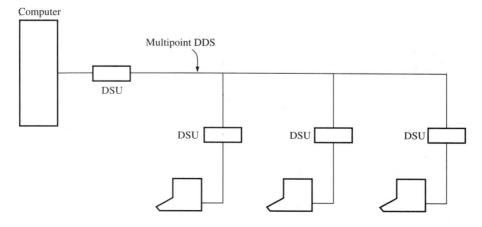

**Figure 13-9** **A Multipoint DDS Connecting Three Terminals or Workstations to a Computer**

The T1 system was designed originally to carry 24 voice channels from central office to central office. At each transmitting central office the analog voice signals are converted into digital form using **pulse code modulation** (PCM). If the voice has a 4K-hertz bandwidth for normal conversation, then sampling the signal at a rate of 8000 samples per second allows a receiver to reproduce the signal. Figure 13-10 shows an analog signal sampled a number of times per cycle. The amplitude at each sample point is converted to an 8-bit pattern and this binary number is sent over the T1 carrier. The binary value for sample point #1, channel #1 is sent, then sample point #1, channel #2 is sent, and so forth. Figure 13-11 shows the frame format for a T1 carrier. There are 24 channel slots per frame and each channel slot contains 8 bits. There is one additional bit per frame for synchronization. Thus each frame contains $(24 \times 8) + 1 = 193$ bits. In order for the receiver to reproduce the analog signal, the information in each channel slot must be updated

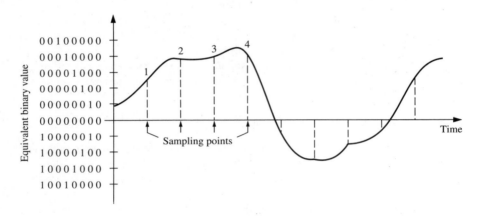

**Figure 13-10   An Analog Signal is Sampled and the Corresponding Amplitude is Converted to a Binary Pattern (Such as Sign Magnitude as Shown or Two's Complement)**

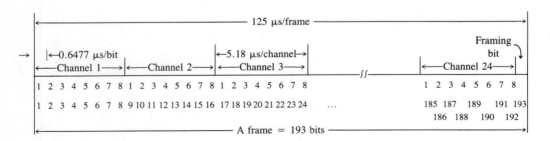

**Figure 13-11    T1 Transmission Format**

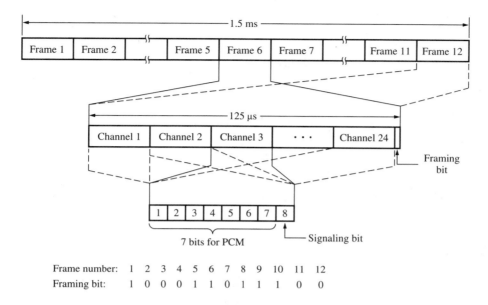

**Figure 13-12   For Transmitting Voice, Every Sixth Frame in a Multiframe Sequence is Used for Signaling Information.**

8000 times per second. This requires that 8000 frames be sent in 1 second. The result is a data rate of 8000 frame/s $\times$ 193 bits/frame = 1.544 M bps.

The time per bit is 1/1.544 M bps = 0.6477 $\mu$s. The time per channel, frame, and multiframe (12 frames) is given in Figures 13-11 and 13-12. The framing bits have a 12-bit pattern of 100011011100 as shown in Figure 13-12.

In voice applications, five frames are sent using 8 bits for PCM. Every sixth frame uses 7 bits for PCM. The eighth bit of each channel slot in every sixth frame is used for signaling information. This signaling information could be used to establish a connection or terminate a call, or for routing or control information.

Although the T1 carrier system was originally designed for voice communication, it is a convenient medium for transmitting digital data. Since the data is already in digital form, then 8 bits of data are transmitted in each channel slot and each channel is sent 8000 times per second. This yields a data rate per channel of 8 $\times$ 8000 = 64K bps. Although the bit rate is 64K bps, bit rates of 56K bps will be seen. The reason for this is that each channel contains only 7 bits for data and the eighth bit is for signaling. This yields a bit rate of 7 $\times$ 8000 = 56K bps. Some systems use 23 channels for data and the 24th channel for signaling.

Customers can now purchase T1 CSU equipment that allows them to connect 24 channels to a leased T1 line. So now users can send digital data from one plant to another using T1 capability. If customers do not require all 24 channels in a T1 carrier, they may lease a fraction of a T1 carrier.

### 13-6.3   Fractional T1

In the previous section, the term T1 refers to a carrier facility including the hardware and line to transmit digital signals at a bit rate of 1.544 M bps using TDM. Telephone companies provide a service called **fractional T1.** This service is designed for customers who need T1 capabilities but do not require all 24 channels. A customer selects one or more T1 channels and pays accordingly. The telephone company combines fractional T1 service from a number of different customers as shown in Figure 13-13 for a "full" T1 line.

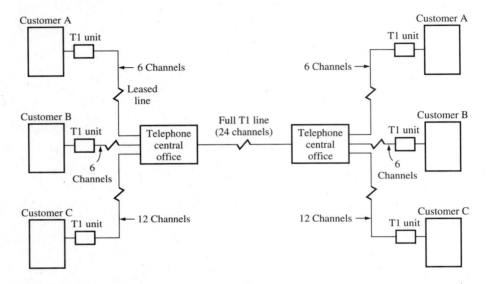

**Figure 13-13    An Application of Fractional T1 Carrier Which is to Combine Customers Who Need T1 Capability into a "Full" T1**

### 13-6.4   Fiber Distributed Data Interface

Fiber distributed data interface (FDDI) is a fiber optic based network whose standards have been developed by American National Standards Institute (ANSI). It specifies a 100 M bps local area network (LAN) ring topology using a token passing method. Presently no other network technology is close to FDDI's transmission rates. However ANSI's X3T9.5 committee has approved a proposal for a new family of standards to be known as FDDI follow-on LAN (FFOL). The data rate in the proposal is for speeds in excess of 600 M bps. Although the subcommittee's work may not be completed until 1995, it does show the future direction and speeds that may be needed by some data communication customers.

FDDI is used by workstations performing mainly computations and also video imaging applications that require exchanging large files and data bases. Interconnecting workstations, minicomputers, and mainframes require high speed LANs.

## 13-7   Line Coding

For most applications, binary data is transmitted by encoding each bit into a voltage pulse using various techniques. This section introduces some of the line coding methods that are used to encode data bits to voltage pulses.

### 13-7.1   Non-Return to Zero Code

Binary signals within computers are mainly transistor-transistor logic (TTL) levels, 0 volts and +5 volts, as shown in Figure 13-14b for the binary pattern given in Figure 13-14a. This type of signal is known as non-return to zero (NRZ) because the voltage does not return to 0 volts between adjacent logic 1s. More specifically, this waveform is called unipolar-NRZ because the voltage is always one polarity. This type of waveform is at +volts for a logic 1 and 0 volts for a logic 0 for the entire bit time. These TTL levels are adequate between components within computers and other DTE or DCE because the components are close together and very little residual dc voltage occurs. As transmission paths become longer, this dc voltage may become significant and prevent a receiver from recovering the data and clocking signals. To avoid the dc residual build-up over long distances, manufacturers of DCE use other signal patterns.

A polar NRZ line code shown in Figure 13-14c can eliminate most of the dc residual problems if the data being transmitted has a significant number of alternating ones and zeros. However, if a long string of ones or zeros occurs, the dc problem is still present and can be worse depending on the voltage levels +volts and −volts. The waveform in Figure 13-14c is at +volts for a logic 1 and −volts for a logic 0 for the entire bit time. This waveform is similar to RS-232 electrical signals, except for RS-232, a logic 1 is at −volts and a logic 0 is at +volts.

### 13-7.2   Alternate Mark Inversion Code

Digital transmission for the T1 carrier uses a scheme called alternate mark inversion (AMI) as shown in Figure 13-14d. The format for this waveform is that alternating ones are transmitted by reversing the voltage polarity. The logic 1 pulse has only a 50% duty cycle; this refers to the fact that the pulse width is only one-half as wide as the bit time allows. In this format, there are actually three voltage levels, +volts, 0 volts, and −volts.

The receiver uses the alternate logic 1 pulse to recover not only the data but also the clock signal. If a long sequence of logic 0s is being transmitted, the receiver could lose the timing information. To overcome this problem the CSU provides logic 1s within the long sequence of logic 0s to provide timing information. (DSUs may not have this feature. Some manufacturers sell their products as DSU/CSU.) The CSU at the receiver extracts the timing information and the data. As shown in Figure 13-13d, a logic 1 pulse occurs in the first half of a bit interval and alternates polarity from logic 1 pulse to the next logic 1 pulse. A logic 0 remains at 0 volts.

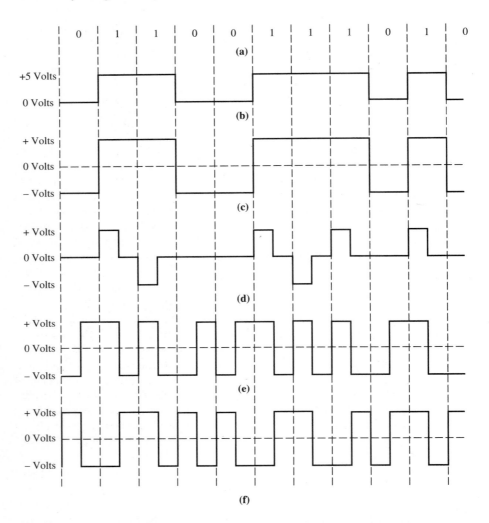

**Figure 13-14   Some Types of Digital Signals for Encoding the Binary Pattern in (a).
(b) Unipolar NRZ Waveform. (c) Polar NRZ Waveform. (d) Alternate Mark
Inversion. (e) Manchester. (f) Differential Encoded.**

### 13-7.3   Diphase Code

The coding used in Figure 13-14e is called digital biphase, diphase, or Manchester
encoding. There is a transition for every bit regardless of whether it is a logic 0
or 1. For a logic 0, there is a transition from low to high in the middle of the bit
interval. For a logic 1, there is a transition from high to low in the middle of the
bit interval.

A modified version of the diphase is the differentially encoded diphase waveform shown in Figure 13-14f. In this waveform, a transition occurs at the beginning

of the bit interval indicating a logic 0 and no transition at the beginning of the bit interval indicates a logic 1. A logic 1 does have a transition in the middle of the bit interval.

## Summary

As a business' data communication needs grow, it looks to solutions that do not require the number of communication channels to grow proportionally. As each new terminal is added, a company does not want to add another long distance communication channel; the cost would quickly become prohibitive. A method of sharing a communication channel is known as multiplexing. This chapter introduced the three most commonly used multiplexing techniques: FDM, TDM, and STDM. Sections 13-2, 13-3, and 13-4 identified the advantages and disadvantages of each type.

If the number of ports on a host computer is limited and more terminals are to be added, then a port concentrator may be the solution. Section 13-5 showed how this type of equipment can be used to offload the problem from the host. Section 13-5 also introduced port selectors and showed how they can interface among a number of terminals and a variety of computers.

Although many data communication applications use a telephone network that requires the data to be sent in analog form over a portion of the channel, it is possible to have the data sent digitally from sender to receiver. This method of transmission is known as DDS. Section 13-6 introduced DDS and showed how the T1 carrier system originally designed for voice conversations has been introduced for digital data transmission. A single T1 carrier system transmits 24 channels. If a business does not require all 24 channels, it may select a fractional T1 service and pay accordingly.

Several different forms of digital signals that are used for encoding data are covered in Section 13-7. They are unipolar NRZ, bipolar NRZ, AMI, Manchester, and differential.

## Problems

**13.1** What is the major advantage of using multiplexers?

**13.2** List the three basic types of multiplexing techniques used in data communication.

**\*13.3** What type of multiplexing technique would you expect to find in slow speed modems?

* *See* Answers to Selected Problems.

**13.4** **(a)** Using the telephone bandwidth from 360 to 3360 hertz, show that 25 75-baud units could be connected to the communication channel.

**(b)** Determine the center frequency used by each unit.

**\*13.5** **(a)** How many 450-baud units could be connected to the telephone bandwidth shown in Figure 13-3?

**(b)** What would be the bandwidth of each unit of part (a)?

**(c)** Calculate the center frequency for each 450-baud unit.

**13.6** Why do synchronous multiplexers ''strip away'' the start and stop bits if they receive data asynchronously?

**13.7** What is a major disadvantage of TDM?

**13.8** Assume that a pair of STDMs is connected to a 9600-bps communication channel. How many 1200-bps terminals would you expect could be connected to the multiplexers?

**31.9** What is a port concentrator?

**13.10** What is a port selector?

**\*13.11** In Europe, the telephone companies combine 30 voice channels and 128K bps for control and synchronization in the equivalent of a T1 carrier. If each voice channel is coded as 8 bits and the sample rate is 8000, calculate the data rate of this international standard.

**13.12** In the United States, AT&T multiplexes a number of T1 carrier lines to form a T series transmission hierarchy. Complete the following table to determine the data rate for each T type line. **Note:** Column 3 is the additional bits per second needed for framing and control for a particular T series.

| T Series | Number of T1 Lines | Control and Framing (bps) | Data Rate (bps) |
|----------|--------------------|--------------------------|-----------------|
| T1C | 2 | 64K | |
| T2 | 4 | 136K | |
| T3 | 28 | 1.504M | |
| T4 | 168 | 14.784M | |

**13.13** What would be an advantage of using differentially encoded diphase instead of AMI?

**13.14** Plot the AMI waveform for the following bit stream.

0 0 1 1 0 1 1 1 0 1 1 1 1

**13.15** For the bit stream given in Problem 13.14, plot the waveform using the Manchester encoding techniques.

# Integrated Digital Voice and Data Communication System

14

## OBJECTIVES

Upon completion of this chapter on integrated digital voice and data communication system, the student will be able to

- Describe how future office systems may be designed using all digital transmission.

- Show how universal digital loop transceivers (UDLTs) exchange voice and data between a telephone and a company's private branch exchange (PBX).

- Understand and explain the basic principles of how other support chips such as data set interfaces (DSIs), pulse code modulations (PCMs), Teleset Audio Interface Circuits (TAICs), and time slot assignment circuits (TSACs) operate and are used in a digital PBX system.

- Plot a modified differential phase shift keying (MDPSK) waveform.

## Introduction

As a company's business expands and many more employees need access to files stored in the central computer from a terminal at their desk, employers are faced either with rewiring every office to the main computer or finding an alternate solution. The cost of installing a direct link to the computer for every new terminal can far exceed what a company can afford. What is needed is a low cost solution that can use already installed telephone lines. Such a system must allow the employee to use the telephone for voice communication while simultaneously being able to transfer data to the computer. The key to this system is the simultaneous transmission of voice and data. Remember that a system designed around a modem can be used to transmit either voice or data, but not both simultaneously.

The reasons for using the telephone twisted pair are (1) it is the backbone of the telephone system, (2) it has probably already been installed in every nook and cranny of a building (new and old), and (3) the lines are most likely to terminate at one central location—the company's PBX. Thus the PBX system can provide a way for interconnecting word processors, CRT terminals, gateways, or bridges to local area networks, as well as provide the link for voice communication as shown in Figure 14-1. The use of twisted pair instead of either coaxial or fiber optic cable provides a cost-effective and flexible way of installing voice and data processing equipment anywhere within a company's plant.

Most manufacturers of digital PBXs offer both analog and digital line cards, as shown in Figure 14-2. The analog line cards (*see* Fig. 14-2b) allow easy interface connection between the millions of analog telephones and the newer digital transmission telephone systems. The subscriber loop interface circuit (SLIC) performs the 2- to 4-wire conversion. The PCM mono-circuit is used for coding and decoding voice. The TSAC is used for logic supervision. On the digital line card (*see* Fig. 14-2c) the master universal digital loop transfer replaces the PCM and SLIC circuitry. Another PCM mono-circuit is now located in the phone. This permits an all-digital phone and a digital PBX.

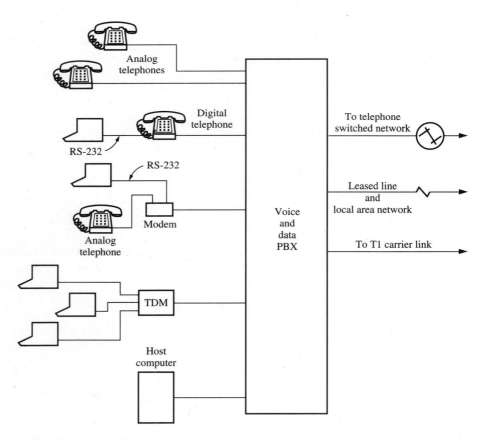

**Figure 14-1   A Company's PBX Can be Used for Both Analog and Digital Interconnections**

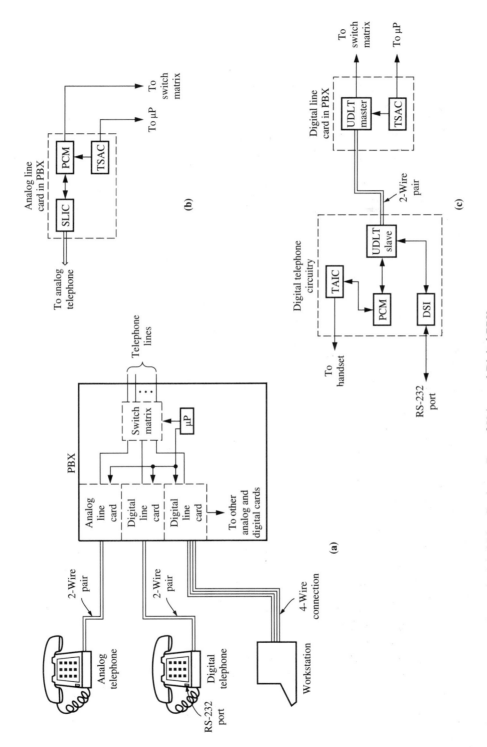

**Figure 14-2** (a) Analog and Digital Line Cards are Part of Voice and Digital PBX. (b) Circuitry on the Analog Line Card. (c) Circuitry Within a Digital Telephone and on the Digital Line Card.

The PCM operates at a rate of 64K bits per second (bps). This allows the voice signals to be sampled at 8000 samples per second and each sample to be 8 bits. If the system was designed only for voice communication, transmission could take place at this time. However, the UDLTs are capable of operating at 80K bps over a twisted pair. This allows 16K bps (80K bps–64K bps) of data to be included. The 16K bps can be divided into 8K bps for signaling data and 8K bps for user data. The signaling data is used for transmitting the hook status and receiving the ring-control signal for the telephone. The user data comes from an RS-232 port on the telephone or from the central computer.

The UDLTs modulate the data and use a half-duplex burst mode transmission technique. The voice and data are collected in 10-bit groups and sent from one UDLT to another. The line is then "turned around" and 10 bits of information are burst in the opposite direction. The function of each integrated circuit (IC) seen in Figure 14-2 will now be examined.

## 14-1   Data Set Interface

An interface circuit is needed to provide asynchronous to synchronous and synchronous to asynchronous conversion. This conversion is essential to transfer data from an asynchronous terminal to a synchronous transmission link and then to a host computer. The reverse process is also essential to convert synchronous data from the computer to asynchronous data to be sent to the terminal. Such a device is Motorola's MC145428 DSI IC. In addition to providing the interface between asynchronous data ports and synchronous transmission links, other features designed into this chip are

**1.** On board bit rate clock generator.

**2.** Acceptance of either 8 or 9 bits in asynchronous words.

**3.** Automatic synchronous flag insertion and detection.

**4.** Automatic zero insertion.

Figure 14-3 shows the pin assignments and an internal block diagram of the MC145428.

### 14-1.1   Transmitting and Receiving Data

Data that is sent from an asynchronous device is received by the DSI chip on the Transmit Data pin (TxD pin 2). Thus the phrase "transmit data" refers to what the asynchronous device is doing and not what communication function the DSI chip is performing. The reason for this is that the DSI chip is part of the data communication equipment (DCE) and not part of the data terminal equipment (DTE). As studied in previous chapters, all data transfer is in relation to the DTE and not the DCE.

The DSI chip expects to receive asynchronous characters beginning with a start bit (low logic level), followed by 8 or 9 data bits, and ending with 1 or 2

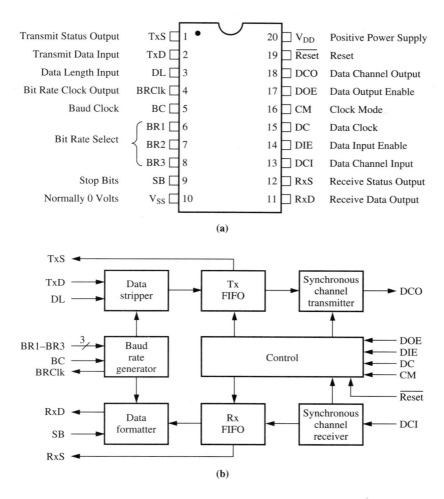

**Figure 14-3** (a) Pin Assignments and (b) Internal Block Diagram of the MC145428 DSI Chip *(Courtesy of Motorola, Inc.)*

stop bits. The user is able to select the number of data bits and stop bits as well as the baud rate. On the Data Length Input pin (DL pin 3) a low selects 8 data bits and a high selects 9 data bits. On the Stop Bit pin (SB pin 9) a low selects 1 stop bit and a high selects 2 stop bits. In most applications, a 4.096 MHz clock signal is applied to the Baud Clock (BC pin 5). This frequency is internally divided by 16 and with the binary pattern applied to the Baud Rate Select inputs BR1, 2, and 3, which in turn set the asynchronous bit rate as shown in the Appendix data sheet for the MC14528.

When an asynchronous character is inputted to the DSI chip, the start and stop bit(s) are stripped away and the data bits are loaded into a four-word deep FIFO (First In First Out) register. When no data is available for transmission, the synchronous channel transmitter portion of the DSI chip automatically sends the flag pattern (01111110). This portion also does an automatic zero insertion after five consecutive binary 1s of data. This concept of zero insertion is also called bit stuffing and was covered in Chapter 12.

In most applications, this system can be designed so that incoming asynchronous data is transmitted at a slower rate than the rate at which the DSI chip transmits the synchronous data. If, however, the FIFO register should fill, the Transmit Status Output (TxS) line goes low. Actually, the TxS line goes low whenever the FIFO register contains two or more data words. The TxS line can be used as a clear-to-send (CTS) signal for the asynchronous interface.

The DSI chip receives synchronous data at its Data Channel Input (DCI) pin (pin 13). The number of bits that will be accepted for each word is selected by the DL pin (pin 3). The synchronous channel receiver removes any inserted zeros and transfers either 8 or 9 data bits to the receive FIFO register. Data words are taken from the top of the FIFO register and transferred to the data formatter. This portion of the DSI chip adds a start and stop bit(s). The number of stop bits has been preselected by the user applying a low or high level at the SB pin.

The Receive Status Output (RxS) pin (pin 12) is used to indicate a loss of framing. A loss of framing occurs for synchronization data if the flag pattern is not detected. This line also goes low if the receive FIFO register is overwritten. This condition occurs if the rate of the incoming synchronous data is greater than the rate at which the DSI chip can send an asynchronous word.

### 14-1.2   Timing Diagram

Although the synchronous channel can be operated in one of three modes, we will concentrate on one mode for our particular application. It is a continuous mode. A new synchronous data bit is sent and received on each falling edge of the DC clock pulse. A synchronous data bit is received at the DCI pin (pin 13) and sent at the Data Channel Output (DCO) pin (pin 18). The timing diagrams for this mode of operation are shown in Figure 14-4. This mode of operation is typical for interfacing a DSI chip to a UDLT so that 8K bps can be transferred between them.

## 14-2   PCM Circuit

The PCM IC houses a CODEC, voltage references, and filtering circuitry all within a dual-in-line package. A family of devices are available from manufacturers. The MC145502 (*see* Fig. 14-5) from Motorola contains all the features needed for this application. This device performs the digitizing of an incoming voice signal as well as the conversion of the digital signal to an analog signal. The voice signal is sampled at a rate of 8K hertz and each sample is converted to 8 bits.

$$\frac{8000 \text{ samples}}{\text{second}} \times \frac{8 \text{ bits}}{\text{sample}} = 64\text{K bps}$$

The digitized voice data coming from the PBX is converted to an analog signal and sent to the earpiece in the phone.

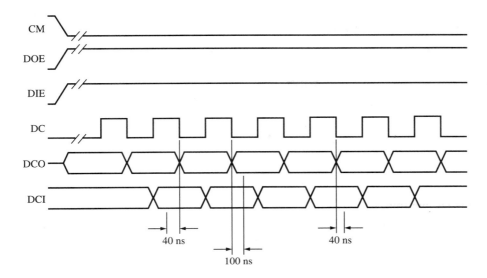

**Figure 14-4**   Typical Waveforms for the DSI Chip *(Courtesy of Motorola, Inc.)*

## 14-3   Teleset Audio Interface Circuit

A TAIC, such as the MC145429, is the interface between the PCM and the handset (which includes the mouthpiece and earpiece) as well as the ringer/speaker amplifier. The TAIC device can be programmed by a microcomputer through a serial port on the TAIC. Hence analog adjustments can be made by software and not hardware. Figure 14-6 shows the pin assignments and internal block diagram for the MC145429.

## 14-4   Universal Digital Loop Transceivers

The UDLTs are high speed data transceivers. They are capable of providing 80K bps digital transmission over 26 AWG twisted pair. There are two parts to the UDLT team. One is the master UDLT, which is located on the digital line card in the PBX. The other part is the slave UDLT, which is designed into the phone set (*see* Fig. 14-2). These devices use a 256-kilobaud burst modulation technique for transmission, are protocol independent, and use complementary metal oxide semiconductor (CMOS) technology for low power. The slave unit also has automatic power up and power down feature. Figure 14-7 shows the pin-outs of both devices.

### 14-4.1   Master-to-Slave Data Transfer

Digitized voice data from the line card is loaded into the Rx register of the master. After the eighth bit, the voice data is then transferred to the transmit data buffer.

*(Text continued on page 310.)*

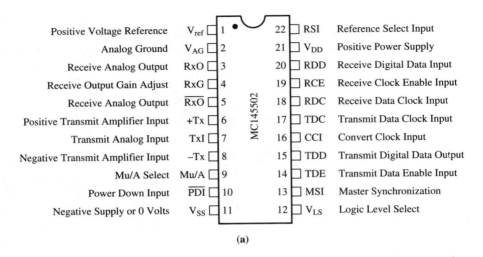

(a)

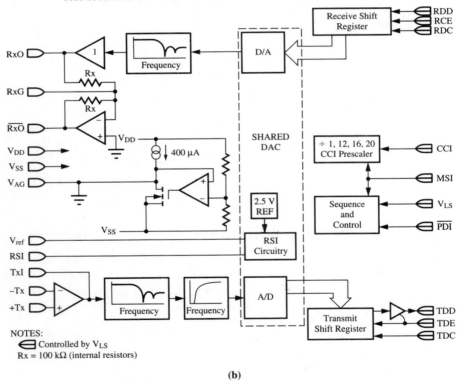

NOTES:
⊑ Controlled by $V_{LS}$
Rx = 100 kΩ (internal resistors)

(b)

**Figure 14-5   The Pin Assignments in (a) and Internal Block Diagram in (b) for the MC145502 CODEC-Filter PCM-Mono-Circuit** *(Courtesy of Motorola, Inc.)*

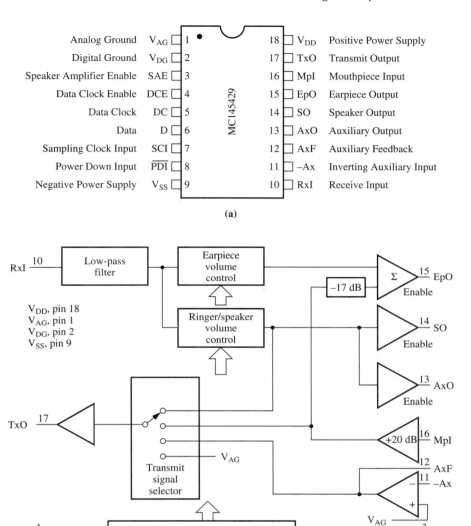

**Figure 14-6** (a) Pin Assignments and (b) Internal Block Diagram for the MC145429 TAIC *(Courtesy of Motorola, Inc.)*

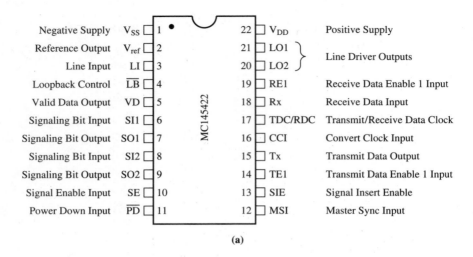

| | | | | | | | |
|---|---|---|---|---|---|---|---|
| Negative Supply | $V_{SS}$ | 1 | | 22 | $V_{DD}$ | Positive Supply |
| Reference Output | $V_{ref}$ | 2 | | 21 | LO1 | Line Driver Outputs |
| Line Input | LI | 3 | | 20 | LO2 | |
| Loopback Control | $\overline{LB}$ | 4 | | 19 | RE1 | Receive Data Enable 1 Input |
| Valid Data Output | VD | 5 | | 18 | Rx | Receive Data Input |
| Signaling Bit Input | SI1 | 6 | | 17 | TDC/RDC | Transmit/Receive Data Clock |
| Signaling Bit Output | SO1 | 7 | | 16 | CCI | Convert Clock Input |
| Signaling Bit Input | SI2 | 8 | | 15 | Tx | Transmit Data Output |
| Signaling Bit Output | SO2 | 9 | | 14 | TE1 | Transmit Data Enable 1 Input |
| Signal Enable Input | SE | 10 | | 13 | SIE | Signal Insert Enable |
| Power Down Input | $\overline{PD}$ | 11 | | 12 | MSI | Master Sync Input |

(MC145422)

**(a)**

Master UDLT Block Diagram

**(b)**

**Figure 14-7** UDLTs, Master-to-Slave IC is Shown in (a) and its Internal Block Diagram in (b). The Slave-to-Master Unit is Shown in (c) and (d) *(Courtesy of Motorola, Inc.)*

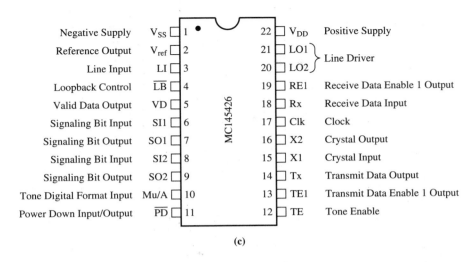

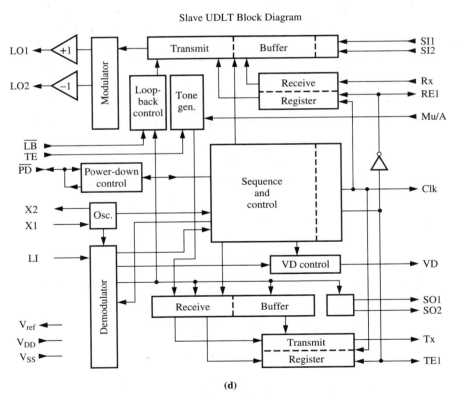

(d)

**Figure 14-7** *continued*

This buffer register accepts the voice data plus 1 bit of signal data and 1 bit of digital data. The signal bit comes in on the Signaling Bit Input (SI1) pin (pin 6) and the digital data comes in on the SI2 pin (pin 8). The signal bit is used to activate the ring circuitry in the phone, while the digital data bit can come from a computer through the microprocessor in the PBX. After the 10 bits are received in the buffer, the data is then transmitted in a 256K-hertz burst to the slave UDLT.

In the slave unit, the incoming data is demodulated. After demodulation, the data is moved to the received data buffer register. Here the signal and data bits are separated. The signal bits are outputted on the Signaling Bit Output (SO1) line (pin 7) while the digital data bits are outputted on the SO2 line (pin 9). (Remember that the digital data is sent to the DSI unit. After 8 bits are collected in the DSI unit, start and stop bits are attached and then outputted to an asynchronous terminal.)

The voice data that is demodulated by the slave unit in the telephone is outputted on Transmit Data Output (Tx) (pin 14) to the PCM circuit. As previously mentioned, the PCM code unit converts the digitized voice data to an analog signal and outputs it to the earpiece.

After the slave has received the 10th bit and the line has had time to settle (approximately 8 $\mu$s), the slave UDLT is now ready to transmit data to the master.

### 14-4.2   Slave-to-Master Data Transfer

The slave unit inputs 8 bits of digitized voice data from the PCM on the Receive Data Input (Rx) pin (pin 18). It also collects 1 bit from the SI1 pin (pin 6) and 1 bit from the SI2 pin (pin 8). The 10 bits are formatted in the transmit buffer and serially shifted to the modulator. The data is transmitted from the slave to the master at a 256K-hertz bit rate. The master unit demodulates the burst signal. The digitized voice data is transferred from the demodulator to the receive buffer, where the signal and data bits are separated and outputted on the SO1 and SO2 pins, respectively.

### 14-4.3   Modulation Signal

We have studied three different modulation techniques for transmitting digital data by analog signals, namely amplitude modulation or amplitude shift keying (ASK), frequency modulation or frequency shift keying (FSK), and phase modulation or phase shift keying (PSK). In all three cases, the resulting signal occupies a bandwidth centered on the carrier frequency. This application uses a modified version of FSK and PSK. This modulation technique is known as modified differential phase shift keying (MDPSK). Figure 14-8 illustrates a binary pattern modulated as a modified differential PSK for a master to slave and slave to master burst. This modulation technique is similar to FSK. The burst always begins and ends with a half cycle of 256K hertz which locates the bit boundaries. The line does not charge up between bursts because each bit period has no dc level. Therefore, no dc balancing bits or neutralizing networks have to be added.

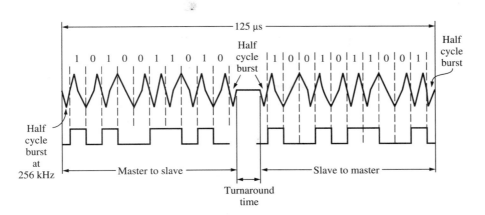

**Figure 14-8    UDLT Devices Transfer Data in Bursts Which is Referred to as "Ping Pong."**

## 14-5    Time Slot Assigner Circuit

The TSAC IC, as shown in Figure 14-9, performs all the supervisory and control functions required in a single-party telephone line circuit. This device is programmable and allows for variable time slot assignments. A TSAC has three basic functions: the serially programmable microprocessor port, the supervisor controls, and the time slot computation. The microprocessor port allows the microprocessor in the PBX system to address and send a binary pattern to the TSAC to program it. This binary pattern can assign a TSAC a particular time slot to transmit data, receive data, or both. For example, TSAC $^\#16$ may be assigned time slot $^\#0$ for both transmitting and receiving data. For a T1 carrier application, time slot $^\#0$ is known as channel slot $^\#0$.

The new ICs that are making their way to the marketplace are allowing designers to develop cost-effective solutions for transmitting voice and data over a single channel. This chapter presented five ICs that are available to aid in the design of such a system. New ICs are emerging for the central office equipment and the evolving Integrated Service Digital Network (ISDN) systems.

## Summary

This chapter introduced a method of having an all-digital communication system for both voice and data. The handset includes the circuitry to convert voice (analog signals) into digital signals and then 2 bits of data are added. This digital sequence is transmitted over a conventional telephone cable to the company's central PBX. The communication outlined in this chapter is a half-duplex operation. Therefore, after the combined voice and data information is sent from the handset to the PBX, the line is "turned around." Now information (voice and data), all in digital form,

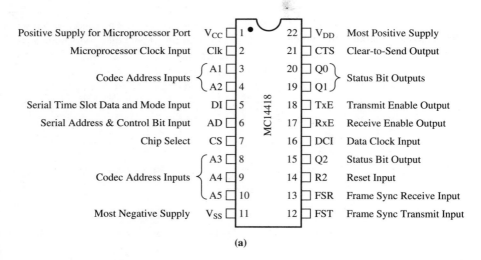

**(a)**

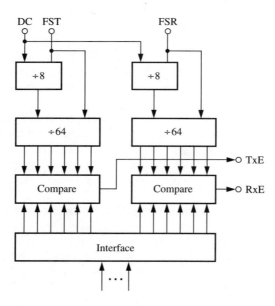

**(b)**

**Figure 14-9   The Pin Assignments for the MC14418 TSAC are Shown in (a) and a Simplified Block Diagram in (b)** *(Courtesy of Motorola, Inc.)*

is transmitted from the PBX system to an individual's handset. The circuitry within the handset separates the voice and data information. The voice information is converted from digital form to analog and then routed to the earpiece. The data information is routed directly to the handset's RS-232 port. In order for a telephone conversation to appear normal, the combined voice and data is sent in bursts at a rate of 80K bps. This chapter introduced the function of the different ICs that would go into designing such a system.

## Problems

**\*14.1** What do the following abbreviations represent?
  **(a)** LAN       **(d)** PCM
  **(b)** PBX       **(e)** DSI
  **(c)** UDLT

**14.2** Define the following terms (refer to library reference if necessary):
  **(a)** Bridges       **(d)** Off Hook
  **(b)** CODEC         **(e)** Subscriber Line Interface Circuit
  **(c)** Gateway

**14.3** The following bit stream is to be sent from the master UDLT to the slave UDLT. Sketch the waveform using modified differential PSK.

1 1 0 0 1 1 1 0 1 0

**14.4** In the circuit of Figure 14-2, what is the function of the TSAC?

* *See* Answers to Selected Problems.

# Answers to Selected Problems

## Chapter 1

**1.3** 15.7%

**1.5** 144

**1.7** a and c—half duplex
b and d—simplex

## Chapter 2

**2.1** **(a)** SP (space)    **(b)** <    **(c)** \    **(d)** x

**2.3** **(a)** $20_{hex}$    **(b)** bit 6 {logic 0—upper case, logic 1—lower case}

**2.5** 44 61 74 61 20 43 6F 6D 6D 75 6E 69 63 61 74 69 6F 6E

**2.7** **(a)** NUL
**(b)** LF
**(c)** DC1

**2.9** No

**2.11** No

**2.13** The ASCII character would be the address, and the data at that address would be the EBCDIC character.

## Chapter 3

**3.1** MARK; SPACE

**3.3** Yes

**3.5** Even, Odd

**3.6** **(a)** (1) 1  **(b)** (1) 0
      (2) 1       (2) 0
      (3) 0       (3) 1
      (4) 1       (4) 0
      (5) 1       (5) 0

**3.7** C = 43 = 100 0011 0
      h = 68 = 110 1000 0
      e = 65 = 110 0101 1
      c = 63 = 110 0011 1
      k = 6B = 110 1011 0
     sp = 20 = 010 0000 0
      # = 23 = 010 0011 0
      3 = 33 = 011 0011 1
      8 = 38 = 011 1000 0
      7 = 37 = 011 0111 0
      4 = 34 = 011 0100 0
      2 = 32 = 011 0010 0

                    MSB    LSB   parity

**3.9** No. A parity error checking scheme can catch only an odd number of bits that change state.

**3.11** **(a)** No      **(b)** No

**3.13** Marking distortion; spacing distortion

**3.15** **(a)** 4800 bps      **(b)** 1200 bps

# Chapter 4

**4.1** Status register; receive data register

**4.3** Yes

**4.5** No

**4.7** So that the internal registers are in consecutive locations

**4.9** 7 data bits, odd parity, 2 stop bits

**4.11** $\overline{\text{CTS}}$ and $\overline{\text{DCD}}$

**4.13** Carrier present; wired low

**4.15** **(a)** 2400 bps      **(b)** 1200 bps      **(c)** 300 bps

# Chapter 5

**5.1** DTE transmits and/or receives data and uses communication equipment for data transfer over communication channels. Examples: computers, terminals, printers.
DCEs are connected to communication lines for the purpose of transferring data. Examples: modems, digital line drivers.

**5.3** Mechanical, electrical, and functional

**5.5** No

**5.7** DTE

**5.9** Total effective capacitance associated with the terminator. $C_L \leq 2500pF$

**5.11** **(a)** 500pF      **(b)** 1000pF      **(c)** 1250pF

**5.13** **(a)** No      **(b)** Yes

# Chapter 6

**6.1** A—ground
B—data
C—control
D—timing
S—secondary

**6.3** To allow DTE to be connected to DTE or DCE to be connected to DCE

**6.5** An ON condition on CTS

**6.7** Yes

**6.9** Data Carrier Detect

**6.11** The DTE needs to receive a CTS signal

**6.13** Wire DSR

**6.15** 9.9%

**6.17** Local DCE

# Chapter 7

**7.1** Differential or Balanced

**7.3** Electrical characteristics

**7.5** To improve noise immunity

**7.7** 2000 ft

**7.9** 10k Baud

**7.11** 3460 ft

**7.13** For secondary channels

**7.15** Category I circuits

**7.17** 0  mA = SPACE
20 mA = MARK

**7.19** Yes

# Chapter 8

| **8.1** | $a$ | $b$ | $c$ |
|---|---|---|---|
| Peak amplitude | 3 | 670Hz | 45° |
| Frequency | 10 | 1672Hz | 60° |
| Phase angle in degrees | 4 | 1000Hz | 90° |

**8.3** **(a)** Quadrature Phase Shift Keying
**(b)** Quadrature Amplitude Modulation
**(c)** Trellis Code Modulation
**(d)** Quadrature Diphase Modulation

**8.5** No

**8.7** MARK = 2225 Hz
SPACE = 2025 Hz

**8.9** Yes

**8.11** **(a)** The MARK and SPACE frequencies are different
**(b)** No

**8.13** Bell 212 225°, 135°, 315°, 315°, 45°, 135°, 225°, 45°
CCITT V.23 180°, 90°, 270°, 270°, 0°, 90°, 180°, 0°

**8.15** **(a)** The dc term from multiplier #2 is negative and from multiplier #1 is positive
**(b)** The dc term from multiplier #2 is positive and from multiplier #1 is positive

**8.17** **(a)** second      **(b)** third

# Chapter 9

**9.1** Lower channel; 1070 Hz—SPACE    1270 Hz—MARK

**9.3** An interface between the modem and the communication channel

**9.5** MARK condition

**9.7** $V_1 = 0.148V$; $V_2 = 0.29V$; $V_3 = 0.29V$

**9.11** 60 mV

**9.13** The limiter produced equal half-cycle periods

**9.15** **(a)** 3.37%    **(b)** 3.7%

**9.17** 4.37%

# Chapter 10

**10.1** **(a)** 4 bits    **(b)** 15 bits    **(c)** 115 bits

**10.3** **(a)** No    **(b)** Yes    **(c)** No    **(d)** Yes    **(e)** No

**10.5** **(a)** No    **(b)** Yes

**10.7** VRC only

**10.9** LRC only

**10.11** **(a)** 1010    **(b)** 1101    **(c)** 0011

**10.15** a—4
b—1
c—2
d—5
e—3

**10.17** **(a)** 5    **(b)** 6    **(c)** 5    **(d)** 4    **(e)** 6

# Chapter 11

**11.3** Mechanical, electrical, and functional characteristics of a particular interface

**11.5** Byte control protocol

**11.7** Optional

**11.9** **(a)** SYN SYN ACK0
**(b)** SYN SYN WACK

**11.11** No

**11.13** SYN SYN RVI

**11.17** Yes

**11.19** No

**11.21** Full duplex operation, synchronous or asynchronous, serial or parallel, fully transparent

**11.23** 882 decimal

**11.25** 25 decimal

## Chapter 12

**12.5** (a) S–frame
(b) I–frame
(c) U–frame
(d) U–frame
(e) S–frame

**12.7** (a) Address field
(b) Frame check sequence

**12.11** 01111111

**12.13** Yes

**12.15** (a) S–frame
(b) I–frame
(c) S–frame
(d) U–frame
(e) I–frame

**12.19** No

**12.21** Step 9 becomes step 7 and step 10 becomes step 8

**12.23** Bits 1 and 2 of the control field are logic 1s

**12.27** No

## Chapter 13

**13.3** Frequency division multiplexing

**13.5** (a) 4 units

    **(b)** #1 360 to 1080 Hz
        #2 1080 to 1800 Hz
        #3 1800 to 2520 Hz
        #4 2520 to 3240 Hz
    **(c)** 720 Hz; 1440 Hz; 2160 Hz; 2880 Hz

**13.11** 2.048M bps

# Chapter 14

**14.1** **(a)** Local Area Network
    **(b)** Private Branch Exchange
    **(c)** Universal Digital Loop Transceivers
    **(d)** Pulse Code Modulation
    **(e)** Data Set Interface

# Bibliography

Bates, Paul, *Practical Digital and Data Communications with LSI Applications,* Reston-Prentice Hall, Inc., 1987.

Brewster, R. L., *Telecommunications Technology,* Ellis Horwood Limited, 1986.

Carne, E. Bryan, *Modern Telecommunication,* Plenum Press, 1984.

Coughlin, Robert F., and Frederick F. Driscoll, *Operational Amplifiers & Linear Integrated Circuits,* (4th Ed.), Prentice Hall, Inc., 1991.

da Silva, Ed, *Introduction to Data Communications and LAN Technology,* BSP Professional Books, 1986.

Driscoll, Frederick F., *Analysis of Electric Circuits,* Prentice-Hall, Inc., 1973.

Driscoll, Frederick F., *Introduction to 6800/68000 Microprocessors,* Breton Publishers, 1987.

Driscoll, Frederick F., *Microprocessor-Microcomputer Technology,* Breton Publishers, 1983.

Driscoll, Frederick F., and Robert F. Coughlin, *Solid State Devices and Applications,* Prentice-Hall, Inc., 1975.

Effron, Joel, *Data Communications Techniques and Technologies,* Van Nostrand Reinhold Co., 1984.

Fike, John, and George Friend, *Understanding Telephone Electronics,* Radio Shack, 1983.

Glasgal, Ralph, *Techniques in Data Communications,* Artech House, Inc., 1983.

Halsall, Fred, *Data Communications, Computer Networks and OSI,* (2nd Ed.), Addison-Wesley, 1988.

Held, Gilbert, *Data Communications Networking Devices: Characteristics, Operation, Applications,* John Wiley & Sons, 1986.

Hewlett Packard, *Optoelectronics Designer's Catalog,* 1985.

IBM, *Synchronous Data Link Concepts,* GA27-3093-3, 1986.

Institute of Electrical and Electronics Engineers, Inc., *802.2 Logical Link Control,* 1984.

Karp, Harry R., ed., *Basics of Data Communication,* McGraw-Hill, Inc., 1976.

Karp, Harry R., ed., *Practical Applications of Data Communications: A User's Guide,* McGraw-Hill, Inc., 1980.

Lane, Malcolm G., *Data Communications Software Design,* Boyd & Fraser Publishing Co., 1985.

McNamara, John, *Technical Aspects of Data Communications,* (3rd Ed.), Digital Equipment Corporation, 1988.

Motorola, Inc., *Telecommunications Device Data Catalog,* 1984.

Motorola, Inc., *Telecommunications Device Data Catalog,* 1989.

Nichols, Elizabeth, Joseph Nichols, and Keith Musson, *Data Communications for Microcomputers with Practical Applications and Experiments,* McGraw-Hill, Inc., 1982.

Proakis, John G., *Digital Communications,* McGraw-Hill, Inc., 1987.

Proakis, John G., *Digital Communications,* (2nd Ed.), McGraw-Hill, Inc., 1989.

Proakis, John G., and Dimitris G. Manolakis, *Introduction to Digital Signal Processing,* Macmillan Publishing Co., 1988.

Roden, Martin S., *Digital and Data Communication Systems,* Prentice-Hall, Inc., 1982.

Sherman, Kenneth, *Data Communications,* Reston Publishing Co., 1981.

Spragins, J., with J. Hammond and K. Paulikowski, *Telecommunications Protocols and Design,* Addison-Wesley, 1991.

Stallings, William, *Data and Computer Communications,* (2nd Ed.), Macmillan Publishing Co., 1988.

Stone, Harold, *Microcomputer Interfacing,* Addison-Wesley Publishing Co., 1982.

Texas Instruments, Inc., *Understanding Data Communications,* 1984.

Vilips, Vess V., *Data Modem,* Artech House, Inc., 1972.

Ziemer, R., and W. Tranter, *Principles of Communications Systems, Modulation, and Noise,* (3rd Ed.), Houghton Mifflin Co., 1990.

# *Appendix*

These data sheets are for reference purposes only. They are not necessarily complete because some of the electrical parameters have not been included due to space limitations. Readers may contact the manufacturer for the latest, most complete data sheets. Data sheets courtesy of Motorola Corporation.

**MOTOROLA**
**■ SEMICONDUCTOR ■**
**TECHNICAL DATA**

# MC1488

## QUAD LINE DRIVER

The MC1488 is a monolithic quad line driver designed to inter-face data terminal equipment with data communications equipment in conformance with the specifications of EIA Standard No. RS-232C.

Features:

- Current Limited Output
  ±10 mA typ
- Power-Off Source Impedance
  300 Ohms min
- Simple Slew Rate Control with External Capacitor
- Flexible Operating Supply Range
- Compatible with All Motorola MDTL and MTTL Logic Families

### QUAD MDTL LINE DRIVER
### RS-232C
SILICON MONOLITHIC
INTEGRATED CIRCUIT

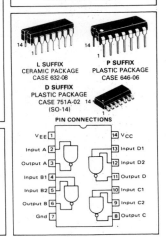

L SUFFIX
CERAMIC PACKAGE
CASE 632-08

P SUFFIX
PLASTIC PACKAGE
CASE 646-06

D SUFFIX
PLASTIC PACKAGE
CASE 751A-02
(SO-14)

**PIN CONNECTIONS**

| | |
|---|---|
| V EE 1 | 14 V CC |
| Input A 2 | 13 Input D1 |
| Output A 3 | 12 Input D2 |
| Input B1 4 | 11 Output D |
| Input B2 5 | 10 Input C1 |
| Output B 6 | 9 Input C2 |
| Gnd 7 | 8 Output C |

### TYPICAL APPLICATION

LINE DRIVER
MC1488

INTERCONNECTING
CABLE

LINE RECEIVER
MC1489

MDTL LOGIC INPUT — INTERCONNECTING CABLE — MDTL LOGIC OUTPUT

### CIRCUIT SCHEMATIC
(1/4 OF CIRCUIT SHOWN)

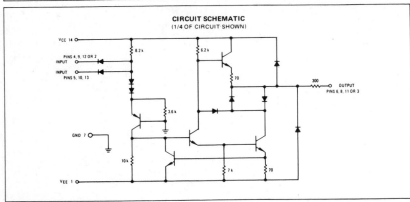

MDTL and MTTL are trademarks of Motorola Inc.

MOTOROLA TELECOMMUNICATIONS DEVICE DATA

*Courtesy of Motorola, Inc. Used by permission.*

MC1488

**TYPICAL CHARACTERISTICS**

($T_A$ = +25°C unless otherwise noted.)

**FIGURE 7 — TRANSFER CHARACTERISTICS
versus POWER-SUPPLY VOLTAGE**

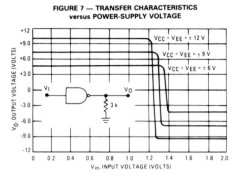

**FIGURE 8 — SHORT-CIRCUIT OUTPUT CURRENT
versus TEMPERATURE**

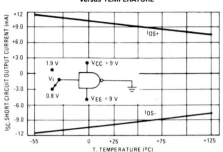

**FIGURE 9 — OUTPUT SLEW RATE
versus LOAD CAPACITANCE**

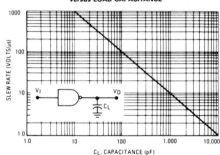

**FIGURE 10 — OUTPUT VOLTAGE
AND CURRENT-LIMITING CHARACTERISTICS**

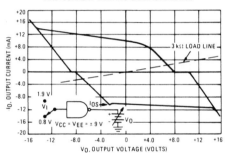

**FIGURE 11 — MAXIMUM OPERATING TEMPERATURE
versus POWER-SUPPLY VOLTAGE**

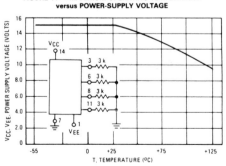

MOTOROLA TELECOMMUNICATIONS DEVICE DATA

*Courtesy of Motorola, Inc. Used by permission.*

**MC1488**

## APPLICATIONS INFORMATION

The Electronic Industries Association (EIA) RS232C specification detail the requirements for the interface between data processing equipment and data communications equipment. This standard specifies not only the number and type of interface leads, but also the voltage levels to be used. The MC1488 quad driver and its companion circuit, the MC1489 quad receiver, provide a complete interface system between DTL or TTL logic levels and the RS232C defined levels. The RS232C requirements as applied to drivers are discussed herein.

The required driver voltages are defined as between 5 and 15-volts in magnitude and are positive for a logic "0" and negative for a logic "1". These voltages are so defined when the drivers are terminated with a 3000 to 7000-ohm resistor. The MC1488 meets this voltage requirement by converting a DTL/TTL logic level into RS232C levels with one stage of inversion.

The RS232C specification further requires that during transitions, the driver output slew rate must not exceed 30 volts per microsecond. The inherent slew rate of the MC1488 is much too

### FIGURE 12 — SLEW RATE versus CAPACITANCE
### FOR $I_{SC}$ = 10 mA

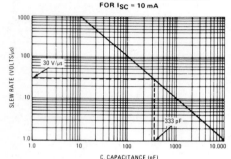

fast for this requirement. The current limited output of the device can be used to control this slew rate by connecting a capacitor to each driver output. The required capacitor can be easily determined by using the relationship $C = I_{OS} \times \Delta T / \Delta V$ from which Figure 12 is derived. Accordingly, a 330-pF capacitor on each output will guarantee a worst case slew rate of 30 volts per microsecond.

The interface driver is also required to withstand an accidental short to any other conductor in an interconnecting cable. The worst possible signal on any conductor would be another driver using a plus or minus 15-volt, 500-mA source. The MC1488 is designed to indefinitely withstand such a short to all four outputs in a package as long as the power-supply voltages are greater than 9.0 volts (i.e., $V_{CC} \geqslant 9.0$ V; $V_{EE} \leqslant -9.0$ V). In some power-supply designs, a loss of system power causes a low impedance on the power-supply outputs. When this occurs, a low impedance to ground would exist at the power inputs to the MC1488 effectively shorting the 300-ohm output resistors to ground. If all four outputs were then shorted to plus or minus 15 volts, the power dissipation in these resistors

### FIGURE 13 — POWER-SUPPLY PROTECTION TO MEET POWER-OFF FAULT CONDITIONS

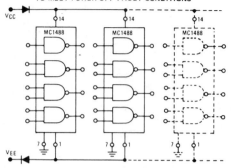

would be excessive. Therefore, if the system is designed to permit low impedances to ground at the power-supplies of the drivers, a diode should be placed in each power-supply lead to prevent over-heating in this fault condition. These two diodes, as shown in Figure 13, could be used to decouple all the driver packages in a system. (These same diodes will allow the MC1488 to withstand momentary shorts to the ±25-volt limits specified in the earlier Standard RS232B.) The addition of the diodes also permits the MC1488 to withstand faults with power-supplies of less than the 9.0 volts stated above.

The maximum short-circuit current allowable under fault conditions is more than guaranteed by the previously mentioned 10 mA output current limiting.

### Other Applications

The MC1488 is an extremely versatile line driver with a myriad of possible applications. Several features of the drivers enhance this versatility:

1. Output Current Limiting — this enables the circuit designer to define the output voltage levels independent of power-supplies and can be accomplished by diode clamping of the output pins. Figure 14 shows the MC1488 used as a DTL to MOS translator where the high-level voltage output is clamped one diode above ground. The resistor divider shown is used to reduce the output voltage below the 300 mV above ground MOS input level limit.

2. Power-Supply Range — as can be seen from the schematic drawing of the drivers, the positive and negative driving elements of the device are essentially independent and do not require matching power-supplies. In fact, the positive supply can vary from a minimum seven volts (required for driving the negative pulldown section) to the maximum specified 15 volts. The negative supply can vary from approximately –2.5 volts to the minimum specified –15 volts. The MC1488 will drive the output to within 2 volts of the positive or negative supplies as long as the current output limits are not exceeded. The combination of the current-limiting and supply-voltage features allow a wide combination of possible outputs within the same quad package. Thus if only a portion of the four drivers are used for driving RS232C lines, the remainder could be used for DTL to MOS or even DTL to DTL translation. Figure 15 shows one such combination.

---

**MOTOROLA**
**■ SEMICONDUCTOR ■■■■■■■■■■■■■**
**TECHNICAL DATA**

**MC1489**
**MC1489A**

### QUAD LINE RECEIVERS

The MC1489 monolithic quad line receivers are designed to interface data terminal equipment with data communications equipment in conformance with the specifications of EIA Standard No. EIA-232D.

- Input Resistance — 3.0 k to 7.0 kilohms
- Input Signal Range — ± 30 Volts
- Input Threshold Hysteresis Built In
- Response Control
  a) Logic Threshold Shifting
  b) Input Noise Filtering

**QUAD MDTL**
**LINE RECEIVERS**
**EIA-232D**

**SILICON MONOLITHIC**
**INTEGRATED CIRCUIT**

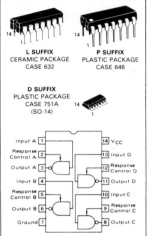

**L SUFFIX**
CERAMIC PACKAGE
CASE 632

**P SUFFIX**
PLASTIC PACKAGE
CASE 646

**D SUFFIX**
PLASTIC PACKAGE
CASE 751A
(SO-14)

Input A 1 — 14 V_CC
Response Control A 2 — 13 Input D
Output A 3 — 12 Response Control D
Input B 4 — 11 Output D
Response Control B 5 — 10 Input C
Output B 6 — 9 Response Control C
Ground 7 — 8 Output C

**TYPICAL APPLICATION**

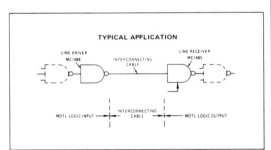

LINE DRIVER
MC1488

INTERCONNECTING
CABLE

LINE RECEIVER
MC1489

MDTL LOGIC INPUT — INTERCONNECTING CABLE — MDTL LOGIC OUTPUT

**EQUIVALENT CIRCUIT SCHEMATIC** (1/4 OF CIRCUIT SHOWN)

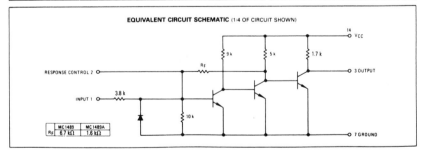

14 V_CC

9 k    5 k    1.7 k

R_F

RESPONSE CONTROL 2

3 OUTPUT

INPUT 1    3.8 k

10 k

7 GROUND

| | MC1489 | MC1489A |
|---|---|---|
| R_F | 6.7 kΩ | 1.6 kΩ |

MOTOROLA LINEAR/INTERFACE DEVICES

*Courtesy of Motorola, Inc. Used by permission.*

**MC1489, MC1489A**

**TYPICAL CHARACTERISTICS**
($V_{CC}$ = 5.0 Vdc, $T_A$ = +25°C unless otherwise noted)

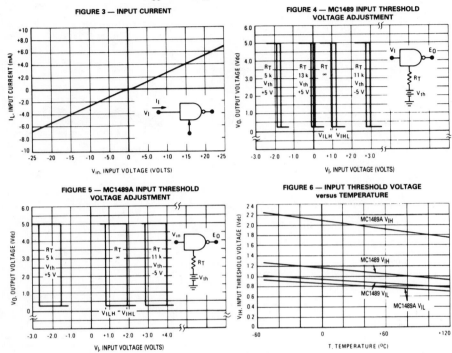

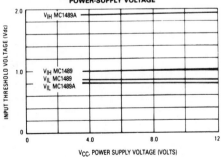

FIGURE 7 — INPUT THRESHOLD versus
POWER-SUPPLY VOLTAGE

**MOTOROLA TELECOMMUNICATIONS DEVICE DATA**

*Courtesy of Motorola, Inc. Used by permission.*

## MC1489, MC1489A

### APPLICATIONS INFORMATION

**General Information**

The Electronic Industries Association (EIA) has released the EIA-232D specification detailing the requirements for the interface between data processing equipment and data communications equipment. This standard specifies not only the number and type of interface leads, but also the voltage levels to be used. The MC1488 quad driver and its companion circuit, the MC1489 quad receiver, provide a complete interface system between DTL or TTL logic levels and the EIA-232D defined levels. The EIA-232D requirements as applied to receivers are discussed herein.

The required input impedance is defined as between 3000 ohms and 7000 ohms for input voltages between 3.0 and 25 volts in magnitude; and any voltage on the receiver input in an open circuit condition must be less than 2.0 volts in magnitude. The MC1489 circuits meet these requirements with a maximum open circuit voltage of one $V_{BE}$.

The receiver shall detect a voltage between $-3.0$ and $-25$ volts as a Logic "1" and inputs between $+3.0$ and $+25$ volts as a Logic "0." On some interchange leads, an open circuit of power "OFF" condition (300 ohms or more to ground) shall be decoded as an "OFF" condition or Logic "1." For this reason, the input hysteresis thresholds of the MC1489 circuits are all above ground. Thus an open or grounded input will cause the same output as a negative or Logic "1" input.

**Device Characteristics**

The MC1489 interface receivers have internal feedback from the second stage to the input stage providing input

hysteresis for noise rejection. The MC1489 input has typical turn-on voltage of 1.25 volts and turn-off of 1.0 volt for a typical hysteresis of 250 mV. The MC1489A has typical turn-on of 1.95 volts and turn-off of 0.8 volt for typically 1.15 volts of hysteresis.

Each receiver section has an external response control node in addition to the input and output pins, thereby allowing the designer to vary the input threshold voltage levels. A resistor can be connected between this node and an external power supply. Figures 2, 4 and 5 illustrate the input threshold voltage shift possible through this technique.

This response node can also be used for the filtering of high-frequency, high energy noise pulses. Figures 8 and 9 show typical noise-pulse rejection for external capacitors of various sizes.

These two operations on the response node can be combined or used individually for many combinations of interfacing applications. The MC1489 circuits are particularly useful for interfacing between MOS circuits and MDTL/MTTL logic systems. In this application, the input threshold voltages are adjusted (with the appropriate supply and resistor values) to fall in the center of the MOS voltage logic levels. (See Figure 10)

The response node may also be used as the receiver input as long as the designer realizes that he may not drive this node with a low impedance source to a voltage greater than one diode above ground or less than one diode below ground. This feature is demonstrated in Figure 11 where two receivers are slaved to the same line that must still meet the EIA-232D impedance requirement.

**FIGURE 8 — TYPICAL TURN-ON THRESHOLD versus CAPACITANCE FROM RESPONSE CONTROL PIN TO GND**

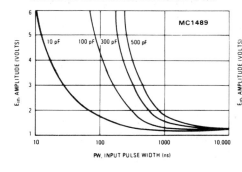

**FIGURE 9 — TYPICAL TURN-ON THRESHOLD versus CAPACITANCE FROM RESPONSE CONTROL PIN TO GND**

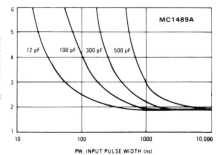

 **MOTOROLA**

# MC3486

## QUAD RS-422/423 LINE RECEIVER

Motorola's Quad RS-422/3 Receiver features four independent receiver chains which comply with EIA Standards for the Electrical Characteristics of Balanced/Unbalanced Voltage Digital Interface Circuits. Receiver outputs are 74LS compatible, three-state structures which are forced to a high impedance state when the appropriate output control pin reaches a logic zero condition. A PNP device buffers each output control pin to assure minimum loading for either logic one or logic zero inputs. In addition, each receiver chain has internal hysteresis circuitry to improve noise margin and discourage output instability for slowly changing input waveforms. A summary of MC3486 features include:

* Four Independent Receiver Chains
* Three-State Outputs
* High Impedance Output Control Inputs (PIA Compatible)
* Internal Hysteresis — 30 mV (Typ) @ Zero Volts Common Mode
* TTL Compatible
* Single 5 V Supply Voltage
* DS 3486 Second Source

**QUAD RS-422/3 LINE RECEIVER WITH THREE-STATE OUTPUTS**

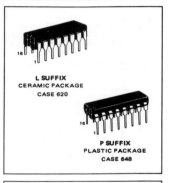

**L SUFFIX**
CERAMIC PACKAGE
CASE 620

**P SUFFIX**
PLASTIC PACKAGE
CASE 648

**RECEIVER CHAIN BLOCK DIAGRAM**

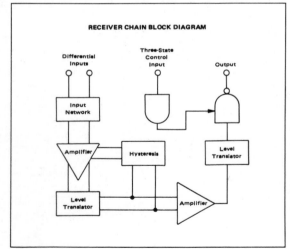

**PIN CONNECTIONS**

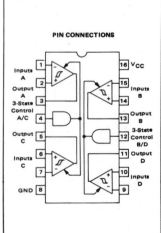

*Courtesy of Motorola, Inc. Used by permission.*

## MC3486

### ABSOLUTE MAXIMUM RATINGS (Note 1)

| Rating | Symbol | Value | Unit |
|---|---|---|---|
| Power Supply Voltage | $V_{CC}$ | 8.0 | Vdc |
| Input Common Mode Voltage | $V_{ICM}$ | ±15 | Vdc |
| Input Differential Voltage | $V_{ID}$ | ±25 | Vdc |
| Three-State Control Input Voltage | $V_I$ | 8.0 | Vdc |
| Output Sink Current | $I_O$ | 50 | mA |
| Storage Temperature | $T_{stg}$ | −65 to +150 | °C |
| Operating Junction Temperature | $T_J$ | | °C |
| Ceramic Package | | +175 | |
| Plastic Package | | +150 | |

Note 1: "Absolute Maximum Ratings" are those values beyond which the safety of the device cannot be guaranteed. They are not meant to imply that the devices should be operated at these limits. The "Table of Electrical Characteristics" provides conditions for actual device operation.

### RECOMMENDED OPERATING CONDITIONS

| Rating | Symbol | Value | Unit |
|---|---|---|---|
| Power Supply Voltage | $V_{CC}$ | 4.75 to 5.25 | Vdc |
| Operating Ambient Temperature | $T_A$ | 0 to +70 | °C |
| Input Common Mode Voltage Range | $V_{ICR}$ | −7.0 to +7.0 | Vdc |
| Input Differential Voltage Range | $V_{IDR}$ | 6.0 | Vdc |

### ELECTRICAL CHARACTERISTICS (Unless otherwise noted minimum and maximum limits apply over recommended temperature and power supply voltage ranges. Typical values are for $T_A$ = 25°C, $V_{CC}$ = 5.0 V and $V_{IK}$ = 0 V. See Note 1.)

| Characteristic | Symbol | Min | Typ | Max | Unit |
|---|---|---|---|---|---|
| Input Voltage — High Logic State (Three-State Control) | $V_{IH}$ | 2.0 | − | − | V |
| Input Voltage — Low Logic State (Three-State Control) | $V_{IL}$ | − | − | 0.8 | V |
| Differential Input Threshold Voltage (Note 4) ($-7.0$ V ≤ $V_{IC}$ ≤ 7.0 V, $V_{IH}$ = 2.0 V) | $V_{TH(D)}$ | | | | V |
| ($I_O$ = 0.4 mA, $V_{OH}$ ≥ 2.7 V) | | − | − | 0.2 | |
| ($I_O$ = 8.0 mA, $V_{OL}$ ≥ 0.5 V) | | − | − | −0.2 | |
| Input Bias Current ($V_{CC}$ = 0 V or 5.25) (Other Inputs at 0 V) | $I_{IB(D)}$ | | | | mA |
| ($V_I$ = −10 V) | | − | − | −3.25 | |
| ($V_I$ = −3.0 V) | | − | − | −1.50 | |
| ($V_I$ = +3.0 V) | | − | − | +1.50 | |
| ($V_I$ = +10 V) | | − | − | +3.25 | |
| Input Balance and Output Level ($-7.0$ V ≤ $V_{IC}$ ≤ 7.0 V, $V_{IH}$ = 2.0 V, See Note 3) | | | | | V |
| ($I_O$ = 0.4 mA, $V_{ID}$ = 0.4 V) | $V_{OH}$ | 2.7 | − | − | |
| ($I_O$ = 8.0 mA, $V_{ID}$ = 0.4 V) | $V_{OL}$ | − | − | 0.5 | |
| Output Third State Leakage Current | $I_{OZ}$ | | | | μA |
| ($V_{I(D)}$ = +3.0 V, $V_{IL}$ = 0.8 V, $V_{OL}$ = 0.5 V) | | − | − | −40 | |
| ($V_{I(D)}$ = −3.0 V, $V_{IL}$ = 0.8 V, $V_{OL}$ = 2.7 V) | | − | − | 40 | |
| Output Short-Circuit Current ($V_{I(D)}$ = 3.0 V, $V_{IH}$ = 2.0 V, $V_O$ = 0 V) See Note 2) | $I_{OS}$ | −15 | − | −100 | mA |
| Input Current — Low Logic State (Three-State Control) ($V_{IH}$ = 0.5 V) | $I_{IL}$ | − | − | −100 | μA |
| Input Current — High Logic State (Three-State Control) | $I_{IH}$ | | | | μA |
| ($V_{IH}$ = 2.7 V) | | − | − | 20 | |
| ($V_{IH}$ = 5.25 V) | | − | − | 100 | |
| Input Clamp Diode Voltage (Three-State Control) ($I_{IK}$ = −10 mA) | $V_{IK}$ | − | − | −1.5 | V |
| Power Supply Current ($V_{IL}$ = 0 V) | $I_{CC}$ | − | − | 85 | mA |

*Courtesy of Motorola, Inc. Used by permission.*

 **MOTOROLA**

## MC3487

### QUAD LINE DRIVER WITH THREE-STATE OUTPUTS

Motorola's Quad RS-422 Driver features four independent driver chains which comply with EIA Standards for the Electrical Characteristics of Balanced Voltage Digital Interface Circuits. The outputs are three-state structures which are forced to a high impedance state when the appropriate output control pin reaches a logic zero condition. All input pins are PNP buffered to minimize input loading for either logic one or logic zero inputs. In addition, internal circuitry assures a high impedance output state during the transition between power up and power down. A summary of MC3487 features include:

- Four Independent Driver Chains
- Three-State Outputs
- PNP High Impedance Inputs (PIA Compatible)
- Fast Propagation Times (Typ 15 ns)
- TTL Compatible
- Single 5 V Supply Voltage
- Output Rise and Fall Times Less Than 20 ns
- DS 3487 Second Source

### QUAD RS-422 LINE DRIVER WITH THREE-STATE OUTPUTS

**SILICON MONOLITHIC INTEGRATED CIRCUIT**

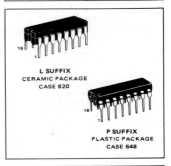

L SUFFIX
CERAMIC PACKAGE
CASE 620

P SUFFIX
PLASTIC PACKAGE
CASE 648

### PIN CONNECTIONS

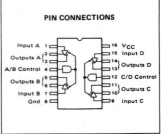

Input A  1          16  V$_{CC}$
Outputs A {2 / 3    15  Input D
A/B Control  4      14 / 13 } Outputs D
Outputs B {5 / 6    12  C/D Control
Input B  7          11 / 10 } Outputs C
Gnd  8              9  Input C

### DRIVER BLOCK DIAGRAM

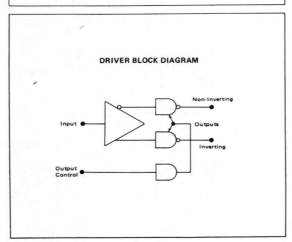

Input

Output Control

Non-Inverting
Outputs
Inverting

### TRUTH TABLE

| Input | Control Input | Non-Inverting Output | Inverting Output |
|-------|---------------|----------------------|------------------|
| H | H | H | L |
| L | H | L | H |
| X | L | Z | Z |

L = Low Logic State
H = High Logic State
X = Irrelevant
Z = Third-State (High Impedance)

*Courtesy of Motorola, Inc. Used by permission.*

## MC3487

MAXIMUM RATINGS

| Rating | Symbol | Value | Unit |
|---|---|---|---|
| Power Supply Voltage | $V_{CC}$ | 8.0 | Vdc |
| Input Voltage | $V_I$ | 5.5 | Vdc |
| Operating Ambient Temperature Range | $T_A$ | 0 to +70 | °C |
| Operating Junction Temperature Range<br>Ceramic Package<br>Plastic Package | $T_J$ | <br>175<br>150 | °C |
| Storage Temperature Range | $T_{stg}$ | -65 to +150 | °C |

ELECTRICAL CHARACTERISTICS (Unless otherwise noted specifications apply 4.75 V ≤ $V_{CC}$ ≤ 5.25 V and 0°C ≤ $T_A$ ≤ 70°C. Typical values measured at $V_{CC}$ = 5.0 V, and $T_A$ = 25°C.)

| Characteristic | Symbol | Min | Typ | Max | Unit |
|---|---|---|---|---|---|
| Input Voltage — Low Logic State | $V_{IL}$ | — | — | 0.8 | Vdc |
| Input Voltage — High Logic State | $V_{IH}$ | 2.0 | — | — | Vdc |
| Input Current — Low Logic State<br>($V_{IL}$ = 0.5 V) | $I_{IL}$ | — | — | -400 | µA |
| Input Current — High Logic State<br>($V_{IH}$ = 2.7 V)<br>($V_{IH}$ = 5.5 V) | $I_{IH}$ | <br>—<br>— | <br>—<br>— | <br>+50<br>+100 | µA |
| Input Clamp Voltage<br>($I_{IK}$ = -18 mA) | $V_{IK}$ | — | — | -1.5 | V |
| Output Voltage — Low Logic State<br>($I_{OL}$ = 48 mA) | $V_{OL}$ | — | — | 0.5 | V |
| Output Voltage — High Logic State<br>($I_{OH}$ = -20 mA) | $V_{OH}$ | 2.5 | — | — | V |
| Output Short-Circuit Current<br>($V_{IH}$ = 2.0 V, Note 1) | $I_{OS}$ | -40 | — | -140 | mA |
| Output Leakage Current — Hi-Z State<br>($V_{IL}$ = 0.5 V, $V_{IL(Z)}$ = 0.8 V)<br>($V_{IH}$ = 2.7 V, $V_{IL(Z)}$ = 0.8 V) | $I_{OL(Z)}$ | <br>—<br>— | <br>—<br>— | <br>±100<br>±100 | µA |
| Output Leakage Current — Power OFF<br>($V_{OH}$ = 6.0 V, $V_{CC}$ = 0 V)<br>($V_{OL}$ = -0.25 V, $V_{CC}$ = 0 V) | $I_{OL(off)}$ | <br>—<br>— | <br>—<br>— | <br>+100<br>-100 | µA |
| Output Offset Voltage Difference (Note 2) | $V_{OS} - \overline{V}_{OS}$ | — | — | ±0.4 | V |
| Output Differential Voltage (Note 2) | $V_{OD}$ | 2.0 | — | — | V |
| Output Differential Voltage Difference (Note 2) | $|\Delta V_{OD}|$ | — | — | ±0.4 | V |
| Power Supply Current<br>(Control Pins = Gnd, Note 3)<br>(Control Pins = 2.0 V) | <br>$I_{CCX}$<br>$I_{CC}$ | <br>—<br>— | <br>—<br>— | <br>105<br>85 | mA |

Notes: 1. Only one output may be shorted at a time.
2. See EIA Specification EIA-422 for exact test conditions.
3. Circuit in three-state condition.

SWITCHING CHARACTERISTICS ($V_{CC}$ - 5.0 V, $T_A$ - 25°C unless otherwise noted.)

| Characteristic | Symbol | Min | Typ | Max | Unit |
|---|---|---|---|---|---|
| Propagation Delay Times<br>High to Low Output<br>Low to High Output | <br>$t_{PHL}$<br>$t_{PLH}$ | <br>—<br>— | <br>—<br>— | <br>20<br>20 | ns |
| Output Transition Times — Differential<br>High to Low Output<br>Low to High Output | <br>$t_{THL}$<br>$t_{TLH}$ | <br>—<br>— | <br>—<br>— | <br>20<br>20 | ns |
| Propagation Delay — Control to Output<br>($R_L$ = 200 Ω, $C_L$ = 50 pF)<br>($R_L$ = 200 Ω, $C_L$ = 50 pF)<br>($R_L$ = ∞, $C_L$ = 50 pF)<br>($R_L$ = 200 Ω, $C_L$ = 50 pF) | <br>$t_{PHZ(E)}$<br>$t_{PLZ(E)}$<br>$t_{PZH(E)}$<br>$t_{PZL(E)}$ | <br>—<br>—<br>—<br>— | <br>—<br>—<br>—<br>— | <br>25<br>25<br>30<br>30 | ns |

## MC3488A
## MC3488B

### Product Preview

DUAL
RS-423/RS-232C
DRIVERS

SILICON MONOLITHIC
INTEGRATED CIRCUIT

#### DUAL RS-423/RS-232C LINE DRIVERS

The MC3488A and MC3488B dual single-ended line drivers have been designed to satisfy the requirements of EIA standards RS-423 and RS-232C, as well as CCITT X.26, X.28 and Federal Standard FIDS1030. They are suitable for use where signal wave shaping is desired and the output load resistance is greater than 450 ohms. Output slew rates are adjustable from 1.0 $\mu$s to 100 $\mu$s by a single external resistor. Output level and slew rate are independent of power supply variations or matching. Input undershoot diodes limit transients below ground; output current limiting is provided in both output states. They can be operated with supply voltages from ±9.0 to ±15 V.

The MC3488A has a standard 1.5 V input logic threshold for TTL or NMOS compatibility. The MC3488B input logic threshold is set at $V_{CC}/2$ for use with CMOS logic systems.

- PNP Buffered Inputs to Minimize Input Loading
- Wide Power Supply Operating Range
- Adjustable Slew Rate Limiting
- Option of Either 1.5 V or $V_{CC}/2$ Input Threshold
- MC3488A Equivalent to 9636A
- Logic Levels and Slew Rate Independent of Power Supply Voltages or Matching

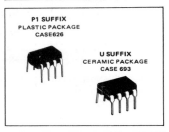

P1 SUFFIX
PLASTIC PACKAGE
CASE626

U SUFFIX
CERAMIC PACKAGE
CASE 693

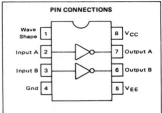

**PIN CONNECTIONS**

| | | |
|---|---|---|
| Wave Shape | 1 | 8 $V_{CC}$ |
| Input A | 2 | 7 Output A |
| Input B | 3 | 6 Output B |
| Gnd | 4 | 5 $V_{EE}$ |

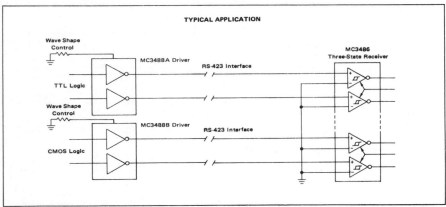

**TYPICAL APPLICATION**

Wave Shape Control

MC3488A Driver

TTL Logic

Wave Shape Control

MC3488B Driver

CMOS Logic

RS-423 Interface

RS-423 Interface

MC3486
Three-State Receiver

This is advance information and specifications are subject to change without notice.

*Courtesy of Motorola, Inc. Used by permission.*

## MC3488A, MC3488B

### ABSOLUTE MAXIMUM RATINGS (Note 1)

| Rating | Symbol | Value | Unit |
|---|---|---|---|
| Power Supply Voltages | $V_{CC}$<br>$V_{EE}$ | +15<br>−15 | V |
| Output Current<br>Source<br>Sink | <br>$I_{0+}$<br>$I_{0-}$ | <br>+150<br>−150 | mA |
| Operating Ambient Temperature | $T_A$ | 0 to +70 | °C |
| Junction Temperature Range<br>Ceramic Package<br>Plastic Package | $T_J$ | <br>175<br>150 | °C |
| Storage Temperature Range | $T_{stg}$ | −65 to +150 | °C |

Note 1:  "Absolute Maximum Ratings" are those values beyond which the safety of the device cannot be guaranteed. They are not meant to imply that the devices should be operated at these limits. The "Table of Electrical Characteristics" provides conditions for actual device operation.

### RECOMMENDED OPERATING CONDITION

| Characteristic | Symbol | Min | Typ | Max | Unit |
|---|---|---|---|---|---|
| Power Supply Voltages | $V_{CC}$<br>$V_{EE}$ | 10.8<br>10.8 | 12<br>−12 | 13.2<br>−13.2 | V |
| Operating Temperature Range | $T_A$ | 0 | 25 | 70 | °C |
| Wave Shaping Resistor | $R_W$ | 10 | − | 500 | kΩ |

### TARGET ELECTRICAL CHARACTERISTICS (Unless otherwise noted specifications apply over $0°C \leq T_A \leq 70°C$, $9.0 \text{ V} \leq |V_{CC}, V_{EE}| \leq 15 \text{ V}$ and $2.0 \text{ k} \leq R_W \leq 400 \text{ k}$)

| Characteristic | Symbol | Min | Typ | Max | Unit |
|---|---|---|---|---|---|
| Input Voltage — Low Logic State<br>MC3488A<br>MC3488B | $V_{IL}$ | <br>−<br>− | <br>−<br>− | <br>0.8<br>$V_{CC}/2 - 2.0$ | V |
| Input Voltage — High Logic State<br>MC3488A<br>MC3488B | $V_{IH}$ | <br>2.0<br>$V_{CC}/2 + 2.0$ | <br>−<br>− | <br>−<br>− | V |
| Input Current — Low Logic State<br>($V_{IL} = 0.4$ V) | $I_{IL}$ | <br>− | <br>− | <br>−80 | µA |
| Input Current — High Logic State<br>($V_{IH} = 2.4$ V)    MC3488A<br>($V_{IH} = 5.5$ V)    MC3488A<br>($V_{IH} = V_{CC}$)    MC3488B | $I_{IH}$ | <br>−<br>−<br>− | <br>−<br>−<br>− | <br>10<br>100<br>100 | µA |
| Input Clamp Diode Voltage<br>($I_{IK} = -15$ mA) | $V_{IK}$ | <br>− | <br>− | <br>−1.5 | V |
| Output Voltage — Low Logic State<br>($R_L = \infty$)    RS-423<br>($R_L = 3.0$ kΩ) RS-232C<br>($R_L = 450$ Ω) RS-423 | $V_{OL}$ | <br>−5.0<br>−5.0<br>−4.0 | <br>−<br>−<br>− | <br>−6.0<br>−6.0<br>−6.0 | V |
| Output Voltage — High Logic State<br>($R_L = \infty$)    RS-423<br>($R_L = 3.0$ kΩ) RS-232C<br>($R_L = 450$ Ω) RS-423 | $V_{OH}$ | <br>5.0<br>5.0<br>4.0 | <br>−<br>−<br>− | <br>6.0<br>6.0<br>6.0 | V |
| Output Short-Circuit Current | $I_{SC+}$<br>$I_{SC-}$ | +15<br>−15 | −<br>− | 150<br>−150 | mA |
| Output Leakage Current<br>($V_{CC} = V_{EE} = 0$ V, $-6.0 \text{ V} \leq V_o \leq 6.0 \text{ V}$) | $I_{ox}$ | −100 | − | 100 | µA |
| Power Supply Current<br>($R_W = 2.0$ kΩ)<br>($R_W = 2.0$ kΩ) | <br>$I_{CC}$<br>$I_{EE}$ | <br>−<br>− | <br>−<br>− | <br>+18<br>−18 | mA |
| Output Resistance<br>($R_L \geq 450$ Ω) | $R_O$ | <br>− | <br>25 | <br>50 | Ω |

Note: A diode is connected in series with $V_{EE}$ for all test conditions.

*Courtesy of Motorola, Inc. Used by permission.*

## MC3488A, MC3488B

**TRANSITION TIMES** (Unless otherwise noted, $C_L$ = 30 pF, f = 1.0 kHz, $V_{CC}$ = 12 V, $V_{EE}$ = –12 V, $T_A$ = 25°C, $R_L$ = 450 Ω. Transition times measure 10% to 90% and 90% to 10%)

| Characteristic | Symbol | Min | Typ | Max | Unit |
|---|---|---|---|---|---|
| Transition Time, Low to High State Output | $t_{TLH}$ | | | | μs |
| ($R_W$ = 10 kΩ) | | 0.8 | – | 1.4 | |
| ($R_W$ = 100 kΩ) | | 8.0 | – | 14 | |
| ($R_W$ = 500 kΩ) | | 40 | – | 70 | |
| ($R_W$ = 1000 kΩ) | | 80 | – | 140 | |
| Transition Time, High to Low State Output | $t_{THL}$ | | | | μs |
| ($R_W$ = 10 kΩ) | | 0.8 | – | 1.4 | |
| ($R_W$ = 100 kΩ) | | 8.0 | – | 14 | |
| ($R_W$ = 500 kΩ) | | 40 | – | 70 | |
| ($R_W$ = 1000 kΩ) | | 80 | – | 140 | |

**FIGURE 1 — TEST CIRCUIT & WAVEFORMS
FOR TRANSITION TIMES**

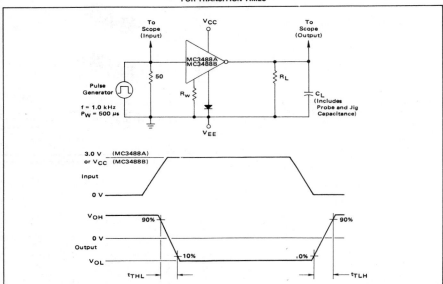

**FIGURE 2 — OUTPUT TRANSITION TIMES
versus WAVE SHAPE RESISTOR VALUE**

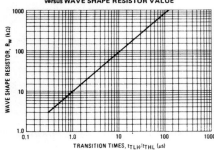

*Courtesy of Motorola, Inc. Used by permission.*

 **MOTOROLA**

**MC6860**

## 0-600 bps DIGITAL MODEM

The MC6860 is a MOS subsystem designed to be integrated into a wide range of equipment utilizing serial data communications.

The modem provides the necessary modulation, demodulation and supervisory control functions to implement a serial data communications link, over a voice grade channel, utilizing frequency shift keying (FSK) at bit rates up to 600 bps. The MC6860 can be implemented into a wide range of data handling systems, including stand alone modems, data storage devices, remote data communication terminals and I/O interfaces for minicomputers.

N-channel silicon-gate technology permits the MC6860 to operate using a single-voltage supply and be fully TTL compatible.

The modem is compatible with the M6800 microcomputer family, interfacing directly with the Asynchronous Communications Interface Adapter to provide low-speed data communications capability.

● Originate and Answer Mode
● Crystal or External Reference Control
● Modem Self Test
● Terminal Interfaces TTL-Compatible
● Full-Duplex or Half-Duplex Operation
● Automatic Answer and Disconnect
● Compatible Functions for 100 Series Data Sets
● Compatible Functions for 1001A/B Data Couplers

## MOS

(N-CHANNEL, SILICON-GATE)

### 0-600 bps
### DIGITAL MODEM

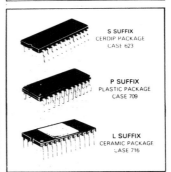

S SUFFIX
CERDIP PACKAGE
CASE 623

P SUFFIX
PLASTIC PACKAGE
CASE 709

L SUFFIX
CERAMIC PACKAGE
CASE 716

FIGURE 1 — TYPICAL MC6860 SYSTEM CONFIGURATION

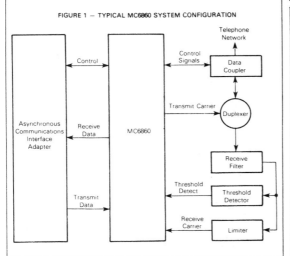

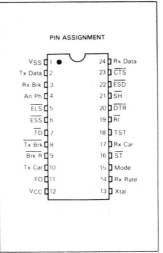

PIN ASSIGNMENT

| Pin | Signal | | Pin | Signal |
|---|---|---|---|---|
| 1 | V$_{SS}$ | | 24 | Rx Data |
| 2 | Tx Data | | 23 | $\overline{CTS}$ |
| 3 | Rx Brk | | 22 | $\overline{ESD}$ |
| 4 | An Ph | | 21 | SH |
| 5 | $\overline{ELS}$ | | 20 | $\overline{DTR}$ |
| 6 | $\overline{ESS}$ | | 19 | $\overline{RI}$ |
| 7 | $\overline{TD}$ | | 18 | TST |
| 8 | $\overline{Tx\ Brk}$ | | 17 | Rx Car |
| 9 | $\overline{Brk\ R}$ | | 16 | $\overline{ST}$ |
| 10 | Tx Car | | 15 | Mode |
| 11 | FO | | 14 | Rx Rate |
| 12 | V$_{CC}$ | | 13 | Xtal |

*Courtesy of Motorola, Inc. Used by permission.*

## MC6860

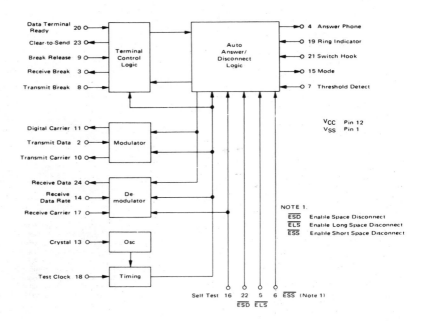

FIGURE 3 — BLOCK DIAGRAM

NOTE 1.
$\overline{ESD}$   Enable Space Disconnect
$\overline{ELS}$   Enable Long Space Disconnect
$\overline{ESS}$   Enable Short Space Disconnect

$V_{CC}$  Pin 12
$V_{SS}$  Pin 1

## DEVICE OPERATION*

### GENERAL

Figure 1 shows the modem and its interconnections. The data to be transmitted is presented in serial format to the modulator for conversion to FSK signals for transmission on the telephone line (refer to Figure 3). The modulator output is buffered before driving the line.

The FSK signal from the remote modem is received via the telephone line and filtered to remove extraneous signals such as the local Transmit Carrier. This filtering can be either a bandpass which passes only the desired band of frequencies or a notch which rejects the known interfering signal. The desired signal is then limited to preserve the axis crossings and fed to the demodulator where the data is recovered from the received FSK carrier.

The Supervisory Control provides the necessary commands and responses for handshaking with the remote modem, along with the interface signals to the data coupler and communication terminal. If the modem is a built-in unit,

*See Tables 1 and 2 for delay time tolerances.

all input-output (I/O) logic need not be RS-232 compatible. The use of MC1488 and MC1489A line drivers and receivers will provide a RS-232 interface conforming to the EIA specification.

### ANSWER MODE

Automatic answering is first initiated by a receipt of a Ring Indicator ($\overline{RI}$) signal. This can be either a low level for at least 51 ms as would come from a CBS data coupler, or at least 20 cycles of a 20-47 Hz ringing singal (low level ≥ 50% of the duty cycle) as would come from a CBT data coupler. The presence of the Ring Indicator signal places the modem in the Answer Mode; if the Data Terminal Ready line is low, indicating the communication terminal is ready to send or receive data, the Answer Phone output goes high. This output is designed to drive a transistor switch which will activate

*Courtesy of Motorola, Inc. Used by permission.*

## MC6860

the Off Hook (OH) and Data Transmission (DA) relays in the data coupler. Upon answering the phone the 2225-Hz Transmit Carrier is turned on.

The originate modem at the other end detects this 2225-Hz signal and after a 450 ms delay (used to disable any echo suppressors in the telephone network) transmits a 1270-Hz signal which the local answering modem detects, provided the amplitude and frequency requirements are met. The amplitude threshold is set external to the modem chip. If the signal level is sufficient the $\overline{TD}$ input should be low for 20 $\mu$s at least once every 32 ms. The absence of a threshold indication for a period greater than 51 ms denotes the loss of Receive Carrier and the modem begins hang-up procedures. Hang-up will occur 17 s after $\overline{RI}$ has been released provided the handshaking routine is not re-established. The frequeny tolerance during handshaking is $\pm$ 100 Hz from the Mark frequency.

After the 1270-Hz signal has been received for 150 ms, the Receive Data is unclamped from a Mark condition and data can be received. The Clear-to-Send output goes low 450 ms after the receipt of carrier and data presented to the answer modem is transmitted. Refer to Figure 4.

### AUTOMATIC DISCONNECT

Upon receipt of a space of 150 ms or greater duration, the modem clamps the Receive Break high. This condition exists until a Break Release command is issued at the receiving station. Upon receipt of a 0.3 s space, with Enable Short Space Disconnect at the most negative voltage (low), the modem automatically hangs up. If Enable Long Space Disconnect is low, the modem requires 1.5 s of continuous space to hang up. Refer to Figure 5 .

### ORIGINATE MODE

Upon receipt of a Switch Hook ($\overline{SH}$) command the modem function is placed in the Originate Mode. If the Data Terminal Ready input is enabled (low) the modem will provide a logic high output at Answer Phone. The modem is now ready to receive the 2225-Hz signal from the remote answering modem. It will continue to look for this signal until 17 s after $\overline{SH}$ has been released. Disconnect occurs if the handshaking routine is not established.

Upon receiving 2225 $\pm$ 100 Hz for 150 ms at an acceptable amplitude, the receive Data output is unclamped from a Mark condition and data reception can be accomplished. 450 ms after receiving a 2225-Hz signal, a 1270-Hz signal is transmitted to the remote modem. 750 ms after receiving the 2225-Hz signal, the Clear-to-Send output is taken low and data can now be transmitted as well as received. Refer to Figure 6.

### INITIATE DISCONNECT

In order to command the remote modem to automatically hang up, a disconnect signal is sent by the local modem. This is accomplished by pulsing the normally low Data Terminal Ready into a high state for greater than 34 ms. The local modem then sends a 3 s continuous space and hangs up provided the Enable Space Disconnect is low. If the remote modem hangs up before 3 s, loss of Threshold Detect will cause loss of Clear-to-Send, which marks the line in Answer Mode and turns the carrier off in the Originate Mode.

If $\overline{ESD}$ is high the modem will transmit data until hang-up occurs 3 s later. Receive Break is clamped 150 ms following the Data Terminal Ready interrupt. Refer to Figure 7.

### INPUT/OUTPUT FUNCTIONS

Figure 8 shows the I/O interface for the low speed modem. The following is a description of each individual signal:

### Receiver Carrier (Rx Car)

The Receive Carrier is the FSK input to the demodulator. The local Transmit Carrier must be balanced or filtered out and the remaining signal hard limited. The conditioned receive carrier is measured by the MC6860. Any half-cycle period greater than or equal to 429 $\pm$ 1.0 $\mu$s for the low band or 235 $\pm$ 1.0 $\mu$s for the high band is detected as a space. Resultant peak phase jitter is as follows:

| Data Rate Bits per Second | Answer Mode $\phi_J$ (Peak %) | Originate Mode $\phi_J$ (Peak %) |
|---|---|---|
| 300 | 7.0 | 3.7 |
| 200 | 4.7 | 2.5 |
| 150 | 3.5 | 1.8 |
| 110 | 2.6 | 1.4 |

### Ring Indicator ($\overline{RI}$)

The modem function will recognize the receipt of a call from the CBT data coupler if at least 20 cycles of the 20-47 Hz ringing singal (low level $\geq$ 50% of the duty cycle) are present. The CBS data coupler $\overline{RI}$ signal must be level-converted to TTL according to the EIA RS-232 specification before interfacing it with the modem function. The receipt of a call from the CBS data coupler is recognized if the $\overline{RI}$ signal is present for at least 51 ms. This input is held high except during ringing. An $\overline{RI}$ signal automatically places the modem function in the Answer Mode.

### Switch Hook ($\overline{SH}$)

$\overline{SH}$ interfaces directly with the CBT data coupler and via the EIA RS-232 level conversion for the CBS data coupler. An $\overline{SH}$ signal automatically places the modem function in the Originate Mode.

$\overline{SH}$ is low during origination of a call. The modem will automatically hang up 17 s after releasing $\overline{SH}$ if the handshaking routine has not been accomplished.

### Threshold Detect ($\overline{TD}$)

This input is derived from an external threshold detector. If the signal level is sufficient, the $\overline{TD}$ input must be low for 20 $\mu$s at least once every 32 ms to maintain normal operation. An insufficient signal level indicates the absence of the Receive Carrier; an absence for less than 32 ms will not cause channel establishment to be lost; however, data during this interval will be invalid.

If the signal is present and the level is acceptable at all times, then the threshold input can be low permanently.

Loss of threshold for 51 ms or longer results in a loss of Clear-to-Send. The Transmit Carrier of the originate modem is clamped off and a constant Mark is transmitted from the answer modem.

*Courtesy of Motorola, Inc. Used by permission.*

# MC6860

TIMING DIAGRAMS

FIGURE 4 — ANSWER MODE

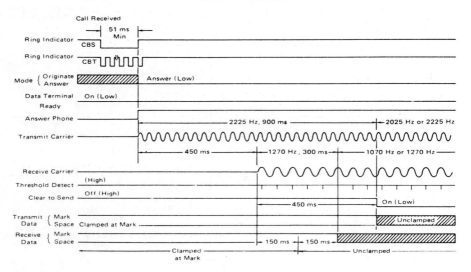

FIGURE 5 — AUTOMATIC DISCONNECT — LONG OR SHORT SPACE

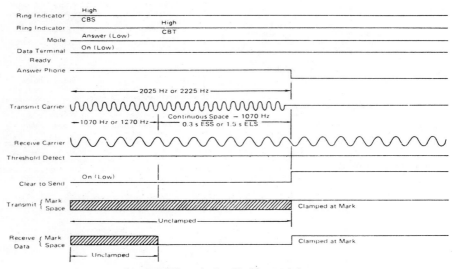

*Courtesy of Motorola, Inc. Used by permission.*

MC6860

FIGURE 6 — ORIGINATE MODE

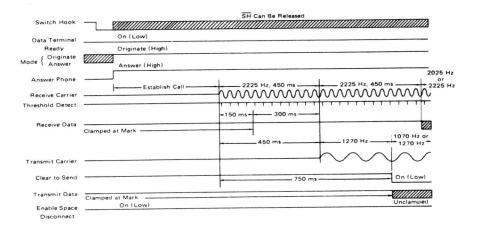

FIGURE 7 — INITIATE DISCONNECT

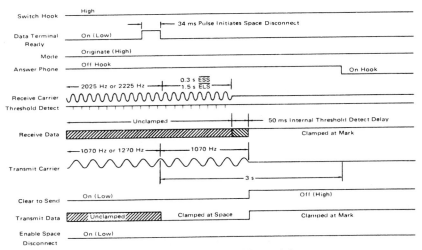

*Courtesy of Motorola, Inc. Used by permission.*

## MC6860

### Receive Data Rate (Rx Rate)

The demodulator has been optimized for signal-to-noise performance at 300 bps and 600 bps. The Receive Data Rate input must be low for 0-600 bps and should be high for 0-300 bps.

### Transmit Data (Tx Data)

Transmit Data is the binary information presented to the modem function for modulation with FSK techniques. A high level represents a Mark.

### Data Terminal Ready (DTR)

The Data Terminal Ready signal must be low before the modem function will be enabled. To initiate a disconnect, DTR is held high for 34 ms minimum. A disconnect will occur 3 s later.

### Break Release (Brk R)

After receiving a 150 ms space signal, the clamped high condition of the Receive Break output can be removed by holding Break Release low for at least 20 μs.

### Transmit Break (Tx Brk)

The Break command is used to signal the remote modem to stop sending data.

A Transmit Break (low) greater than 34 ms forces the modem to send a continuous space signal for 233 ms. Transmit Break must be initiated only after CTS has been established. This is a negative edge sense input. Prior to initiating Tx Brk, this input must be held high for a minimum of 34 ms.

### Enabled Space Disconnect (ESD)

When ESD is strapped low and DTR is pulsed to initiate a disconnect, the modem transmits a space for either 3 s or until a loss of threshold is detected, whichever occurs first. If ESD is strapped high, data instead of a space is transmitted. A disconnect occurs at the end of 3 s.

### Enable Short Space Disconnect (ESS)

ESS is a strapping option which, when low, will automatically hang up the phone upon receipt of a continuous space for 0.3 s. *ESS and ELS must not be simultaneously strapped low.*

### Enable Long Space Disconnect (ELS)

ELS is a strapping option which, when low, will automatically hang up the phone upon receipt of a continuous space for 1.5 s.

### Crystal (Xtal)

A 1.0 MHz crystal with the following parameters is required to utilize the on-chip oscillator. A 1.0-MHz square wave can also be fed into this input to satisfy the clock requirement.

| | |
|---|---|
| Mode: | Parallel |
| Frequency: | 1.0 MHz ±0.1% |
| Series Resistance: | 750 ohms max |
| Shunt Capacitance: | 7.0 pF max |
| Temperature: | 0-70°C |
| Test Level: | 1.0 mW |
| Load Capacitance: | 13 pF |

**FIGURE 8 — I/O INTERFACE CONNECTIONS FOR MC6860
(ORIGINATE/ANSWER MODEM)**

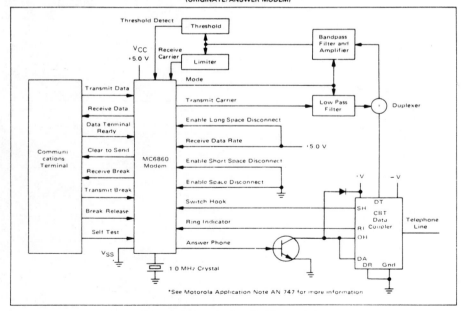

*Courtesy of Motorola, Inc. Used by permission.*

# MC6860

When utilizing the 1.0 MHz crystal, external parasitic capacitance, including crystal shunt capacitance, must be ≤9 pF at the crystal input. Reliable crystal oscillator start-up requires that the $V_{CC}$ power-on transition time be >15 milliseconds.

### Test Clock (TST)

A test signal input is provided to decrease the test time of the chip. In normal operation this input *must be strapped low.*

### Self Test (ST)

When a low voltage level is placed on this input, the demodulator is switched to the modulator frequency and demodulates the transmitted FSK signal. Channel establishment, which occurred during the initial handshake, is not lost during self test. The Mode Control ouput changes state during Self Test, permitting the receive filters to pass the local Transmit Carrier.

| ST | SH | RI | Mode |
|----|----|----|------|
| H | ⎍* | H | H |
| H | H | L | L |
| L | ⎍* | H | L |
| L | H | L | H |

*Note maximum SH low time in Table 1.

### Answer Phone (An Ph)

Upon receipt of Ring Indicator or Switch Hook signal and Data Terminal Ready, the Answer Phone output goes high [(SH + RI)•DTR]. This signal drives the base of a transistor which activates the Off Hook, and Data Transmission control lines in the data coupler. Upon call completion, the Answer Phone signal returns to a low level.

### Mode

The Mode output indicates the Answer (low) or Originate (high) status of the modem. This output changes state when a Self Test command is applied.

### Clear-To-Send (CTS)

A low on the CTS output indicates the Transmit Data input has been unclamped from a steady Mark, thus allowing data transmission.

### Receive Data (Rx Data)

The Receive Data output is the data resulting from demodulating the Receive Carrier. A Mark is a high level.

### Receive Break (Rx Brk)

Upon receipt of a continuous 150 ms space, the modem automatically clamps the Receive Break output high. This output is also clamped high until Clear-to-Send is established.

### Digital Carrier (FO)

A test signal output is provided to decrease the chip test time. The signal is a square wave at the transmit frequency.

### Transmit Carrier (Tx Car)

The Transmit Carrier is a digitally-synthesized sine wave (Figure 9) derived from the 1.0 MHz crystal reference. The frequency characteristics are as follows:

| Mode | Data | Transmit Frequency | Tolerance* |
|------|------|--------------------|-----------|
| Originate | Mark | 1270 Hz | −0.15 Hz |
| Originate | Space | 1070 Hz | 0.90 Hz |
| Answer | Mark | 2225 Hz | −0.31 Hz |
| Answer | Space | 2025 Hz | −0.71 Hz |

*The reference frequency tolerance is not included.

The proper output frequency is transmitted within 3.0 μs following a data bit change with no more than 2.0 μs phase discontinuity. The typical output level is 0.35 V (RMS) into 100 k ohm load impedance.

The second harmonic is typically 32 dB below the fundamental (see Figure 10).

## POWER-ON RESET

Power-on reset is provided on-chip to insure that when power is first applied the Answer Phone output is in the low (inactive) state. This holds the modem in the inactive or idle mode until a SH or RI signal has been applied. Once power has been applied, a momentary loss of power at a later time may not be of sufficient time to guarantee a chip reset through the power-on reset circuit.

To insure initial power-on reset action, the external parasitic capacitance on RI and SH should be <30 pF. Capacitance values >30 pF may require the use of an external pullup resistor to $V_{CC}$ on these inputs in addition to the pullup devices already provided on chip.

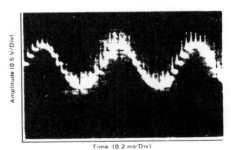

FIGURE 9 — TRANSMIT CARRIER SINE WAVE

FIGURE 10 — TRANSMIT CARRIER FREQUENCY SPECTRUM

*Courtesy of Motorola, Inc. Used by permission.*

## MC6860

TABLE 1 — ASYNCHRONOUS INPUT PULSE WIDTH AND OUTPUT DELAY VARIATIONS
(Time delays specified do not include the 1-MHz reference tolerance.)

Due to the asynchronous nature of the input signals with respect to the circuit internal clock, a delay variation or input pulse width requirement will exist. Time delay A is the maximum time for which no response will occur. Time delay B is the minimum time required to guarantee an input response. Input signal widths in the cross hatched region (i.e., greater than A but less than B) may or may not be recognized as valid.

For output delays, time A is the minimum delay before an output will respond. Time B is the maximum delay for an output to respond. Output signal response may or may not occur in the cross-hatched region (i.e., greater than A but less than B).

**INPUT PULSES**        **OUTPUT DELAYS**

* Digital Representation

(continued)

*Courtesy of Motorola, Inc. Used by permission.*

## MC6860

TABLE 1 – OUTPUT DELAY VARIATIONS (continued)

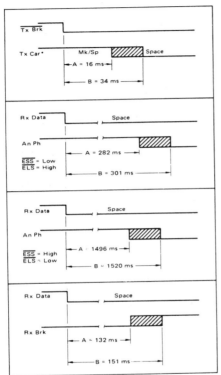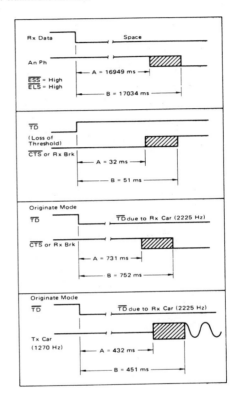

*Digital Representation

TABLE 2 – TRANSMIT BREAK AND DISCONNECT DELAYS

| Function Description | Min | Max | Unit |
|---|---|---|---|
| $\overline{\text{Tx Brk}}$ (Space Duration) | 232 | 235 | ms |
| Space Disconnect (Space Duration) ($\overline{\text{DTR}}$ = High, $\overline{\text{ESD}}$ and $\overline{\text{TD}}$ = Low) | 3010 | 3023 | ms |
| Loss of Carrier Disconnect (Measured from positive edge of $\overline{\text{CTS}}$ to negative edge of An Ph, with $\overline{\text{RI}}$, $\overline{\text{SH}}$, and $\overline{\text{TD}}$ = High) | 16965 | 17034 | ms |
| Override Disconnect (Measured from positive edge of $\overline{\text{RI}}$ or $\overline{\text{SH}}$ to negative edge of An Ph, with $\overline{\text{TD}}$ = High) | 16916 | 17101 | ms |

*Courtesy of Motorola, Inc. Used by permission.*

**MOTOROLA**
**■ SEMICONDUCTOR ■**
**TECHNICAL DATA**

**MC14416**
**MC14418**

### PER CHANNEL, ADDRESSABLE TIME SLOT ASSIGNER CIRCUITS (TSACs)

The MC14416 and MC14418 are per channel devices that allow variable codec time slot assignment to be programmed through a serial microprocessor port (0-63 time slots). Both devices have independent transmit and receive frame syncs and enables. They also include chip select and clear to send signals which simplify system design.

The MC14418 provides the additional addressing capability which allows a parallel bus back plane in the channel group. In addition, the MC14418 provides control bits which can be used for the power down, ring enable and ring trip functions on a line circuit.

The MC14416 provides the ability to multiplex off hook signals for a bank of TSACs.

Both devices are fabricated using the CMOS technology for reliable low power performance. The MC14418 is the full featured device produced in a 22-pin package. The MC14416 without the addressing capability is offered in a 16-pin package.

- Low Power
- 5-Volt Interface on Microprocessor Port
- 5-16 Volt Output Logic Levels
- Independent Transmit and Receive Frame Syncs and Enables
- Up to 64 Time Slots Per Frame
- For Use With Up to 2.56 MHz Clocks
- Provides Power Down Control for Line Circuits
- Compatible with MC14400/01/02/03/05 and MK5116 Codecs
- Provides the Ring Enable and Ring Trip Functions (MC14418)
- Allows Use of a Parallel Backplane for Line Circuits Due to the Hard Wired Address Feature (MC14418)
- Off-Hook Multiplex Control (MC14416)
- CMOS Metal Gate for High Reliability

**MOS LSI**
(LOW-POWER COMPLEMENTARY MOS)

**TSAC**
**TIME SLOT ASSIGNER**
**CIRCUITS**

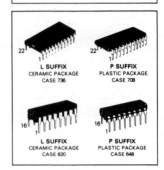

| | |
|---|---|
| **L SUFFIX**<br>CERAMIC PACKAGE<br>CASE 736 | **P SUFFIX**<br>PLASTIC PACKAGE<br>CASE 708 |
| **L SUFFIX**<br>CERAMIC PACKAGE<br>CASE 620 | **P SUFFIX**<br>PLASTIC PACKAGE<br>CASE 648 |

**BLOCK DIAGRAM**

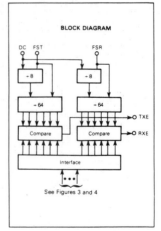

See Figures 3 and 4

### PIN ASSIGNMENTS

**MC14416**

| | | | |
|---|---|---|---|
| V_CC | 1 | 16 | V_DD |
| CLK | 2 | 15 | CTS |
| DI | 3 | 14 | TXE |
| CS | 4 | 13 | RXE |
| DC2 | 5 | 12 | DC1 |
| OHO | 6 | 11 | OHI |
| PD | 7 | 10 | FSR |
| V_SS | 8 | 9 | FST |

**MC14418**

| | | | |
|---|---|---|---|
| V_CC | 1 | 22 | V_DD |
| CLK | 2 | 21 | CTS |
| A1 | 3 | 20 | Q0 |
| A2 | 4 | 19 | Q1 |
| DI | 5 | 18 | TXE |
| AD | 6 | 17 | RXE |
| CS | 7 | 16 | DC1 |
| A3 | 8 | 15 | Q2 |
| A4 | 9 | 14 | R2 |
| A5 | 10 | 13 | FSR |
| V_SS | 11 | 12 | FST |

---

**MOTOROLA TELECOMMUNICATIONS DEVICE DATA**

*Courtesy of Motorola, Inc. Used by permission.*

## MC14416, MC14418

### GENERAL DEVICE DESCRIPTION

The MC14416 and MC14418 TSACs are microprocessor peripherals intended to be used to control and supervise per channel codec subscriber channel units. The TSACs consist of three basic functions.

**The Serially Programmable Microprocessor Port** consists of V$_{CC}$, CLK, DI, CS and CTS for the MC14416 and further includes AD and A1 through A5 for the MC14418. This port allows the call processing microprocessor to access load data into each TSAC. See the applications section for a detailed description of the microprocessor port. Figure 5 defines the data word bit assignments.

**The Supervision Controls** consist of Q0, Q1, Q2, R2 on the MC14418 and OHI, $\overline{OHO}$ and $\overline{PD}$ on the MC14416. These functions provide data path for the supervision and control of user selected requirements in the subscriber channel unit. Figure 3 shows some typical uses of these bits.

**The Time Slot Computation** section of the chip derives separate transmit and receive time slot outputs (TXE and RXE) for the controlled codec from the bit rate clock and sync pins DC1, DC2, FST and FSR, respectively. The computed time slot is then derived from the information received through the microprocessor port.

### PIN DESCRIPTIONS

**V$_{CC}$ (Positive Supply for Microprocessor Port)** — If this is a 5-volt supply, AD, DI, CS and CLK are TTL compatible CMOS inputs. V$_{CC}$ may be any voltage from 4.5 V to V$_{DD}$ allowing either TTL or CMOS compatibility.

**CS (Chip Select Input)** — For the MC14418, the pin is used to select a bank of TSACs.

For the MC14416, the CS is used to select that individual TSAC. All CSs are normally held low. To PROGRAM A SPECIFIC TSAC, CS must go high prior to the first falling edge of CLK. CS must stay high until the selected CTS goes low to guarantee a valid access.

CS is synchronous with DI, AD and CLK. CS can be asynchronous with DC1, DC2, FST or FSR. (This pin is normally intended to be set by a microprocessor.)

**CLK (Microprocessor Clock Input)** — Serial data is entered through the AD and DI pins under the control of CLK. The data is entered on the trailing edge of CLK. CLK is synchronous with CS, AD and DI and can be asynchronous with the TSAC's data clocks (DC1 or DC2).

**DI (Serial Time Slot Data and Mode Input)** — 8-bit words are clocked into the device through DI under the control of CLK after CS is brought high. The first 2 bits of DI control the various programming modes while the last 6 bits are time slot data. (See Figure 5 for the format of the DI word.)

**AD (Serial Address and Control Bits Input — MC14418 only)** — 8-bit words are clocked into the device through AD under the control of CLK after CS is brought high. AD words are loaded in parallel with the DI words. The first 3 bits of AD program the control bits Q0, Q1, and Q2 while the last 5 bits are compared with the hardware address on A1 through A5 to identify a specific TSAC in a bank. (See Figure 5 for the format of the AD words.)

**A1-A5 (Codec Address Inputs — MC14418 only)** — These five pins provide a unique identity for each TSAC. The TSAC address pins are either hardwired on the PC board or in the channel bank backplane. The processor loads the 5-bit address data into AD, and each MC14418 in the selected bank compares this data to the hardwired address set by its A1-A5 to determine if the time slot data loaded into DI is intended for that TSAC. By this process, only one of 32 TSACs in a bank will accept the transmitted time slot data. A1-A5 are CMOS inputs, logical "1" = V$_{DD}$ and logical "0" = V$_{SS}$.

**Q0, Q1, Q2 (Status Bit Outputs — MC14418 Only)** — These three bits are programmed by the first 3 bits of the 8-bit word which is loaded into AD. The bits are used for the basic control functions of a line circuit. See the applications section (ref. Figure 11) for an example of how these status bits are used. In this example, Q1 selects to receive data streams, Q0 is used for the power down control, and Q2 is used for the ring enable. These are CMOS outputs.

**R2 (Reset Input for Q2)** — The R2 input provides a direct reset of the Q2 output. When R2 is taken high, Q2 is set to "0" independent of all other TSAC functions. See the applications section (ref Figure 11) for an example of how this reset is used, i.e., the ring trip signal is used to reset Q2 which is the ring enable. This combination of R2 and Q2 allows a simple solution to the ring trip function.

**CTS (Clear to Send Output)** — This output provides a simple diagnostic capability for the processor TSAC combination. The selected TSAC outputs the CTS signal after it has accepted data. This output goes low three data clock cycles after the next FST, and returns high on the subsequent FST. For the MC14418, only the TSAC which accepts transmitted data will respond with CTS low. All other TSACs in the bank will leave CTS high. The CTS output is an open drain transistor with a weak internal pullup. Normally a bank of CTS outputs are wire ORed together to provide a single diagnostic bus, which can be used to verify that transmitted data was properly acknowledged by some TSAC in the bank.

CTS may also be used to strobe additional supervision data into a selected channel unit, due to its dependence upon the address selection logic of the MC14418.

**DC1, DC2 (Data Clock Input)** — The data clock input establishes the bit rate of the TSAC and its associated codec. It is intended to be between 1.536 and 2.56 MHz and is the same as the codec's bit rate clock. Both TSACs divide these inputs by eight to derive the time slot rate. For the MC14418, DC1 provides the data rate clock for both transmit and receive time slot computation. The MC14416 derives transmit timing from DC1 and receive timing from DC2. They are CMOS compatible inputs.

**FST, FSR (Frame Sync Transmit and Frame Sync Receive Inputs)** — These inputs are leading-edge sensitive synchronization pulses for establishing the position of time slot zero in the transmit and receive frames, respectively.

The rising edge of DC (1 or 2) associated with the rising edge of FST or FSR identifies the sign bit period of time slot zero. See Figures 6 and 7 for detailed timing. In the MC14418, both zero time slots are derived from DC1 but may be different by an integral number of bits. In the MC14416, FST and DC1 derive the transmit time slot zero, while FSR and DC2 derive the receive time slot zero independently. DC1 and DC2 can be asynchronous. FSR and FST are CMOS inputs.

---

## MC14416, MC14418

**TXE, RXE (Transmit Enable and Receive Enable Outputs)** — These are the outputs of the time slot computation circuitry. Each output is high for eight data clocks; i.e., an integral number of time slots after the rising edge of FST and FSR for TXE and RXE, respectively. The binary number entered in the last 6 bits of the DI input indicates the number of eight data clock intervals (time slots) between FST or FSR and the eight data clock time slot, when TXE or RXE will be high. These are CMOS B series outputs which will drive one TTL LS input when $V_{DD}$ is five volts. See Figure 6 and Figure 7 for detailed timing and numbering.

TABLE 1 — BASIC OPERATION OF MC14418

| Input Conditions | | | | | Action to Outputs After Next FST | | | | | |
|---|---|---|---|---|---|---|---|---|---|---|
| TS Data Received | Address Compare | b0 | b1 | CTS | TX Reg. Load | RX Reg. Load | TXE Disabled | RXE Disabled | Data Reg. (Q0-Q2) Load | Time Slot Counters Running |
| No | X | X | X | 1 | No | No | No Change | No Change | No | No Change |
| Yes | No | X | X | 1 | No | No | No Change | No Change | No | No Change |
| Yes | Yes | 0 | 0 | 0 | Yes | Yes | No | No | Yes | Yes |
| Yes | Yes | 0 | 1 | 0 | Yes | No | No | No | Yes | Yes |
| Yes | Yes | 1 | 0 | 0 | No | Yes | No Change | No | Yes | Yes |
| Yes | Yes | 1 | 1 | 0 | X | Yes | Yes | Yes | Yes | No |

TABLE 2 — BASIC OPERATION OF MC14416

| Input Conditions | | | | | Action to Outputs After Next FST | | | |
|---|---|---|---|---|---|---|---|---|
| TX Data Received | CS | b0 | b1 | CTS | TX Reg. Load | RX Reg. Load | TXE Disabled | PD Output |
| No | X | X | X | 1 | No | No | No Change | No Change |
| Yes | 0 | X | X | 1 | No | No | No Change | No Change |
| Yes | 1 | 0 | 0 | 0 | Yes | Yes | No | 1 |
| Yes | 1 | 0 | 1 | 0 | Yes | No | No | 1 |
| Yes | 1 | 1 | 0 | 0 | No | Yes | No Change | 1 |
| Yes | 1 | 1 | 1 | 0 | No | No | Yes | 0 |

Note 1: The $\overline{OHO}$ output remains operational when TXE is disabled.

FIGURE 5 — FORMAT FOR DI AND AD WORDS

| MC14418 | DI Word Input | | | | | | | | AD Word Input | | | | | | | |
|---|---|---|---|---|---|---|---|---|---|---|---|---|---|---|---|---|
| | First Bit Sent | | | | | | | | First Bit Sent | | | | | | | |
| Results of Bit Pattern | Mode | | Time Slot Data | | | | | | Status Bits | | | Address Data | | | | |
| | b0 | b1 | t6 | t5 | t4 | t3 | t2 | t1 | q2 | q1 | q0 | a5 | a4 | a3 | a2 | a1 |
| Assign TSAC 16 to the first time slot (TSO) for both receive and transmit and set its status bit to 011 | 0 | 0 | 0 | 0 | 0 | 0 | 0 | 0 | 0 | 1 | 1 | 1 | 0 | 0 | 0 | 0 |
| Assign TSAC 1 to time slot 8 for receive only and set status bits to 011 | 1 | 0 | 0 | 0 | 1 | 0 | 0 | 0 | 0 | 1 | 1 | 0 | 0 | 0 | 0 | 1 |
| Assign TSAC 8 to time slot 2 for transmit only and set status bits to 011 | 0 | 1 | 0 | 0 | 0 | 0 | 1 | 0 | 0 | 1 | 1 | 0 | 1 | 0 | 0 | 0 |
| Program TSAC 4 to idle (no time slot outputs) and set status bits to 011 | 1 | 1 | X | X | X | X | X | X | 0 | 1 | 1 | 0 | 0 | 1 | 0 | 0 |
| Codec 1 is powered down (80 = 0) | X | X | X | X | X | X | X | X | 0 | 1 | 0 | 0 | 0 | 0 | 0 | 1 |
| Line circuit associated with codec 2 is programmed to ring the line (See Fig. 13) | X | X | X | X | X | X | X | X | 1 | 1 | 1 | 0 | 0 | 0 | 1 | 0 |

| MC14416 | | | | | | | | |
|---|---|---|---|---|---|---|---|---|
| Assign the selected TSAC to the first time slot (TSO) for both receive and transmit and set PD = 1 | 0 | 0 | 0 | 0 | 0 | 0 | 0 | 0 |
| Assign the selected TSAC to time slot 8 for receive only and set PD = 1 | 1 | 0 | 0 | 0 | 1 | 0 | 0 | 0 |
| Assign the selected TSAC to time slot 2 for transmit only and set PD = 1 | 0 | 1 | 0 | 0 | 0 | 0 | 1 | 0 |
| Power down the selected TSAC, i.e., PD to "0" | 1 | 1 | X | X | X | X | X | X |

*See Figures 12 and 13 for the hardware implementations using MC14418 and MC14416.

MOTOROLA TELECOMMUNICATIONS DEVICE DATA

*Courtesy of Motorola, Inc. Used by permission.*

## MC14416, MC14418

$\overline{PD}$ (Power Down Output — MC14416 Only) — The $\overline{PD}$ output is normally high. It is set high whenever b0 or b1 is a zero and the TSAC is programmed. If b0 and b1 are both one, then PD will be set low. This output is intended to be used to power down other circuitry in the channel unit when the channel unit is idle. This is a CMOS B series output which will drive one TTL LS load when $V_{DD}$ is five volts.

OHI (Off Hook Input — MC14416 Only) — The OHI is a CMOS input with an internal pull-down resistor. A DC level at this pin will appear at the OHO output during the programmed TXE time slot.

$\overline{OHO}$ (Off Hook Output Inverted — MC14416 Only) — During the programmed transmit time slot, the data at OHI appears inverted at $\overline{OHO}$; otherwise $\overline{OHO}$ will be pulled high passively. The $\overline{OHO}$ output is an open drain N-channel transistor with a weak pull-up to $V_{DD}$. A number of these outputs can be wire ORed together to form a hook status bus consisting of a serial stream of hook information from a bank of channels. When the MC14416 powers down its codec, the TXE output is disabled; but the $\overline{OHO}$ output continues to multiplex out OHI and transmit time slot information during the previously entered transmit time slot.

$V_{SS}$ — This is the most negative supply pin and digital ground for the package.

$V_{DD}$ — This is the most positive supply. $V_{DD}$ is typically 12 V with an operation range of 5 to 16 volts. All logic outputs swing the full supply voltage.

### APPLICATIONS

The following section is intended to facilitate device understanding through several application examples. Included are Data Multiplex Timing Diagrams, a description of the TSAC Microprocessor port, a sample program, two circuit configurations using Motorola's devices, a systems drawing and two suggested clock circuits for obtaining codec data and control clocks.

In Figures 6 and 7 are shown Data Multiplex Timing Diagrams for 2.048 MHz and 1.544 MHz data clocks. The major points to be seen from these examples are:

1) Receive and transmit programming for the MC14418 are bit synchronous and word asynchronous. The MC14416 can be completely asynchronous.

2) The rising edges of FST and FSR initiate the programming frame for transmit and receive channels, respectively, and identify transmit and receive time slot "0," respectively.

3) Time slots identify eight data clock words. In this example: the transmit time slot is programmed as time slot "1." Therefore, bits 8 through 15 after FST are time slot "1."

4) For the 1.544 MHz clock, the framing bit is at the very end of the frame.

**TSAC Microprocessor Port (MC14418 and MC14416)** — The MC14418 provides four pins with 5-volt microprocessor input characteristics. These are AD, CS, CLK, and DI. The input supply for these inputs is $V_{CC}$. The CTS output is an open drain device with a weak pull up to

$V_{DD}$. Typically, these five pins are bused in parallel to 24 or 32 TSACs per processor port. If desired, AD, CLK, DI, and CTS may be bused to greater than 32 TSACs by using the CS input as a group select. A microprocessor port of eight bits can thus control four groups of 32 TSACs with no additional decoding, as shown in Figure 8.

In order to program any given codec to a transmit or receive time slot, the processor simply exercises the corresponding 8-bit port.

Beginning with CS1 to CS4 low, all TSACs in the bank have their data registers in the Ready for Data Mode. The microprocessor takes the appropriate CS high and clocks in two bits of data into the 32 selected TSACs through DI and AD using CLK. The microprocessor presents data on the leading edge of CLK and the TSACs clock in data on the trailing edge of CLK. After eight CLK pulses (high, then low) the 32 selected TSACs will have two new 8-bit words; one in the data register through DI and one in the address register through AD. The unique TSAC, whose last 5 bits of the address register match its hardwired address on A1 through A5, acknowledges the new data. After the next FST, the selected TSAC will pull CTS low. This event notifies the processor that its transmission has been recognized. If CTS occurs at any other time, the processor can recognize the fault condition and restart the transmission using the reset function of the TSAC chip select. The uniquely selected TSAC will load its new program data into the appropriate TIME SLOT register on the next leading edge of FST. The bank of 32 TSACs will internally reset to the Ready for Data Mode when the transmission is completed, after the next FST. The TSAC, which was uniquely selected, and which has CTS low, will clear CTS to the pulled-up condition with the next FST. The processor may now program a new time slot immediately, with or without returning the selected CS low. Time Slot data can thus be sent at the rate of once every 256 μsec. for 8 kHz sampling (FST). The processor need not operate in an interrupt mode even though the TSAC's DC and CLK are asynchronous.

The processor port of the MC14416 works similarly to the MC14418, but will accept data if CS is high, and does not compare a hardwired address to the address word.

Figure 11 shows the typical signal timing for programming the microprocessor port.

To demonstrate the programming of the TSAC, consider the following configuration. A microprocessor is used to control four groups of thirty-two TSACs through an eight-bit PIA port. Four of the PIA lines are used for group select lines. The other four lines are dedicated to CLK, DI, AD, and CTS. The TSACs are programmed by serially loading bits into the DI and AD leads. Data bits are latched on the falling edge of CLK. The PIA port is connected as shown in Figure 9. The flow chart in Figure 10 and the following program illustrate one method of TSAC programming.

Before running the following program, the address, time slot, and group number must be entered in appropriate locations. During execution, CS (group select), AD, and DI words are arranged for serial presentation to the TSACs. The bits are presented with CLK high and are latched in with the falling edge of CLK. After eight passes through the loop, the TSAC is programmed, and CTS falls on the third data clock pulse after the next FST. The program waits for CTS to go high again before removing CS to prevent aborting the TSAC's programming. This program allows a maximum rate of programming equal to one TSAC per two frames.

MOTOROLA
■ **SEMICONDUCTOR** ■
TECHNICAL DATA

*Advance Information*
## Universal Digital-Loop Transceivers (UDLT)

The MC145422 and MC145426 UDLTs are high-speed data transceivers that provide 80 kilobits per second full duplex data communication over 26 AWG and larger twisted pair cable up to two kilometers in distance. Intended primarily for use in digital subscriber voice/data telephone systems, these devices can also be used in remote data acquisition and control systems. These devices utilize a 256 kilobaud modified differential phase shift keying burst modulation technique for transmission to minimize RFI/EMI and crosstalk. Simultaneous power distribution and duplex data communication can be obtained using a single twisted pair wire.

These devices are designed for compatibility with existing, as well as evolving, telephone switching hardware and software architectures.

The UDLT chip-set consists of the MC145422 master UDLT for use at the telephone switch linecard and the MC145426 slave UDLT for use at the remote digital telset and/or data terminal.

The devices employ CMOS technology in order to take advantage of its reliable low-power operation and proven capability for complex analog/digital LSI functions.

- Provides Full Duplex Synchronous 64 Kilobits-Per-Second Voice/Data Channel and Two Eight Kilobits-Per-Second Signaling Data Channels Over One 26 AWG Wire Pair Up to Two Kilometers
- Compatible with Existing and Evolving Telephone Switch Architectures and Call Signaling Schemes
- Automatic Detection Threshold Adjustment for Optimum Performance Over Varying Signal Attenuations
- Protocol Independent
- Single Five Volt Power Supply
- 22 Pin Package

### MC145422 Master UDLT
- Pin Controlled Power-Down and Loop-Back Features
- Signaling and Control I/O Capable of Sharing Common Bus Wiring with Other UDLTs
- Variable Data Clock — 64 kHz to 2.56 MHz
- Pin Controlled Insertion/Extraction of Eight Kilobits/Second Channel into LSB of 64 Kilobits/Second Channel for Simultaneous Routing of Voice and Data Through PCM Voice Path of Telephone Switch

### MC145426 Slave UDLT
- Compatible with MC14400 Series PCM Mono-Circuits
- Pin Controlled Loop-Back Feature
- Automatic Power-Up/Down Feature
- On-Chip Data Clock Recovery and Generation
- Pin Controlled 500 Hz D3 or CCITT Format PCM Tone Generator for Audible Feedback Applications

## MC145422
## MC145426

**L SUFFIX
CERAMIC
CASE 736**

**PIN ASSIGNMENTS**

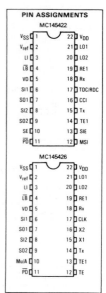

MC145422

| | | | |
|---|---|---|---|
| V$_{SS}$ | 1 | 22 | V$_{DD}$ |
| V$_{ref}$ | 2 | 21 | LO1 |
| LI | 3 | 20 | LO2 |
| $\overline{LB}$ | 4 | 19 | RE1 |
| VD | 5 | 18 | Rx |
| SI1 | 6 | 17 | TDC/RDC |
| SO1 | 7 | 16 | CCI |
| SI2 | 8 | 15 | Tx |
| SO2 | 9 | 14 | TE1 |
| SE | 10 | 13 | SIE |
| $\overline{PD}$ | 11 | 12 | MSI |

MC145426

| | | | |
|---|---|---|---|
| V$_{SS}$ | 1 | 22 | V$_{DD}$ |
| V$_{ref}$ | 2 | 21 | LO1 |
| LI | 3 | 20 | LO2 |
| $\overline{LB}$ | 4 | 19 | RE1 |
| VD | 5 | 18 | Rx |
| SI1 | 6 | 17 | CLK |
| SO1 | 7 | 16 | X2 |
| SI2 | 8 | 15 | X1 |
| SO2 | 9 | 14 | Tx |
| Mu/A | 10 | 13 | TE1 |
| $\overline{PD}$ | 11 | 12 | TE |

MOTOROLA TELECOMMUNICATIONS DEVICE DATA

*Courtesy of Motorola, Inc. Used by permission.*

**MC145422, MC145426**

## MC145422 MASTER UDLT PIN DESCRIPTIONS

### V$_{DD}$ — POSITIVE SUPPLY
Normally 5 volts.

### V$_{SS}$ — NEGATIVE SUPPLY
This pin is the most negative supply pin, normally 0 volts.

### V$_{ref}$ — REFERENCE OUTPUT
This pin is the output of the internal reference supply and should be bypassed to V$_{DD}$ and V$_{SS}$ by 0.1 $\mu$F capacitors. No external dc load should be placed on this pin.

### LI — LINE INPUT
This input to the demodulator circuit has an internal 100 k resistor tied to the internal reference node so that an external capacitor and/or line transformer may be used to couple the input signal to the part with no dc offset.

### $\overline{LB}$ — LOOP-BACK CONTROL
A low on this pin disconnects the LI pin from internal circuitry, drives LO1, LO2 to V$_{ref}$ and internally ties the modulator output to the demodulator input which loops the part on itself for testing in the system. The state of this pin is internally latched if the SE pin is brought and held low. Loop-Back is active only when $\overline{PD}$ is high.

### VD — VALID DATA OUTPUT
A high on this pin indicates that a valid line transmission has been demodulated. A valid transmission is determined by proper sync and the absence of detected bit errors. VD changes state on the leading edge of MSI when $\overline{PD}$ is high. When $\overline{PD}$ is low, VD changes state at the end of demodulation of a line transmission. VD is a standard B-series CMOS output and is high impedance when SE is held low.

### SI1, SI2 — SIGNALING BIT INPUTS
Data on these pins is loaded on the rising edge of MSI for transmission to the slave. The state of these pins is internally latched if SE is held low.

### SO1, SO2 — SIGNALING BIT OUTPUTS
These outputs are received signaling bits from the slave UDLT and change state on the rising edge of MSI if $\overline{PD}$ is high, or at the completion of demodulation if $\overline{PD}$ is low. These outputs have standard B-series CMOS drive capability and are high impedance if the SE pin is held low.

### SE — SIGNAL ENABLE INPUT
If held high, the $\overline{PD}$, $\overline{LB}$, SI1, SI2, and SIE inputs and the SO1, SO2, and VD outputs function normally. If held low, the state of these inputs are latched and held internally while the outputs are high impedance. This allows these pins to be bussed with those of other UDLTs to a common controller.

### $\overline{PD}$ — POWER-DOWN INPUT
If held low, the UDLT ceases modulation. In power-down, the only active circuitry is that which is necessary to demodulate an incoming burst and output the signal and valid data bits. Internal data transfers to the transmit and receive registers cease. When brought high, the UDLT powers-up, and waits three positive MSI edges or until the end of an incoming transmission from the slave UDLT and begins transmitting every MSI period to the slave UDLT on the next rising edge of the MSI.

### MSI — MASTER SYNC INPUT
This pin is the system sync and initiates the modulation on the twisted pair. MSI should be approximately leading-edge aligned with TDC/RDC.

### SIE — SIGNAL INSERT ENABLE
This pin, when held high, inserts signal bit 2 received from the slave into the LSB of the outgoing PCM word at Tx and will ignore the SI2 pin and use in place the LSB of the incoming PCM word at Rx for transmission to the slave. The PCM word to the slave will have LSB forced low in this mode. In this manner, signal bit 2 to/from the slave UDLT is inserted into the PCM words the master sends and receives from the backplane for routing through the PABX for simultaneous voice/data communication. The state of this pin is internally latched if the SE pin is brought and held low.

### TE1 — TRANSMIT DATA ENABLE 1 INPUT
This pin controls the outputting of data on the Tx pin. While TE1 is high, the Tx data is presented on the eight rising edges of TDC/RDC. TE1 is also a high-impedance control of the Tx pin. If MSI occurs during this period, new data will be transferred to the Tx output register in the ninth high period of TDC/RDC after TE1 rises; otherwise, it will transfer on the rising edge of MSI. TE1 and TDC/RDC should be approximately leading-edge aligned.

### Tx — TRANSMIT DATA OUTPUT
This three-state output pin presents new voice data during the high periods of TDC/RDC when TE1 is high (see TE1).

### CCI — CONVERT CLOCK INPUT
A 2.048 MHz clock signal should be applied to this pin. The signal is used for internal sequencing and control. This signal should be coherent with MSI for optimum performance but may be asynchronous if slightly worse error rate performance can be tolerated.

### TDC/RDC — TRANSMIT/RECEIVE DATA CLOCK
This pin is the transmit and receive data clock and can be 64 kHz to 2.56 MHz. Data is output at the Tx pin while TE1 is high on the eight rising edges of TDC/RDC after the rising edge of TE1. Data on the Rx pin is loaded into the receive register of the UDLT on the eight falling edges of TDC/RDC after a positive transition on RE1. This clock should be approximately leading-edge aligned with MSI.

## MC145422, MC145426

### Rx—RECEIVE DATA

Voice data is clocked into the UDLT from this pin on the falling edges of TDC/RDC under the control of RE1.

### RE1—RECEIVE DATA ENABLE 1 INPUT

A rising edge on this pin will enable data on the Rx pin to be loaded into the receive data register on the next eight falling edges of the data clock, TDC/RDC. RE1 and TDC/RDC should be approximately leading-edge aligned.

### LO1, LO2—LINE DRIVER OUTPUTS

These outputs drive the twisted pair line with 256 kHz modified DPSK bursts each frame and are push-pull. These pins are driven to $V_{ref}$ when not modulating the line.

### MC145426 SLAVE UDLT PIN DESCRIPTIONS

### $V_{DD}$—POSITIVE SUPPLY

Normally 5 volts.

### $V_{SS}$—NEGATIVE SUPPLY

This pin is the most negative supply pin, normally 0 volts.

### $V_{ref}$—REFERENCE OUTPUT

This pin is the output of the internal reference supply and should be bypassed to $V_{DD}$ and $V_{SS}$ by 0.1 $\mu$F capacitors. No external dc load should be placed on this pin.

### LI—LINE INPUT

This input to the demodulator circuit has an internal 100 kilohm resistor tied to the internal reference node ($V_{ref}$) so that an external capacitor and/or line transformer may be used to couple the signal to this part with no dc offset.

### $\overline{LB}$—LOOP-BACK CONTROL

When this pin is held low and $\overline{PD}$ is high (the UDLT is receiving transmissions from the master), the UDLT will use the eight bits of demodulated PCM data in place of the eight bits of Rx data in the return burst to the master, thereby looping the part back on itself for system testing. SI1 and SI2 operate normally in this mode. CLK will be held low during loop-back operation.

### VD—VALID DATA OUTPUT

A high on this pin indicates that a valid line transmission has been demodulated. A valid transmission is determined by proper sync and the absence of detected bit errors. VD changes state on the leading edge of TE1. If no transmissions from the master have been received in the last 250 $\mu$s (derived from the internal oscillator), VD will go low without TE1 rising since TE1 is not generated in the absence of received transmissions from the master (see TE pin description for the one exception to this).

### SI1, SI2—SIGNALING BIT INPUTS

Data on these pins is loaded on the rising edge of TE1 for transmission to the master. If no transmissions from the master are being received and $\overline{PD}$ is high, data on these pins will be loaded into the part on an internal signal. Therefore, data on these pins should be steady until synchronous communication with the master has been established, as indicated by the high on VD.

### SO1, SO2—SIGNALING BIT OUTPUTS

These outputs are received signaling bits from the master UDLT and change state on the rising edge of TE1. These outputs have standard B-series CMOS output drive capability.

### $\overline{PD}$—POWER-DOWN INPUT/OUTPUT

This is a bidirectional pin with weak output drivers such that it can be overdriven externally. When held low, the UDLT is powered down and the only active circuitry is: that which is necessary for demodulation, TE1/RE1/CLK generation upon demodulation the outputting of data received from the master and updating of VD status. When held high, the UDLT is powered-up and transmits in response to received transmissions from the master. If no received bursts from the master have occurred when powered-up, for 250 $\mu$s (derived from the internal oscillator frequency), the UDLT will generate a free running 125 $\mu$s internal clock from the internal oscillator and will burst a transmission to the master every other internal 125 $\mu$s clock using data on the SI1 and SI2 pins and the last data word loaded into the receive register. The weak output drivers will try to force $\overline{PD}$ high when a transmission from the master is demodulated and will try to force it low if 250 $\mu$s have passed without a transmission from the master. This allows the slave UDLT to self power-up and down in demand powered loop systems.

### TE—TONE ENABLE

A high on this pin generates a 500 Hz square wave PCM tone and inserts it in place of the demodulated voice PCM word from the master to the Tx pin to the telset mono-circuit. A high on TE will generate TE1 and CLK from the internal oscillator when the slave is not receiving bursts from the master so that the PCM square wave can be loaded into the mono-circuit. This feature allows the user to provide audio feedback for the telset keyboard depressions except during Loop-Back. During Loop-Back of the slave UDLT, CLK is defeated so a tone cannot be generated in this mode.

### TE1—TRANSMIT DATA ENABLE 1 OUTPUT

This is a standard B-series CMOS output which goes high after the completion of demodulation of an incoming transmission from the master. It remains high for eight CLK periods and then low until the next burst from the master is demodulated. While high, the voice data just demodulated is output on the first eight rising edges of CLK at the Tx pin. The signaling data just demodulated is output on SO1 and SO2 on TE1's rising edge, as is VD.

### Tx—TRANSMIT DATA OUTPUT

This is a standard B-series CMOS output. Voice data is output on this pin on the rising edges of CLK while TE1 is high and is high impedance when TE1 is low.

### X1—CRYSTAL INPUT

A 4.096 MHz crystal is tied between this pin and X2. A 10 megohm resistor across X1 and X2 and 25 pF capacitors from X1 and X2 to $V_{SS}$ are required for stability and to insure start-up. X1 may be driven by an external CMOS clock signal if X2 is left open.

## MC145422, MC145426

### X2-CRYSTAL OUPUT

This pin is capable of driving one external CMOS input and 15 pF of additional capacitance. (SEE X1)

### CLK — CLOCK OUTPUT

This is a standard B-series CMOS output which provides the data clock for the telset mono-circuit. It is generated by dividing the oscillator down to 128 kHz and starts upon the completion of demodulation of an incoming burst from the master. At this time, CLK begins and TE1 goes high. CLK will remain active for 16 periods, at the end of which it will remain low until another transmission from the master is demodulated. In this manner, sync from the master is established in the slave and any clock slip between the master and the slave is absorbed each frame. CLK is generated in response to an incoming burst from the master; however, if TE is brought high, then CLK and TE1/RE1 are generated from the internal oscillator until TE is brought low or an incoming burst from the master is received. CLK is disabled when $\overline{LB}$ is held low.

### Rx — RECEIVE DATA INPUT

Voice data from the telset mono-circuit is input on this pin on the first eight falling edges of CLK after RE1 goes high.

### Mu/A — TONE DIGITAL FORMAT INPUT

This pin determines if the PCM code of the 500 Hz square wave tone, generated when TE is high, is D3 (Mu/A = 1) or CCITT (Mu/A = 0) format.

### RE1-RECEIVE DATA ENABLE 1 OUTPUT

This is a standard B-series CMOS output which is the inverse of TE1 (see TE1).

### LO1, LO2 — LINE DRIVER OUTPUTS

These outputs drive the twisted pair line with 256 kHz modified DPSK bursts each frame and are push-pull. These pins are driven to $V_{ref}$ when the device is not modulating.

### BACKGROUND

The MC145422 master and MC145426 slave UDLT transceiver ICs main application is to bidirectionally transmit the digital signals present at a codec/filter-digital PABX backplane interface over normal telephone wire pairs. This allows the remoting of the mono-circuit in a digital telephone set and enables each set to have a high speed data access to the PABX switching facility. In effect, the UDLT allows each PABX subscriber direct access to the inherent sixty-four kilobits per second data routing capabilities of the PABX.

The UDLT provides a means for transmitting and receiving sixty-four kilobits of voice data and sixteen kilobits-per-second of signaling data in two wire format over normal telephone pairs. The UDLT is a two chip set consisting of a master and a slave. The master UDLT replaces the codec/filter and SLIC on the PABX line card, and transmits and receives data over the wire pair to the telset. The UDLT appears to the linecard and backplane as if it were a PCM codec/filter and has almost the same digital interface features as the MC14400 series mono-circuits. The slave UDLT is located in the telset and interfaces the mono-circuit to the wire pair. By hooking two UDLTs

back-to-back, a repeater can also be formed. The master and slave UDLTs operate in a frame synchronous manner, sync being established at the slave by the timing of the master's transmission. The master's sync is derived from the PABX frame sync.

The UDLT operates using one twisted pair. Eight bits of voice data and two bits of signaling data are transmitted and received each frame in a half duplex manner; i.e., the slave waits until the transmission from the master is completely received before transmitting back to the master. Transmission occurs at 256 kilohertz bit rate using a modified form of DPSK. This "ping-pong" mode will allow transmission of data at distances up to two kilometers before turnaround delay becomes a problem. The UDLT is so defined as to allow this data to be handled by the linecard, backplane, and PABX as if it were just another voice conversation. This allows existing PABX hardware and software to be unchanged and yet provides switched sixty-four kilobits per second voice or data communications throughout its service area by simply replacing a subscriber's linecard and telset. A feature in the master allows one of the two signaling bits to be inserted and extracted from the backplane PCM word to allow simultaneous voice and data transmission through the PABX. Both UDLTs have a loop-back feature by which the device can be tested in the user system.

The slave UDLT has the additional feature of providing a 500 hertz Mu or A-law coded square wave to the mono-circuit when the TE pin is brought high. This can be used to provide audio feedback in the telset during keyboard depressions.

### CIRCUIT DESCRIPTION

#### GENERAL

The UDLT consists of a modulator, demodulator, two intermediate data buffers, sequencing and control logic, and transmit and receive data registers. The data registers interface to the linecard or mono-circuit digital interface signals, the modulator and demodulator interface the twisted pair transmission medium, while the intermediate data registers buffer data between these two sections. The UDLT is intended to operate on a single five volt supply and can be driven by TTL or CMOS logic.

#### MASTER OPERATION

In the master, data from the linecard is loaded into the receive register each frame from the Rx pin under the control of the TDC/RDC clock and the receive data enable, RE1. RE1 controls loading of eight serial bits, henceforth referred to as the voice data word. Each MSI, these words are transferred out of the receive register to the modulation buffer for subsequent modulation onto the line. The modulation buffer takes the received voice data word and the two signaling data input bits on SI1 and SI2 loaded on the MSI transition and formats the ten bits into a specific order. This data field is then transmitted in a 256 kilohertz modified DPSK burst onto the line to the remote slave UDLT.

Upon demodulating the return burst from the slave, the decoded data is transferred to the demodulation buffer and the signaling bits are stripped ready to be output on SO1 and SO2 at the next MSI. The voice data word is loaded into the transmit register as described in the TE1 pin description for outputting via the Tx pin at the TDC/RDC data clock rate under the control of TE1. VD is output on the rising edge of MSI. Timing diagrams for the master are shown in Figure 10.

---

*Courtesy of Motorola, Inc. Used by permission.*

**MC145422, MC145426**

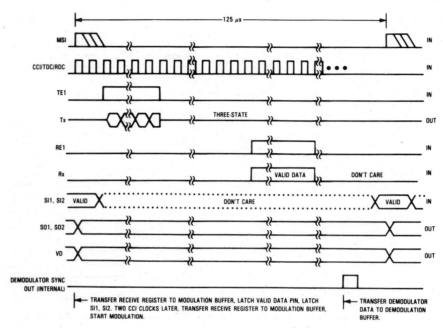

**Figure 10. Master UDLT Timing**

## SLAVE OPERATION

In the slave, the synchronizing event is the detection of an incoming line transmission from the master as indicated by the completion of demodulation. When an incoming burst from the master is demodulated, several events occur. As in the master, data is transferred from the demodulator to the demodulation buffer and the signaling bits are stripped for outputting at SO1 and SO2. Data in the receive register is transferred to the modulation buffer. TE1 goes high loading in data at SI1 and SI2, which will be used in the transmission burst to the master along with the data in the transmit data buffer, and outputting SO1, SO2, and VD. Modulation of the burst begins four 256 kilohertz periods after the completion of demodulation.

While TE1 is high, voice data is output on Tx to the telset mono-circuit on the rising edges of the data clock output on the CLK pin. On the ninth rising edge of CLK, TE1 goes low, RE1 goes high, and voice data from the mono-circuit is input to the receive register from the Rx pin on the next eight falling edges of CLK. RE1 is TE1 inverted and is provided to facilitate interface to the mono-circuit.

The CLK pin 128 kilohertz output is formed by dividing down the 4.096 megahertz crystal frequency by thirty-two. Slippage between the frame rate of the master (as represented

by the completion of demodulation of an incoming transmission from the master) and the crystal frequency is absorbed by holding the sixteenth low period of CLK until the next completion of demodulation. This is shown in the slave UDLT timing diagram of Figure 11.

### POWER-DOWN OPERATION

In the master, when $\overline{PD}$ is low, the UDLT stops modulating and only that circuitry necessary to demodulate the incoming bursts and output the signaling and VD data bits is active. In this mode, if the UDLT receives a burst from the slave, the SO1, SO2, and VD pins will change state upon completion of the demodulation instead of the rising edge of MSI. The state of these pins will not change until either three rising MSI edges have occurred without the reception of a burst from the slave or until another burst is demodulated, whichever occurs first.

When $\overline{PD}$ is brought high, the master UDLT will wait either three rising MSI edges or until the MSI rising edge following the demodulation of an incoming burst before transmitting to the slave. The data for the first transmission to the slave after power—up is loaded into the UDLT during the RE1 period prior to the burst in the case of voice, and on the present rising edge of MSI for signaling data.

---

*Courtesy of Motorola, Inc. Used by permission.*

**MC145422, MC145426**

In the slave, $\overline{PD}$ is a bidirectional pin with weak output drivers such that it can be overdriven externally. When held low, the UDLT slave is powered—down and only that circuitry necessary for demodulation, TE1/RE1/CLK generation upon demodulation, and the outputting of voice and signaling bits is active. When held high, the UDLT slave is powered-up and transmits normally in response to received transmissions from the master. If no bursts have been received from the master within 250 $\mu$s after power-up (derived from the internal oscillator frequency), the UDLT generates an internal 125 $\mu$s free-running clock from the internal oscillator. The slave UDLT then bursts a transmission to the master UDLT every other 125 $\mu$s clock period using data loaded into the Rx pin during the last RE1 period and SI1, SI2 data loaded in on the internal 125 $\mu$s clock edge. The weak output drivers will try to force $\overline{PD}$ high when a transmission from the master is demodulated and will try to force it low if 250 $\mu$s have passed without a transmission from the master. This allows the slave UDLT to self power-up and down in demand powered-loop systems.

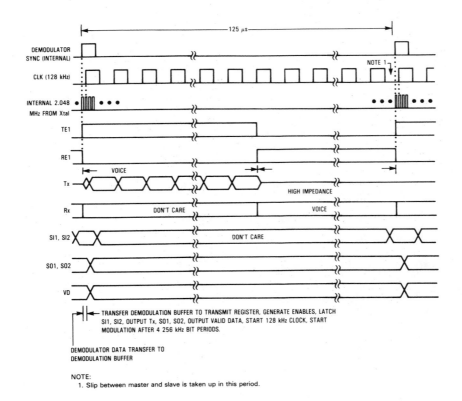

NOTE:
1. Slip between master and slave is taken up in this period.

**Figure 11. Slave UDLT Timing**

*Courtesy of Motorola, Inc. Used by permission.*

MC145422, MC145426

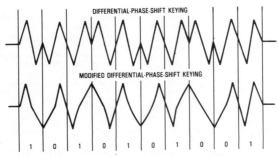

Figure 12. Modified Differential Phase Shift Keying

Both the Differential-Phase Shift Keying and the Modified Differential-Phase-Shift Keying waveforms are shown above. The DPSK encodes data as phase reversals of a 256 kHz carrier. A "0" is indicated by a 180 degree phase shift between bit boundaries, while the signal continues in phase to indicate a "1". This method needs no additional bits to indicate the start of the burst.

The Modified DPSK waveform actually used in the transceivers is a slightly modified form of DPSK, as shown in the figure. The phase-reversal cusps of the DPSK waveform have been replaced by a 128 kHz half cycle to lower the spectral content of the waveform, which, save for some key differences, appears quite similar to frequency-shift keying. The burst always begins and ends with a half cycle of 256 kHz, which helps locate bit boundaries.

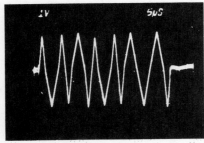
13a—BIT PATTERN—1010101000

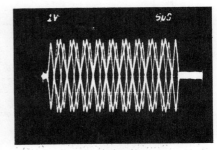
13b—BIT PATTERN—RANDOM

The bit pattern shown above in Figure 13a shows a stable waveform due to the even number of phase changes or zeros. The waveform shown in Figure 13b shows random data patterns being modulated.

Figure 13. Typical Modulated Waveforms

## MC145422, MC145426

"Ping pong" signals on 3000 feet of 26 AWG twisted pair wire as viewed at LI (Line Input) of the master ULDT and the slave UDLT.

MASTER

SLAVE

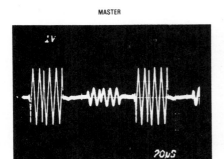 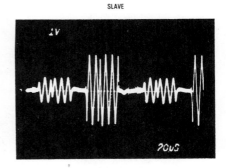

BIT PATTERN—1010101000

MASTER

SLAVE

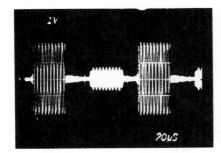 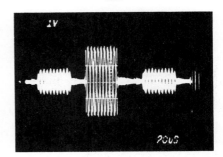

BIT PATTERN—RANDOM

**Figure 14. Typical Signal Waveforms at Demodulator**

## MOTOROLA
# ◼ SEMICONDUCTOR ◼
### TECHNICAL DATA

**MC145428**

*Advance Information*

# Data Set Interface
### Asynchronous-To-Synchronous
### Synchronous-To-Asynchronous Converter

The MC145428 Data Set Interface provides asynchronous to synchronous and synchronous to asynchronous data conversion. It is ideally suited for voice/data digital telsets supplying an RS-232 compatible data port into a synchronous transmission link. Other applications include, data multiplexers, concentrators, data-only switching and PBX-based local area networks. This low power CMOS device directly interfaces with either the 64 kbps or 8 kbps channel of Motorola's MC145422 and MC145426 Universal Digital Loop Transceivers (UDLTs), as well as the MC145418 and MC145419 Digital Loop Transceivers (DLTs).

- Provides the Interface Between Asynchronous Data Ports and Synchronous Transmission Links
- Up to 128 kbps Asynchronous Data Rate Operation
- Up to 2.1 Mbps Synchronous Data Rate Operation
- On-board Bit Rate Clock Generator with Pin Selectable Bit Rates of 300, 1200, 2400, 4800, 9600, 19200 and 38400 bps or an Externally Supplied 16 Times Bit Rate Clock
- Accepts Asynchronous Data Words of Eight or Nine Bits in Length
- False Start Detection Provided
- Automatic Sync Insertion and Checking
- Single 5 Volt Power Supply
- Low Power Consumption of 5 mW Typical
- Applications Notes AN943 and AN946

L SUFFIX
CERAMIC
CASE 732

P SUFFIX
PLASTIC
CASE 738

**PIN ASSIGNMENT**

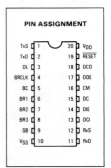

| | | | |
|---|---|---|---|
| TxS | 1 | 20 | V_DD |
| TxD | 2 | 19 | RESET |
| DL | 3 | 18 | DCO |
| BRCLK | 4 | 17 | DOE |
| BC | 5 | 16 | CM |
| BR1 | 6 | 15 | DC |
| BR2 | 7 | 14 | DIE |
| BR3 | 8 | 13 | DCI |
| SB | 9 | 12 | RxS |
| V_SS | 10 | 11 | RxD |

**BLOCK DIAGRAM**

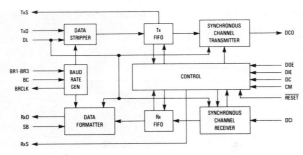

**MOTOROLA TELECOMMUNICATIONS DEVICE DATA**

*Courtesy of Motorola, Inc. Used by permission.*

## MC145428

**MAXIMUM RATINGS** (Voltages Referenced to V$_{SS}$)

| Rating | Symbol | Value | Unit |
|---|---|---|---|
| DC Supply Voltage | V$_{DD}$ · V$_{SS}$ | −0.5 to 6.0 | V |
| Voltage, Any Pin to V$_{SS}$ | V | −0.5 to V$_{DD}$ +0.5 | V |
| DC Current, Any Pin (Excluding V$_{DD}$, V$_{SS}$) | I | +10 | mA |
| Operating Temperature | T$_A$ | −40 to +85 | °C |
| Storage Temperature | T$_{stg}$ | −85 to +150 | °C |

**DIGITAL CHARACTERISTICS** (V$_{DD}$ = 4.5 to 5.5 V, T$_A$ = 0 to 70°C)

| Parameter | Symbol | V$_{DD}$ | Min | Max | Unit |
|---|---|---|---|---|---|
| Input High Level | V$_{IH}$ | 5 | 3.5 | — | V |
| Input Low Level | V$_{IL}$ | 5 | — | 1.5 | V |
| Input Current | I$_{in}$ | — | — | +1.0 | µA |
| Input Capacitance | C$_{in}$ | — | — | 7.5 | pF |
| Output High Current (Source) V$_{OH}$ = 2.5 V  V$_{OH}$ = 4.6 V | I$_{OH}$ | 5  5 | −1.7  −0.36 | —  — | mA |
| Output Low Current V$_{OL}$ = 0.4 V  V$_{OL}$ = 0.8 V | I$_{OL}$ | 5  5 | 0.36  0.8 | —  — | mA |
| Operating Current (DC = 128 kHz, BC = 4.096 MHz) | I$_{DD}$ | 5 | — | 2.0 | mA |

**SWITCHING CHARACTERISTICS** (C$_L$ = 50 pF, V$_{DD}$ = 5 V, T$_A$ = 25°C)

| Characteristic | Min | Typ | Max | Unit |
|---|---|---|---|---|
| Baud Clock Bit Rate Input Frequency (BR1, BR2, BR3) = (0,0,0)  (BR1, BR2, BR3) = non-zero | —  — | —  — | 2.1  4.1 | MHz |
| Baud Clock Pulse Width | 100 | — | — | ns |
| Data Clock Frequency | — | — | 2.1 | MHz |
| Data Clock Pulse Width | 200 | — | — | ns |

## MC145428 DSI PIN DESCRIPTIONS

### V$_{DD}$, POSITIVE POWER SUPPLY

The most positive power supply pin, normally 5 volts.

### V$_{SS}$, NEGATIVE POWER SUPPLY

The most negative supply pin, normally 0 volts.

### TxD, TRANSMIT DATA INPUT

Input for asynchronous data. Idle is logic high; break is 11 baud or more of logic low. One stop bit is required.

### RxD, RECEIVE DATA OUTPUT

Output for asynchronous data. The number of stop bits and the data word length are selected by the SB and DL pins. Idle is logic high; break is a continuous logic low.

### TxS, TRANSMIT STATUS OUTPUT

This pin will go low if the transmit FIFO holds 2 or more data words or if RESET is low.

### RxS, RECEIVE STATUS OUTPUT

This pin will go low if framing of the synchronous channel is lost or not established or if RESET is low, or if the receive FIFO is overwritten.

### SB, STOP BITS INPUT

This pin controls the number of stop bits the DATA FORMATTER will re-create when outputting data at the RxD asynchronous output. A high on this pin selects two stop bits; a low selects one stop bit.

### DL, DATA LENGTH INPUT

This pin instructs the DSI to look for either 8 or 9 bits of data to be input at the TxD asynchronous input between the start and stop bits. The DL input also instructs the DSI's SYNCHRONOUS CHANNEL RECEIVER and SYNCHRONOUS CHANNEL TRANSMITTER to expect 8 or 9 bit data words and also instructs the DSI's DATA FORMATTER to re-create 8 or 9 data bits between the start and stop bits when outputting data at its RxD asynchronous output. A high on this pin selects a 9 bit data word; a low selects an 8 bit data word length.

---

**MOTOROLA TELECOMMUNICATIONS DEVICE DATA**

*Courtesy of Motorola, Inc. Used by permission.*

**MC145428**

### MC145428 DSI PIN DESCRIPTIONS — cont'd.

#### BC, BAUD CLOCK INPUT

This pin serves as an input for an externally supplied 16 times data clock. Otherwise, the BC pin expects a 4.096 MHz clock signal which is internally divided to obtain the 16 times clock for the most frequently used standard bit rates (see BR1-BR3 pin description).

#### BRCLK, 16 TIMES CLOCK INTERNAL OUTPUT

This pin outputs the internal 16 times asynchronous data rate clock.

#### BR1, BR2, BR3, BIT RATE SELECT INPUTS

These three pins select the asynchronous bit rate, either externally supplied at the BC pin (16 times clock) or one of the internally supplied bit rates. (See Table 1.)

#### DCO, DATA CHANNEL OUTPUT

This pin is a three-state output pin. Synchronous data is output when DOE is high. This pin will go high impedance when DOE or RESET are low. When CM is low, synchronous data is output on DCO on the falling edges of DC as long as DOE is high. When CM is high, synchronous data is output on DCO on the rising edges of DC, while DOE is held high. No more than eight data bits can be output during a given DOE high interval when CM = high. This feature allows the DSI to interface directly with the MC145422/26 Universal Digital Loop Transceivers (UDLT's) and PABX time division multiplexed highways.

#### DOE, DATA OUTPUT ENABLE INPUT

See DCO pin description and the SYNCHRONOUS CHANNEL INTERFACE section.

#### DIE, DATA INPUT ENABLE INPUT

See DCI pin description and the SYNCHRONOUS CHANNEL INTERFACE section.

#### DC, DATA CLOCK INPUT

See DCI and DCO pin descriptions and the SYNCHRONOUS CHANNEL INTERFACE section.

#### CM, CLOCK MODE INPUT

See the SYNCHRONOUS CHANNEL INTERFACE section and the SYNCHRONOUS CLOCKING MODE SUMMARY. (See Table 2.)

#### RESET, RESET INPUT

When held low, this pin clears the internal FIFO's, forces the TxD asynchronous input to appear high to the DSI's internal circuitry, forces TxS and RxS low. When returned high, normal operation results.

When the RESET input is returned high the DSI's SYNCHRONOUS CHANNEL RECEIVER will not accept or transfer any incoming data words on the DCI pin to the Rx FIFO until one "flag" word is input at the DCI pin. (Also see RxS pin description.)

#### DCI, DATA CHANNEL INPUT

Synchronous data is input on this pin on the falling edges of DC when DIE is high.

**Table 1. Programmable Baud Rates**

| BR3 | BR2 | BR1 | Bit Rate (bps) | BC in MHz | BRCLK |
|-----|-----|-----|----------------|-----------|-------|
| 0 | 0 | 0 | Variable 0 to 128 kbps | 0 to 2.1 MHz | 0 to 2.1 MHz |
| 0 | 0 | 1 | 38.4 k | 4.096 | 614.4 kHz |
| 0 | 1 | 0 | 19.2 k | 4.096 | 307.2 kHz |
| 0 | 1 | 1 | 9600 | 4.096 | 153.6 kHz |
| 1 | 0 | 0 | 4800 | 4.096 | 76.8 kHz |
| 1 | 0 | 1 | 2400 | 4.096 | 38.4 kHz |
| 1 | 1 | 0 | 1200 | 4.096 | 19.2 kHz |
| 1 | 1 | 1 | 300 | 4.096 | 4.8 kHz |

**MC145428**

### CM = LOW, SYNCHRONOUS CHANNEL RECEIVER INPUT SWITCHING CHARACTERISTICS

($C_L$ = 50 pF, $V_{DD}$ = 5 V, $T_A$ = 25°C) (See Figure 1A)

| Characteristic | Symbol | Min | Typ | Max | Unit | Notes |
|---|---|---|---|---|---|---|
| DIE Fall Before DC Falls | $t_{su1}$ | 40 | –9 | — | ns | 1 |
| DIE Rise After Rise of DC | $t_{su2}$ | 40 | +24 | — | ns | 2 |
| DCI Data Stable Before DC Falling Edge | $t_{su3}$ | 40 | –5 | — | ns | 3 |
| DCI Data Stable After DC Falling Edge | $t_{h1}$ | 40 | 0 | — | ns | 4 |

NOTES:
1. Time DIE must fall before DC falls in order to avoid reading the bit after B3.
2. Time DC must be high before DIE rise in order to avoid clocking in the bit before B1. (See Synchronous Channel Interface for further details and see Figure 1A.)
3. Time data must be stable on the DCI pin before falling edge of the data clock DC.
4. Time data must be stable on the DCI pin after the falling edge of the data clock DC.

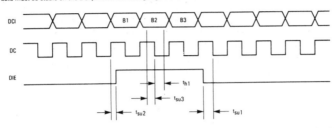

NOTE: When CM = 0, data bits are read into the DSI's SYNCHRONOUS CHANNEL RECEIVER at the DCI pin on the falling edge of the signal formed by the LOGICAL NAND of $\overline{DC}$ and DIE.
i.e. $\downarrow$ of $\overline{DC}$ • DIE

**Figure 1A. CM = Low, Synchronous Channel Receiver Input Switching Characteristics**

### CM = LOW, SYNCHRONOUS CHANNEL TRANSMITTER OUTPUT SWITCHING CHARACTERISTICS

($C_L$ = 50 pF, $V_{DD}$ = 5 V, $T_A$ = 25°C) (See Figure 1B)

| Characteristic | Symbol | Min | Typ | Max | Unit | Notes |
|---|---|---|---|---|---|---|
| DC Falling to DOE Rising | $t_{su4}$ | 0 | 10 | — | ns | 5 |
| DOE Falling to DC Rising | $t_{su5}$ | 40 | –5 | — | ns | 6 |
| DOE Rising to DCO Active | $t_{p1}$ | 50 | 28 | — | ns | 7 |
| DOE Falling to High-Z of DCO | $t_{p2}$ | 50 | 26 | — | ns | 8 |
| DC Falling to DCO | $t_{p3}$ | 80 | 71 | — | ns | 9 |

NOTES:
5. Time DC must be low before the rising edge of DOE in order to avoid clocking out a data bit before B1. (See Synchronous Channel Interface section for further details and also Figure 1B.)
6. Time DOE must be low before the rising edge of DC in order for the (*) bit to be output in the B1 position in the next cycle.
7. Propagation delay time from the rising edge of DOE to the low output impedance state of the DCO pin.
8. Propagation delay time from the falling edge of DOE to the high output impedance state of the DCO pin.
9. Propagation delay time from the falling edge data of the data clock DC to valid data on the DCO pin.

---

*Courtesy of Motorola, Inc. Used by permission.*

**MC145428**

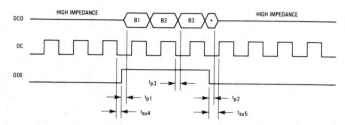

*This bit will be output in the B1 position on the next cycle of DOE.

NOTE: When CM = Low, data bits are advanced from the DSI's SYNCHRONOUS CHANNEL TRANSMITTER at the DCO pin on the rising edge of the signal formed by the LOGICAL NAND of DC and DOE.  i.e. ⬆ of $\overline{DC \bullet DOE}$

**Figure 1B. CM = Low, Synchronous Channel Transmitter Output Switching Characteristics**

**CM = HIGH, SYNCHRONOUS CHANNEL RECEIVER INPUT SWITCHING CHARACTERISTICS**
($C_L$ = 50 pF, $V_{DD}$ = 5 V, $T_A$ = 25°C) (See Figure 1C)

| Characteristic | Symbol | Min | Typ | Max | Unit | Notes |
|---|---|---|---|---|---|---|
| DIE Rising to DC Falling | $t_{su6}$ | 100 | 76 | — | ns | 10 |
| DCI to DC Falling | $t_{su7}$ | 40 | – 4 | — | ns | 11 |
| DC Falling to DCI | $t_{h2}$ | 20 | 0 | — | ns | 12 |

NOTES:
10. Time DIE must be high before the falling edge of DC in order for the data bit to be accepted by the synchronous data input of the DSI. (See Synchronous Channel Interface for further details.)
11. Time DCI data must be stable before the falling edge of the data clock DC.
12. Time DCI data must be stable after the falling edge of the data clock DC.

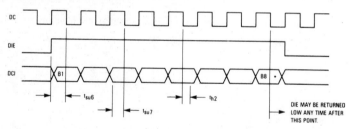

*Last bit accepted.

NOTE: When CM = 1, data bits are read into the DSI's SYNCHRONOUS CHANNEL RECEIVER at the DCI pin on the falling edge of the signal formed by the LOGICAL AND of DC and DIE. (DC ● DIE)

**Figure 1C. CM = High, Synchronous Channel Receiver Input Switching Characteristics**

# MC145428

**CM = HIGH, SYNCHRONOUS CHANNEL TRANSMITTER OUTPUT SWITCHING CHARACTERISTICS**

($C_L$ = 50 pF, $V_{DD}$ = 5 V, $T_A$ = 25°C) (See Figure 1D)

| Characteristic | Symbol | Min | Typ | Max | Unit | Notes |
|---|---|---|---|---|---|---|
| DC Falling to DOE Rising | $t_{su8}$ | 100 | 82 | — | ns | 13 |
| DOE Rising to Active Data on DCO | $t_{p4}$ | 105 | 87 | — | ns | 14 |
| DOE Falling to High-Z on DCO | $t_{p5}$ | 50 | 28 | — | ns | 15 |
| DC Rising to DCO | $t_{p6}$ | 100 | 74 | — | ns | 16 |

NOTES:
13. Time DOE must be high before the falling edge of the data clock DC.
14. Time delay between the rise of the DOE pin and the time the DCO reaches the low impedance state.
15. Time delay between the fall of the DOE pin and the time the DCO pin reaches the high impedance state.
16. Delay from the rising edge of the data clock DC to the valid data on the DCO pin.

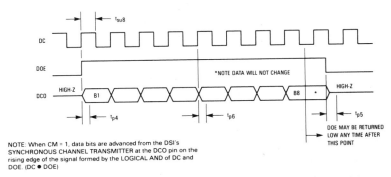

NOTE: When CM = 1, data bits are advanced from the DSI's SYNCHRONOUS CHANNEL TRANSMITTER at the DCO pin on the rising edge of the signal formed by the LOGICAL AND of DC and DOE. (DC ● DOE)

**Figure 1D. CM = High, Synchronous Channel Transmitter Output Switching Characteristics**

## CIRCUIT DESCRIPTION

The MC145428 Data Set Interface provides a means for conversion of an asynchronous (start/stop format) data channel to a synchronous data channel and synchronous to asynchronous data channel conversion. Although primarily intended to facilitate the implementation of RS-232 compatible asynchronous data ports in digital telephone sets using the MC145422/26 UDLTs, this device is also useful in many applications that require the conversion of synchronous and asynchronous data.

## TRANSMIT CIRCUIT

Asynchronous data is input on the TxD pin. This data is expected to consist of a start bit (logic low) followed by eight or nine data bits and one or more stop bits (logic high). The length of the data word is selected by the DL pin. The data baud rate is selected with the BR1, BR2, and BR3 pins to obtain the internal sampling clock. This internal sampling clock is selected to be 16 times the baud rate at the TxD pin. An externally supplied 16 times clock may also be used, in which case, the BR1, BR2, and BR3 pins should all be at logic zero and the 16 times sampling clock supplied at the BC pin.

Data input at the TxD pin is stripped of start and stop bits and is loaded into a four-word deep FIFO register. A break condition is also recognized at the TxD pin and this information is relayed to the synchronous channel transmitter which codes this condition so it may be re-created at the remote receiving device.

The synchronous channel transmitter sends one bit at a time under control of the DC, CM, and DOE pins. The synchronous channel transmitter transmits one of three possible data patterns based on whether or not the top of the Tx FIFO is full and whether or not a break condition has been recognized by the data stripper. When no data is available at the top of the Tx FIFO for transmission, the synchronous data transmitter sends a special synchronizing flag pattern (01111110). When a break condition is detected by the data stripper and no data is available at the top of the Tx FIFO, the break pattern (11111110) is sent. Figure 2A depicts this operation.

## MC145428

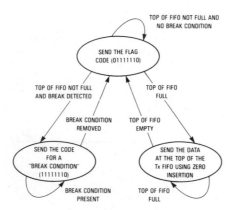

**Figure 2A. Synchronous Data Channel
Transmitter Operation**

When stripped data words reach the top of the Tx FIFO they are loaded into the SYNCHRONOUS CHANNEL TRANS-MITTER and are sent using a special zero insertion technique. When stripped data is being transmitted, the synchronous data transmitter will insert a binary 0 after any succession of five continuous 1's of data. Therefore, using this technique, no pattern of (01111110) or (11111110) can occur while sending data. This also allows the DSI to synchronize itself to the incoming synchronous data word boundaries based on the data alone.

The receive section of the DSI (synchronous channel receiver) performs the reverse operation by removing a binary 0 that follows five continuous 1's in order to recover the transmitted data. (Note that a binary 1 which follows five continuous 1's is not removed so that flags and breaks may be detected.) Figure 2B shows an example of this process.

ASYNCHRONOUS DATA WORD RECEIVED AT THE TxD PIN
11111111, 11000000, 11111100

ACTUAL SYNCHRONOUS WORDS TRANSMITTED BY THE SYNCHRONOUS
CHANNEL TRANSMITTER
FLAG, 01111110, 111110111, 110000000, 111110100, 01111110, FLAG, FLAG, ···

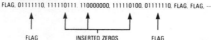

FLAG          INSERTED ZEROS          FLAG

**Figure 2B. Data Format Protocol**

If the incoming data rate at TxD exceeds the rate at which it is output at DCO, the FIFO will fill. The TxS pin will go low when the FIFO contains two or more words. TxS may, therefore, be used as a local Clear-to-Send control line at the asynchronous interface port to avoid transmit data over-runs.

In order to insure synchronization during the transfer of a continuous stream of data the DSI's synchronous channel transmitter will insert a flag synchronizing word (01111110) every 61st data word. The DSI's synchronous channel receiver checks for this synchronizing word and if not present, the loss of synchronization will be indicated by the RxS pin being latched low until the flag synchronizing word is received. Note that under these conditions the data will continue to output at RxD.

### RECEIVE CIRCUIT

Data incoming from the synchronous channel is loaded into the MC145428 at the DCI pin under the control of the DC and DIE pins (see SYNCHRONOUS CHANNEL INTERFACE section). Framing information, break code detection, and data word recovery functions are performed by the SYNCHRON-OUS CHANNEL RECEIVER. Recovered data words are loaded into the four word deep Rx FIFO. When the recovered data words reach the top of the Rx FIFO they are taken by the DATA FORMATTER, start and stop bits are re-inserted and the re-constructed asynchronous data is output at the RxD pin at the same baud rate as the transmit side. The number of stop bits and word length are those selected by the SB and DL pins.

Loss of framing, if it occurs, is indicated by the RxS pin going low. Data will continue to be output under these conditions, but RxS will remain low until frame synchronization, i.e., the detection of a framing flag word, is re-established. If the output data rate is less than the data rate of the incoming synchronous data channel, data will be lost at a rate of one word at a time due to the bottom word on the Rx FIFO being overwritten. In order to prevent data loss (in the form of asynchronous terminal to asynchronous terminal over-runs) due to clock slip between remote DSI links, (during long bursts of continuous data) the DSI purposely reduces the length of the stop bit which it re-creates at its RxD output by 1/32nd. This action allows the originator of a transmission (of asyn-chronous data) to be up to 3% faster than the receive device is expecting for any given data rate. This tolerance is well within the normally expected differences in clock frequencies between remote stations. If the Rx FIFO is overwritten the RxS line will pulse low for one DC clock period following the over-writing of the bottom level of the Rx FIFO.

### INITIALIZATION

Initialization is accomplished by use of the $\overline{\text{RESET}}$ pin. When held low, the internal FIFOs are cleared, the TxD input appears high to the data strippers internal circuitry, DCO is forced to a high impedance state, TxS and RxS are forced low. When brought high normal operation resumes and the synchronous channel transmitter sends the flag code until data has reached the top of the Tx FIFO. Note that the TxS line will immediately go high after $\overline{\text{RESET}}$ goes high, while RxS

**MC145428**

will remain low until framing is detected. The synchronous channel receiver section of the DSI is forced into a "HOLD" state while the $\overline{\text{RESET}}$ line is low. The synchronous channel receiver remains in the "HOLD" state after $\overline{\text{RESET}}$ goes high until a flag code word (01111110) is received at the DCI pin. While in the "HOLD" state no data words can be transferred to the Rx FIFO and, therefore, the DATA FORMATTER and RxD line are held in the MARK idle state. After receiving the flag code pattern the RxS line goes high and normal operation proceeds. $\overline{\text{RESET}}$ should be held low when power is first applied to the DSI. $\overline{\text{RESET}}$ may be tied high permanently, if a short period of undefined operation at initial power application can be tolerated.

### SYNCHRONOUS CHANNEL INTERFACE

The synchronous channel interface is generally operated in one of three basic modes of operation. The first is a continuous mode. A new data bit is clocked out of the DCO pin on each successive falling edge of the DC clock, and a new data bit is accepted by the DSI at its DCI pin on each successive falling edge of the DC clock. In this mode of operation, the CM control line is always low and the DOE and DIE enable control lines are always high. This is the typical setup when interfacing the DSI to the 8 kbps signal bit inputs and outputs of the MC145422/26 UDLTs. (See Figures 3A and 4.)

The second synchronous clocking mode is one in which 8 bits at a time are clocked out of the SYNCHRONOUS CHANNEL TRANSMITTER, and 8 bits are read by the SYNCHRONOUS CHANNEL RECEIVER at a time. The transferring of these 8 bit groups of data would normally be repeated on some cyclic basis. An example is a time division multiplexed data highway. In this mode (CM = 1), the rising edge of the enable signal DIE and DOE should be roughly aligned to the rising edge of the DC clock signal. When enabled, the data is clocked out on the rising edge of the DC clock through the DCO pin and clocked in on the falling edge of the DC clock through the DCI pin. A variation of this clocking mode is to transfer less than 8 bits of data into or out of the DSI on a cyclic basis. If less than eight bits are to be transmitted and received, enable pins DIE and DOE should be returned low while the DC clock is low. This is illustrated in Figure 3D where five bits are being clocked out of the DSI through the DCO pin and four bits are being input to the DSI through the DCI pin.

This restriction does not apply if eight bits are to be clocked into or out of the synchronous channels of the DSI; i.e., the DSI has internal circuitry to prevent more than eight clocks following the rising edge of the respective enable signals). Figure 3B illustrates a timing diagram depicting an eight bit data format. If the DOE enable is held high beyond the eight clock periods the last data bit B8 will remain at the output of

the DCO pin until the DOE enable is brought low to reinitialize the sequence. Similarly the DSI's SYNCHRONOUS CHANNEL RECEIVER will read (at its DCI input) a maximum of eight data bits for any given DIE high period.

The CM = high mode, using 8 bits of data, is the typical setup for interfacing the DSI to the 64 kbps channel of the MC145422 or MC145426 Universal Digital Loop Transceivers. (See Figure 3B and Figure 5.)

In the third mode of operation, an unlimited variable number of data bits may be clocked into or out of the synchronous side of the DSI at a time. When the CM line is low, any number of data bits may be clocked into or out of the DSI's synchronous channels provided that the respective enable signal is high. Figure 3C illustrates three data bits being clocked out of the DCO pin and three data bits being clocked into the DCI pin.

In the CM = low mode of operation, an internal clock is formed, which is the logical NAND of DC, DOE and $\overline{\text{CM}}$, (DC $\bullet$ DOE $\bullet$ $\overline{\text{CM}}$). It is on the rising edge of this signal that a new data bit is clocked out of the DCO pin. Therefore, the DOE signal should be raised and lowered following the falling edge of the DC clock (i.e., when the DC clock is low).

Also in the CM = low mode of operation, another internal clock is formed which is the logical NAND of $\overline{\text{DC}}$, DIE, and $\overline{\text{CM}}$ ($\overline{\text{DC}}$ $\bullet$ DIE $\bullet$ $\overline{\text{CM}}$). It is on the falling edge of this signal that a new bit is clocked into the DCI pin. Therefore the DIE signal should be raised and lowered following the rising edge of the DC clock (i.e., when the DC clock is high).

The following table summarizes when data bits are advanced from the synchronous channel transmitter and when data bits are read by the synchronous channel receiver dependent on the CM control line. (Shown below in Table 2.)

**Table 2. Synchronous Clocking Mode Summary**

| Mode | Bits Advanced From The Synchronous Channel Transmitter On; | Bits Read By The Synchronous Channel Receiver On: |
|------|------------------------------------------------------------|----------------------------------------------------|
| CM = 0 | The rising edge of an internal clock formed by the logical NAND of DOE and DC. i.e. $\uparrow$ of $\overline{\text{DOE} \bullet \text{DC}}$ | The falling edge of an internal clock formed by the logical NAND of DIE and $\overline{\text{DC}}$. i.e. $\downarrow$ of $\overline{\text{DIE} \bullet \overline{\text{DC}}}$ |
| CM = 1 | The rising edge of an internal clock formed by the logical AND of DOE and DC. i.e. $\uparrow$ of DOE $\bullet$ DC | The falling edge of an internal clock formed by the logical AND of DIE and DC. i.e. $\downarrow$ of DIE $\bullet$ DC |

**MOTOROLA**
## ■ SEMICONDUCTOR ■
**TECHNICAL DATA**

| MC145429 |
| :---: |

### Advance Information

#### TELSET AUDIO INTERFACE CIRCUIT

The MC145429 is a silicon-gate CMOS Telset Audio Interface Circuit (TAIC) intended for microcomputer controlled digital or analog telset applications. The device provides the interface between a codec/filter or analog speech network and the telset mouthpiece, earpiece, ringer/speaker amplifier, and an auxiliary input and output. The configuration of the device is programmed via a serial digital data port. Features provided on the device include:

- Independent Adjustment of Earpiece, Speaker, and Ringer Volume
- Transient Suppression Circuitry to Prevent Acoustic "Pops"
- Receive Low-Pass Filter for 8 kHz Attenuation
- Sixteen Possible Audio Configurations
- Power-Down Mode with Data Retention
- 20 dB Mouthpiece Input Gain
- Receive to Transmit Loopback Test Mode
- Provision for Auxiliary Input and Output
- Externally Adjustable Auxiliary Input Gain
- PCM Mono-circuit Compatible Power Supply Range
- Digital Output for Speaker Amplifier Control
- Versatile Logic Input Levels
- 18-Pin Package

### CMOS
(LOW-POWER COMPLEMENTARY MOS)

TELSET
AUDIO INTERFACE
CIRCUIT

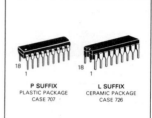

**P SUFFIX**
PLASTIC PACKAGE
CASE 707

**L SUFFIX**
CERAMIC PACKAGE
CASE 726

SIMPLIFIED BLOCK DIAGRAM

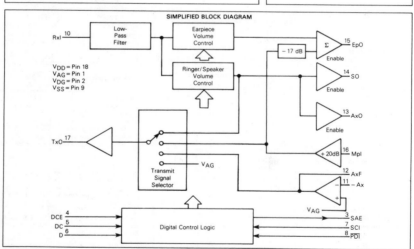

This document contains information on a new product. Specifications and information herein are subject to change without notice.

*Courtesy of Motorola, Inc. Used by permission.*

## MC145429

### MAXIMUM RATINGS

| Rating | Symbol | Value | Unit |
|---|---|---|---|
| DC Supply Voltage | $V_{DD} - V_{SS}$ | $-0.5$ to 13 | V |
| Voltage, Any Pin to $V_{SS}$ | V | $-0.5$ to $V_{DD} + 0.5$ | V |
| DC Current Drain per Pin (Excluding $V_{DD}$, $V_{SS}$) | I | 10 | mA |
| Operating Temperature Range | $T_A$ | $-40$ to $+85$ | °C |
| Storage Temperature Range | $T_{stg}$ | $-85$ to $+150$ | °C |

### RECOMMENDED OPERATING CONDITIONS

| Parameter | Symbol | Min | Typ | Max | Unit |
|---|---|---|---|---|---|
| DC Supply Voltage | $V_{DD} - V_{SS}$ | 6 | 10 to 12 | 13 | V |
| DC Supply Voltage Nominally $(V_{DD} - V_{SS})/2$ | $V_{DD} - V_{DG}$ | 3 | 5 to 7 | 7.5 | V |
| Power Dissipation | $P_D$ | | | | mW |
| $V_{DD} - V_{SS} = 10$ V | | — | 25 | 50 | |
| $V_{DD} - V_{SS} = 12$ V | | — | 30 | 60 | |
| Power-Down Dissipation | $P_D$ | | | | mW |
| $V_{DD} - V_{SS} = 12$ V | | — | 3 | 5 | |
| Full Scale Input Levels | | | | | Vpk |
| $V_{DD} - V_{SS} = 10$ V     Rxl, AxF | | — | — | 3.15 | |
| Mpl | | — | — | 0.315 | |
| $V_{DD} - V_{SS} = 12$ V     Rxl, AxF | | — | — | 3.8 | |
| Mpl | | — | — | 0.38 | |
| Sampling Clock Input Frequency | | — | 128 | — | kHz |

### PIN ASSIGNMENTS

| | | | |
|---|---|---|---|
| $V_{AG}$ | 1 | 18 | $V_{DD}$ |
| $V_{DG}$ | 2 | 17 | TxO |
| SAE | 3 | 16 | Mpl |
| DCE | 4 | 15 | EpO |
| DC | 5 | 14 | SO |
| D | 6 | 13 | AxO |
| SCI | 7 | 12 | AxF |
| $\overline{PDI}$ | 8 | 11 | $-$ Ax |
| $V_{SS}$ | 9 | 10 | Rxl |

### TRANSMISSION CHARACTERISTICS

($V_{DD}$ to $V_{SS} = 10$ to 12 V $\pm 5\%$; $T_A = 0$ to 70°C; 0 dBm0 = 6 dBm ref 600 Ω; $+3.17$ dBm0 = 3.15 Vp; SCI = 128 kHz)

| Characteristic | | Min | Max | Unit |
|---|---|---|---|---|
| Gain | | | | dB |
| 840 Hz @ 0 dBm0, Max Gain Setting | Rxl to EpO | $-0.3$ | 0.3 | |
| | Rxl to SO | $-0.3$ | 0.3 | |
| | Rxl to AxO | $-0.3$ | 0.3 | |
| | Rxl to TxO | $-0.3$ | 0.3 | |
| | AxF to TxO | $-0.3$ | 0.3 | |
| 840 Hz @ $-20$ dBm0 | Mpl to TxO | 19.5 | 20.5 | |
| | Mpl to EpO | 2.5 | 3.5 | |
| Gain vs Volume | | | | dB |
| Relative to Volume Setting, with 840 Hz @ 0 dBm0 Input | | | | |
| ($-3$ to $-21$ dB) | Rxl to EpO | $-0.5$ | 0.5 | |
| ($-5$ to $-35$ dB) | Rxl to SO or AxO | $-0.5$ | 0.5 | |
| Idle Noise | | | | dBm0 |
| 0 to 15 kHz, AxF = $-$ Ax, Rxl = Mpl = 600 Ω to $V_{AG}$ | TxO, EpO, SO, or AxO | — | $-75.0$ | |
| C-Message | | — | 9.0 | dBrnC0 |
| In-Band Spurious Outputs | | | | dBm0 |
| 840 Hz @ 0 dBm0, 0.3 to 3.4 kHz, 2nd and 3rd Harmonic | | — | $-43.0$ | |
| Out-Band Spurious Outputs | | | | dBm0 |
| 840 Hz @ 0 dBm0, 0 to 20 kHz | | — | $-40.0$ | |
| Gain vs Frequency | | | | dB |
| Relative to 840 Hz @ 0 dBm0 | | | | |
| (0.3 to 3.0 kHz, All Gain Paths) | | $-0.25$ | 0.25 | |
| (3.4 kHz, Rx Path) | | $-1.0$ | 0.25 | |
| (8.0 kHz, Rx Path) | | — | $-26.0$ | |
| Crosstalk | | | | dBm0 |
| 840 Hz @ 0 dBm0 | Rx to Tx and Tx to Rx | — | $-65.0$ | |
| Isolation from Any Input to Any Deselected Output | | | | dBm0 |
| Input = 840 Hz @ 0 dBm0 | | — | $-75.0$ | |

*Courtesy of Motorola, Inc. Used by permission.*

## MC145429

**ANALOG ELECTRICAL CHARACTERISTICS** ($V_{DD} - V_{SS}$ = 10 to 12 V ±5%, $T_A$ = 0 to 70°C)

| Characteristic | | Min | Typ | Max | Unit |
|---|---|---|---|---|---|
| Input Leakage Current | SCI, D, DC, DCE, Rxl, − Ax | − | ± 10 | ± 30 | nA |
| | $V_{AG}$, Mpl | − | ± 50 | ± 60 | μA |
| AC Input Impedance | Rxl | 100 | 200 | − | kΩ |
| | Mpl to $V_{AG}$ | 8 | 10 | − | |
| PDI Internal Input Pull Down Resistor Impedance to $V_{SS}$ | | 50 | 100 | 200 | kΩ |
| Output Voltage Range | TxO, EpO, SO, AxO | | | | V |
| $V_{DD} - V_{SS}$ = 10 V, $R_L$ = 600 to $V_{AG}$ | | − 3.2 | − | 3.2 | |
| $V_{DD} - V_{SS}$ = 12 V, $R_L$ = 900 to $V_{AG}$ | | − 3.8 | − | 3.8 | |
| Output Current | TxO, EpO, SO, AxO | | | | mA |
| Source | | − 5.5 | − | − | |
| Sink | | 5.5 | − | − | |
| Power Supply Rejection Ratio | TxO, EpO, SO, AxO | 20 | 30 | − | dB |
| $V_{AC}$ = 100 mVrms, 0 to 20 kHz, $V_{DD}$, $V_{SS}$ | | | | | |

**DIGITAL ELECTRICAL CHARACTERISTICS** ($T_A$ = 0 to 70°C, $V_{DD}$ = 5.0 V, $V_{SS}$ = − 5.0 V, $V_{DG}$, $V_{AG}$ = 0)

| Characteristic | | Symbol | Min | Max | Unit |
|---|---|---|---|---|---|
| Logic Input Voltage ($V_{DG}$ = 0 V) | SCI, D, DC, DCE, $\overline{PDI}$ | | | | V |
| $V_{SS}$ to $V_{DD}$ Mode | | $V_{IL}$ | − | − 3.5 | |
| | | $V_{IH}$ | 2.0 | − | |
| $V_{DG}$ to $V_{DD}$ Mode | | $V_{IL}$ | − | 0.8 | |
| | | $V_{IH}$ | 2.0 | − | |
| $V_{SS}$ to $V_{DG}$ Mode | | $V_{IL}$ | − | − 3.5 | |
| | | $V_{IH}$ | − 1.5 | − | |
| Logic Output Voltage ($V_{DG}$ = 0 V, $|I_O|$ < 1 μA) | SAE | $V_{OL}$ | − | − 4.95 | V |
| | | $V_{OH}$ | 4.95 | − | |
| Output Current ($V_O$ = − 4.5 V) | SAE | $I_{OL}$ | 0.9 | − | mA |
| ($V_O$ = 4.5 V) | | $I_{OH}$ | − 0.3 | − | |

**SWITCHING CHARACTERISTICS** ($T_A$ = 0 to 70°C, $V_{DD}$ = 5.0 V, $V_{SS}$ = − 5.0 V, $V_{DG}$, $V_{AG}$ = 0)

| Characteristic | | Symbol | Min | Max | Unit |
|---|---|---|---|---|---|
| Maximum Frequency | DC (Data Clock) | $f_{max}$ | − | 1.0 | MHz |
| Minimum Pulse Width | DC | $t_{w1}$ | 0.5 | − | μs |
| Minimum Pulse Width Low (SCI = 128 kHz) | DCE | $t_{w2}$ | 33 | − | |
| Propagation Delay (SCI = 128 kHz) | DCE to SAE | $t_p$ | 30 | 60 | μs |
| Setup Times | DCE to DC | $t_{su1}$ | 0.5 | − | μs |
| | D to DC | $t_{su2}$ | 0.5 | − | |
| Hold Times | D to DC | $t_{h1}$ | 0.5 | − | μs |
| | DCE to DC | $t_{h2}$ | 0.5 | − | |

FIGURE 1 — DATA INPUT TIMING

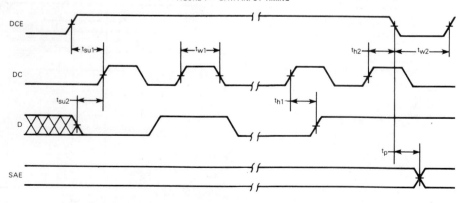

*Courtesy of Motorola, Inc. Used by permission.*

**MC145429**

## PIN DESCRIPTIONS

$V_{DD}$, POSITIVE POWER SUPPLY (PIN 18) — Typically +3 to +6.5 volts with $V_{AG} = 0$ volts.

$V_{SS}$, NEGATIVE POWER SUPPLY (PIN 9) — Typically −3 to −6.5 with $V_{AG} = 0$ volts.

$V_{AG}$, ANALOG GROUND (PIN 1) — Typically 0 volts supplied by a mono-circuit in digital telset applications. All analog signals are referenced to this pin.

$V_{DG}$, DIGITAL GROUND (PIN 2) — Typically common to logic ground. All internal digital logic operates between $V_{DG}$ and $V_{DD}$. $V_{DG}$ preferably equals $(V_{DD} - V_{SS})/2$.

SAE, SPEAKER AMPLIFIER ENABLE (PIN 3) — The SAE output will be at $V_{DD}$ whenever the external speaker amplifier is required, otherwise SAE is at $V_{SS}$.

DCE, DATA CLOCK ENABLE (PIN 4) — This digital input enables the serial data entry circuitry and also latches the serial data into the appropriate data register.

DC, DATA CLOCK (PIN 5) — This digital input allows data on the D pin to be shifted into the serial input data register on rising edges of DC whenever DCE is active.

D, DATA (PIN 6) — Digital data, required to set the configuration or gain of the audio interface, is applied to the D pin and will be shifted into the serial input register by DC whenever DCE is active.

SCI, SAMPLING CLOCK INPUT (PIN 7) — The clock applied to this digital input is used to sample the audio signals. This frequency is nominally 128 kHz and is typically provided by the slave Universal Digital Loop Transceiver such as the MC145426 in digital telset applications. This clock must be applied during data transfers.

PDI, POWER-DOWN INPUT (PIN 8) — This pin allows all analog circuitry on the device to be powered down while retaining all digital data. An internal pull-down resistor connected to $V_{SS}$ will insure the powered-down state during system power up.

RxI, RECEIVE INPUT (PIN 10) — This pin is the input to the receive low-pass filter and volume controls, and is typically driven from RxO of a mono-circuit in digital telset applications.

−Ax, INVERTING AUXILIARY INPUT (PIN 11), AxF, AUXILIARY FEEDBACK (PIN 12) — These two pins are the inverting input and output, respectively, of the auxiliary input operational amplifier and are used to set the gain of the auxiliary input. The noninverting input of the Ax amp is internally connected to $V_{AG}$.

AxO, AUXILIARY OUTPUT (PIN 13) — This output drives the input to an external auxiliary circuit and will be at $V_{AG}$ when disabled.

SO, SPEAKER OUTPUT (PIN 14) — This output drives an external speaker amplifier, and when disabled will be at $V_{AG}$.

EpO, EARPIECE OUTPUT (PIN 15) — This output drives the handset earpiece which may require a series resistor to set the correct signal level. This output will be at $V_{AG}$ when disabled.

MpI, MOUTHPIECE INPUT (PIN 16) — The mouthpiece microphone circuit is connected to this pin.

TxO, TRANSMIT OUTPUT (PIN 17) — This is the audio output pin of the device and is typically used to drive the TxI pin of a mono-circuit in digital telset applications.

## DEVICE OPERATION

The telset audio interface IC consists of two major sections: an analog subsystem and a digital subsystem. The digital subsystem provides an interface to a microcomputer and generates the necessary control signals to configure the analog subsystem as desired.

### ANALOG SUBSYSTEM

The analog subsystem provides the low-pass filtering, audio-signal routing, gain adjustment, and signal summing required for a digital or analog telset application. This subsystem consists of a receive and a transmit signal path.

### RECEIVE SIGNAL PATH

The receive audio signal, typically from the RxO output of a PCM mono-circuit or a speech network, is input to the audio interface via the RxI pin. Once buffered into the device and passed through the low-pass filter, the audio signal has four possible destinations: earpiece output, speaker output, auxiliary output, or loopback to the TxO output.

The audio path to the earpiece output consists of an earpiece volume control and summing output amplifier. The volume control is an eight-step attenuation circuit with −3 dB steps and unity gain at the maximum setting. The steps are selected by a 3-bit binary code with $0_8$ and $7_8$, the minimum and maximum settings, respectively. The output of the earpiece volume control is summed (0 dB gain) with a sidetone (−17 dB gain) from the mouthpiece input. The earpiece output is capable of driving an earpiece transducer which typically requires 200 mVp-p into 150 ohms. The gain to the earpiece to attain the proper sound pressure level may be adjusted with a resistor in series with the earpiece. When the audio interface is configured such that the earpiece is not selected, the earpiece volume control and the summing output amplifier are powered down.

The audio path to the speaker output consists of a volume control and an output driver. The volume control is an eight-step attenuation circuit with −5 dB steps and unity gain at the maximum setting. The steps are selected by a 3-bit binary code with $0_8$ and $7_8$, the minimum and maximum settings, respectively. The binary code may be from either of two volume registers: the speaker volume register, selected when the speaker is used for voice, or the ringer volume register, selected when the speaker is used for ringing. The register used is determined by the current configuration of the audio interface. The output of the volume control is fed into a unity gain output buffer which is intended to drive a speaker power amplifier. The speaker/ringer volume control and output buffer power down when not selected.

The auxiliary output is similar to the speaker output and is powered down when not needed. This output can be used to drive a conference phone circuit or the receive portion of a modem.

The three analog outputs, EpO, SO, and AxO, have a transient suppression circuit which eliminates the possibility of acoustic "pops" during configuration or volume changes. This same circuit keeps the output at $V_{AG}$ when it is not selected. When enabled, the output signal slews directly from $V_{AG}$ to the audio signal.

The other possible destination for the receive audio is the TxO audio output. This is an audio loopback configuration

---

## MC145429

which allows a system to test the operation of the audio path in the telset. In the loopback configuration, the output of the ringer/speaker volume control is switched into the TxO output amplifier input.

### TRANSMIT SIGNAL PATH

The transmit portion of the analog subsystem consists of a unity gain output driver which has three possible inputs. The input selection depends upon the current configuration of the audio interface. One of these inputs is used in the loopback configuration discussed above. The auxiliary inputs, AxF and − Ax, allow gain adjustment from an auxiliary circuit, and the third input, MpI, is from the mouthpiece microphone and is amplified 20 dB by the input amplifier. Two configurations allow use of the auxiliary inputs as a mouthpiece input without sidetone, which is useful in analog telset applications.

### DIGITAL SUBSYSTEM

The digital subsystem provides a three-wire serial input which allows a microcomputer to program the audio configuration of the audio interface.

Data is clocked into the audio interface using the DCE, DC, and D pins. DCE going high enables the data input circuitry. While DCE is high, data appearing on the D pin is clocked into the serial input data register on rising edges of DC. The falling edge of DCE latches the serial data into the appropriate register.

The serial data input format consists of five bits as shown in Figure 2.

Configuration/$\overline{\text{Volume}}$ bit (C/$\overline{\text{V}}$), loaded last, indicates the type of data contained in the data field D0-D3. When C/$\overline{\text{V}}$ is a "1", the data indicates the device configuration to be established. When C/$\overline{\text{V}}$ is a "0", the data indicates a volume level. The volume control which receives the data depends upon the current configuration of the audio interface.

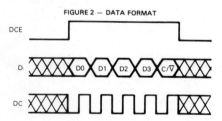

**FIGURE 2 — DATA FORMAT**

When C/$\overline{\text{V}}$ is "1", D0-D3 are loaded into the configuration register. The four configuration register bits then address a ROM which has outputs to control the analog subsystem elements, enable the appropriate volume register, select the appropriate volume register for the speaker/ringer volume control, and provide the SAE output.

When C/$\overline{\text{V}}$ is "0", the data bits D1-D3 are loaded into the volume register which has been selected by the ROM. For

volume changes, only D1-C/$\overline{\text{V}}$ need be transferred. However, if five bits are loaded into the serial input data register and C/$\overline{\text{V}}$ is low, D0 will be ignored.

If six or more data bits are clocked in while DCE is high, the last five bits clocked will be accepted when DCE goes low.

The digital input SCI is used by the analog subsystem as a sampling clock for signal processing and by the data input circuitry as a sequencing clock during data transfers.

The $\overline{\text{PDI}}$ input, when low, powers down the analog subsystem; however, all data is retained in the data registers and data may still be loaded into the serial input data register as usual as long as SCI is present. An internal pull-down resistor to $V_{SS}$ is connected to $\overline{\text{PDI}}$ to insure the power-down state upon application to $V_{DD}$ and $V_{SS}$.

The five digital inputs are DCE, DC, D, SCI and PDI. After one logic transition change, the input logic determines which of the three possible input voltage swings is used, and responds accordingly to future input levels.

There are two input logic circuits per input pin. The first operates from $V_{DG}$ to $V_{DD}$ with TTL levels referenced from $V_{DG}$. The second circuit uses $V_{DG}$ as the positive supply and $V_{SS}$ as the negative, sensing CMOS input levels from $V_{SS}$ to $V_{DG}$. The internal logic looks at the output of these two circuits and determines the input logic levels used. This permits logic level swings of $V_{SS}$ to $V_{DG}$, $V_{DG}$ to $V_{DD}$, or $V_{SS}$ to $V_{DD}$.

### CONFIGURATION MODES

The audio interface configuration set provides a total of 16 possible configurations. A description of each of the modes follows.

### LOOPBACK

This is a system test mode which loops received audio through the ringer/system volume control and out the TxO output amp.

The ring volume register controls the ringer/speaker volume control and new volume data enters the same register.

### STANDBY

This mode accomplishes the same result as the $\overline{\text{PDI}}$ pin except for powering down the TxO amplifier. All other amplifiers are powered down and all transmission gates are turned off. Volume data is latched into the ring volume register.

### STANDARD A

The standard A mode resembles that of the ordinary telephone. Rxl audio is passed through the earpiece volume control and summed with a sidetone from the mouthpiece before being presented to the earpiece. Tx audio originates at the mouthpiece input, receives 20 dB of gain, and is then passed to the TxO output. New volume data is stored in the earpiece volume register. Transmit mute in this mode disable the path from the mouthpiece amplifier to the TxO amplifier.

---

## MC145429

### RING

This is a receive only mode in which the receive audio is passed through the ringer/speaker volume control and output via the SO output. The ring volume register is selected to properly attenuate the ringing signal in the ringer/speaker volume control and any new volume data is written into the same register. Transmit mute has no effect in this mode and SAE goes high.

### ON HOOK DIALING

This mode will allow a user to dial without taking the handset off hook. Audible feedback from the speaker could indicate dial tone, key depressions, etc. Receive audio passes through the ringer/speaker volume control and out the SO output. The transmit signal will originate at the auxiliary input which could be used for a DTMF dialer input. The speaker volume register is applied to the volume control and new volume data is latched into the same register. Mute will disable the transmit path from the auxiliary input. SAE will be high in this mode, enabling the speaker amplifier.

### RECEIVER MONITOR A

This mode is similar to the standard A mode except the receive audio is also applied to the speaker output. Receive audio passes through both volume controls and out the EpO and SO pins. The speaker volume register controls the ringer/speaker volume control and new volume data is written into the speaker volume register. Transmit audio is taken from the mouthpiece input and output via the TxO amplifier. Transmit mute disables and mouthpiece amp to TxO amp path. SAE is high, enabling the speaker amplifier.

### AUXILIARY

A suggested application for this mode would be for an optional conference phone circuit to be connected to the auxiliary input and output pins. Basically, a conference phone is a voice activated half-duplex controller which allows hands free conversation without audio feedback problems. Another useful application would be to connect a modem to the auxiliary input and output, thus eliminating the requirement for several components. In this mode the receive audio is passed through the ringer/speaker volume control and out the AxO pin. The SAE pin goes high, enabling the speaker amplifier. The transmit audio enters the audio interface via the auxiliary input amplifier and is connected directly to the TxO output amp. The speaker volume register controls the volume control and new volume data enters the same register. Transmit mute disables AxF from the input to the TxO output amp, disables AxO and enables the SO output.

### STANDARD B

This mode is identical to the Standard A mode with one exception: the TxO signal originates at the auxiliary input instead of Mpl. This allows use of the Telset Audio Interface in applications that generate sidetone in a speech network. Mute disables the transmit path from the auxiliary input.

### RECEIVE MONITOR B

This mode is identical to the Receive Monitor A mode with the same exception as the Standard B mode described above.

## MODE AND VOLUME CONTROL

The data patterns required to program the audio interface mode or set the volume levels are summarized in Figures 3 and 4.

MOTOROLA TELECOMMUNICATIONS DEVICE DATA

*Courtesy of Motorola, Inc. Used by permission.*

## MC145429

FIGURE 3 — MODE CONTROL SUMMARY

| Mode | C/V̄ | D3 | D2 | D1 | D0 | Volume Register Selected | SAE State |
|---|---|---|---|---|---|---|---|
| Loopback | 1 | 0 | 0 | 0 | 0 | Ring | 0 |
| Standby | 1 | 0 | 0 | 0 | 1 | Ring | 0 |
| Standard A | 1 | 0 | 0 | 1 | 0 | Earpiece | 0 |
| Standard A/Mute | 1 | 0 | 0 | 1 | 1 | Earpiece | 0 |
| Ring | 1 | 0 | 1 | 0 | 0 | Ring | 1 |
| Ring/Mute | 1 | 0 | 1 | 0 | 1 | Ring | 1 |
| On-Hook Dialing | 1 | 0 | 1 | 1 | 0 | Speaker | 1 |
| On-Hook Dialing/Mute | 1 | 0 | 1 | 1 | 1 | Speaker | 1 |
| Receive Monitor A | 1 | 1 | 0 | 0 | 0 | Speaker | 1 |
| Receiver Monitor A/Mute | 1 | 1 | 0 | 0 | 1 | Speaker | 1 |
| Auxiliary | 1 | 1 | 0 | 1 | 0 | Speaker | 1 |
| Auxiliary/Mute | 1 | 1 | 0 | 1 | 1 | Speaker | 1 |
| Standard B | 1 | 1 | 1 | 0 | 0 | Earpiece | 0 |
| Standard B/Mute | 1 | 1 | 1 | 0 | 1 | Earpiece | 0 |
| Receive Monitor B | 1 | 1 | 1 | 1 | 0 | Speaker | 1 |
| Receive Monitor B/Mute | 1 | 1 | 1 | 1 | 1 | Speaker | 1 |

FIGURE 4 — VOLUME CONTROL SUMMARY

| Attenuation (dB) | | C/V̄ | D3 | D2 | D1 | D0 |
|---|---|---|---|---|---|---|
| Earpiece | Speaker/Ringer | | | | | |
| 0 | 0 | 0 | 1 | 1 | 1 | X |
| 3 | 5 | 0 | 1 | 1 | 0 | X |
| 6 | 10 | 0 | 1 | 0 | 1 | X |
| 9 | 15 | 0 | 1 | 0 | 0 | X |
| 12 | 20 | 0 | 0 | 1 | 1 | X |
| 15 | 25 | 0 | 0 | 1 | 0 | X |
| 18 | 30 | 0 | 0 | 0 | 1 | X |
| 21 | 35 | 0 | 0 | 0 | 0 | X |

X = Don't Care

MOTOROLA
■ ■ **SEMICONDUCTOR** ■■■■■■■
TECHNICAL DATA

*Advance Information*
# PCM Codec/Filter Mono-Circuit

The MC145500, MC145501, MC145502, MC145503, and MC145505 are all per channel PCM codec/filter mono-circuits. These devices perform the voice digitization and reconstruction as well as the band limiting and smoothing required for PCM systems. The MC145500 and MC145503 are general purpose devices that are offered in a 16-pin package. They are designed to operate in both synchronous and asynchronous applications and contain an on chip precision reference voltage. The MC145501 is offered in an 18-pin package and adds the capability of selecting from three peak overload voltages (2.5, 3.15, and 3.78 V). The MC145505 is a synchronous device offered in a 16-pin DIP and wide body SOIC package intended for instrument use. The MC145502 is the full-featured device which presents all of the options of the chip. This device is packaged in a 22-pin DIP and a 28-pin chip carrier package and contains all the features of the MC145500 and MC145501 plus several more. Most of these features can be made available in a lower pin count package tailored to a specific user's application. Contact the factory for further details.

These devices are pin-for-pin replacements for Motorola's first generation of MC14400/01/02/03/05 PCM mono-circuits and upwardly compatible with the MC14404/06/07 codecs and other industry standard codecs. They also maintain compatibility with Motorola's family of TSACs and MC3419 SLIC products.

The MC145500 family of PCM codec/filter mono-circuits utilizes CMOS due to its reliable low-power performance and proven capability for complex analog/digital VLSI functions.

**MC145500**
- 16-Pin Package
- Transmit Bandpass and Receive Low-Pass Filters on Chip
- Pin Selectable Mu/A Law Companding with Corresponding Data Format
- On Chip Precision Reference Voltage (3.15 V)
- Power Dissipation of 50 mW, Power Down of 0.1 mW at ±5 Volts
- Automatic Prescaler Accepts 128 kHz, 1.536, 1.544, 2.048, and 2.56 MHz for Internal Sequencing

**MC145501**—All of the Above Plus:
- 18-Pin Package
- Selectable Peak Overload Voltages (2.5, 3.15, 3.78 Volts)
- Access to the Inverting Input of the TxI Input Operational Amplifier

**MC145502**—All of the Above Plus:
- 22-Pin Package
- Variable Data Clock Rates (64 kHz to 4.1 MHz)
- Complete Access to the Three Terminal Transmit Input Operational Amplifier
- An External Precision Reference May Be Used

**MC145503**—All the Above Features of the MC145500 Plus:
- 16-Pin Package
- Complete Access to the Three Terminal Transmit Input Operational Amplifier

**MC145505**—Same as MC145503 Except:
- 16-Pin Package
- Common 64 kHz to 4.1 MHz Transmit/Receive Data Clock

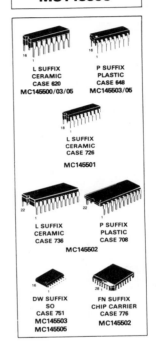

**MC145500**
**MC145501**
**MC145502**
**MC145503**
**MC145505**

L SUFFIX
CERAMIC
CASE 620
MC145500/03/05

P SUFFIX
PLASTIC
CASE 648
MC145503/05

L SUFFIX
CERAMIC
CASE 726
MC145501

L SUFFIX
CERAMIC
CASE 736

P SUFFIX
PLASTIC
CASE 708
MC145502

DW SUFFIX
SO
CASE 751
MC145503
MC145505

FN SUFFIX
CHIP CARRIER
CASE 776
MC145502

This document contains information on a new product. Specifications and information herein are subject to change without notice.

MOTOROLA TELECOMMUNICATIONS DEVICE DATA

*Courtesy of Motorola, Inc. Used by permission.*

## MC145500, MC145501, MC145502, MC145503, MC145505

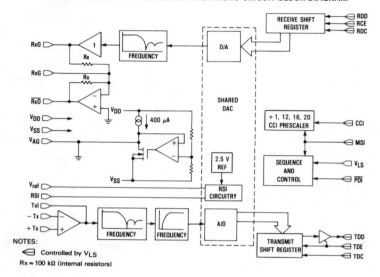

**MC145500/01/02/03/05 PCM CODEC/FILTER MONO-CIRCUIT BLOCK DIAGRAM**

NOTES:
⊏ Controlled by $V_{LS}$
Rx ≈ 100 kΩ (internal resistors)

### PIN ASSIGNMENT
(Drawings Do Not Reflect Relative Size)

**MC145500L**

| | | | |
|---|---|---|---|
| $V_{AG}$ | 1 ● | 16 | $V_{DD}$ |
| RxO | 2 | 15 | RDD |
| $\overline{RxO}$ | 3 | 14 | RCE |
| TxI | 4 | 13 | RDC |
| Mu/A | 5 | 12 | TDC |
| $\overline{PDI}$ | 6 | 11 | TDD |
| $V_{SS}$ | 7 | 10 | TDE |
| $V_{LS}$ | 8 | 9 | MSI |

**MC145503L,P**

| | | | |
|---|---|---|---|
| $V_{AG}$ | 1 ● | 16 | $V_{DD}$ |
| RxO | 2 | 15 | RDD |
| +Tx | 3 | 14 | RCE |
| TxI | 4 | 13 | RDC |
| −Tx | 5 | 12 | TDC |
| Mu/A | 6 | 11 | TDD |
| $\overline{PDI}$ | 7 | 10 | TDE |
| $V_{SS}$ | 8 | 9 | $V_{LS}$ |

**MC145505L,P**

| | | | |
|---|---|---|---|
| $V_{AG}$ | 1 ● | 16 | $V_{DD}$ |
| RxO | 2 | 15 | RDD |
| +Tx | 3 | 14 | RCE |
| TxI | 4 | 13 | DC |
| −Tx | 5 | 12 | CCI |
| Mu/A | 6 | 11 | TDD |
| $\overline{PDI}$ | 7 | 10 | TDE |
| $V_{SS}$ | 8 | 9 | $V_{LS}$ |

**MC145501L**

| | | | |
|---|---|---|---|
| RSI | 1 ● | 18 | $V_{DD}$ |
| $V_{AG}$ | 2 | 17 | RDD |
| RxO | 3 | 16 | RCE |
| $\overline{RxO}$ | 4 | 15 | RDC |
| TxI | 5 | 14 | TDC |
| −Tx | 6 | 13 | TDD |
| Mu/A | 7 | 12 | TDE |
| $\overline{PDI}$ | 8 | 11 | MSI |
| $V_{SS}$ | 9 | 10 | $V_{LS}$ |

**MC145502L,P**

| | | | |
|---|---|---|---|
| $V_{ref}$ | 1 ● | 22 | RSI |
| $V_{AG}$ | 2 | 21 | $V_{DD}$ |
| RxO | 3 | 20 | RDD |
| RxG | 4 | 19 | RCE |
| $\overline{RxO}$ | 5 | 18 | RDC |
| +Tx | 6 | 17 | TDC |
| TxI | 7 | 16 | CCI |
| −Tx | 8 | 15 | TDD |
| Mu/A | 9 | 14 | TDE |
| $\overline{PDI}$ | 10 | 13 | MSI |
| $V_{SS}$ | 11 | 12 | $V_{LS}$ |

**MC145503DW**

| | | | |
|---|---|---|---|
| $V_{AG}$ | 1 ● | 16 | $V_{DD}$ |
| RxO | 2 | 15 | RDD |
| +Tx | 3 | 14 | RCE |
| TxI | 4 | 13 | RDC |
| −Tx | 5 | 12 | TDC |
| Mu/A | 6 | 11 | TDD |
| $\overline{PDI}$ | 7 | 10 | TDE |
| $V_{SS}$ | 8 | 9 | $V_{LS}$ |

**MC145505DW**

| | | | |
|---|---|---|---|
| $V_{AG}$ | 1 ● | 16 | $V_{DD}$ |
| RxO | 2 | 15 | RDD |
| +Tx | 3 | 14 | RCE |
| TxI | 4 | 13 | DC |
| −Tx | 5 | 12 | CCI |
| Mu/A | 6 | 11 | TDD |
| $\overline{PDI}$ | 7 | 10 | TDE |
| $V_{SS}$ | 8 | 9 | $V_{LS}$ |

**MC145502FN 28-PIN PLCC (TOP VIEW)**

Top pins: RxO, $V_{AG}$, $V_{ref}$, NC, RSI, $V_{DD}$, RDD (4, 3, 2, 1, 28, 27, 26)

| | | |
|---|---|---|
| RxG | 5 | 25  RCE |
| RxO | 6 | 24  RDC |
| +Tx | 7 | 23  TDC |
| NC | 8 | 22  NC |
| NC | 9 | 21  NC |
| TxI | 10 | 20  CCI |
| −Tx | 11 | 19  TDD |

Bottom pins (12–18): Mu/A, $\overline{PDI}$, $V_{SS}$, NC, $V_{LS}$, MSI, TDE

---

**MOTOROLA TELECOMMUNICATIONS DEVICE DATA**

*Courtesy of Motorola, Inc. Used by permission.*

# MC145500, MC145501, MC145502, MC145503, MC145505

## DEVICE DESCRIPTIONS

A codec/filter is a device which is used for digitizing and reconstructing the human voice. These devices were developed primarily for the telephone network to facilitate voice switching and transmission. Once the voice is digitized, it may be switched by digital switching methods or transmitted long distance (T1, microwave, satellites, etc.) without degradation. The name codec is an acronym from "coder" for the A/D used to digitize voice, and "decoder" for the D/A used for reconstructing voice. A codec is a single device that does both the A/D and D/A conversions.

To digitize intelligible voice requires a signal to distortion of about 30 dB for a dynamic range of about 40 dB. This may be accomplished with a linear 13-bit A/D and D/A, but will far exceed the required signal to distortion at amplitudes greater than 40 dB below the peak amplitude. This excess performance is at the expense of data per sample. Two methods of data reduction are implemented by compressing the 13-bit linear scheme to companded 8-bit schemes. These companding schemes follow a segmented or "piecewise-linear" curve formatted as sign bit, three chord bits, and four step bits. For a given chord, all 16 of the steps have the same voltage weighting. As the voltage of the analog input increases, the four step bits increment and carry to the three chord bits which increment. With the chord bits increment, the step bits double their voltage weighting. This results in an effective resolution of 6-bits (sign + chord + four step bits) across a 42 dB dynamic range (7 chords above zero, by 6 dB per chord). There are two companding schemes used; Mu-255 Law specifically in North America, and A-Law specifically in Europe. These companding schemes are accepted world wide. The tables show the linear quantization levels to PCM words for the two companding schemes.

In a sampling environment, Nyquist theory says that to properly sample a continuous signal, it must be sampled at a rate higher than twice the signal's highest frequency component. Voice contains spectral energy above 3 kHz, but its absence is not detrimental to intelligibility. To reduce the digital data rate, which is proportional to the sampling rate, a sample rate of 8 kHz was adopted, consistent with a bandwidth of 3 kHz. This sampling requires a low-pass filter to limit the high frequency energy above 3 kHz from distorting the inband signal. The telephone line is also subject to 50/60 Hz power line coupling which must be attenuated from the signal by a high-pass filter before the A/D converter.

The D/A process reconstructs a staircase version of the desired inband signal which has spectral images of the inband signal modulated about the sample frequency and its harmonics. These spectral images are called aliasing components which need to be attenuated to obtain the desired signal. The low-pass filter used to attenuate these aliasing components is typically called a reconstruction or smoothing filter.

The MC145500 series PCM codec/filters have the codec, both presampling and reconstruction filters, a precision voltage reference on chip, and require no external components. There are five distinct versions of the Motorola MC145500 Series.

### MC145500

The MC145500 PCM mono-circuit is intended for standard byte interleaved synchronous and asynchronous applications.

The TDC pin on this device is the input to both the TDC and CCI functions in the pin description. Consequently, for MSI = 8 kHz, TDC can be one of five discrete frequencies. These are 128 kHz (40 to 60% duty cycle) 1.536, 1.544, 2.048, or 2.56 MHz. (For other data clock frequencies see MC145502 or MC145505.) The internal reference is set for 3.15 volts peak full scale, and the full scale input level at TxI and output level at RxO is 6.3 volts peak-to-peak. This is the +3 dBm0 level of the PCM codec/filter. All other functions are described in the pin description.

### MC145501

The MC145501 PCM codec/filter offers the same features and is for the same application as the MC145500, but offers two additional pins and features. The reference select input allows the full scale level of the device to be set at 2.5 Vp, 3.15 Vp, or 3.78 Vp. The −Tx pin allows for external transmit gain adjust and simplifies the interface to the MC3419 SLIC. Otherwise, it is identical to MC145500.

### MC145502

The MC145502 PCM codec/filter is the full feature 22-pin device. It is intended for use in applications requiring maximum flexiblity. The MC145502 contains all the features of the MC145500 and MC145501. The MC145502 is intended for bit interleaved or byte interleaved applications with data clock frequencies which are nonstandard or time varying. One of the five standard frequencies (listed above) is applied to the CCI input, and the data clock inputs can be any frequency between 64 kHz and 4.096 MHz. The Vref pin allows for use of an external shared reference or selection of the internal reference. The RxG pin accommodates gain adjustments for the inverted analog output. All three pins of the input gain-setting operational amplifier are present which provide maximum flexibility for the analog interface.

### MC145503

The MC145503 PCM mono-circuit is intended for standard byte interleaved synchronous or asynchronous applications. TDC can be one of five discrete frequencies. These are 128 kHz (40 to 60% duty cycle), 1.536, 1.544, 2.048, or 2.56 MHz. (For other data clock frequencies see MC145502 or MC145505.) The internal reference is set for 3.15 volts peak full scale, and the full scale input level at TxI and output level at RxO is 6.3 volts peak-to-peak. This is the +3 dBm0 level of the PCM codec/filter. The +Tx and −Tx inputs provide maximum flexibility for analog interface. All other functions are described in the pin description.

### MC145505

The MC145505 PCM mono-circuit is intended for byte interleaved synchronous applications. The MC145505 has all the features of the MC145503 but internally connects TDC and RDC (see pin description) to the DC pin. One of the five standard frequencies (listed above) should be applied to CCI. The data clock input (DC) can be any frequency between 64 kHz and 4.096 MHz.

*Courtesy of Motorola, Inc. Used by permission.*

## MC145500, MC145501, MC145502, MC145503, MC145505

### PIN DESCRIPTION

#### DIGITAL

#### $V_{LS}$—Logic Level Select Input and TTL Digital Ground

$V_{LS}$ controls the logic levels and digital ground reference for all digital inputs and the digital output. These devices can operate with logic levels from full supply ($V_{SS}$ to $V_{DD}$) or with TTL logic levels using $V_{LS}$ as digital ground. For $V_{LS} = V_{DD}$, all I/O is full supply ($V_{SS}$ to $V_{DD}$ swing) with CMOS switch points. For $V_{SS} < V_{LS} < (V_{DD} - 4$ volts), all inputs and outputs are TTL compatible with $V_{LS}$ being the digital ground. The pins controlled by $V_{LS}$ are inputs MSI, CCI, TDE, TDC, RCE, RDC, RDD, $\overline{PDI}$, and output TDD.

#### MSI—Master Synchronization Input

MSI is used for determining the sample rate of the transmit side and as a time base for selecting the internal prescale divider for the convert clock input (CCI) pin. The MSI pin should be tied to an 8 kHz clock which may be a frame sync or system sync signal. MSI has no relation to transmit or receive data timing, except for determining the internal transmit strobe as described under the TDE pin description. MSI should be derived from the transmit timing in asynchronous applications. In many applications MSI can be tied to TDE. (MSI is tied internally to TDE in MC145503/05.)

#### CCI—Convert Clock Input

CCI is designed to accept five discrete clock frequencies. These are 128 kHz, 1.536 MHz, 1.544 MHz, 2.048 MHz, or 2.56 MHz. The frequency at this input is compared with MSI and prescale divided to produce the internal sequencing clock at 128 kHz (or 16 times the sampling rate). The duty cycle of CCI is dictated by the minimum pulse width except for 128 kHz, which is used directly for internal sequencing and must have a 40 to 60% duty cycle. In asynchronous applications, CCI should be derived from transmit timing. (CCI is tied internally to TDC in MC145500/01/03.)

#### TDC—Transmit Data Clock Input

TDC can be any frequency from 64 kHz to 4.096 MHz, and is often tied to CCI if the data rate is equal to one of the five discrete frequencies. This clock is the shift clock for the transmit shift register and its rising edges produce successive data bits at TDD. TDE should be derived from this clock. (TDC and RDC are tied together internally in the MC145505 and are called DC.)

#### TDE—Transmit Data Enable Input

TDE serves three major functions. The first TDE rising edge following an MSI rising edge generates the internal transmit strobe which initiates an A/D conversion. The internal transmit strobe also transfers a new PCM data word into the transmit shift register (sign bit first) ready to be output at TDD. The TDE pin is the high impedance control for the transmit digital data (TDD) output. As long as this pin is high, the TDD output stays low impedance. This pin also enables the output shift register for clocking out the 8-bit serial PCM word. The logical AND of the TDE pin with the TDC pin clocks out a new data bit at TDD. TDE should be held high for eight consecutive TDC cycles to clock out a complete PCM word for byte interleaved applications. The transmit shift register feeds back on itself to allow multiple reads of the transmit data. If the PCM word is clocked out once per frame in a byte interleaved system, the MSI pin function is transparent and may be connected to TDE.

The TDE pin may be cycled during a PCM word for bit interleaved applications. TDE controls both the high impedance state of the TDD output and the internal shift clock. TDE must fall before TDC rises ($t_{su8}$) to ensure integrity of the next data bit. There must be at least two TDC falling edges between the last TDE rising edge of one frame and the first TDE rising edge of the next frame. MSI must be available separate from TDE for bit interleaved applications.

#### TDD—Transmit Digital Data Output

The output levels at this pin are controlled by the $V_{LS}$ pin. For $V_{LS}$ connected to $V_{DD}$, the output levels are from $V_{SS}$ to $V_{DD}$. For a voltage of $V_{LS}$ between $V_{DD} - 4$ V and $V_{SS}$, the output levels are TTL compatible with $V_{LS}$ being the digital ground supply. The TDD pin is three-state output controlled by the TDE pin. The timing of this pin is controlled by TDC and TDE. When in TTL mode, this output may be made high-speed CMOS compatible using a pullup resistor. The data format (Mu-Law, A-Law, or sign magnitude) is controlled by the Mu/A pin.

#### RDC—Receive Data Clock Input

RDC can be any frequency from 64 kHz to 4.096 MHz. This pin is often tied to the TDC pin for applications that can use a common clock for both transmit and receive data transfers. The receive shift register is controlled by the receive clock enable (RCE) pin to clock data into the receive digital data (RDD) pin on falling RDC edges. These three signals can be asynchronous with all other digital pins. The RDC input is internally tied to the TDC input on the MC145505 and called DC.

#### RCE—Receive Clock Enable Input

The rising edge of RCE should identify the sign bit of a receive PCM word on RDD. The next falling edge of RDC, after a rising RCE, loads the first bit of the PCM word into the receive register. The next seven falling edges enter the remainder of the PCM word. On the ninth rising edge, the receive PCM word is transferred to the receive buffer register and the A/D sequence is interrupted to commence the decode process. In asynchronous applications with an 8 kHz transmit sample rate, the receive sample rate should be between 7.5 and 8.5 kHz. Two receive PCM words may be decoded and analog summed each transmit frame to allow on chip conferencing. The two PCM words should be clocked in as two single PCM words, a minimum of 31.25 $\mu$s apart, with a receive data clock of 512 kHz or faster.

#### RDD—Receive Digital Data Input

RDD is the receive digital data input. The timing for this pin is controlled by RDC and RCE. The data format is determined by the Mu/A pin.

---

## MC145500, MC145501, MC145502, MC145503, MC145505

**Mu/A Select**

This pin selects the companding law and the data format at TDD and RDD.

Mu/A = V$_{DD}$; Mu255 Companding D3 Data Format with Zero Code Suppress

Mu/A = V$_{AG}$; Mu255 Companding with Sign Magnitude Data Format

Mu/A = V$_{SS}$; A-law Companding with CCITT Data Format Bit Inversions

| CODE | SIGN/MAGNITUDE | Mu-LAW | A-LAW (CCITT) |
|---|---|---|---|
| + FULL SCALE | 1111 1111 | 1000 0000 | 1010 1010 |
| + ZERO | 1000 0000 | 1111 1111 | 1101 0101 |
| − ZERO | 0000 0000 | 0111 1111 | 0101 0101 |
| − FULL SCALE | 0111 1111 | 0000 0010 | 0010 1010 |

| SIGN BIT | CHORD BITS | | | STEP BITS | | | |
|---|---|---|---|---|---|---|---|
| 0 | 1 | 2 | 3 | 4 | 5 | 6 | 7 |

NOTE: Starting from sign magnitude, to change format:
To Mu-Law—
  MSB is unchanged (sign)
  Invert remaining seven bits
  If code is 0000 0000, change to 0000 0010 (for zero code suppression)
To A-Law—
  MSB is unchanged (sign)
  Invert odd numbered bits
  Ignore zero code suppression

**$\overline{PDI}$—Power Down Input**

The power down input disables the bias circuitry and gates off all clock inputs. This puts the V$_{AG}$, TxI, RxO, $\overline{RxO}$, and TDD outputs into a high impedance state. The power dissipation is reduced to 0.1 mW when $\overline{PDI}$ is a low logic level. The circuit operates normally with $\overline{PDI}$ = V$_{DD}$ or with a logic high as defined by connection at V$_{LS}$. TDD will not come out of high impedance for two MSI cycles after $\overline{PDI}$ goes high.

**DC—Data Clock Input**

DC—in the MC145505, TDC and RDC are internally connected to this pin.

## ANALOG

**V$_{AG}$—Analog Ground Input/Output Pin**

V$_{AG}$ is the analog ground power supply input/output. All analog signals into and out of the device use this as their ground reference. Each version of the MC145500 PCM codec/filter family can provide its own analog ground supply internally. The dc voltage of this internal supply is 6% positive of the midway between V$_{DD}$ and V$_{SS}$. This supply can sink more than 8 mA but has a current source limited to 400 µA. The output of this supply is internally connected to the analog ground input of the part. The node where this supply and the analog ground are connected is brought out to the V$_{AG}$ pin. In symmetric dual supply systems (±5, ±6, etc.), V$_{AG}$ may be externally tied to the system analog ground supply. When RxO or $\overline{RxO}$ drive low impedance loads tied to V$_{AG}$, a pullup

resistor to V$_{DD}$ will be required to boost the source current capability if V$_{AG}$ is not tied to the supply ground. All analog signals for the part are referenced to V$_{AG}$, including noise, therefore, decoupling capacitors (0.1 µF) should be used from V$_{DD}$ to V$_{AG}$ and V$_{SS}$ to V$_{AG}$.

**V$_{ref}$—Positive Voltage Reference Input (MC145502 Only)**

The V$_{ref}$ pin allows an external reference voltage to be used for the A/D and D/A conversions. If V$_{ref}$ is tied to V$_{SS}$, the internal reference is selected. If V$_{ref}$ > V$_{AG}$, then the external mode is selected and the voltage applied to V$_{ref}$ is used for generating the internal converter reference voltage. In either internal or external reference mode, the actual voltage used for conversion is multiplied by the ratio selected by the RSI pin. The RSI pin circuitry is explained under its pin description below. Both the internal and external references are inverted within the PCM codec/filter for negative input voltages such that only one reference is required.

External Mode—In the external reference mode (V$_{ref}$ > V$_{AG}$), a 2.5 volt reference like the MC1403 may be connected from V$_{ref}$ to V$_{AG}$. A single external reference may be shared by tying together a number of V$_{ref}$ and V$_{AG}$ pins from different codec/filters. In special applications, the external reference voltage may be between 0.5 and 5 volts. However, the reference voltage gain selection circuitry associated with RSI must be considered to arrive at the desired codec/filter gain.

Internal Mode—In the internal reference mode (V$_{ref}$ = V$_{SS}$), an internal 2.5 volt reference supplies the reference voltage for the RSI circuitry. The V$_{ref}$ pin is functionally connected to V$_{SS}$ for the MC145500, MC145501, MC145503, and MC145505 pinouts.

**RSI—Reference Select Input (MC145501/02 Only)**

The RSI input allows the selection of three different overload or full scale A/D and D/A converter reference voltages independent of the internal or external reference mode. The RSI pin is a digital input that senses three different logic states; V$_{SS}$, V$_{AG}$, and V$_{DD}$. For RSI = V$_{AG}$, the reference voltage is used directly for the converters. The internal reference is 2.5 volts. For RSI = V$_{SS}$, the reference voltage is multiplied by the ratio of 1.26, which results in an internal converter reference of 3.15 volts. For RSI = V$_{DD}$, the reference voltage is multiplied by 1.51, which results in an internal converter reference of 3.78 volts. The device requires a minimum of 1.0 volt of headroom between the internal converter reference to V$_{DD}$. V$_{SS}$ has this same absolute valued minimum, also measured from V$_{AG}$ pin. The various modes of operation are summarized in the table below. The RSI pin is functionally connected to V$_{SS}$ for the MC145500, MC145503, and MC145505 pinouts.

**RxO, $\overline{RxO}$—Receive Analog Outputs**

These two complimentary outputs are generated from the output of the receive filter. They are equal in magnitude and out of phase. The maximum signal output of each is equal to the maximum peak-to-peak signal described with the reference. If a 3.15 volt reference is used with RSI tied to V$_{AG}$

## MC145500, MC145501, MC145502, MC145503, MC145505

and a +3 dBm0 sine wave is decoded, the RxO output will be a 6.3 volt peak-to-peak signal. $\overline{RxO}$ will also have an inverted signal output of 6.3 volt peak-to-peak. External loads may be connected from RxO to $\overline{RxO}$ for a 6 dB push-pull signal gain or from either RxO or $\overline{RxO}$ to $V_{AG}$. With a 3.15 volt reference each output will drive 600 Ω to +9 dBm. With RSI tied to $V_{DD}$, each output will drive 900 Ω to +9 dBm.

### RxG—Receive Output Gain Adjust (MC145502 Only)

The purpose of the RxG pin is to allow external receive gain adjustment for the $\overline{RxO}$ pin. If RxG is left open, then the output signal at RxO will be inverted and output at $\overline{RxO}$. Thus the push-pull gain to a load from RxO to $\overline{RxO}$ is two times the output level at RxO. If external resistors are applied from RxO to RxG (RI) and from RxG to $\overline{RxO}$ (RG), the gain of $\overline{RxO}$ can be set differently from inverting unity. These resistors should be in the range of 10 kΩ. The RxO output level is unchanged by the resistors and the $\overline{RxO}$ gain is approximately equal to minus RG/RI. The actual gain is determined by taking into account the internal resistors which will be in parallel to these external resistors. The internal resistors have a large tolerance, but they match each other very closely. This matching tends to minimize the affects of their tolerance on external gain configurations. The circuit for RxG and $\overline{RxO}$ is shown in the block diagram.

### TxI—Transmit Analog Input

TxI is the input to the transmit filter. It is also the output of the transmit gain amplifiers of the MC145501/02/03/05. The input impedance is greater than 100 k to $V_{AG}$ in the MC145500. The TxI input has an internal gain of 1.0, such that a +3 dBm0 signal at TxI corresponds to the peak converter reference voltage as described in the $V_{ref}$ and RSI pin descriptions. For 3.15 volt reference, the +3 dBm0 input should be 6.3 volts peak-to-peak.

### +Tx-Positive Tx Amplifier Input (MC145502/03/05 Only)
### −Tx-Negative Tx Amplifier Input (MC145501/02/03/05 Only)

The TxI pin is the input to the transmit band-pass filter. If +Tx or −Tx are available, then there is an internal amplifier preceding the filter whose pins are +Tx, −Tx, and TxI. These pins allow access to the amplifier terminals to tailor the input gain with external resistors. The resistors should be in the range of 10 kΩ. If +Tx is not available, it is internally tied to $V_{AG}$. If −Tx and +Tx are not available, the TxI is a unity gain high impedance input.

### Power Supplies

$V_{DD}$—Most Positive Supply $V_{DD}$ is typically 5 to 12 volts.

$V_{SS}$—Most Negative Supply. $V_{SS}$ is typically 10 to 12 volts negative of $V_{DD}$.

For a ±5 volt dual-supply system, the typical power supply configuration is $V_{DD} = +5$ V, $V_{SS} = -5$ V, $V_{LS} = 0$ V (digital ground accommodating TTL logic levels), and $V_{AG} = 0$ V being tied to system analog ground.

For single-supply applications, typical power supply configurations include:

$V_{DD} = 10$ V to 12 V
$V_{SS} = 0$ V

$V_{AG}$ generates a mid supply voltage for referencing all analog signals.

$V_{LS}$ controls the logic levels. This pin should be connected to $V_{DD}$ for CMOS logic levels from $V_{SS}$ to $V_{DD}$. This pin should be connected to digital ground for true TTL logic levels referenced to $V_{LS}$.

### Testing Considerations (MC145500/01/02 Only)

An analog test mode is activated by connecting MSI and CCI to 128 kHz. In this mode, the input of the A/D (the output of the Tx filter) is available at the $\overline{PDI}$ pin. This input is direct coupled to the A/D side of the codec. The A/D is a differential design, this results in the gain of this input being effectively attenuated by half. If monitored with a high-impedance buffer, the output of the Tx low-pass filter can also be measured at the $\overline{PDI}$ pin. This test mode allows independent evaluation of the transmit low-pass filter and A/D side of the codec. The transmit and receive channels of these devices are tested with the codec/filter fully functional.

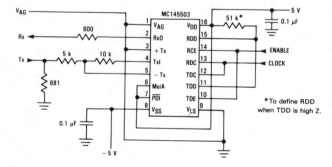

**Figure 1. Test Circuit**

---

MOTOROLA TELECOMMUNICATIONS DEVICE DATA

*Courtesy of Motorola, Inc. Used by permission.*

# Index